The Journals of

PATRICK GASS

Member of the Lewis and Clark Expedition

THE JOURNALS OF PATRICK GASS
Member of the Lewis and Clark Expedition

Edited and Annotated by
CAROL LYNN MACGREGOR

Mountain Press Publishing Company
Missoula, Montana
1997

The Journals of Patrick Gass,
Member of the Lewis and Clark Expedition

Book I

*A Journal of the Voyages and
Travels of a Corps of Discovery . . .*

Book II

The Account Book of Patrick Gass,
1826–1837 and 1847–1848

Edited and Annotated by
Carol Lynn MacGregor

© 1997, Carol Lynn MacGregor
Fifth Printing, June 2003

cover art: Missoula County Courthouse Murals, Panel Five
(Capt. Meriwether Lewis, Sgt. Patrick Gass, and others crossing
the Clark Fork River at Grant Creek), by Edgar S. Paxson
© 1914, 1997 Missoula County

Map and Appendices X, Y, Z assisted by Jennifer Hamelman

PRINTED IN THE U.S.A.

Library of Congress Cataloging-in-Publication Data

Gass, Patrick, 1771–1870.
    The journals of Patrick Gass : member of the Lewis and Clark
Expedition / edited and annotated by Carol Lynn MacGregor.
        p.   cm.
    The journal was originally published in 1807; the account book has
never before been published.
    Includes bibliographical references and index.
    Contents: bk. 1. A journal of the voyages and travels of a corps of
discovery — bk. 2. The account book of Patrick Gass, 1826–1837 and
1847–1848.
    ISBN 0-87842-350-8 (alk. paper). — ISBN 0-87842-351-6 (alk. paper)
    1. Lewis and Clark Expedition (1804–1806)   2. Gass, Patrick, 1771–
1870—Diaries.   3. West (U.S.)—Discovery and exploration. 4. West
(U.S.)—Description and travel.   5. Missouri River—Description and
travel.   6. Columbia River—Description and travel.   7. West (U.S.)—
History—To 1848.   I. MacGregor, Carol Lynn, 1942–   .   II. Title.
F592.5.G2   1997
917.804'2—dc21   97-15350

MOUNTAIN PRESS PUBLISHING COMPANY
P.O. Box 2399 • Missoula, MT 59806
406-728-1900 • 1-800-234-5308

Book I:
To my late father, Gordon MacGregor,
a man of the West

and

to Dr. Patricia Ourada,
my friend and mentor

Book II:
To Ludd A. Trozpek,
invaluable colleague and friend

CONTENTS

LIST OF ILLUSTRATIONS

ACKNOWLEDGMENTS

Thanks to my mother, Nell MacGregor, for giving me the Patrick Gass journal of 1807 in the 1960s.

At Boise State University, I began this project at Dr. Patricia Ourada's suggestion. Her influence was both seminal and constant. She is what a mentor is meant to be, and much more. Two other professors at BSU lent many hours to assist me: Dr. Sandra Schackel in the Department of History and Dr. James Maguire, editor of the Western Writers Series and professor in the Department of English. Also at BSU, computer expert David Law-Smith rescued me from trepidation and bungling repairmen to get a good system.

Ludd A. Trozpek deserves many vacations at my Raspberry Ranch. His editing suggestions were time-consuming, accurate, and numerous.

Ron Laycock and the late Robert Lange, friends from the Lewis and Clark Heritage Trail Foundation, offered helpful critique and encouragement, and Don Nell has been generous in sharing his copies of documents. Arlen J. Large's comments proved thought-provoking and accurate.

Dr. James Ronda, with whom I shared the podium in Boise in April 1990 and Sioux City in August 1996, offered encouragement and interesting ideas.

Jeanette Taranik contributed the excellent photograph of Patrick Gass, her ancestor.

The staff in the Special Collections and Preservation Division of the University of Washington Libraries made my research there enjoyable and efficient.

Betty Lou Donnelley manifested her enduring friendship and support in typing, proofreading, and editing.

Laura, Catherine, and Janelle, my three daughters, sacrificed daily time with me and encouraged me anyway. J.G., my son, meanwhile pioneered his way around the globe, "proceeding on" to adventures of his own.

Other loving friends who offered support, though not listed, are not forgotten.

Book I

—◆—

A Journal of the Voyages and Travels of a Corps of Discovery...

INTRODUCTION

The Lewis and Clark Expedition: Purpose, Legend, and Reality

The voyage of Lewis and Clark into unknown wilderness has become legendary in the consciousness of Americans since May 14, 1804, when the Corps of Discovery left St. Louis to explore, observe, and record what lay between that city and the Pacific Ocean. The first federally sponsored overland expedition in the United States, the voyage continues to loom large as the greatest episode of the nation's exploration period. Patrick Gass, a member of this epic group, kept a journal of the trip that has been published several times since its original 1807 publication. His simple account allows us to view the trip and the corps from the perspective of one of its working members.

The seed for the expedition was sown by Thomas Jefferson long before he ascended to the presidency. Jefferson discussed a proposal for an expedition to the Pacific with George Rogers Clark in 1783, but financing proved elusive. His second design for exploration sponsored John Ledyard to trek across Russia and return to the United States by way of the Bering Sea and the Northwest Coast. Catherine the Great granted Ledyard permission, then suddenly withdrew it in 1788, stopping the adventurer in Siberia and ordering him home. Trying again in 1793, Jefferson solicited members of the American Philosophical Society to send André Micheaux west. Meriwether Lewis, then just eighteen, wanted to join this group. However, sponsors quashed the plan when Micheaux's French nationality became a diplomatic issue in the sensitive international rivalry for the western region.[1]

After these three abortive attempts, the idea to secure an overland expedition finally came to fruition at the same time that Robert Livingston, Jefferson's emissary to France, successfully negotiated the Louisiana Purchase in 1803. The Congress of the United States voted a secret appropriation of $2,500 for an expedition before the land title of Louisiana officially changed. Plans for the trip were not made public until title changed in the spring of

1804. The $2,500 appropriation certainly did not represent the cost of the voyage, but it did give official congressional sanction to the trip. The War Department financed it as an official expedition of the U.S. Army. A modern study estimates the total cost was $38,722.25.[2]

England, the United States, Spain, and Russia all competed for the riches of the Northwest Coast prior to the Lewis and Clark expedition. England's claim to the northwestern territories strengthened with the explorations of Sir Frances Drake, Captain James Cook, and Alexander Mackenzie. By 1778 Cook had begun his third voyage in search of a water passage connecting the Orient with the east coast of North America. Heading north toward the Arctic Ocean during a storm, he passed the mouth of the Columbia River without seeing it. In 1792–93, Alexander Mackenzie and a crew of ten men crossed the Canadian Rockies and found the passage by water extremely arduous. In spite of Cook's and Mackenzie's findings, wishful thinking sustained belief in a Northwest Passage. Lewis and Clark's confrontation with the geographical realities of the Bitterroot Mountains in the late summer of 1805 finally dashed the myth of an easy waterway to the Pacific coast.

The political need for American exploration westward beyond the Louisiana Territory rested within this context of international imperialistic rivalries. Exploration of the continent's interior would promote the future security, growth, and settlement of the United States. American commercial seaman Robert Gray, of Boston, named the Columbia River after his ship in 1792. Yet claims to the Oregon country remained in dispute until 1846 when a treaty between England and the United States established the boundary at the 49th parallel. Spain's maritime exploration of the Northwest Coast took Juan Pérez beyond Vancouver Island in 1774. Hezeta's second in command, Bodega y Quadra, sailed as far north as the 58th parallel in 1775, naming bays and capes along his way, while Hezeta himself saw the mouth of the great river but did not enter the Columbia's dangerous estuary. From the reign of Peter the Great in 1696, Russians had sailed east to the Aleutian Islands and the west coast of North America on trade missions. In 1803, Russians established a post at Sitka, Alaska. Moving south in 1812, Russia established Fort Ross at Bodega Bay, sixty miles north of present-day San Francisco. Indeed, when Lewis and Clark began their exploration at the turn of the nineteenth century, the international game of laying claim to the western coast of North America had several major players.

Meanwhile, Spain ceded the title of Louisiana Territory back to France in 1800 by the Second Treaty of San Ildefonso. Almost immediately, title passed to the United States with the Louisiana

Purchase of 1803. Because actual transfer to the United States did not occur until the spring of 1804, the Lewis and Clark Corps of Discovery stayed on the American side of the Mississippi River at Camp DuBois during the winter of 1803–1804. Jefferson's preparations to meet military or diplomatic threats to the United States posed by the transfer of Louisiana included negotiations abroad, troop deployment along the Missouri River, and the Lewis and Clark expedition.[3]

The weight given to various missions of the Lewis and Clark expedition continues as a topic of scholarly interpretation. William Goetzmann asserts in *Exploration and Empire* that purpose drives exploration.[4] From conception, exploration becomes a seeking activity with specific goals in mind. Applying Goetzmann's paradigm to the Lewis and Clark voyage, one can understand its lasting significance by reviewing its purposes. A brief review of the expedition's contributions to politics, economics, geography, cartography, anthropology, ethnography, botany, zoology, history, and literature lends fruitful background for reading Gass's journal.

While interest in searching for the mythical Northwest Passage lingered, in spite of various failed attempts to find it, political, economic, and scientific motives overshadowed that quest. The expedition would acquaint the young nation with the Louisiana Purchase, an area that more than doubled the size of the United States. It would inform the native inhabitants of the vast area about the change of government. The nation's security would be enhanced with the settlement of contiguous land extending to the natural boundary of the Pacific Ocean. Jefferson hoped that rich trade would result from contacts with natives not already part of the economic network beyond the Mississippi. Certainly, the observations of the Corps of Discovery would be welcomed by the president and his colleagues in the American Philosophical Society, who possessed keen interest in knowing more about the people, land, plants, and animals of the unexplored lands to the west.

Political, economic, and scientific motives converged when the Corps of Discovery met native occupants of the vast Louisiana Territory. Expedition members tried to promote peace and trade with American Indians while recording simple descriptions of them. The party exercised diplomacy as it moved through territories of Native Americans, groups of whom were sometimes at war with one another when the corps visited. For the most part, native groups allowed peaceful passage. When the corps felt threatened by Teton Sioux (or Lakota) and Blackfeet Indians, it used firm tactics. The speed with which the corps moved through different cultural areas precluded sensitive or extensive observations of Native American culture except at the Mandan villages, Fort Clatsop, and the Long Camp on the Clearwater.

Lewis and Clark and their men operated from Euro-American diplomatic premises that were not compatible with Indian cultures. They presented gifts to recognize chiefs or leaders, promised indigenous peoples the protection of their "father" in Washington, and announced the change of title in the land by giving flags and presidential peace medals—all unilateral actions that could not have been understood by American Indians. Native recipients of official United States policy messages understood gift giving and responded to ceremonies generally with impressive pomp, but they could not understand the concepts of the American presidency, its assumptive power, or ownership of land. Native people gave lip service to the white men's advice about peaceful relations with neighbors, sometimes hoping that promised protection might aid them. Often, the bestowal of gifts on perceived leaders did not reflect tribal organization. Never were American concepts of land title and ownership versus native concepts of land use and sanctity mutually understood. Despite profound differences in their cultures, however, mutual humanity, curiosity, and kindness allowed Native Americans and the Lewis and Clark party to share food, drink, and entertainment. Most experiences of their contact consisted of rich interchanges.

Jefferson placed great importance on mapping uncharted areas of the West, setting cartography as a significant goal for the expedition. Clark proved to be a genius in mapmaking. Both Lewis and Clark took astronomical readings throughout the trip to ascertain points of latitude and longitude. Clark's engraved 1814 map shattered geographic misconceptions about the West, including hopes of a Northwest Passage and short portages between major rivers.[5]

President Jefferson's enthusiasm for Enlightenment science prompted him to train Lewis to document scientific observations on the journey. Lewis, in turn, encouraged the other men to record all they observed in weather, topography, minerals, plants, birds, animals, and Indian dress, food, language, and habits. Paul Russell Cutright's *Lewis and Clark: Pioneering Naturalists* (1969) enumerates the expedition's immense contribution in classifying new plants and animals. Science was clearly a motivation for the trip: A March 1803 letter from the English chargé d'affaires in the United States to the British secretary of state for foreign affairs stated that it was Jefferson's intention as a man of letters and of science to distinguish his presidency by accomplishing the only remaining discovery on the continent, that portion linking the northwest territories with the Missouri River. The expedition would not carry articles of commerce except as necessary to obtain favorable reception and passage through native villages.[6] This letter overplayed Jefferson's scientific motive while ignoring his instructions to Lewis to find a practicable water route for purposes of commerce. Speculation that Jefferson used scientific discovery for political advancement must contend with the fact that the president had always been fascinated by scientific discovery and description. Jefferson's previous attempts to sponsor this particular exploration demonstrated his avid commitment to scientific knowledge.

Jefferson's letter of instruction admonished Lewis and Clark to bring home scientific, anthropological, and geological information.

> Your observations are to be taken with great pains & accuracy, to be entered distinctly, & intelligibly for others as well as for yourself . . . several copies of these, as well as of your other notes, should be made at leisure times & put into the care of the most trustworthy of your attendants to guard by multiplying them, against the accidental losses to which they will be exposed.[7]

Thus, writing itself became a mission of the journey. Jefferson's instructions reflected popular curiosity about wilderness territory at home and in Europe. Gass's daily journal testifies to the voyage's political, scientific, and literary accomplishments, even though geography defied the expectation of easy trade routes to the West. Nevertheless, fur traders, mountain men, and, later, precious metal prospectors followed Lewis and Clark, eventually pushing the area open for settlement. Several members of the corps returned to the West after their release from the expedition.

To lead his favorite project, Jefferson chose Captain Meriwether Lewis, First Infantry, U.S. Army. Prior to his inauguration, Jefferson requested Lewis from General James Wilkinson on February 23, 1801, to serve as his private secretary.[8] Lewis's skills as a frontiersman surpassed those of a secretary, so the Sage of Monticello clearly was nurturing Lewis for the voyage he had so long promoted. As the expedition gained approval and funding, the president made sure that Lewis received the basic and varied education needed for the trip. Lewis studied medicinal cures under Benjamin Rush. In 1803, Jefferson sent Lewis to spend three weeks with Andrew Ellicot, an astronomer who instructed him in the use of the sextant and advised him which navigational instruments to buy. Lewis studied natural history under Caspar Wistar in Philadelphia. Another friend of Jefferson and author of the first textbook on botany in the United States, Benjamin Barton, personally guided Lewis's keen interest in the study of plants. Lewis shopped extensively for the supplies his party would need for living in the wilderness and trading with Indians.

In 1794, Meriwether Lewis had served in a rifle company as an ensign under William Clark, who resigned from the army after the Battle of Fallen Timbers. Lewis admired him greatly. Knowing him to be familiar with American Indians and life in the wilderness, Lewis invited Clark to share the command for the Voyage of Discovery. Lewis requested a captain's commission for Clark but the War Department refused, granting Clark the rank of second lieutenant in the Corps of Artillery. Clark, nevertheless, was addressed as "Captain" throughout the trip. The two men ignored the disparity and honored the promise of shared command in a spirit quite rare in human relations and unique in the military.

Lewis and Clark chose members of the expedition for their hardy practicality. No gentlemen's sons were encouraged to sally forth into the vast unknown. They were looking for "some good hunters, stout, healthy, unmarried men, accustomed to the woods, and capable of bearing bodily fatigue in a pretty considerable degree."[9] Hunters would labor with the rest of the party. No jobs would be exclusive. Captain Lewis received army authorization to select volunteers from the companies of Captain Russell Bissell, Captain Daniel Bissell, and Captain Amos Stoddard, then at Fort Massac and Fort Kaskaskia. Patrick Gass and John Ordway volunteered at Kaskaskia. Captain Russell Bissell did not want to release Gass because of his skills as a carpenter, but Gass persisted, asking Lewis to intervene on his behalf. With Lewis as Gass's advocate, Bissell had to release Gass.[10]

Other volunteers exhibited skills needed for the voyage. John Shields and Alexander Willard were talented blacksmiths. The "nine young men from Kentucky" included excellent hunters: Nathaniel Pryor, Charles Floyd, William Bratton, John Colter, Joseph Field, Reuben Field, George Gibson, George Shannon, and Joseph Whitehouse (see Appendix B, Table of Hunters). Lewis and Clark engaged French riverboatmen (engagés) who knew the waterways of the Missouri and its tributaries. Peter Cruzatte, a permanent member, used these skills past the Mandan villages. Some of the men facilitated negotations with American Indians by interpreting. Perhaps the most valuable man in the party was not in the army. Employed as an interpreter, George Drouillard, half French and half Shawnee (called "Drewyer" in the journals), used the art of gesticulation to communicate with Indians. An excellent hunter and tracker, he killed much of the game that fed the expedition.[11]

Fifty-one men (not forty-three, as Gass reported) began the journey from St. Louis, according to the biographical roster compiled by Charles G. Clarke.[12] They included two captains, a slave, three sergeants, eight corporals, twenty-four privates, an interpreter, and approximately a dozen temporary engagés. These men left Camp DuBois in three boats, a fifty-five-foot-long by eight-foot-wide keelboat with twenty-two oars, and two pirogues, or large, deep rowboats. Lewis had ordered the keelboat built at Pittsburgh and used it to descend the Ohio into the Mississippi.[13]

The men rowed and towed the boats against the current of the Missouri River to what is now North Dakota. Names of rivers, streams, notable geographic sites, animals, and Indian tribes they encountered reflected earlier French presence in the region. The party moved north up the Missouri to spend the first winter among the Mandan Indians. In April 1805, a party of men including Richard Warfington and six other corporals, pilot Joseph Gravelines, two Frenchmen, two engagés (Francois Rivet and Phillipe Degie), two expelled members (Private Moses Reed and Corporal John Newman), and one Arikara Indian returned down the Missouri River to St. Louis. The return party took maps, writings, and samples of fauna and flora so at least the first leg of the trip would be forever preserved.

Thirty-three people proceeded westward from the fortification at the Mandan village on April 7, 1805. Interpreter Toussaint Charbonneau, his Lemhi Shoshone wife, Sacagawea, and their newborn infant, Jean Baptiste ("Pomp"), joined the party. Continuing up the Missouri River, the travelers saw no Indians on this portion of the trip. At Great Falls, Montana, they portaged around the awesome series of waterfalls. The party left the water to cross the Continental Divide. At the Bitterroot Mountains dividing present-day Idaho and Montana, they at last met Sacagawea's people, the Shoshone. Cameahwait, whom Sacagawea called her brother, traded with the first Euro-Americans his people had ever seen, providing the horses that the corps needed to cross the mountains. He also furnished the party with an old guide, Toby. Crossing the Continental Divide a second time in present-day Montana, the party acquired more horses from the Flathead Indians at Ross's Hole and proceeded to Travellers Rest, near present-day Missoula. Then the Corps of Discovery crossed the arduous Lolo Trail, with Toby as their guide, to Nez Perce country at Weippe Prairie. After leaving the Nez Perce Indians, another Idaho tribe who had never previously encountered whites, the travelers descended rivers now known as the Clearwater, the Snake, and the Columbia. The corps encountered many groups of native peoples on both banks of the Columbia below Walla Walla, Washington, and arrived at the Pacific Ocean in November 1805.

During the expedition, the corps made three protracted stops. The first lasted from November 2, 1804, to April 7, 1805, at the Mandan villages in what is now North Dakota. Under the direction of Patrick Gass, the men built a fortification where they spent the winter. The following winter, on December 7, 1805, the travelers located their encampment on the Pacific coast near the Clatsop Indians. Gass and the men built Fort Clatsop, where they remained until March 23, 1806. In its haste to return home, the expedition set out too early and met snow in the Bitterroot mountains, which made them impassable. The party built temporary shelters (called the "Long Camp") near Nez Perce villages on the Clearwater River and waited for warmer weather from May 13 to June 10, 1806. Anxious to proceed, the group prematurely set out across the mountains and faced its only "retrograde march." Then, with Nez Perce guides, the men crossed the snow-laden mountains.

After traversing the difficult Lolo Trail east across the Bitterroots, the party divided. Clark explored the Yellowstone River to the south while Lewis headed north to the Marias River. Gass, Ordway, and Pryor had separate assignments with other personnel. The vulnerability of Lewis's group of four that ascended the Marias contributed to an unfortunate dispute with several Piegan Blackfeet, two of whom were killed. Returning from this sad encounter at breakneck speed, Lewis's party miraculously met the combined groups under Sergeants Ordway and Gass, who, after portaging the Great Falls, had descended farther down the Missouri. Days later, with a deep wound through his hip after being shot by the chagrined and partially blind Cruzatte, who had mistaken him for an elk, Lewis joined Clark slightly downstream from the mouth of the Yellowstone. At the Mandan villages, the Charbonneau family left the party and the corps released John Colter to head west with Illinois traders in search of beaver.

When the ragged and travel-weary Corps of Discovery reached civilization and other boats along the Missouri River, it was greeted with amazement. People had thought the men lost. Two years, four months, and ten days had elapsed since the explorers had departed St. Louis. They had covered more than 8,000 miles walking, rowing and hauling boats, or riding horseback. Their return to St. Louis September 23, 1806, ended the adventure, but the legend grew.

Interpretations of this famous "tour," as the captains called it, have construed events and imbedded values in the consciousness of Westerners. Traits of independence, bravery, curiosity, and adventure have been regularly ascribed to the voyagers, assigned to western American culture at large, and embraced by individuals as part of their own heritage. Rather than raw courage and individuality, however, intelligence and cooperation provide key themes for the successful legacy of the expedition. Mutual understanding among members of the Corps of Discovery showed daily in the purposeful activity of exploration. Human relations on this voyage showed the merits of interdependence, mutual respect, and shared responsibility.

Another look at original sources allows us to check the myths against what really happened. An annotated original journal account offers the best way to review events. The Patrick Gass journal of 1807, edited by David McKeehan, provides an interesting and easy way to read an original account. The concise Gass journal, the rich, inclusive observations of Clark and Lewis, the detail of Ordway, the charming descriptions of Whitehouse—each account documents the exploration.

All of the Lewis and Clark journals embody the earliest written accounts of western tribes and their lifestyles, describing events such as Shoshone women carrying baggage across the river for the corps, Mandans generously giving corn in appreciation for repairs executed with the corps' primitive forge, and Nez Perces, while tottering on the brink of starvation themselves, sharing their meager rations with the white visitors. Some Native Americans who experienced substantial contact with whites, especially those on the lower Columbia River, such as the Chinooks and the Clatsops, challenged expedition members with wily sophistication in bargaining for food and sex. Teton Sioux on the Missouri River posed threats when they nearly prevented the expedition's passage. The tragic fracas with Piegan Blackfeet on the Marias River during the return trip ended the corps' bloodless record.

Overall, however, the Corps of Discovery enjoyed astounding luck. Hugh McNeal's horse threw him off under a grizzly bear that he popped on the head with the muzzle of his gun hard enough to stun the bear so he could climb a tree, where the grizzly held him hostage for three hours. John Potts, a nonswimmer, escaped when a canoe with three men overturned in the Clearwater River during the high flow and strong current of spring thaw of 1806. On three occasions during their westward journey, George Shannon, a young man of nineteen, wandered lost for days, miraculously returning each time to the group. When the nearly blind Cruzatte shot Lewis by mistake, the lead that ripped through his hip missed Lewis's ball and socket by only an inch. None of these events delivered human tragedy. On the other hand, the episode on the Marias River, when Lewis and Reuben Field killed Side Hill Calf and his fellow Piegan warrior, the party's luck turned awry.[14]

When they returned home, members of the expedition scattered to their various fates, all interesting, but only a few of which will be mentioned here. John Colter had already asked to leave at Mandan, where he headed back upriver with two Illinois fur traders. He later became the first white man to report on the natural wonders south of present-day Yellowstone Park. Drouillard also went back upstream, with Manuel Lisa's party, and Blackfeet Indians later killed him. Perhaps they recognized him as one of the party that they had encountered on the Marias River. The junior member of the corps, George Shannon, served under Pryor on the army unit assigned to escort Chief Sheheke (Big White) home to the Mandans. On this mission, Arikara Indians shot him and Shannon lost a leg. After Lewis's death, Shannon assisted Nicholas Biddle in preparing the captains' journals for publication. "Pegleg" Shannon married, studied law, and was elected to the Kentucky House of Representatives in 1820 and 1822. Sergeant Nathaniel Pryor, one of the few married men on the expedition, stayed in the army and became a captain in 1814. On his discharge, he entered the Indian trade, took an Osage woman as his wife, and fathered several children, all with Indian names. William Bratton, who nearly died on the trip, married at age forty-one and raised ten children in Indiana. Sacagawea's baby, Jean Baptiste ("Pomp") Charbonneau, the junior member of the party, was educated by William Clark at St. Louis. In 1823, Baptiste went to Europe with Prince Paul Wilhelm, Duke of Württemburg, for six years, returning to become a fur trader and interpreter for John C. Frémont and others.[15] Patrick Gass became the first of the corps to have a full biography written about him.

Patrick Gass

Patrick Gass fit the model of frontiersman that Lewis and Clark were seeking for the expedition. He was born June 12, 1771, at Falling Springs, Pennsylvania, under the British flag at the dawn of the Age of American Exploration. There the Gass family operated a fulling mill, which treated cloth for garments. His biographer, J. G. Jacob, described him in 1859 as Irish; however, a modern writer, Dr. E. G. Chuinard, argues that Gass was descended from the clan of Gasg or Gask in Scotland. The clan changed its name to Gass in the sixteenth century.[16] Gass's mother was a McLean of Scottish descent.

Gass's peripatetic father moved the family to Maryland when Patrick was four, settling within earshot of Revolutionary War battles. From 1777 to 1780, young Patrick lived with his grandparents, supposedly to receive an education. In spite of the fact that Gass told Jacob the sum of his formal education was only nineteen days, which he received after manhood,[17] his account book between 1826 and 1837 shows Gass's ease with writing, spelling, record-keeping and mathematics.

The Gass family moved in 1780, and again in 1782, when they migrated farther west to Carlisle, Pennsylvania. In April 1784, the family moved on three pack horses to Uniontown, formerly Beasontown, Pennsylvania.[18] Shortly thereafter, they moved to Catfish Camp (modern-day Washington), Pennsylvania. From Catfish Camp, where the Gasses leased a farm, Patrick rode to Hagerstown and Mercersburg occasionally, taking pack horses to bring home salt and iron. Young Gass developed an affinity for travel and self-sufficiency.

In 1792, when the army drafted Gass's father to defend settlers from Indian attacks, Patrick served in his stead. No battles developed, but Gass became acquainted with well-known frontier scouts. He joined a group of flatboatmen on a trading trip to New Orleans in March of 1793, returning to Philadelphia by way of Cuba, a wide swath of travel at that time.

Patrick Gass bound himself as a carpenter's apprentice in Mercersburg, Pennsylvania, in 1794. There he worked on the house owned by James Buchanan, Senior, whose son, young Jimmy, was destined to become the fifteenth president of the United States. Gass worked as a carpenter in Mercersburg until 1799. When conflict with France threatened, Gass lay down his tools to enlist in the army under General Alexander Hamilton. Stationed at Harper's Ferry, Gass was discharged when no skirmish developed. He later reenlisted under Major Jonathan Cass, whose detachment spent the winter of 1800 in tents at Wilkinsville on the Ohio River. In the fall of 1801, Patrick Gass went with Captain Russell Bissell's company up the Tennessee River. The next year, this contingent joined an artillery company at Kaskaskia, Illinois.

In the fall of 1803, the recruitment process began for volunteers to go on an overland expedition to the Pacific Ocean. Meriwether Lewis came to Fort Kaskaskia for recruits. The prospect of a western expedition to venture where no white man had trod appealed to Gass. When Captain Bissell refused to release his carpenter, Gass prevailed by asking Lewis to intercede. Gass joined the small company at Camp DuBois and built living quarters there on the Mississippi, where the recruits stayed during the winter of 1803–1804 while they prepared for the trip west.

At thirty-three, Gass was among the oldest men of the expedition. William Clark was ten months his senior, and John Shields was two years older than Gass. Most of the men were in their twenties. Meriwether Lewis was twenty-nine. The senior member, in his mid-forties, was Toussaint Charbonneau, the French trader who joined them at the Mandan village with Sacagawea and their infant son.[19]

Gass proved to be a practical, flexible member of the expedition, serving as head carpenter, a boatsman in charge of a canoe, an occasional hunter, an experienced horseman, and one of seven known journalists: Lewis, Clark, Ordway, Gass, Floyd, Whitehouse, and Frazer. Pryor and Willard may have kept journals as well. Gass brought a special perspective to the trip—that of a woodsman who knew and identified trees, a laborer who diligently applied himself, whatever the task, and a lover of land where water, timber, and game abounded.

Mention of Gass's contributions lay in the captain's journals, not in his own. On June 29, 1804, during the court-martial of John Collins, accused of being drunk while on sentinel duty, Gass served as a member of the court that sentenced Collins to one hundred lashes. Again, on October 13, 1804, Gass served during the court-martial of John Newman, who was sentenced to seventy-five lashes and expelled from the permanent expedition for mutinous utterances. When Sergeant Charles Floyd died, apparently of appendicitis, on August 20, 1804, the men of the corps elected Gass by popular vote to replace him. Gass received nineteen votes. Bratton and Gibson were runners-up. The captains' appointment of Gass confirmed the popular votes. Gass, a man of "capacity, deligence and integrety,"[20] had a reputation for responsibility, hard work, and good humor. Gass mentioned none of the above in his journal, an indication of his humility or, perhaps, of his laconic style.

Gass often accompanied the leaders on sensitive missions to Native Americans. In September 1804, he went with Clark to take Teton Sioux chiefs ashore when they did not want to go. In February 1805, Gass accompanied Lewis and twenty-four of the party to pursue the Sioux who had robbed Captain Clark's party of two horses. And in July 1806, he separated from Clark's party to join Lewis for the trek up the Marias River. After seven horses were stolen, leaving enough for only four to explore the Marias, he stayed in charge of portaging the canoes around the falls.

More than anything, Gass proved to be a reliable worker and an able carpenter. He toiled for days on the *Experiment,* the iron boat of Lewis's dream. Held together with strips of buffalo and elk hide, it sank for want of proper materials, despite good efforts. Gass was sent to the salt works on the Pacific to render salt and find two tardy companions. He made saddle pads of goat hair, repaired broken canoes and masts, and dug up the cache at the Great Falls on the homeward route. He hunted lost horses and tracked game. The only times Lewis hinted at faulting him occurred when Gass lost Captain Lewis's tomahawk and when Gass could not find the seven missing horses lost before the Marias River foray.

Most of Gass's brief lapses from journal writing indicate days of his greatest responsibility—building the stockade at the Mandan village, accompanying a hunting trip at Mandan, constructing canoes to leave Mandan in the spring of 1805, building the canoes to descend the Clearwater at the Nez Perce village in the fall of 1805, and building Fort Clatsop in December of that year. Other brief omissions occur while the party took leave in St. Charles and while Gass accompanied Lewis to the Mandan village after Christmas. Also, during the last few days before the expedition arrived at St. Louis, when the men received ample spirits from Missouri River traders, Gass failed to keep his journal.

Gass's renowned humor appears less often in his journal than it did in his speech, according to his family's oral tradition and his biographer. He enjoyed liquor and tobacco during the trip and afterward, and a few times he noted the presence or absence of females when other journalists did not. Despite an affinity for liquor and the abuses of frontier life, Gass's health remained superb. Years later, when he was eighty-seven, biographer Jacob described Gass as "a hale, hearty old man, with the apparent promise of many years of life yet to come . . . in stature, somewhat low, never having in his best estate, exceeded five feet seven, stoutly and compactly built, broad-chested and heavy limbed, yet lean, sprightly and quick of motion . . . remarkably alert and [an] active walker [who] can make the four miles from his residence to Wellsburg, in about as good time as most of those of one fourth his years."[21] Gass's military enlistment record described him as a young man having a dark complexion, gray eyes, and dark hair.

During the expedition, Gass noted four bad days. One occurred in Montana, when he slipped and fell in a canoe and sprained his back, forcing him to go on foot a few days. On another occasion, he noted discomfort from eating the dried salmon and the camas roots the charitable Nez Perce of Idaho gave the starving men, to the abdominal chagrin of most of them. He mentioned being "unwell" on July 24, 1806, for only one day. The fourth mention was when he claimed, on leaving the Nez Perce, that he had ague, a form of malaria with accompanying fever. It seems dubious that Gass had ague instead of just a bad fever in light of the fact he lived ninety-nine years, outliving his wife, more than forty years younger than he, and outliving all other members of the expedition by many years.

Gass went home to Wellsburg, Virginia (later West Virginia), when the Corps of Discovery disbanded. He apparently contacted David McKeehan, a bookseller in Pittsburgh, to edit his journal. McKeehan, whose interest in geography shows in his footnotes to Gass's journal, may be the same David McKeehan who graduated from Dickinson College in 1787 and was admitted to the Pennsylvania bar in 1792. J. G. Jacob associated McKeehan with Wellsburg, Virginia, where Gass returned home to after the expedition.

The first edition of Gass's journal appeared a short time later in the early summer of 1807. During its many subsequent publications, little is known about Gass except that he was speculating in lead ore when the War of 1812 began. He enlisted for the war, receiving a $100 cash advance and the promise of $24 more on the expiration of his service. He served at Fort Massac, Kentucky, in 1813, and at Bellefontaine, Missouri. His biographer, J. G. Jacob, learned in an interview that Gass lost his left eye after being struck with a splinter from a falling tree.[22] There was a discrepancy about this in the biographical notes by Earle Forrest in 1958.[23] Later, Donald Jackson pointed out the error in Gass's pension application of December 23, 1851, which stated that he had lost his eye while fighting the Battle of Lundy's Lane in 1814.[24] At age eighty-four, Gass appealed to Congress to enhance his pension because he was a widower with six young children. However, his letter of March 12, 1829, clearly claimed that he lost his eye in service, not in battle. His discharge papers of 1815 also state that Gass lost his left eye in service at Fort Independence on the Mississippi, Territory of Missouri (not Lundy's Lane), in September of 1813, depriving him entirely of the use of it. The army granted Gass a pension for total disability upon his discharge June 10, 1815, because of his useless left eye.[25]

After his military discharge, Gass again returned to Wellsburg, where he lived in a marginal fashion until he met a girl more than forty years his junior. Maria Hamilton's father owned the room-and-board house where Gass was living. In 1831, at age fifty-nine, Gass married Maria, who was at the most sixteen years old.[26] She bore him seven children before dying of measles on February 16, 1847, leaving six (their firstborn, Elizabeth, died at nine months of age in 1832) surviving children, the youngest of whom was then just eleven months old. Their names were Benjamin, William, James, Sara ("Sallie" Bowman), Annie (Smith), and Rachel (Brierley).[27]

When Maria died, Patrick was seventy-five; he lived ninety-nine years. "He died April 2, 1870, in a small log house on the farm of David Waugh, near the first tunnel on the Bethany Pike, on Buffalo Creek, Brooke County, and is buried in Shrimplin's cemetery on Pierce's Run."[28] In about 1920, Patrick and Maria Gass's remains were moved to the Brooke County Cemetery at Wellsburg.

During Gass's lifetime, Forrest noted, our nation grew from thirteen colonies to thirty-eight states. Eighteen men had been president, from Washington to Grant. Four wars were fought: the Revolutionary War, the War of 1812, the Mexican War of 1848, and the Civil War. Patrick Gass had not only observed tremendous change in the growth of America but also he had participated in the expedition that served as a model for United States expansion. Bernard DeVoto pointed out that the development of culture in the West assured the security of American borders, prohibited the nation's division by civil war, and fostered the later strength and prosperity of the United States. The expedition that opened the Louisiana Purchase and the Northwest territories to American expansion proved to be a mission of historic significance beyond what Patrick Gass or other members of the corps could have dreamed.

The Gass Journal in the Historiography of the Expedition

This new edition of Patrick Gass's journal preserves exactly its first printing in textual format and spelling (including the consistent misspelling of Clark's name), but the graphics are added from a later edition. Annotation amplifies the reader's experience by identifying people when possible, pointing out places occasionally for bearings, and describing interesting events from other journals that Gass omitted. Beyond explaining the cryptic and missing, this edition credits Gass for his contribution to the greater literary body of Lewis and Clark expedition journals.

The men on the Lewis and Clark expedition were the "writingest explorers" ever, according to Donald Jackson. Original journals have appeared from 1807 through 1953, with each discovery expanding scholars' opportunities to compare information and amplify the interpretations of the most outstanding saga in the Age of Exploration. Seven men kept journals on the trip: the two captains (Lewis and Clark), three sergeants (Charles Floyd, John Ordway, and Patrick Gass), and two privates (Joseph Whitehouse and Robert Frazer). Six of these are published today, for which five original manuscripts are known to exist. That of Frazer is lost, as is the original manuscript of Patrick Gass.

Numerous searches for the Gass manuscript have been conducted since Reuben Gold Thwaites work in 1904 through March 1990, when I searched for in at the American Philosophical Society and at the Brooke County Library at Wellsburg, West Virginia, where local manuscripts and records of the area are kept. The few clues on record about the Gass manuscript have led nowhere so far.

Only three of the extant six journals—those by Clark, Ordway, and Gass—are continuous accounts of the entire journey. The journal of Patrick Gass was the first to be published upon the return of the voyage, appearing in print in 1807 at Pittsburgh. David McKeehan edited the journal. Gass's choice to have McKeehan edit his journal engendered rebuke from Meriwether Lewis and subsequent criticism from a few scholars.

Meriwether Lewis reacted extremely critically to the advertisement for Gass's journal. He published letters in the *National Intelligencer* on March 18, 25, 27, and 30, and April 1, 1807, stating that he had heard of "several unauthorised and probably some spurious publications now preparing for the press, on the subject of my late tour to the Pacific Ocean by individuals entirely unknown to me." He wished to warn the public that his own work could be depreciated by these less worthy projects, and that the only one he had given permission to publish journals was Frazer, whom Lewis dubbed as unqualified in most subjects of their observations, as were other "unauthorised" authors.

McKeehan answered Lewis's letters with a scathing retort aimed at his less-than-humble assumption of authority over journals that McKeehan said were not claimed by the government and were, therefore, the property of the individuals who had written them. He suggested the royalties Lewis received after the voyage were more appropriate for a prince than for an officer of a republican army. Further, he accused Lewis of being avaricious—too eager for the proceeds of his own journal and fame.[29]

No one will ever know the impact this unfortunate exchange had on Captain Meriwether Lewis or on Sergeant Patrick Gass. For himself, Gass received as compensation the copyright of his book (which was later disregarded), one hundred copies of it (few of which were passed on to his heirs), and perhaps "original purchase money," referred to in McKeehan's Prospectus (see Appendix C). For Lewis, financial problems, emotional instability, and drinking exacerbated his frustration over publishing the expedition journals. Gass's scoop of the story must have dismayed him and perhaps contributed to Lewis's procrastination and eventually diminished the commercial value of his own book (published posthumously). The vast materials he and Clark had written on the voyage, plus the journals of Ordway and Pryor, which he had purchased, weighed heavily on him as time passed. In 1809, before his project was published, Lewis died of apparent suicide at Grinder's Stand on the Natchez Trace in Tennessee.

That Patrick Gass contacted an editor to publish his notes showed his enterprising nature when he knew what he wanted, just as he had convinced Lewis he wanted to accompany the overland expedition. David McKeehan, a schoolmaster and bookseller, came recommended to Patrick Gass after he returned home to Wellsburg. McKeehan wrote in the current genre of exploration literature, much like the writings of Alexander Mackenzie. Members of Captain Cook's expedition published two other well-known journals of the period. John Rickman and John Ledyard "faithfully narrated" their journals from manuscript form to other parties who published them.[30] Gass's decision to have McKeehan, an educated man he knew, edit his journal conformed to the standard of the day.

The discovery of Gass's account book of 1826–1837 and 1847–1848 demonstrates his ability to keep records, spell, and organize data better than his descendants guessed.[31] Gass noted particulars of trees, numbers of moccasins made, and other details, but he never mentioned names of personnel, as Ordway had, or scientific data, as the captains had.

Clear clues exist as to what was written by Gass and what was added by McKeehan in the text of the first edition. Most of the text is simple, clear reporting on daily events; that was Gass's style. The flowery, erudite style of the thirty footnotes, indicated by * or † and attributed to McKeehan, appears heavily in the text on the first day, May 14, 1804, and rarely in subsequent entries.

A comparison with other journals of the Lewis and Clark expedition shows that on many occasions exact wording was copied by two or more journals. None of the expedition journals were entirely "original." Campfire editing was encouraged as a practical way to have several copies of the same material, in case something might be lost.

The Gass journal was published in 1807 in Pittsburgh by Zadok Cramer as *A Journal of the Voyages and Travels of a Corps of Discovery, under the command of Capt Lewis and Capt Clarke of the Army of the United States from the mouth of the River Missouri through the interior parts of North America to the Pacific Ocean, during the years 1804, 1805, & 1806*. J. Budd, bookseller to the Prince of Wales, Pall-Mall, published it in London in 1808. Gass's journal was published in 1810 in France, and in 1814 in Germany. The Mathew Carey publications of 1810, 1811, and 1812 in Philadelphia included six charming woodcuts, the first published graphics of the journey; the 1810 woodcuts are reproduced in Book I herein. Paul Russell Cutright, an eminent voice on the historiography of the expedition, calls them "delightfully preposterous."[32] They have become favorites among Lewis and Clark aficionados. The legality of Carey's copyright, owned by Gass, is questionable.[33] Ells, Claflin, and Company added more illustrations, a few inaccurately imaginative, in their 1847 printing of the Gass journals. In 1904, the same year that Reuben Gold Thwaites published the first complete edition of the original journals, James K. Hosmer edited a new publication called *Gass's Journal of the Lewis and Clark Expedition*. In 1958, Earle E. Forrest presented his *Journal of Patrick Gass*. In 1996, Gary E. Moulton published Gass's journal as volume ten in *The Journals of the Lewis and Clark Expedition*.

None of the above editions varies much in content, although the format varies and spelling errors have been corrected. However, public reception of them has changed. At the outset, enthusiastic international interest greeted the Gass journal. In the twentieth century, however, it has suffered in status and popularity. The discovery and publication of Gass's account book should dispel the notion that Gass's journal met with heavy-handed editing from McKeehan. Clearly, Gass could keep records accurately. His terse style and practical knowledge is unique and easily identifiable. That McKeehan used only a light and occasional hand in the manuscript is evident in the preservation of exact wording in other journals as a result of the campfire editing sessions. Further analysis of editorial intervention in Gass's journal appears in my introduction to "The Account Book of Patrick Gass," Book II of this volume.

The first seven years following the expedition proved most important in the role of the Gass journal. As the only printed record of the voyage, it satisfied the curiosities of many Europeans and Americans. By the time Allen and Biddle published the journals of the captains in 1814, other explorations, the War of 1812, and time itself diverted national attention away from the Lewis and Clark expedition. The number of printings of Gass's journal in three languages and four countries prior to the appearance of the official account in 1814 testified to its large, worldwide audience.

In the twentieth century, criticism of McKeehan's editing and the discovery of others' original journals and letters made Gass's journal less popular. Reuben Gold Thwaite's comprehensive edition of the expedition—including Whitehouse's and Floyd's journals, all of Clark's prose, and much of Lewis's—represented a huge contribution to scholarship. The discovery of Ordway's journal in 1913 in the attic of Edward Biddle, grandson of Nicholas Biddle, accompanied by large portions of Lewis's journal, made these materials available for Milo Quaife's edition of the expedition, published by the Wisconsin Historical Society in 1916. Then, as late as 1953, some of Clark's field notes were found in the attic of a descendant of General John Hammond, who had been employed by the Indian Bureau for a period after the Civil War. Clark's notes from Camp DuBois were with the field notes. They were edited by Ernest Staples Osgood in 1964 and the originals are now housed at Yale University. The most definitive and inclusive work yet to be published on the Lewis and Clark expedition is Gary Moulton's handsome new multivolume hardback edition being published by the University of Nebraska Press. It presents the best cartography of the expedition and will eventually include all of the journals.

This new edition of Gass's journal offers new evidence, in the form of his account ledger, of the sergeant's literacy and brings his journal up-to-date with recent scholarship, all in a single volume and reader-friendly format. Annotation comparing Gass's work to the others provides a clear sketch of the whole journey. The easiest jounal to read because of Gass's straightforward style, it presents material not otherwise noted on the voyage. The result is an excellent opportunity for students and devotees of western history to experience the trip, day by day.

By comparing Gass's daily entries with those of Lewis, Clark, Ordway, Floyd, and Whitehouse, readers gain an enhanced understanding of what happened. Through Gass's unadorned prose we learn how this practical man felt about the rainy coast, the rich Missouri river bottoms, and the mountainous wastelands where horses fell from narrow paths. Overall, Gass kept a positive tone. As a worker and an adventurer, he sought the unknown and was ready for any job. Clearly, his journal lacks an overview of the voyage's purposes and the *espirit de corps* of the men. He omitted scientific data and extensive observations of Indian ethnography. His vocabulary was limited, rendering his journal less exciting to scholars yet more readable for those who want a simple, straightforward account. The rich minutiae in the captains' journals, which fascinates sincere scholars of the expedition, involves wading through difficult spelling, astronomical readings, long descriptions of plants, animals, and Indian linguistics, and arduous repetition of journal entries. The original 1807 Gass journal still effectively points to the real, practical questions necessary to daily survival on the Lewis and Clark expedition.

McKeehan's original footnotes are intact in this new edition, at the bottom of the pages, as they appeared in 1807. Frequent references to Alexander Mackenzie's journey in McKeehan's footnotes of Gass's journal lent an interesting comparison to the earliest observations on the West. With the absence of maps until the Biddle edition, these notes facilitated geographical references.

New comparative annotations parallel the daily journal. This edition includes six appendices: A, B, and C for the journal; X, Y, and Z for the account book. Hunters never identified by name in Gass's journal are sometimes identified in other journals; they are noted in this edition by a superscript plus mark (+) and identified in Appendix B, the Table of Hunters.

A journal comprises inductive history. The story unfolds as it happens, without the embellishment of overview or the perspective of hindsight. Now, readers can enjoy Gass's journal with many of the missing details explained in the end notes. Gass's own words and style allow the reader to feel the hardship of the day-to-day quest for food, the influence of weather on the men, the torments of fleas, mosquitoes, the prickly pear, and the grizzly bears. Readers can see the beauty Gass saw in trees, rivers, plains, and mountains, and his fascination with new sorts of people and animals, as the unknown unfolded each day for a working member of the corps.

Patrick Gass

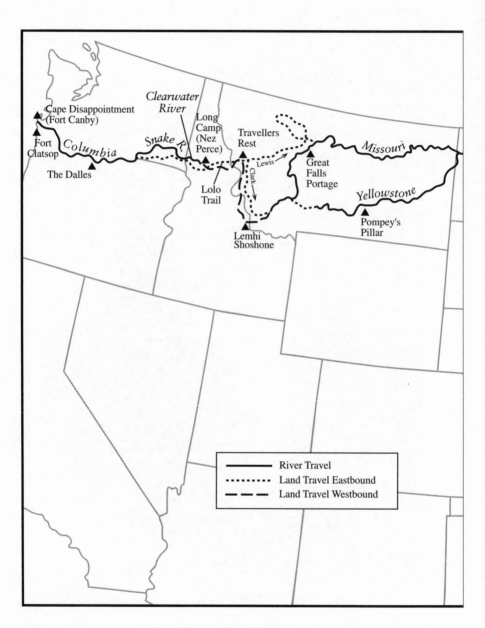

Map of the Lewis and Clark route.

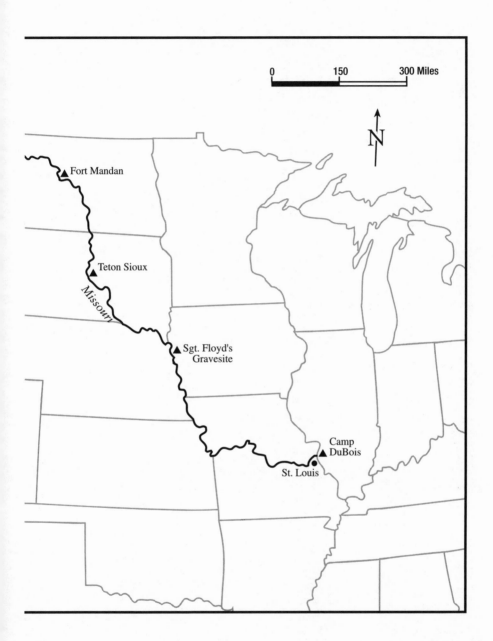

0   150   300 Miles

N

Fort Mandan

Teton Sioux

Missouri

Sgt. Floyd's
Gravesite

Camp
DuBois

St. Louis

A JOURNAL

OF THE

VOYAGES AND TRAVELS
OF A CORPS OF DISCOVERY,

UNDER THE COMMAND OF CAPT. LEWIS AND CAPT.
CLARKE OF THE ARMY OF THE UNITED STATES

FROM

THE MOUTH OF THE RIVER MISSOURI THROUGH THE INTERIOR PARTS OF NORTH AMERICA TO THE PACIFIC OCEAN, DURING THE YEARS 1804, 1805 & 1806.

CONTAINING

An authentic relation of the most interesting transactions
during the expedition,—A description of the country,—
And an account of its inhabitants, soil, climate, curiosities
and vegetable and animal productions.

BY PATRICK GASS
ONE OF THE PERSONS EMPLOYED IN THE EXPEDITION

WITH

GEOGRAPHICAL AND EXPLANATORY NOTES
BY THE PUBLISHER

PITTSBURGH,
PRINTED BY ZADOK CRAMER,
FOR DAVID M'KEEHAN, PUBLISHER AND
PROPRIETOR..........1807.

DISTRICT OF PENNSYLVANIA, TO WIT:

(L. S.) BE IT REMEMBERED, That on the eleventh day of April in the thirty-first year of the Independence of the United States of America, A.D. 1807, *David M'Keehan*, of the said District, hath deposited in this Office, the Title of a Book the Right whereof he claims as Proprietor in the words following, to wit:

"A Journal of the Voyages and Travels of a Corps of Discovery, under the command of Capt. Lewis and Capt. Clarke of the Army of the United States, from the mouth of the river Missouri through the interior parts of North America to the Pacific Ocean, during the years 1804, 1805 and 1806. Containing an authentic relation of the most interesting transactions during the expedition,—A description of the country,—And an account of its inhabitants, soil, climate, curiosities, and vegetable and animal productions [*sic*]. —By *Patrick Gass*, one of the persons employed in the Expedition. With Geographical and Explanatory Notes by the *Publisher.*"

In Conformity to the Act of the Congress of the United States, intituled [*sic*], "An Act for the Encouragement of Learning, by securing the Copies of Maps, Charts, and Books, to the Authors and Proprietors of such Copies during the Times therein mentioned" And also to the Act, entitled "An Act supplementary to Act, entitled, "An Act for the Encouragement of Learning, by securing the Copies of Maps, Charts, and Books, to the Authors and Proprietors of such Copies during the Times therein mentioned," and extending the Benefits thereof to the Arts of designing, engraving, and etching historical and other Prints."

D . CALDWELL, *Clerk of the District of Pennsylvania.*

JOURNAL

OF THE

Voyages and Travels

OF A

CORPS OF DISCOVERY

PREFACE

[to the original 1807 edition]

BY THE PUBLISHER.

⸻

OF the various publications which unite amusement
and information, few can be justly held in higher estima-
tion than the Journals and Narratives of Travellers and
Voyagers: and in our own highly favoured country, the
diffusion of general knowledge, the enterprizing spirit of
the people, their commercial pursuits and habits of emi-
gration, render such works particularly valuable and
interesting; while the vigorous and unrestrained mind of
the free American, by amplifying and embellishing the
scenes presented to its view, enjoys the choicest luxuries
of the entertainment they are calculated to afford. If it is
conceded that discoveries made in North America are more
important to the people of the United States than those
made elsewhere, it will not be difficult to shew that none
could have been made of so much importance to them in
any part of the world as in the large tracts of country
through which the late expedition, under the command
of Captain Lewis and Captain Clarke, passed. For if we
take a view of the different discoveries and settlements
previously made, we will find that those tracts through
which the Missouri and Columbia rivers and their
branches flow, commonly called *unknown regions,* were
the only parts remaining unexplored, which could be
considered valuable.

The first discovery of the Western World by Europeans of which we have any authentick accounts, being near
the southern extremity of North America, drew, as might
be expected, their attention to that quarter: and the rage
which this grand discovery excited for other enterprizes
of the same nature; the avidity, with which avarice was
stimulated to seize the precious metals, known to exist in
those parts; the means held out for gratifying ambition;
and the prospects of a lucrative commerce, with many
other objects and considerations tended largely to extend
them; while the diminution of the Northern Continent to
a narrow isthmus, and its large gulphs, bays and rivers,
furnished and facilitated the means of exploring it. The
spirit of enterprize, however, was not confined to the southern extremity; but extending itself to the climates congenial with those which it had left, and connecting with its
researches the planting of colonies, important discoveries were made along the Atlantic coast. In the meantime
the project of discovering a northwest passage to the East
Indies led the boldest naval commanders of Europe
through the inland seas, bays, and straights of the north;
and at length produced surveys of the shores of the Pacific. To these discoveries, and those occasionally made
during the settlement of the country within the limits of
the United States, and in Canada, the Hudson's Bay Company, though not famed for enterprize added something
to the stock of general information, and by their establishments aided others in their enterprizes. Mr. Hearne
under the direction of this company, in an expedition,
which lasted from the 7th of December 1770 to the 30th
of June 1772, proceeded from Prince of Wales' Fort, on
the Churchhill river in latitude 58 d[egrees] 47 1-2
m[inutes] north, and longitude 94 d. 7 1-2 m. west of
Greenwich, or 19 d. west of Philadelphia, to the mouth of
the Coppermine river, which according to some accounts
is in latitude 72 d. north, and longitude 119 d. west from
Greenwich, or 44 d. west of Philadelphia; but is laid down
by others to be in latitude about 69 d. north, and longi-

tude 112 d. west from Greenwich or 37 d. west from Philadelphia. Whatever the confined views and contracted policy of the Hudson's Bay Company may, however, have omitted in the way of discovery, the enterprize and perseverance of the Canadian traders, sometime since united under the name of the North West Company, have amply supplied. Prior to the year 1789, they had extended their discoveries and establishments along the numerous lakes and rivers situated north of that high tract of country which divides the Mississippi and Missouri waters from those which run towards the north and east, to within a short distance of the Rocky Mountains. In the summer of this year Mr. M'Kenzie made a voyage from Fort Chepewyan on the lake of the Hills in latitude 58 d. 40 m. north, and longitude 110 d. 30 m. west from Greenwich or 35° 22 m. west from Philadelphia, by the way of the Slave river, Slave lake, and a river by which this lake discharges its waters (since called M'Kenzie's River) to the mouth of that river where it falls into the North sea, in latitude 69 d. 14 m. north and longitude 135 d. west from Greenwich, or 59 d. 52 m. west from Philadelphia. He again in the year 1793 penetrated from an establishment on the Peace river in latitude 56 d. 9 m. north, and longitude 117 d. 35 m. west from Greenwich, or 41 d. 27 m. west from Philadelphia, to the Pacific ocean in latitude 52 d. 24 m. north, and longitude 128 d. 2 m. west from Greenwich, or 52 d. 54 m. west from Philadelphia.

By the discoveries alluded to, and those occasionally made during the rapid settlement of the country and the progress of the enterprize, the principal divisions of this Northern Continent has been explored and become known. The line separating these from the parts which remained unexplored and unknown, may be considered as commencing at the Pacific ocean in latitude about 38 d. north and running along the high lands and mountains between the waters which fall into the gulphs [sic] of California and Mexico and those which fall into the Missouri river, and continuing in that direction to the Mississippi; thence up the river to the source of its highest north western branch; thence along the high tract of country which divides the waters of the Missouri from those which fall into Hudson's Bay and the North sea; from whence it will continue across the Rocky Mountains to the Pacific ocean in latitude about 52 d. north. To the south of this general division line, the known countries will be Old and New Mexico and a part of Louisiana; to the southeast, West and East Florida; to the east, the United States; to the northeast, Canada, the Labrador country, part of New South Wales and of other countries round Hudson's Bay; and to the north, part of New South Wales, New North Wales, the Athabasca and other countries containing the establishments of the Hudson's Bay and North West Companies, and those explored by Hearne and M'Kenzie: leaving unknown and unexplored (except so far as the surveys made by navigators of the coast of the Pacific, and the imperfect accounts of traders who have ascended the Missouri have furnished information) all that large intermediate tract, containing in breadth about 1000 miles; and in length in a direct line, about 1800 miles, and by the way of the Missouri and Columbia rivers nearly twice that distance. This tract from its situation may be supposed to contain the chief part of those lands in the great western division of the continent of North America fit for tillage: and this circumstance will therefore in a special manner claim the attention of an agricultural people, render more interesting a description of them, and attach additional value to the history of the country. It will not be forgotten that an immense sum of treasure has been expended in the purchase of this country, and that it is now considered as belonging to the United States. Here at no distant period settlements may be formed; and in a much shorter term than has elapsed since the first were made in America, from which hath arisen a great, powerful, and independent nation, the prosperity of the present inhabitants of the Union may unfurl the standard of independence on the plains of the Missouri and Columbia.

With respect to the accuracy of the relations given in the following pages, it may be necessary to inform those readers not acquainted with the fact, that the principal object in sending out the expedition was to gain some correct account of the country: and that this might be done more effectually, and the information collected, preserved with more certainty, it was enjoined upon the several persons belonging to the corps, who were considered capable, to keep journals, and every necessary information and assistance given them for that purpose: these journals were also from time to time compared, corrected and any blanks, which had been left, filled up, and unavoidable omissions supplied. By thus multiplying the journals, revising and correcting them, the chances of securing to the country a true account of the progress of the expedition and of the discoveries which should be made, especially should the party be attacked and defeated by the savages or meet with any other disasters in their hazardous enterprize, were also multiplied.

The following is an extract of a certificate delivered by Captain Lewis to Mr. Gass, dated St. Louis Oct. 1806:

"As a tribute justly due to the merits of the said Patrick Gass, I with chearfulness declare, that the ample support, which he gave me, under every difficulty; the manly firmness, which he evinced on every necessary occasion; and the fortitude with which he bore the fatigues and painful sufferings incident to that long voyage, intitles [sic] him to my highest confidence and sincere thanks, while it eminently recommends him to the consideration and respect of his fellow citizens."

In determining the form in which the work should appear, the publisher had some difficulty. Two plans presented themselves. The one was to preserve the form of a daily journal (in which the original had been kept) and give a plain description of the country and a simple relation of occurrences equally intelligible to all readers; leaving to every person an opportunity of embellishing the

scenes presented to him in his own way. The other plan
was to more fully digest the subject, make the narrative
more general, and, assuming less of the journal form and
style, describe and clothe the principal parts of it as his
fancy might suggest. However far the latter might have
been proper had a foreign country been the subject, and
the principal object of the publication, mere amusement,
many objects occurred to it in the present case; and rendered the former the most eligible, especially as by it the
climate and face of the country will be more satisfactorily
described. And Mr. Gass having declared that the beau-
ties and deformities of its grandest scenes were equally
beyond the power of description, no attempts have been
made either by him or the publisher to give adequate rep-
resentations of them.

The publisher hopes that the curiosity of the reader
will be in some degree gratified; that the information furnished will not be uninteresting; and that some aid will
be furnished those who wish to acquire a Geographical
knowledge of their country.

26th March, 1807

JOURNAL.

<hr>

CHAP. I.

On Monday the 14th of May 1804, we left our establishment at the mouth of the river du Bois or Wood river, a small river which falls into the Mississippi, on the east side, a mile below the Missouri, and having crossed the Mississippi proceeded up the Missouri on our intended voyage of discovery, under the command of Captain Clarke. Captain Lewis was to join us in two or three days on our passage.*

The corps consisted of forty-three men (including Captain Lewis and Captain Clarke, who were to command the expedition) part of the regular troops of the United States, and part engaged for this particular enterprize. The expedition was embarked on board a batteau and two periogues [sic]. The day was showery and in the evening we encamped on the north bank six miles up the river. Here we had leisure to reflect on our situation, and the nature of our engagements: and, as we had all entered this service as volunteers, to consider how far we stood pledged for the success of an expedition, which the government had projected; and which had been undertaken for the benefit and at the expence [sic] of the Union: of course of much interest and high expectation.

The best authenticated accounts informed us, that we were to pass through a country possessed by numerous, powerful and warlike nations of savages, of gigantic stature, fierce, treacherous and cruel; and particularly hostile to white men. And fame had united with tradition in opposing mountains to our course, which human enterprize and exertion would attempt in vain to pass. The determined and resolute character, however, of the corps, and the confidence which pervaded all ranks dispelled every emotion of fear, and anxiety for the present; while a sense of duty, and of the honour,

<hr>

*The confluence of the Missouri and Mississippi rivers is in latitude about 38 degrees and forty minutes north, and in longitude 92 degrees and an half west of London, or 17 and a third west of Philadelphia. The town of St. Louis is 14 miles below the mouth of the Missouri on the west side of the Mississippi; and Cahokia about 4 or 5 miles lower down on the east side. The longitude of these places is nearly the same with that of the mouth of the river St. Louis at the west end of lake Superior in 46 degrees 45 minutes north latitude; about 2 degrees west of New Orleans in latitude 30 degrees north, and the same number of degrees east of the most western point of Hudson's Bay in latitude about 59 degrees north: So that a line drawn from New Orleans to Fort Churchill, at the mouth of Churchhill river on the west side of Hudson's Bay, would pass very near the mouth of the Missouri and the west end of lake Superior.

which would attend the completion of the object of the expedition; a wish to gratify the expectations of the government, and of our fellow citizens, with the feelings which novelty and discovery invariably inspire, seemed to insure to us ample support in our future toils, suffering and dangers.

On the 15th we continued our voyage. It rained in the morning; but in the afternoon we had clear weather, and encamped at night on the north side of the river.

Wednesday 16th. We had a fine pleasant morning; embarked early, and at 2 o'clock in the afternoon arrived at St. Charles, and fired a gun. A number of the inhabitants came to see us. This is an old French village; in the country around which, a number of Americans have settled.

We remained at St. Charles until the 21st, where Captain Lewis arrived from St. Louis and joined us. At 4 o'clock in the afternoon we left this place under a salute of three cheers from the inhabitants, which we returned with three more and a discharge of three guns. This evening was showery, and we again encamped on the north side of the river.[34]

Tuesday 22nd. We continued our voyage; passed Bonum [Bon Homme] creek on the south side, and having made fifteen miles, encamped at the Cliffs on the north side of the river. Here we were visited by some Indians.[35]

Wednesday 23rd. At 6 o'clock in the morning we proceeded on our voyage with pleasant weather. Passed the mouth of the Osage* river[36] on the south side, about a mile and an half below the Tavern Cove, a noted place among the French traders. One mile above this is the Tavern Creek. We encamped this evening on the south side of the river, and had our arms and ammunition inspected.

Thursday 24th. We continued our voyage, and encamped at night on the south side. This day our boat turned in a ripple, and nearly upset.

Friday 25th. We proceeded three miles and passed a creek on the south side, called Wood river; the banks of the river are here high and the land rich: arrived at St. Johns, a small French village situated on the north side, and encamped a quarter of a mile above it. This is the last settlement of white people on the river.

---

*Perhaps Little Osage

Saturday 26th. This morning two of our people set out by land with a couple of horses. At seven we embarked and had loud thunder and heavy rain; passed Otter creek on the north side, and encamped near its mouth.[37]

Sunday 27th. We passed Ash creek where there are high cliffs on the south side, and at five in the afternoon arrived at the mouth of Gaskenade river. On the south side one of our party[38+] killed a deer. We encamped for the night on an island oppposite the mouth of Gaskenade river. This is a very handsome place,—a rich soil and pleasant country:

Monday 28th. Our provisions and stores were put out to air and dry, and several of our men sent out to hunt. One of them killed a deer.[+] The mouth of the Gaskenade river is 157 yards wide.

Tuesday 29th. Seven men were sent out to hunt; six of whom returned. We waited here until 5 o'clock P.M. for the man, who had not come in,[39] and then proceeded three miles, passed Deer creek on the south side, and encamped a short distance above it on the same side. A periogue and eight men had been left for the hunter who had not returned.

Wednesday 30th. After experiencing a very disagreeable night, on account of the rain, we continued our voyage at seven o'clock A.M. and passed a cove where there were high cliffs on the north side opposite an island, called Mombran's tavern. At twelve we had a heavy shower of rain, accompanied with hail; passed a creek called Rush creek, on the north side; and four miles further, Mud creek on the same side. Here the soil is good, with cotton wood, sycamore, oak, hickory, and white walnut; with some grape vines, and an abundance of rushes.[40] We halted and encamped at Grindstone creek on the south side of the river.

Thursday 31st. We were obliged to remain at this encampment all day, on account of a strong wind from the west. An Indian man and a squaw came down the river with two canoes, loaded with fur and peltry, and remained with us all night. Some of our hunters went out and killed a deer.[+]

Friday 1st June, 1804. Before daylight we embarked and proceeded on our voyage; passed Big Muddy creek on the north side; and on the opposite side saw high banks. Two and an half miles higher up, we passed Bear creek; and at 4 o'clock P.M. arrived at the Osage river; where we remained during the evening and the next day. The Osage river is 197 yards wide at its confluence with the Missouri, which, at this place, is 875 yards broad. The country on the south side is broken, but rich: and the land on the other of a most excellent quality. The two men who went by land with the horses came to us here: they represented the land they had passed through as the best they had ever seen, and the timber good, consisting chiefly of oak, ash, hickory and black walnut. They had killed in their way five deer. The periogue left at the mouth of the Gaskenade river came up with the man, who had been lost.[41] Here our hunters went out and killed three deer. The Osage nation of Indians live about two hundred miles up this river. They are of a large size and well proportioned, and a very warlike people. Our arms and ammunition were all inspected here and found in good order.

Sunday 3rd. Captain Lewis, with one of the men went out and killed a deer. At five in the afternoon we embarked, and having proceeded six miles, encamped at the mouth of Marrow creek[42] on the south side.

Monday 4th. Three hunters went out this morning. We continued our voyage, and during the day broke our mast by steering too close to the shore. In the evening we encamped on the south side near lead mines; when our hunters came in with seven deer.

Tuesday 5th. We passed Mine creek on the south side, and Little Goodwoman creek on the north: also the creek of the Big Rock. We met two Frenchmen in two canoes laden with peltry; passed a high cliff of rocks on the south side, and encamped on the north side.[43] The land about this place is good and well timbered.

On the 6th we passed Saline creek on the south side;[44] and on the 7th the river of the Big Devil on the north; and Big Goodwoman's creek on the same side, where we encamped.[45]

Friday 8th. We embarked and proceeded five miles, when we met four canoes loaded with fur and peltry: and passed the Mine river on the south side, which is 150 yards wide. This land here is also good and well timbered.

Saturday 9th. We passed the Prairie of Arrows and Arrow creek[46] on the south side.[†] This is a beautiful country and the land excellent. The Missouri here is only 300 yards wide, and the current very strong. Three miles further we passed Blackbird creek on the north side, and encamped. This day going round some drift wood, the stern of the boat became fast, when she immediately swung round, and was in great danger; but we got her off without much injury.

[†]Prairies are natural meadows, or pastures, without trees and covered with grass.

Sunday 10th. We proceeded five miles and passed a creek called Deer-lick creek[47] on the north side; and three miles further the Two Charlottes[48] on the same side. The mouths of these two rivers are very near each other: the first 70 and the other 100 yards wide. We encamped on the south side of the river at a prairie, and remained there the whole of the next day, the wind blowing too violent for us to proceed.[49]

Tuesday 12th.[50] We set out early, and proceeded until five o'clock in the afternoon, when we met five periogues loaded with fur and peltry from the Sioux nation of Indians. We remained with the people to whom these periogues belonged all night; and got from them an old Frenchman, who could speak the languages of the different nations of Indians up the Missouri, and who agreed to go with us as an interpreter.[51]

Wednesday 13th. We proceeded early on our voyage; passed a small creek on the north side in a long bend of the river, and encamped at the mouth of Grand River on the North side. This is as handsome a place as I ever saw in an uncultivated state.

Thursday 14th. At five o'clock in the morning we continued our voyage. The river having risen during the night was difficult to ascend. At noon we passed some Frenchmen from the Poenese or Ponis [Pawnee] nation of Indians, where they spent the last winter. In the evening we passed Snake creek on the north side and encamped on the same.

Friday 15th. We renewed our voyage at five in the morning, and had very rapid water. There is a beautiful Prairie on the south side and the land high. Mulberries are in great abundance almost all along the river. We encamped on the north side, opposite an old Indian village.

Saturday 16th. Three men went out this morning to look for timber to make oars, but could find none suitable. On their return we continued our voyage; had cloudy weather and rapid water all day and encamped on the north side.

Sunday 17th. This morning was clear and at five we renewed our voyage. Having proceeded about a mile we halted to get timber for oars; and while we remained here to make them our hunters came in and brought with them a handsome horse, which they had found astray. They also brought a bear, which they had killed.

Monday 18th. We remained here all day; and our hunters killed five deer and a bear.[+] On the south side there is high land and a long prairie; on the north the land is level and well timbered, with ash, sugar tree, black walnut, buck-eye, cotton wood and some other timber.

Tuesday 19th. We passed Tabo creek on the south side, and a small creek on the north; and encamped on the south side opposite a small lake about two miles distant.

Wednesday 20th. At five in the morning we continued our voyage, passed Tiger creek, a large creek that flows in from the north, and encamped on an island. The land along here is good on both sides of the river.

On the 21st we had rapid water, and for about a mile had to warp up our boat by a rope. A creek called Du Beau or Du Bois, falls in on the south side behind an island. We encamped in the evening on the south side.

Friday 22nd. It rained hard from four to seven in the morning, when we continued our voyage. About 12, one of our men went out and killed a large bear.[+] We encamped at a handsome prairie on the south side opposite a large creek, called the Fire-prairie, and which is 60 yards wide.

Saturday 23rd. We set out at five in the morning; at 12 the wind blew so strong down the river that we were unable to proceed, and we encamped on an island and inspected the arms and ammunition.—Captain Clarke went out with one of the men and did not return this evening.

Sunday 24th. We had a fine morning, embarked at five and pursued our voyage: at nine Captain Clarke came to us and brought with him two deer and a bear.[+] We passed a creek on the south side called Depie. At 12 we stopped to jirk* our meat, and again proceeded at two; passed a creek on the north side and encamped on the south bank of the river.

Monday 25th. The morning was foggy, and at seven o'clock we pursued our voyage. The river here is narrow with high land on the south side. We passed a creek on the south side called Labenile, and encamped on an island.

Tuesday 26th. We embarked and set out at five o'clock in the morning; passed a creek on the south side, called Blue-water. This afternoon we had some difficulty in passing a sandbar, the tow-rope[52]

---

*Jirk is meat cut into small pieces and dried in the sun or by a fire. The Indians cure and preserve their meat in this way without salt.

having broke; but by the exertions of those on board, the boat was brought to shore without injury. We encamped on the south side on a point at the confluence of the Canzan, or Kanzas river with the Missouri. It was agreed to remain here during the 27th and 28th where we pitched our tents and built bowers in front of them. Canzan or Kanzas, is 230 and a quarter yards wide, and navigable to a great distance. Our hunters killed 4 deer, and a young wolf, and caught another alive.[+] In the afternoon of the 29th we again proceeded on our voyage, and encamped on the north side of the river.

Saturday 30th. The day was clear and we continued our voyage; found high land on both sides of the river; and passed a large creek on the north side, called Platt, fifty yards wide. We broke our mast and encamped on the south side, where there were the most signs of game I ever saw.

Sunday 1st, July, 1804. We set out at five in the morning, and having advanced 12 miles, encamped on an island opposite a prairie on the south side of the river.

Monday 2nd. At sunrise we continued our voyage, and met a quantity of driftwood which was carried down the stream; this morning we passed a creek on the south side and encamped on the north opposite an old French village and fort, but all vacant.[53]

Tuesday 3d. We proceeded again at five, and continued our voyage until 12, when we stopt [*sic*] at an old trading place on the south side of the river. There we found a grey horse; but saw no appearance of any persons have lately encamped at that place.

Wednesday 4th. We fired a swivel at sunrise in honour of the day, and continued our voyage; passed a creek on the north side, called Pond Creek, and at one o'clock stopt to dine. One of our people got snake bitten, but not dangerously.[54] After dinner we renewed our voyage, passed a creek on the north side, which we called INDEPENDENCE, encamped on the north side at an old Indian village situated in a handsome prairie, and saluted the departing day with another gun.

Thur. 5th. We proceeded on our voyage at five in the morning; and found the land high on the south side. We went through a large bend full of sand bars where we had some difficulty in passing; and encamped on the south side at high prairie land.

Friday 6th. We set out early this morning; had a fine day, and made a good day's voyage: and encamped on the south side at Whipperwell Creek.

Saturday 7th. At an early hour we proceeded on our voyage; passed a high handsome prairie on the north side, and killed a wolf[+] and a large wood rat on the bank. The principal difference between it and the common rat is, its having hair on its tail.

Sunday 8th. We were under way this morning before day light. The river here is crooked and narrow. At one we came to a large island, with only a small stream on the north side which we went up. A large creek called Nadowa flows in from the north; and on this side we encamped.

Monday 9th. Early this morning we continued our voyage. It rained hard till 12 o'clock. We passed a creek on the south side, called Wolf creek. The man that was snake bitten is become well. We encamped on the south side.

Tuesday 10th. We set out early this morning and had a fair day and fair wind. There is a handsome prairie on the south side opposite an island. We encamped on the north side.

Wednesday 11th. We also embarked early this morning; passed a creek on the north side, called Tarico, and halted at an island, opposite a creek called Moha on the south side of the river. Seven hunters went out to day [*sic*] and two of them brought in five deer.[+] Here we found another horse on the bank of the river, supposed to have been left by a hunting party last winter. Two of our men, who had gone to hunt on the south side of the river, did not return at night.

Thursday 12th. We remained here this day, that the men, who were much fatigued, might take some rest. The hunters, who had remained on the south side of the river all night, came in, but had killed nothing. Two more went to hunt on the north side and killed two deer.[55+]

Friday 13th. We were early under way this morning with a fair wind. The day was fine. We passed a creek on the north side, and having made 20 miles and an half, encamped on a large sand bar.

Saturday 14th. At day break it began to rain and continued until seven when it abated, and we set forward: but in a short time a gust of wind and rain came on so violent, that all hands had to leap into the water to save the boat. Fortunately this storm did not last long, and we went on to a convenient place and landed. Here we continued two hours and then proceeded. We saw some elk, but could not kill any of them; passed a river on the north side, called Washba-to-nan, and encamped on the south side.

Sunday 15th. We got under way at six o'clock; passed a creek on the south side; and gathered some ripe grapes. There is high land and prairies on this side. Captain Clarke and two men went by land.[56] At the head of an island, called Elk island, we found some pummice stone among the drift wood. We passed a creek on the south side, called Na-ma-ha, and encamped on the same.

Monday 16th. Early in the morning we proceeded on our voyage opposite a prairie; had a fine day and fair wind, and passed a long island, above which is a place where the bank has slipped into the river. There are high rocky cliffs on the south side, and hills and prairies on the north: on which side we encamped. The river here is two miles wide with rapid water. Two of our hunters met us here with two deer.[57+]

Tuesday 17th. We remained here all day; and one of our hunters killed three deer.[+]

Wednesday 18th. Early this morning we prosecuted our voyage with a fair wind and pleasant weather. This is the most open country I ever beheld, almost one continued prairie. Two of our hunters went by land with the horses as usual. On the south side we passed high handsome banks or bluffs of red and blue strata;* found some iron ore here, and encamped on the south side, where one of the hunters brought us two deer.[+]

Thursday 19th. At sun rise we renewed our voyage, and passed a number of sand bars, and high land on the south side. Where we halted for dinner we found a great quantity of cherries, called by some choak-cherries. We encamped for the night on an island of Willows.

Friday 20th. We embarked early; passed high yellow banks on the south side and a creek, called the Water-which-cries, or the Weeping stream, opposite a willow island, and encamped on a prairie on the south side.

Saturday 21st. We set out early. It rained this morning but we had a fine breeze of wind. There are a great many willow islands and sand-bars in this part of the river. At nine the wind fell, and at one we came to the great river Platte, or shallow river, which comes in on the south side, and at the mouth is three quarters of a mile broad. The land is flat about the confluence. Up this river live three nations of Indians, the Otos, Panis and Loos, or Wolf Indians. On the south side there is also a creek, called Butterfly creek.

Sunday 22nd. We left the river Platte and proceeded early on our voyage, with fair weather. There is high prairie land on the south

---

*By Bluffs in the Western Country is understood high steep banks, which come close to and are washed at their base by the rivers.

side, with some timber on the northern parts of the hills. We came nine miles from the mouth of Platte river, and landed on a willow bank. The hunters killed five deer and caught two beaver.

Monday 23rd. Six men were sent out to make oars; and two to a nation of Indians up the Platte river, to inform them of the change of government in this country, and that we were here ready to treat with them.[58] We hoisted a flag, and sent them another.[59]

Our people were all busily engaged in hunting, making oars, dressing skins, and airing our stores, provisions and baggage. We killed two deer and caught two beaver.[+] Beaver appear plenty in this part of the country.

We continued here to the 27th.—On the 24th there were some showers; but during the remainder of the time there was clear weather. Our people were generally employed as before. The hunters killed five more deer;[+] and the two men returned from the Indian village, without finding any of the natives.

CHAP. II.

Friday 27th [July 1804]. This forenoon we were engaged in loading the boats and preparing to start. At 12 we proceeded with a fair wind, and pleasant weather; went twelve miles, and encamped on a handsome prairie on the south side.[60]

Saturday, 28th. We set out early; had a cloudy morning: passed some beautiful hills and prairies, and a creek called Round-Knob creek,[61] on the north side; and high bluffs on the south. We encamped on the north side. Here two of our hunters came to us, accompanied by one of the Oto Indians.[62]

Sunday, 29th. We embarked early, and continued our voyage. One of our Frenchmen went with the Indian to bring more of them to meet us at some convenient landing place. At 12 one of our hunters came in with a deer and some elk meat.+ We renewed our voyage at 3, passed a bank, where there was a quantity of fallen timber, and encamped on the north side.

Monday 30th. Our grey horse died last night. We set out early, and the hunters met us with a deer. At 9 we came to some timber land at the foot of a high bluff and encamped there in order to wait for the Indians. At the top of the bluff is a large handsome prairie, and a large pond, or small lake about two miles from camp on the south side of the river. Two of our hunters+ went out and killed an animal, called a prarow,[63] about the size of a ground hog and nearly of the same colour. It has a head similar to that of a dog, short legs and large claws on its fore feet; some of the claws are an inch and an half long. Our hunters again went out, but did not return this day.

Tuesday 31st One of our men went to visit some traps he had set, and in one found a young beaver, but little hurt and brought it in alive.[64] In a short time he went out again and killed a large buck.+ Two other hunters came in about 12, who had killed two deer; but lost the horses.[65] One of them with two other persons were sent out to hunt them, who returned at dark without finding them; and supposed they had been stolen by the Indians.

Wednesday 1st Aug. 1804. Three of our men again went out to hunt the horses, but returned without them. They brought a deer, and two of our other hunters killed two more.[+]

Thursday 2nd. Some hunters went out this morning; and two of them returned with the horses and an elk they had killed.[+] The others brought in two large bucks and a fawn.[+] The Indians we expected came at dark; but our Frenchman was not with them.[66] We supposed he had been lost. This place we named Council-Bluff, and by observation we found to be in latitude 41d. 17m. north.[67]

Friday 3rd. Captain Lewis and Captain Clarke held a council with the Indians, who appeared well pleased with the change of government, and what had been done for them. Six of them were made chiefs, three Otos and three Missouris.[68]

We renewed our voyage at 3 o'clock; went six miles and encamped on the south side; where we had a storm of wind and rain, which lasted two hours.

Saturday 4th. We were early under way this morning, and had a fair day. We passed a creek on the south side, which came out of ponds. One of our men went out this morning and did not return:[69] another came to us and brought a deer. We encamped on the south side.

Sunday 5th. We set out early, but a storm of rain and wind obliged us to stop two hours. It then cleared and we continued our voyage; passed prairies on both sides, and encamped on the north side. The river here is very crooked and winding. To arrive at a point only 370 yards from this place, the passage by water is twelve miles.

Monday 6th. We proceeded at an early hour this morning, after a stormy night of wind and rain; passed a creek on the north side, at the back of an island, called Soldiers creek; and encamped on the south side.

Tuesday 7th. We set out early this morning and continued our voyage till 12, when four of our people were dispatched to the Oto nation of Indians after the man who had not returned on the 4th, with orders to take him, dead or alive, if they could see him.[70] There is no timber in this country except some cotton wood and willows in the bends of the river. All the high land is a continued prairie. We encamped on the north side. The musquetoes [*sic*] here are very numerous and troublesome.

Wednesday 8th. We embarked early, passed a small river on the north side, called Little Sioux. Captain Clarke and one of the men went out to hunt and killed an elk.[+] One of the hunters killed a pelican on a sand bar,[+] and Captain Lewis killed another, very large. We encamped on the north bank. In the bag under the bill and neck of the pelican, which Captain Lewis killed, we put five gallons of water.[71]

Thursday 9th. The fog was so thick this morning, that we could not proceed before 7, when we went on under a gentle breeze, and having advanced eleven miles, came to a place where the river by cutting through a narrow neck of land, reduced the distance fifteen miles. Captain Clarke and one of the men went out to hunt and killed a small turkey.[+] We encamped on the south side, where we found the musquetoes very troublesome.

Friday 10th. We embarked early, passed high yellow banks on the south side, and encamped on the north.

Saturday 11th. A storm came on at three o'clock this morning and continued till nine; notwithstanding which, we kept under way till ten, when we came to a high bluff, where an Indian chief had been buried, and placed a flag upon a pole, which had been set up at his grave. His name was Blackbird, king of the Mahas; an absolute monarch while living, and the Indians suppose can exercise the power of one though dead.[72] We encamped in latitude 42d. 1m. 3s. 8 [42 degrees 1 minute 3.8 seconds], as ascertained by observation.

Sunday 12th. We embarked and got under way before day light. The musketoes [*sic*] last night were worse than I ever experienced. We went round a bend, of eighteen miles, the neck of which was only 974 yards across; passed high bluffs of yellow clay on the south side of the river and low land on the north; and encamped on a sand island.

Monday 13th. We proceeded this morning with a fair wind; and at 2 landed on a sandy beach, near the Maha village, on the south side of the river. A sergeant and one man were sent to the village, who did not return this day.[73]

Tuesday 14th. The sergeant and man returned from the village; but they had found no Indians there. Some of our hunters went out but killed nothing. Game appears scarce here. While at this place we provided ourselves with a new mast.

Wednesday 15th. Captain Clarke and ten of the party went to the Maha creek to fish, and caught 387 fish of different kinds.[74] We discovered smoke on the opposite side of the river, and four men crossed to see if any of the Mahas or Sioux Indians were there; but could not discover any. There had been fire there some days, and the wind lately blowing hard had caused the fire to spread and smoke to rise. We continued at this place until the 20th. Captain Lewis went with a party of twelve men to fish and took 709 fish, 167 of which were large pike. The fish here are generally pike, cat, sun perch and other common fish. What we caught were taken with trails or brush nets. On the 18th the party who had been sent in pursuit of the man who had been absent since the 4th. returned with him, and eight Indians and a Frenchman; but left our Frenchman behind who had gone out to hunt the horses.[75] On the 19th a council was held with these Indians, who appeared to wish to make peace with all nations. This day sergeant Floyd became very sick and remained so all night. He was seized with a complaint somewhat like a violent colick.

Monday 20th. Sergeant Floyd continued very ill. We embarked early, and proceeded, having a fair wind and fine weather, till 2 o'clock, when we landed for dinner. Here sergeant Floyd died, notwithstanding every possible effort was made by the commanding officers, and other persons, to save his life. We went on about a mile to high prairie hills on the north side of the river, and there interred his remains in the most decent manner our circumstances would admit; we then proceeded a mile further to a small river on the same side and encamped. Our commanding officers gave it the name of Floyd's river; to perpetuate the memory of the first man who had fallen in this important expedition.[76]

Tuesday 21st. We set out early; passed handsome pale coloured bluffs, willow creek and the Sioux river on the north side: and having come upwards of 20 miles, encamped on the south side.

Wednesday 22nd. We proceeded early upon our voyage; passed bluffs on the south side, where there is copperas, allum and ore of some kind; also passed a creek. The high land on the south side for nine or ten miles runs close to the river, where there are cedar bluffs of various colours. We encamped on the north side.[77]

Thursday 23d. We proceeded early this morning with a fair wind. The river here becomes more straight than we had found it for a great distance below. Captain Clarke and one of the men killed a deer and a buffaloe,[+] and some of the men were sent to dress and bring the buffaloe to the boat.[78] We stopped at a prairie on the north side, the largest and handsomest, which I had seen. Captain Clarke called it Buffaloe prairie. The men having returned, we again went on; but the wind changed and we were obliged to halt for the present. While we were detained here we salted two barrels of buffaloe meat. At five in the evening we proceeded some distance and encamped on the south side.

Friday 24th. This morning was cloudy with some rain. Captain Clarke went by land. We passed cedar bluffs on the north side, a part of which were burning; and there are here to be found mineral substances of various kinds. There is also a quantity of small red berries, the Indian name for which in English means rabbit berries. They are handsome small berries and grow upon bushes about 10 feet high. Captain Clarke came to us and had killed two elk and a fawn, we passed a creek called White-stone creek; landed and remained here all night to jirk our meat.

Saturday 25th. Two of our men last night caught nine catfish, that would together weigh three hundred pounds. The large catfish are caught in the Missouri with hook and line. Captain Lewis and Captain Clarke went to see a hill on the north side of the river where the natives will not or pretend that they will not venture to go, and say that a small people live there, whom they are afraid of.[79] At 11 o'clock, the gentlemen not having returned, we set sail with a gentle breeze from the S.E. passed black bluffs on the south side, and continued on nine miles and encamped. Two of our hunters came in who had killed a large elk.[+] Captains Lewis and Clarke did not return this evening.

Sunday 26th. Some of the men went out to dress and bring in the elk. About 10 o'clock Captain Lewis and Captain Clarke with the party accompanying them came to camp; but had not been able to discover any of those small people. The hill is in a handsome prairie: and the party saw a great many buffaloe near it. About 11 we renewed our voyage and passed some timber land on the south side; and black and white bluffs on the same side, we encamped on the north side opposite a creek called Pettit-Ark, or Little-bow.

Monday 27th. Got under way at sunrise, and passed white bluffs on the south side. At 2 we stopped for dinner, and an Indian of the Mahas nation, who lives with the Sioux came to us here, at the mouth of the Sacque river; and while we remained here two more came in. A sergeant with our old Frenchman and another man went with two of the Indians to their camps, and the other went with us in the boat.[80] We encamped on a sand beach on the north side.

Tuesday 28th. We set forward early. The day was pleasant, and a fair wind from S.E. At 8 we halted for breakfast, when our young Indian left us to go to his camp at a handsome prairie, gently rising from the river on the north side; a small distance above which are beautiful groves of Cotton wood [*sic*] on both sides of the river. About 12 one of the periogues run against a snag which broke a hole in it. We then crossed to the south side to mend the periogue, and to wait to receive the Indians we expected; and landed a little below some high bluffs. Our camp is in a wide bottom, in which are large elm and oak trees.[81]

Wednesday 29th. At 8 o'clock last night a storm of wind and rain came on from the N. west, and the rain continued the greater part of the night. The morning was cloudy with some thunder. We are generally well supplied with Catfish, the best I have ever seen. Some large ones were taken last night. In the afternoon the men who had gone to the Indian camp returned and brought with them sixty Indians of the Sioux nation.[82] They encamped for the evening upon the opposite shore, and some corn and tobacco were sent over to them. The sergeant who had gone to their camp informed me that their lodges, forty in number, are about nine miles from the Missouri on the Sacque river. They are made of dressed buffaloe and elk skins, painted red and white and are very handsome. He said the women are homely and mostly old; but the young men likely and active. They killed a dog as a token of friendship. One of our men killed a deer.[+]

Thursday 30th. A foggy morning, and heavy dew. At nine o'clock the Indians came over the river. Four of them, who were musicians went backwards and forwards, through and round our camp, singing and making a noise. After that ceremony was over they all sat in council. Captain Lewis and Captain Clarke made five of them chiefs, and gave them some small presents. At dark Captain Lewis gave them a grained deer skin to stretch over a half keg for a drum. When that was ready they all assembled round some fires made for the purpose: two of them beat on the drum, and some of the rest had little bags of undressed skins dried, with beads or small pebbles in them, with which they made a noise. These are their instruments of musick. Ten or twelve acted as musicians, while twenty or thirty young men and boys engaged in the dance, which was continued during the night. No Squaws made their appearnce [*sic*] among this party.[83]

Friday 31st. A clear morning. The Indians remained with us all day, and got our old Frenchman to stay and go with their chief to the city of Washington.[84] Some of them had round their necks strings of the white bear's claws, some of the claws three inches long.

CHAP. III.

Saturday 1st Sept. 1804. We renewed our voyage early; passed high bluffs on the south side, and high prairie land on the north; on this side, the hills come close to the river; and are so near on both sides, as not to be more than two miles from each other. During last night we had hard wind and some rain, which continues to fall occasionally during the day.—About 1 o'clock we passed a rich prairie on the south side, and encamped on the north side, at the lower end of an island.

Sunday 2nd. At 1 o'clock last night we had hard thunder, lightning and rain, which continued about two hours. We set out early in the morning, along the north side of the island: there is handsome prairie land on the south. Three of our men went on the island to hunt. When we landed for breakfast we heard several guns fired on the island, and saw six elk swimming across the river about a mile above where we had halted. Two of our men went up and killed one of them;[+] those on the island killed three.[+] About twelve, the wind blew so hard down the river, that we could not proceed, and we landed on the north side, where there is an extensive prairie. It was cloudy and rained till 4 when it cleared up. We remained here for the night and dried our meat. On the bank opposite our camp is an ancient fortification or breastwork, similar to those which have been occasionally discovered on the western waters. The two ends run at right angles to the river, and the outside, which is 2500 yards in length, parallel to it: there is no breastwork thrown up next to the river, the bank as is supposed, serving as a sufficient defence on that side.*

---

*The description of this Breastwork corresponds exactly with the accounts given of numerous antient [sic] fortifications discovered in the Western Country, which are known and represented to be generally of an oblong form, situate on strong and well chosen ground, and contiguous to water. These works from the examinations which have been made, are supposed to have been erected more than 1000 years ago; or 700 years before the discovery of America by Columbus. They appear to have existed about the same period, throughout all, or the greater part of that vast tarct [sic] of Country bounded by the Alleghany Mountains on the east and the Rocky Mountains on the west, and including the most favourable latitudes of North America. Perhaps some have been found east of the Alleghany Mountains. Have numerous antient [sic] nations, more civilized and disposed to labour than any of the modern Indian tribes, inhabited this Country? And have these fortifications been their humble substitutes for the walled and fortified Cities of the old world in remote ages? Or, has this been the Roman Empire of the New World? and has it been destroyed by other hordes of barbarians, as fierce and cruel as those who destroyed that of the old[?] [Gass and McKeehan's supposition has been subsequently deemed erroneous; this natural feature was probably a result of erosion.]

Monday 3d. [*sic*] We set out early, and had a clear day; passed yellow bluffs on the north side and a small creek, called Plumb creek. Here the river turns at right angles to the left, till it reaches the hills on the south side, then winds gradually to the right. There is no timber in this part of the country; but continued prairie on both sides of the river. A person by going on one of the hills may have a view as far as the eye can reach without any obstruction, or intervening object; and enjoy the most delightful prospects. During this day's voyage we found the hills on the opposite sides of the river generally not more than two miles apart, and the river meandering through them in various directions. We encamped on the south side.

Tuesday 4th. We proceeded early on our voyage, passed a creek on the south side about 30 yards wide, called Paint creek; and high yellow bluffs on the same side. About a mile and an half further we passed another creek on the same side 50 yards wide called Whitepaint creek; and yellow bluffs on the north side. About four miles higher up, we passed a river, on the south side, 152 yards wide, called Rapid-water river: Up this river the Poncas nation of Indians lived not long since. We encamped on the south side among some cedar trees.

Wednesday 5th. We set sail early this morning with a fair wind, and had a clear day. We passed a long island covered with timber, and three men went to hunt on it. On the north side are yellow bluffs, out of which issue several beautiful springs. Opposite the head of the island, on the south side, flows in a river, called Pania river; and about three miles higher up, on the north side, a creek, called Goat creek. On the hills above this creek we saw some goats or antelopes, which the French call cabres. About 4 we encamped on an island, where we made and put in a new mast. The three men, who went to hunt on the long island killed a deer and an elk;[+] and two more went out from camp and killed another deer and an elk, both young.[+]

Thursday 6th. We set out early and had a cloudy morning: passed a handsome bottom prairie on the north side; at the upper end of which is a grove of cotton wood, and a long range of dark coloured bluffs on the south side. About 9 o'clock it began to rain and we had strong wind ahead. There are a great number of sand bars, and we had much difficulty in getting along. We encamped on the north side and one of our men killed two deer.[+]

Friday 7th. We set sail early, and had a clear day: passed high prairie land on both sides; but there is some cotton wood on the low points in the bottoms. On the south side we found a scaffold of meat neatly dried. This had been left by one of our men, who had gone out on the 26th of last month to hunt the horses, and supposing we had got a distance ahead, proceeded up the river several days journey, before he discovered his error.[85] Captain Lewis and Captain Clarke with some of the men went to view a round knob of a hill in a prairie, and on their return killed a prairie dog, in size about that of the smallest species of domestic dogs.[+]

Having understood that the village of those small dogs was at a short distance from our camp, Captain Lewis and Captain Clarke with all the party, except the guard, went to it; and took with them all the kettles and other vessels for holding water; in order to drive the animals out of their holes by pouring in water; but though they worked at the business till night they only caught one of them.[86]

Saturday 8th. We proceeded early on our voyage, and had a clear day and fair wind from the S.E. Passed the bed of a creek without water. At 9 I went out with one of our men, who had killed a buffaloe and left his hat to keep off the vermin and beasts of prey; but when we came to the place, we found the wolves had devoured the carcase and carried off the hat.[87] Here we found a white wolf dead, supposed to have been killed in a contest for the buffaloe. We passed high bluffs on the south side and burnt prairie on the north. We encamped on an island covered with timber; and having a number of buffaloe on it. Captain Lewis who had been out with some of the men hunting informed us he had passed a trading house, built in 1796. This day we killed two buffaloe, a large and a small elk, a deer and two beaver.[+]

Sunday 9th. We set out early, and passed two small creeks on the north side, high bluffs on the south, and at 1 o'clock landed for dinner at a small creek on the south side. One of our hunters brought in a deer and two fawns.[+] This day we saw several gangs or herds, of buffaloe on the sides of the hills: One of our hunters killed one,[+] and Captain Clarke's black servant [York] killed two. We encamped at sunset on the south side.

Monday 10th. We had a foggy morning, but moved on early; passed high bluffs on the north side, and saw some timber in the bottom on the south side. At 12 we came to black sulphur bluffs on the south side. On the top of these bluffs we found the skeleton or back bones of a fish, 45 feet long, and petrified: part of these bones were sent to the City of Washington. One of our sergeants[88] discovered a large salt spring about a mile and an half from the river. A hunter went up the bank and killed an elk.[+] We left a periogue for the men who were dressing the elk, and proceeded up the north side of the river two miles, when we were obliged to return on account of sand bars, and to take the south side. Here we saw eight elk swimming the river, and had seen a great many buffaloe during the day. We encamped on an island and killed one buffaloe.[+]

Tuesday 11th. We set sail before day light with a fair wind; passed an island covered with timber, and high hills and prairie on both sides of the river. At 1 o'clock it began to rain. We saw some person coming down the river on horseback, when we came to land and found it was the man who had preceded us with the horses.[89] He had left one of the horses that had failed. We now had only one horse left. This man had been absent 16 days, and his bullets being expended, he subsisted 12 days almost wholly on grapes. The hills here come close to the river on both sides. One of the men went by land with the horse, and we continued our voyage, until night, though it rained very hard; and encamped on the south side. Captain Clarke with two or three of the men who had gone out to hunt, killed two elk, four deer and one porcupine.[+]

Wednesday 12th. We set out as usual and had a cloudy day; passed a long range of black bluffs on the south side, and an island covered with timber, which is all the timber that can be seen from this place. The country round is all hills and prairie. Captain Clarke, myself and another went out to hunt, and did not return till after dark.[90] The boat had much difficulty in passing on account of the sand bars and strong current, and did not make to day more than four miles.

Thursday 13th. Four beaver were taken last night.[+] We set sail early; the morning was cloudy with some rain and wind ahead; passed a creek and a long range of bluffs on the south side. Some of our men went out to hunt;[91] but did not return this evening. We encamped on the north side.

Friday 14th. We proceeded as yesterday, and with the same kind of weather. Had considerable difficulty in getting along, on account of the shallowness of the river; all hands in the water dragging the boat. At 8 we halted for breakfast, and the men who went to hunt yesterday came in, and had only killed a porcupine.[+] Three beaver were caught last night.[92+] The musketoes are as troublesome as they have been any time in summer. We passed black bluffs on the south side, and an island with timber on it. Passed a creek on the same side and encamped on it. The man who had gone by land with the horse came to us here; had killed a hare.[+] Captain Clarke killed a goat or antelope.[93]

Saturday 15th. A cloudy morning. We continued our voyage early, and passed a creek on the south side and black bluffs on the north. Passed White river on the south side; one of the men and myself went up it to examine the country, and encamped about twelve miles from the mouth, where it is 150 yards broad.[94] We found good bottoms on this creek; but timber scarce, and none upon the hills. The current and colour of the water are much like those of the Missouri.

Sunday 16th. We set out for the boat across the hills, on the tops of which are level plains with a great number of goats and buffaloe on them. Came to the head waters of a creek and kept down it a S.E. course, and on our way killed three deer.[+] We proceeded on to its mouth, which I computed to be 14 miles from that of the White river. Having found the boat had passed we proceeded up the river, and came to a handsome bottom, where our people had encamped to dry the provisions and stores.[95] In our absence the men had killed some deer and two buffaloe.[+]

Monday 17th. As the weather was fair we remained here during the day. Captain Lewis and some men went out to hunt, and killed thirteen common, and two black-tailed deer; three buffaloe and a goat.[+] The wild goat in this country differ from the common tame goat, and is supposed to be the real antelope. The black-tailed, or mule deer have much larger ears than the common deer and tails almost without hair, except at the end, where there is a bunch of black hair. There is another species of deer in this country with small horns and long tails. The tail of one which we killed was 18 inches long.[96+] One of our men caught a beaver, and killed a prairie wolf.[+]— These are a small species of wolves, something larger than a fox, with long tails and short ears.[97]

Tuesday 18th. We continued our voyage; the day was clear and pleasant: passed some timber land on the south side, and hills and prairies on the north; also an island and a great number of sand bars. Yesterday captain Lewis while hunting killed a bird not common in the states: it is like a magpie and is a bird of prey. This day we killed eleven deer and a wolf,[+] and halted and encamped on the south side of the river in order to jirk our meat.

Wednesday 19th. We set out early and had a clear day passed large bottoms on both sides of the river covered with timber. We saw some buffaloe swimming the river and killed two of them.[+] There is an island here, opposite which a river flows in on the north side. This river is formed of three, which unite their waters just above its mouth; and immediately above the confluence is a crossing place,

called the Sioux-crossing-place of the three rivers.[98] At the upper
end, a creek, called Elm creek, comes in on the south side, and two
miles above another creek called Wash creek, falls in on the same
side. About two miles further we passed another creek called Night
creek where we encamped on the south side. Three black tailed deer
were killed this day.[+]

Thursday 20th. We renewed our voyage at an early hour, and
had a clear day and fair wind. Passed handsome rising prairies on
the north side, and bottoms covered with timber on the south side.
Two of the men with the horse went across the neck of the Long, or
Grand bend, which we were obliged to go round with the boat, a
distance of 30 miles. At 1 o'clock we stopped for dinner, and Captain
Lewis and one of the men went to hunt, Captain Clarke had gone
out in the morning. At 2 we proceeded again on our voyage, and
passed a long chain of bluffs on the north side, of a dark colour.
From these and others of the same kind the Missouri gets its muddy
colour. The earth of which they are composed dissolves like sugar;
every rain washes down great quantities of it, and the rapidity of
the stream keeps it mixing and afloat in the water, until it reaches
the mouth of the Mississippi. We encamped at 7 o'clock on a sand
beach on the north side. Here Captain Lewis, Captain Clarke and
the other man joined us. They had killed two goats and two deer.[+] At
1 o'clock at night, the bank where we were stationed began to fall so
much, that we were obliged to rouse all hands, and go on a mile and
cross the river before we could again encamp.

Friday 21st. We set out early, the day was clear, and we proceeded on four miles along bluffs on the south side, when we came to
the termination of the Grand bend, about a mile from the place of
our encampment on the 19th.—We again went on, having black bluffs
on the south and a handsome bottom on the north side; and beyond
these a cedar bottom on the south side and bluffs on the north; passed
a creek on the south side, called Tyler's creek; and encamped on the
north side.

Saturday 22nd. We embarked early in a foggy morning, saw some
timber on the south side and high plains on the north. About 3 o'clock
we passed cedar island, one of the Three-Sisters, where Mr. Lucelle[99]
had built a fort of cedar. The space picketed in is about 65 or 70 feet
square, with centry [*sic*] boxes in two of the angles. The pickets are
13 1-2 feet above ground. In this square he built a house 45 1-2 by 32
1-2 feet, and divided it into four equal parts, one for goods, one to
trade in, one to be used as a common hall and the other for a family

Captains Lewis & Clark holding a Council with the Indians.

house.[100] Here the two men came to us with the horse.[101] They had killed a white wolf and some deer.[+] We proceeded on, passed a creek, and islands of the three sisters; and an old Indian camp, where we found some of their dog-poles, which answer for setting poles. The reason they are called dog-poles is because the Indians fasten their dogs to them, and make them draw them from one camp to another loaded with skins and other articles.[*102] We encamped on the north side.

Sunday 23rd. We went on early, and had a clear morning; passed some timber on the north side and high land on the south; also a creek on the north side called Smoke creek; passed Elk island, a handsome bottom on the north side covered with timber and barren hills on the south. At six in the evening we saw four Indians on the south side and encamped on the north. Three of the Indians swam over to us: they belonged to the Sioux, and informed us that there were more of their nation not far distant. We sent them over the river again. One of our men killed an antelope.[+]

---

*Mr. Mackenzie speaking of the Knisteneaux, a numerous nation of Indians spread over a vast extent of country extending south westerly from the coast of Labrador, north of the St. Laurence and its Lakes and the Lake Winnipic, east of Elk river, south of the Lake of the Hills, and west, south and east of James's Bay and the southern part of Hudson's Bay, says, "In the winter when the waters are frozen, they make their journies, which are never of any greatlength [sic], with sledges drawn by dogs." *General History of Fur Trade.*

Monday 24th. We set sail early with fair weather, and passed a small creek on the south side. About 3 o'clock the man who had gone by land with the horse came to us, and informed us that he had gone that morning on an island to kill elk, and that while he was there the Indians had stolen the horse.[103] He had killed three elk,+ and the periogues remained behind to bring on the meat. We saw five Indians on the bank, but we could not understand each other. We cast anchor to wait for the periogues; one of which having came up, we went on to the mouth of the Tinton or Teeton river, where we anchored about 100 yards from the shore on the south side. The guard and cooks only landed, the rest slept in the boat. The five Indians remained with us all night. We had a Frenchman aboard a periogue, who understood and could speak a little of the Sioux language.[104] The Indians gave us to understand the chiefs would come to-morrow, and that if their young men had taken the horse, they would have him given up. These Indians are a band of the Sioux, called the Tinton or Teeton-Band.

Tuesday 25th. We stayed here to wait for the Indians, who were expected to arrive, and at 10 o'clock they came, about 50 in number. The commanding officers made three of them chiefs and gave them some presents. Five of them came on board and remained about three hours. Captain Clarke and some of our men in a periogue went ashore with them; but the Indians did not seem disposed to permit their return. They said they were poor and wished to keep the periogue with them. Captain Clarke insisted on coming to the boat; but they refused to let him, and said they had soldiers as well as he had. He told them his soldiers were good, and that he had more medicine aboard his boat than would kill twenty such nations in one day.[105] After this they did not threaten any more, and said they only wanted us to stop at their lodge, that the women and children might see the boat. Four of them came aboard, when we proceeded on a mile, and cast anchor at the point of an island in the middle of the river. The Indians remained with us all night.

Wednesday 26th. We set out early, and proceeded on four miles. The bank of the river on the south side was covered all the way with Indians; and at 10 o'clock we met the whole band, and anchored about 100 yards from the shore. Captain Lewis, the chiefs, and some men went on shore, the Indians were peaceable and kind. After some time Capt. Lewis returned on board, and Capt. Clarke went on shore. When the Indians saw him coming they met him with a buffaloe robe, spread it out and made him get into it, and then eight of them carried him to the council house. About an hour after some of them came for Captain Lewis, and he landed; and eight of them carried him to the council house in the same manner, they had carried Captain Clarke. They killed several dogs for our people to feast on, and spent the greater part of the day in eating and smoking. At night the women assembled, and danced till 11 o'clock: then the officers came on board with two chiefs, who continued with us until the morning.

Thursday 27th. We remained here all day. Capt. Lewis, myself and some of the men went over to the Indian camp. Their lodges are about eighty in number, and contain about ten persons each; the greater part women and children. The women were employed in dressing buffaloe skins, for clothing for themselves and for covering their lodges. They are the most friendly people I ever saw; but will pilfer if they have an opportunity. They are also very dirty: the water they make use of, is carried in the paunches of the animals they kill, just as they are emptied, without being cleaned. They gave us dishes of victuals of various kinds; I had never seen any thing like some of these dishes, nor could I tell of what ingredients, or how they were made.[106]

About 15 days ago they had had a battle with the Mahas [Omaha Indians], of whom they killed 75 men and took 25 women prisoners, whom they have now with them. They promised to Capt. Lewis that they would send the prisoners back and make peace.[107]

About 3 o'clock we went aboard the boat accompanied with the old chief and his little son. In the evening Captain Clarke and some of the men went over, and the Indians made preparations for a dance. At dark it commenced. Captain Lewis, myself and some of our party went up to see them perform. Their band of musick, or orchestra, was composed of about twelve persons beating on a buffaloe hide, and shaking small bags that made a rattling noise. They had a large fire in the centre of their camp; on one side the women, about 80 in number, formed in a solid column round the fire, with sticks in their hands, and the scalps of the Mahas they had killed, tied on them. They kept moving, or jumping round the fire, rising and falling on both feet at once; keeping a continual noise, singing and yelling. In this manner they continued till 1 o'clock at night, when we returned to the boat with two of the chiefs. On coming aboard, the periogue run [*sic*] across the bow of the boat and broke the cable. All hands were roused to row the boat ashore; the chiefs called aloud, and a number of the warriors came to our assistance, but we did not need it: the circumstance, however, shewed their disposition to be of service. This unfortunate accident lost to us our anchor.

Friday, 28th. This morning we dragged the river all round where the boat lay, but could not find the anchor. At 9 o'clock we made preparations to sail; some of the chiefs were on board, and concluded to go some distance with us. When we went to shove off, some of the Indians took hold of the rope and would not let it go.[108] This conduct had like to be attended with bad consequences, as Captain Lewis was near giving orders to cut the rope and to fire on them. The chiefs, however, went out and talked with them: they said they wanted a carrot of tobacco, and that if we gave that we might go.[109] The tobacco was given them, and we went off under a gentle breeze of wind. We passed high land on the north side and bottom on the south. We proceeded 4 miles, and then saw an Indian following us along the beach, when Captain Lewis went in a periogue and brought him on board. He informed us that 300 more Indians had come to their camp, and desired we should stop and talk with them. We did not then stop, but proceeded on, and he remained on board. We passed a fine bottom covered with timber on the north side, and bare hills on the south. We made two large stones serve the purpose of an anchor, and at sunset anchored for the night, near a small sand-bar in the middle of the river.

While I was at the Indian camp yesterday they yoked a dog to a kind of car, which they have to haul their baggage from one camp to another; the nation having no settled place or village, but are always moving about.† The dogs are not large, much resemble a wolf, and will haul about 70 pounds each.

---

†It appears that these people, (in some respects resembling the wandering Arabs) are an unsettled, ferocious, blood-thirsty race, and have been great destroyers of the Algonquin nation, who inhabit the country about lake Superior. Mr. M'Kenzie states the following circumstance, "Within three miles of the last portage" (a place near lake Superior) "is a remarkable rock, with a smooth face, but split and cracked in different parts, which hang over the water. Into one of its horizontal chasms a great number of arrows have been shot, which is said to have been done by a war party of the Nadowasis or Sieux, who had done much mischief in this country, and left these weapons as a warning to the Chebois or natives, that, notwithstanding its lakes, rivers and rocks, it was not inaccessible to their enemies." *General History of the Fur Trade.*

CHAP. IV.

Saturday 29th [September 1804]. We set sail early and had fair weather; passed a handsome bottom covered with timber on the north side, and bluffs on the south. We saw several Indians on the south side walking up the shore; spoke to them and found they were some of those we left yesterday. There were one or two of the chiefs with them. They requested us to give them a carrot of tobacco for the chiefs of the other band to smoke. We sent them two carrots to a sand bar, where they could get it; but told them we should not go on shore again, untill [*sic*] we came to the nation of the Aricaris, commonly called Rickarees, Rickrees, or Rees. The Missouri is very shallow at this time and full of sand bars. We passed an old village on the south side, where the Rickarees lived five years ago, and raised corn in the bottom, around the village. We encamped on a sand beach on the south side of the river.

Sunday 30th. We set out early in a cloudy morning; passed black buffs [*sic*] on the south side, and handsome bottom prairie on the north; saw an Indian on the shore, and the chief we had on board spoke to him. He said he wished to come on board and go with us to the Rees; but we did not take him. The wind was fair and we made 9 miles by 10 o'clock. We saw a great number of Indians coming down to the river on the south side. We stopt for breakfast about 200 yards from the shore; then proceeded about a mile; near to the place where the Indians were encamped on the south side; we halted and spoke to them and then went on under a fine breeze of wind.[110]

A short time before night, the waves ran very high and the boat rocked a great deal, which so alarmed our old chief, that he would not go any further. We encamped on the north side.

Monday 1st Oct 1804. We early continued our voyage, the morning was cloudy but the wind fair and we sailed rapidly. At 9 we passed the river De Chien, or Dog river,[111] a large river that comes in on the south side. A short distance above this river, the sand bars are so numerous, that we had great difficulty to get along; and encamped on one in the middle of the river. There were some French traders on the other bank of the river, and one of them came over and remained with us all night.[112]

Tuesday 2nd. We set sail before day light. A Frenchman came on board, who could speak English. He mentioned it as his opinion, that we should see no more Indians, until we should arrive at the nation of Rees. We passed a range of black bluffs on the north side and a large bottom on the south, where there was some timber on the bank of the river. About 2 o'clock we discovered some Indians on the hills on the north side, and one of them came down to the bank and fired a gun; the object or intention we did not well understand, but were ready to meet an attack. We passed black bluffs on the south side, an island covered with timber, and a handsome bottom on the north side. We halted and spoke to the Indian, who said he belonged to the Jonkta or Babarole band, and that there were 20 lodges of them. We told him we had seen two of their chiefs, and given them a flag and a medal. We passed a creek on the south side, and encamped on a sand bar in the middle of the river.

Wednesday 3rd. The morning was cloudy, and some rain fell. The land is high on both sides of the river. About 12 o'clock the wind began to blow so hard down the stream, that we were unable to proceed, and we halted under some high bluffs, where drift wood was plenty. At 3 we continued our voyage; passed a long range of dark coloured bluffs on the south side and bottom, with some timber, on the north. We encamped on the south side.

Thursday 4th. We set out early; but were obliged to return to the place where we halted yesterday at 12 and to take the other side of the river; the water was so shallow and sand bars so numerous. At 9 o'clock an Indian swam across the river to see us, when we stopped for breakfast. We informed him that we were not traders, that we had seen his chief and told him all we had to say. We proceeded on, passed a creek on the south side, called Teel creek, and encamped on the upper part of an island.

Friday 5th. This morning there was a white frost; the day clear and pleasant. About 11 we saw some goats swimming the river, when one of our hunters ran up the shore and killed four of them, and we took them into the boat and periogues as they floated down. We passed a creek on the north side, called Hidden creek, and high black bluffs on the south side.* Some of our hunters having gone on an island to hunt scared a prairie wolf into the river, which we killed.

---

*To prevent mistakes, owing to the very winding course of the river, Starboard side and Larboard side were made use of in the original journal, instead of north side and south side; during the remainder of the voyage up the Missouri; but have been changed to north side and south side, as being better understood, and sufficiently representing the general course of the river.

We passed a creek on the south side called White Goat creek and encamped on the north side.

Saturday 6th. We continued our voyage early, and had a clear day; passed bluffs on the south side and a bottom covered with timber on the north. About 11 we passed a handsome bottom, where a band of the Rees lived last winter. They had left a number of round huts covered with earth, some of their water craft made of buffaloe hides, and some garden truck, such as squashes. We proceeded on and passed a small creek on the south side; a handsome bottom on the north; and encamped on a sand beach on the north side.

Sunday 7th. We set forward early and had a clear day: passed a willow bottom on the south side, and a creek on the north. At the beginning of some timber land we passed a small river on the south side, called Cer-wer-cer-na, about 90 yards wide. It is not so sandy as the Missouri, and the water is clear, with a deep channel. At the mouth of this river is a wintering camp of the Rickarees of 60 lodges. We saw two Sioux Indians on the north side, gave them some meat and proceeded on. We passed an island, on which Captain Clarke and one of the men went to hunt and killed a deer and a prarow. We encamped on the north side opposite the head of the island.

Monday 8th. The morning was pleasant and we set out early: passed high land on the south side and bottom on the north. The river here is very shallow and full of sand bars. We passed a run on the south side called slate run. Two of our hunters went out to some timber land on the north side to look for game. At 12 we came to a river on the south side, 120 yards wide, called the Marapa,[113] where we halted for dinner. The hunters came up, but had killed nothing. We passed a long range of hills on the north side; about two miles from the Marapa we passed a creek 25 yards wide; and about four miles further came to an island, where one band of the Rickarees live, and encamped at the upper end.

Tuesday 9th. The day was stormy, and we remained here preparing to hold a Council with the nation. Captain Lewis with some of the men went down to their lodges, and were used very kindly and friendly. Two Frenchmen live with them, one to trade and the other to interpret.[114]

Wednesday 10th. This day I went with some of the men to the lodges, about 60 in number. The following is a description of the form of these lodges and the manner of building them.

In a circle of a size suited to the dimensions of the intended lodge, they set up 16 forked posts five or six feet high, and lay poles from one fork to another. Against these poles they lean other poles, slanting from the ground, and extending about four inches above the cross poles: these are to receive the ends of the upper poles, that support the roof. They next set up four large forks, fifteen feet high, and about ten feet apart, in the middle of the area; and poles or beams between these. The roof poles are then laid on extending from the lower poles across the beams which rest on the middle forks, of such a length as to leave a hole at the top for a chimney. The whole is then covered with willow branches, except the chimney and a hole below to pass through. On the willow branches they lay grass and lastly clay. At the hole below they build a pen about four feet wide and projecting ten feet from the hut; and hang a buffaloe skin, at the entrance of the hut for a door.[115] This labour like every other kind is chiefly performed by the squaws. They raise corn, beans and tobacco. Their tobacco is different from any I had before seen: it answers for smoking, but not for chewing. On our return, I crossed from the island to the boat, with two squaws in a buffaloe skin stretched on a frame made of boughs, wove together like a crate or basket for that purpose. Captain Lewis and Captain Clarke held a Council with the Indians, and gave them some presents.[116]

Thursday 11th. A clear day. We waited for an answer from the Indians. About 12 o'clock, they came, and brought some corn, beans and squashes, which they presented to us. The chief said he was glad to see us, and wished our commanding officers would speak a good word for them to the Mandans; for they wanted to be at peace with them. These are the best looking Indians I have ever seen. At 1 o'clock P.M. we proceeded on our voyage; passed a creek on the south side 20 yards wide and a handsome bottom covered with timber. Having made about four miles, we came to the second Village of the Rickarees, situated in a prairie on the south side. They had the American flag hoisted which Captain Lewis gave them yesterday. Their lodges are similar to those in the first village, and the same, or perhaps more, in number. They are the most cleanly Indians I have ever seen on the voyage; as well as the most friendly and industrious. We anchored about 50 yards from shore, and sent a periogue over the river for wood. We all slept on board except the cooks, who went on shore to prepare provisions for the next day.

Friday 12th. We had a pleasant morning, and remained here the forenoon to hear the chief of this village speak. Last night the Indians stole an axe from our cook, which of course in some degree diminished our confidence, and lessened the amicable character we had conceived of them. At 9 o'clock Captain Lewis, Captain Clarke and myself went to the 2nd Village, and talked with its chief: then to the third Village, about half a mile beyond a small creek, and talked with the chief of that Village; and got some corn and beans from them. The third village is nearly of the same size of the second, and has in it a great number of handsome and smart women and children: the men are mostly out hunting. About 12 we left the village and proceeded on our voyage. One of the natives agreed to go with us as far as the Mandans. We encamped on the north side. After dark we heard some person hallooing on the opposite shore; and a periogue went over and brought an Indian and two squaws, who remained with us all night.

Saturday 13th. We proceeded on early and had a cloudy day; passed Pond river on the north side, about 50 yards wide. One of the squaws went on with us.[117] At 12 it rained some, and we halted to hold a court martial.[118] At 2 continued our voyage, and did not get landing until after dark, the bank was so high and steep on one side and the water so shallow on the other. We encamped on the north side.

Sunday 14th. We had a cloudy morning and some rain. We proceeded early on our voyage; passed a bottom covered with timber on the south side and low ground covered with willows on the north; passed a creek and black bluffs on the south side and encamped on the north. It rained slowly during the whole of the day.

Monday 15th. It rained all last night, and we set out early in a cloudy morning. At 7 we saw a hunting party of the Rickarees, on their way down to the villages. They had 12 buffaloe-skin canoes or boats laden with meat and skins; besides some horses that were going down the bank by land. They gave us a part of their meat. The party consisted of men, women and children. At 8 we went on again; passed a fine bottom covered with cotton wood on the north side, and naked hills on the south. About 10, we saw another party of hunters, who asked us to eat and gave us some meat. One of these requested to speak with our young squaw, who for some time hid herself, but at last came out and spoke with him. She then went on shore and talked with him, and gave him a pair of ear-rings and drops for leave to come with us; and when the horn blew for all hands to come on board, she left them and came to the boat. We passed a creek on the south side, and encamped at dusk on the north; where there was a party of Indians about 30 in number. Our squaw remained with this party: They gave us some meat and appeared very glad to see us.[119]

Tuesday 16th. We early renewed our voyage; and had a clear morning, passed a creek on the south side. The timber is more plenty than it has been for a considerable distance down the river. The sand bars, gave us a great deal of trouble, and much retarded our progress. In the evening a short time before we encamped, we met with another hunting party of the Rickarees. They had a flock of goats, or antelopes, in the river, and killed upwards of forty of them.[120] Captain Lewis, and one of our hunters went out and killed three of the same flock. We encamped on the south side. This day we saw more than an hundred goats.

Wednesday 17th. We renewed our voyage early, and had a clear morning. Last night eight of the Indians came over to see us, brought us some meat and remained all night. Captain Lewis, gave them some presents this morning. At half past ten the wind blew so hard down the river that we were obliged to halt. At four we proceeded on with the assistance of the tow line, though the wind still continued against us, and having made about two miles, encamped on the south side. Several hunters went out this day and killed six deer:[+] one of them did not join us at night.

Thursday 18th. We had a clear pleasant morning with some frost. We set sail early, and a hunter went up each shore. Having proceeded two miles we met a couple of Frenchmen in a canoe,[121] who had been up at the Mandan nation hunting, and met with a party of that nation, who robbed them of their arms, ammunition and some fur which they had; and therefore they had to return down the river; but, meeting us, went back in hopes of recovering their property. We passed a small river, on the south side called Cannon-ball river.[122] Several hunters went out here. We passed a creek on the north side, called Fish creek, on which I killed a deer. At night we encamped on the south side, and all the hunters came in having killed six deer, four goats and a pelican.

Friday 19th. Early this morning we renewed our voyage, having a clear day and a fair wind: passed a creek on the south side. While out hunting yesterday I saw about three hundred goats, and some buffaloe. Deer are not so plenty here as lower down the river, but elk, buffaloe and goats, are very numerous. Four hunters went out to day and in the evening returned with 7 deer and three elk. We encamped on the north side.

Saturday 20th. We were early under way this morning, which was very pleasant. Two hunters went out and at breakfast time brought a deer to the boat; when four more went out. We passed a creek on the north side, about 20 yards wide; bottom covered with timber on both sides, and a small river on the south side opposite the lower point of an island. At the upper end we passed bluffs on the south side and bottom on the north. We, this day, saw a number of buffaloe, and goats on the sides of the hills. We encamped on the south side, and our hunters came in having killed 14 deer,+ a goat and a wolf; and one of them wounded a large white bear.[123]

Sunday 21st. We had a disagreeable night of sleet and hail. It snowed during the forenoon, but we proceeded early on our voyage, passed bottom on the south side and hills on the north. We also passed a small river on the south side called Chischeet river; and encamped on the south side. Two of the hunters, who had gone out in the morning came in, and had killed a buffaloe and an otter.+

Monday 22nd. Some snow fell last night, and the morning was cloudy and cold. We embarked early and went on. At 9 we saw 11 Indians of the Sioux nation coming down from the Mandans, who, notwithstanding the coldness of the weather, had not an article of clothing except their breech-clouts.[124] At 1 o'clock the day became clear and pleasant and we encamped at night on the south side.

Tuesday 23rd. Some snow again fell last night, and the morning was cloudy. At 8 it began to snow, and continued snowing to 11, when it ceased. We passed the place where the Frenchmen had been robbed but no Indians could be seen. The hills here are further from the river than they are for some distance down it; and there are fine large bottoms on both sides covered with cotton wood. We encamped on the south side where we found a great quantity of rabbit berries. Three hunters were out to day, but killed nothing.

CHAP. V.

Wednesday 24th [October 1804]. We set out early in a cloudy morning. At 9 it began to rain and continued to rain for an hour. At 12 we came to a hunting party of the Mandan nation of Indians, and remained with them untill 2 and then continued our voyage. There were three lodges of these Indians on an island, which has been cut off the Grand Bend, a short distance below the Mandan village. We encamped on the north side. Five of the Indians came to us, and our Indian went over with them and returned in the morning.[125]

Thursday 25th. The morning was pleasant, and we set sail early with a fair wind. Passed a beautiful bottom on the south side, and hills on the north. A great many of the natives, some on horseback and some on foot appeared on the hills on the north side, hallooing and singing. At 2, we stopped for dinner, and as we could not get our boat to shore on the north side, the water being shallow, our Indian was sent over to them. In the afternoon we passed a bottom covered with timber on the north side and hills on the south, and encamped on the north side. Here our Indian returned accompanied by one of the Mandans.

Friday 26th. We set out early and had a clear morning; passed a large Willow bottom on the south and high land on the north side. The Mandan Indian left us early in the morning. At 10, we came to a hunting party of the Mandans, consisting of men, women and children. There was an Irishman with them, who had come from the North West Company of traders.[126] We remained here an hour, and then proceeded. A number of the Indians kept along the shore opposite the boat all day, on the south side, on which side we encamped. Some of them remained with us to 12 at night and then returned to their village.

Saturday 27th. The morning was clear and pleasant and we set out early. At half past seven we arrived at the first village of the Mandans, and halted about two hours. This village contains 40 or 50 lodges built in the manner of those of the Rickarees. These Indians have better complexions than most other Indians, and some of the children have fair hair.[127] We passed a bluff on the south side with a stratum of black resembling coal. There is a bottom on the north side, where the second Mandan village is situated. We went about a mile above it, and encamped in the same bottom, for the purpose of holding a council with the natives. This place is 1610 miles from the mouth of the river du Bois, where we first embarked to proceed on the expedition. There are about the same number of lodges, and people, in this village as in the first. These people do not bury their dead, but place the body on a scaffold, wrapped in a buffaloe robe, where it lies exposed.*

Sunday 28th. The day was clear, and we remained here; but could not sit in council, the wind blew so violent.

Monday 29th. We had again a clear day, and some of the principal men came from each village of the Mandans, from the Watasoons, Sioux, and one from the Grossventers; and all sat in council together. At 11 o'clock, when the Council met, a shot was fired from our bow piece, and the commanding officers took the chiefs by the hand. Captain Lewis, through an interpreter, delivered a speech; gave a suit of clothes to each of the chiefs and some articles for their villages. He also sent a suit to the chief of the Grossventers. At three o'clock another gun was fired at the breaking up the council, and they all appeared satisfied. Captain Lewis gave an iron mill to the Mandan nation to grind their corn, with which they were highly pleased.[128]

Tuesday 30th. We remained here to know the answer of the Indians. The day was clear and pleasant. At 10, Captain Lewis with a party of our people, and an Indian or two, went about 6 miles up the river to view an island, in order to ascertain whether or not it would suit for winter quarters. At 5 P.M. they returned and were of opinion that it was not an eligible place.

Wednesday 31st. A pleasant morning. We remained here also to day, the Indians having given no answer. At 12, Captain Clarke and some of the men went down to the village, and the chief gave 9 or 10 bushels of corn, and some buffaloe robes.

Thursday 1st Nov. 1804. At 3 o'clock P.M. we returned down the river, to look for a place where we could fix our winter quarters. At dark we had descended 9 miles and came to a bottom covered with cotton wood, where we encamped.

Friday 2nd. Captain Lewis, myself and some of the men, went up to the first village of the Mandans, who gave us some corn. Captain Clarke and the rest of our party, having dropt half a mile lower

---

*See Mackenzie's account of the funeral rites of the Kristeneaux, in his General History of the Fur Trade.

down the river, began to clear a place for a camp and fort. We pitched our tents and laid the foundation of one line of huts.[129]

Saturday 3rd. A clear day; we continued building, and six men went down the river in a periogue to hunt. They will perhaps have to go 30 or 50 miles before they come to good hunting ground.—The following is the manner in which our huts and fort were built. The huts were in two rows, containing four rooms each, and joined at one end forming an angle. When raised about 7 feet high a floor of puncheons or split plank were laid,[130] and covered with grass and clay; which made a warm loft. The upper part projected a foot over and the roofs were made shed-fashion, rising from the inner side, and making the outer wall about 18 feet high. The part not inclosed [*sic*] by the huts we intend to picket. In the angle formed by the two rows of huts we built two rooms, for holding our provisions and stores.[131]

About the 16th, the weather became very cold, and the ice began to run in the river. We sent a Frenchman down to enquire about the hunters and periogue. He and one of the hunters returned to the fort, having left the periogue and the rest about 30 miles below. The Frenchman was sent down again with a rope, and returned by land. On the 19th the hunters came up with the periogue loaded with the meat of about thirty deer, eleven elk and some buffaloe. In the cold weather we moved into the huts, though not finished. From the 20th to the 27th we had fine pleasant weather, and on the evening of the latter finished the roofs of our huts. These were made of puncheons split out of cotton wood and then hewed. The cotton wood resembles the lombardy poplar, and is a light soft wood. The largest trees are in thickness about eighteen inches diameter. On the night of the 27th the snow fell seven inches deep, and the 28th was stormy.[132]

Thursday 29th. This day was clear, but cold. We went to unrig the boat, and by an accident one of the sergeants had his shoulder dislocated.[133] The 30th the weather continued the same. Early in the morning of this day we saw an Indian on the opposite side of the river, and brought him over. He informed us, that, a few days ago, eight of his nation were out hunting, and were attacked by a party of the Sioux tribe, who killed one and wounded two more; and also carried off their horses. Captain Clarke and twenty-three men immediately set out with an intention of pursuing the murderers. They went up to the first village of the Mandans, but their warriors did not seem disposed to turn out. They suggested the coldness of the weather; that the Sioux were too far gone to be overtaken; and put off the expedition to the spring of the year. Captain Clarke and his party returned the same evening to the fort. We have been daily visited by the Indians since we came here. Our fort is called Fort Mandan, and by observation is in latitude 47. 21. 32. 8.*

Saturday 1st December, 1804. The day was pleasant, and we began to cut and carry pickets to complete our fort. One of the traders from the North West Company came to the fort,[134] and related that the Indians had been troublesome in his way through. An Indian came down from the first Mandan village, and told us that a great number of the Chien or Dog nation had arrived near the village.

Sunday 2nd. The day was pleasant, and the snow melted fast. A party of the Chien Indians with some of the Mandans came to the fort: they appeared civil and good natured.

The 3rd 4th and 5th were moderate and we carried on the work; but the 6th was so cold and stormy, we could do nothing. In the night the river froze over, and in the morning was covered with solid ice an inch and an half thick.

Friday 7th. A clear cold morning. At 9 o'clock, the Big-white head chief, of the first village of the Mandans, came to our garrison and told us that the buffaloe were in the prairie coming into the bottom.[135] Captain Lewis and eleven more of us went out immediately, and saw the prairie covered with buffaloe and the Indians on horseback killing them. They killed 30 or 40 and we killed eleven of them. They shoot them with bows and arrows, and have their horses so

---

*The course of the Missouri, and distances of places on it appear to be very erroneously laid down upon the maps of Louisiana generally. On these the villages of the Mandans are placed in about 43 1-2 degress [sic] of north latitude and 112 1-2 of west longitude from Greenwich. This would place them about 500 miles nearer the mouth of the Columbia on the Pacific ocean, than the mouth of the Missouri: supposing the mouth of the Columbia to be about 124 degrees west of London. But the nearest practicable route from the Mandan villages to the mouth of the Columbia, according to Captain Clarke's estimate, places them 335 miles nearer the mouth of the Missouri than that of the Columbia; and by the route actually taken by the expedition to the mouth of the Columbia, they are 900 miles nearer the mouth of the Missouri. By Captain Lewis's observations these villages are in latitude 47. 21. 32. 8 and according to Mr. Mackenzie, Mr. Thompson astronomer to the North West company, in the year 1798, determined the northern bend of the Missouri to be in latitude 47. 32. north, and longitude 101. 25. west. Now this is probably near the longitude of the Mandan villages; for as it appears by the above statement, and by other observations of Captain Lewis nearer the mouth of the Missouri, that the course up the river is, for a considerable distance, nearly due west, and afterwards nearly due north, the difference of longitude and latitude, between the mouth of the Missouri and the point where Mr. Thompson took his observations, may be added together, in estimating the distance: and this will give about 8 1-2 degrees of latitude [a]nd 9 degrees of longitude making in the whole 17 1-2 degrees, which from the very meandring[sic] course of the Missouri, may be sufficient to include 1610 miles of it, the distance from the mouth to the villages. In the map of North America included in the Atlas accompanying Pinkerton's Geography, published in 1804, this part of the Missouri appears pretty accurately laid down; but in the map of Louisiana in the same set it is equally erroneous with any other.

Captain Clark & his men building a line of Huts.

trained that they will advance very near and suddenly wheel and fly off in case the wounded buffaloe attempt an attack.

Saturday 8th. In our hunt of yesterday, two men had their feet frost-bitten. Captain Clarke and another party went out though the cold was extreme, to hunt the buffaloe; and killed nine and a deer. One man got his hand frozen, another his foot; and some more got a little touched.[136] Two men encamped out to take care of the meat.

Sunday 9th. Captain Lewis and twelve more of us, went down to the bottom where the two men were taking care of the meat. We found some buffaloe had come into the woods, and we killed ten of them and a deer. Having dressed them we loaded four horses with meat and sent them with some of the party to the fort: Captain Lewis and the rest of us encamped out, and had tolerable lodging with the assistance of the hides of the buffaloe we had killed.

Monday 10th. After breakfasting on marrow bones, Captain Lewis and four of us set out for the fort. Four hunters and another man to keep camp remained out. On our return we met one of our men, who said that a party had gone down with the horses for more meat. This day was very cold: an experiment was made with proof spirits, which in fifteen minutes froze into hard ice. In the evening two of our hunters came in with the horses, but had killed nothing. Five encamped out.

Tuesday 11th. Captain Lewis and Captain Clarke thinking the weather too cold to hunt, sent men down to the camp to bring up the remainder of the meat, and orders for the hunters to return. The hunters came in at dark. They had killed four buffaloe, and had dressed two of them. The cold was so severe they could do nothing with the other two.

Wednesday 12th. We all remained at the garrison, the weather being intensely cold. We made three small sleds to haul in the meat with.[137]

Thursday 13th. The weather this day, began to be more moderate. Two hunters went out and killed two buffaloe.[+] One came in, and he and some of the men went out and brought in the meat.

Friday 14th. This day was more moderate, and light snow showers fell. Captain Clarke and fourteen men went out to hunt; and took the three sleds with them. In the evening five of them returned. Captain Clarke and the other 9 encamped out, and killed two deer. The snow fell about three inches deep.

Saturday 15th. A cloudy day. Some of the natives paid us a visit, and brought presents of meat to the commanding officers. About 1 o'clock Captain Clarke and his party returned, but had killed nothing more. The buffaloe were gone from the river. Some slight showers of snow fell during the day.

Sunday 16th. A clear cold day; I went up with some of the men to the 1st and 2nd village of the Mandans, and we were treated with much kindness. Three of the traders from the N.W. Company came to our fort, and brought a letter to our commanding officers.[138] They remained with us all night. The object of the visits we received from the N.W. Company, was to ascertain our motives for visiting that country, and to gain information with respect to the change of government.[*]

---

*The North West Company was first formed in the winter of 1783-4 by the merchants of Canada engaged in the fur trade, uniting their interests. The concern was divided into sixteen shares, without any capital being deposited; each party furnishing his proportion of the articles necessary for carrying on the trade. After a severe struggle and rival competition with others engaged in the trade, in the year 1787 more partners were admitted, the shares extended to twenty and the establishment, which was no more than an association of commercial men agreeing among themselves to carry on the fur trade, founded on a more solid basis.

This and Hudson's Bay Company, has engrossed and carry on almost the whole of the fur trade in that extensive country, situated between Hudson's Bay, the Rocky mountains, and that high tract of country, west of lake Superior, which seperates [sic] the southern from the northern waters: and have factories, forts, and trading establishments on the

Monday 17th. This was a cold clear day, and we all remained in the garrison. A sled was fitted up for one of the N.W. traders to return in.[139] In the evening one of the natives came down and told us the buffaloe were again come to the river.

Tuesday 18th. A very cold day. Six of us went out to look for the buffaloe; but could see nothing but some goats. At 9 we returned and found the men from the N.W. Company had set out on their return, notwithstanding the severity of the weather.

Wednesday 19th. This was a more pleasant day and we began to set up the pickets.[140]

The 20th. and 21st. were quite warm and pleasant, and we advanced with our work.

Saturday 22nd. The weather continued clear, pleasant and warm. A great number of the natives came with corn, beans and mockasins to trade, for which they would take anything—old shirts, buttons, awls, knives and the like articles.

Sunday 23rd. The weather continued pleasant, and we proceeded in our operations in setting up the pickets.

Monday 24th. Some snow fell this morning; about 10 it cleared up, and the weather became pleasant. This evening we finished our fortification. Flour, dried apples, pepper and other articles were distributed in the different messes to enable them to celebrate Christmas in a proper and social manner.[141]

Tuesday 25th.[142] The morning was ushered in by two discharges of a swivel, and a round of small arms by the whole corps. Captain Clarke then presented to each man a glass of brandy, and we hoisted the American flag in the garrison, and its first waving in fort Mandan was celebrated with another glass.—The men then cleared out one of the rooms and commenced dancing. At 10 o'clock we had another glass of brandy, and at 1 a gun was fired as a signal for dinner. At half past 2 another gun was fired, as a notice to assemble at the dance, which was continued in a jovial manner till 8 at night; and without the presence of any females, except three squaws, wives to our interpreter, who took no other part than the amusement of looking on. None of the natives came to the garrison this day; the commanding officers having requested they should not, which was strictly attended to. During the remainder of the month we lived in peace and tranquility in the garrison, and were daily visited by the natives.[143]

Winnipic, Assiniboin, Sturgeon, Saskatchiwine, Elk, and most of the other great lakes and rivers, which communicate with or discharge themselves into Hundson's [sic] Bay, and the North sea. It is said some change has since taken place in the establishment of the North West Company.

CHAP. VI.

Tuesday 1st Jan. 1805. Two shot were fired from the swivel, followed by a round of small arms, to welcome the New year. Captain Lewis then gave each a glass of good old whiskey; and a short time after another was given by Captain Clarke.

About 11 o'clock one of the interpreters and half of our people, went up, at the request of the natives, to the village, to begin the dance;[144] and were followed some time after by Captain Clarke, and three more men. The day was warm and pleasant. Captain Lewis in the afternoon issued another glass of whiskey; and at night Captain Clarke and part of the men returned from the village, the rest remained all night.

Wednesday 2nd. Some snow fell this morning. The men, who remained at the village last night, returned. Captain Lewis, myself and some others went up to the second village and amused ourselves with dancing &c. the greater part of the day. In the evening we in general returned and a great number of the natives, men, women and children, came to see us, and appeared highly pleased.

This day I discovered how the Indians keep their horses during the winter. In the day time they are permitted to run out and gather what they can; and at night are brought into the lodges, with the natives themselves, and fed upon cotton wood branches: and in this way are kept in tolerable case.[145]

Thursday 3rd. From this to the 13th, the weather was generally very cold; but our hunters were frequently out. One of them killed a beautiful white hare. These animals are said to be plenty. We killed a small buffaloe, 3 elk, 4 deer and two or three wolves. Three of the hunters going to a distance down the river, killed nothing for two days, but a wolf, which they were obliged to eat; and said they relished it pretty well, but found it rather tough. A number of the natives being out hunting in a very cold day, one of them gave out on his return in the evening; and was left in the plain or prairie covered with a buffaloe robe. After some time he began to recover and removed to the woods, where he broke a number of branches to lie on, and to keep his body off the snow. In the morning he came to the fort, with his feet badly frozen, and the officers undertook his cure.

Sunday 13th.[146] A clear cold day. A number of the natives went down the river to hunt with our men. In the evening one of our interpreters and another Frenchman[147] who had gone with him to the Assiniboins for fur returned. They had their faces so badly frost bitten that the skin came off; and their guide was so badly froze that they were obliged to leave him with the Assiniboins. This nation lives near the Rocky Mountains, and about 90 miles from fort Mandan.*

Monday 14th. Some snow fell this morning. Six more hunters went out to join those with the natives. In the evening one of the hunters that first went out, returned. They had killed a buffaloe, a wolf and two porcupine;+ and one of the men had got his feet so badly frozen that he was unable to come to the fort.[148]

During the 15th and 16th the weather was warm, and the snow melted fast. Horses were sent for the lame man, and he was brought to the fort his feet were not so bad as we had expected.

On the 17th. it became cold; the wind blew hard from the north, and it began to freeze.

Friday 18th. Clear cold weather. Two of our hunters returned, and had killed four deer, four wolves and a prarow. Two men belonging to the N.W. company, who stay at the Grossventers [Gros Ventres or Hidatsa] village, came to the fort.[149] They say this animal which the French call a prarow, or brarow, is a species of the badger.

Saturday 19th. Two men were sent with horses for meat, to the hunters' Camp, which is thirty miles down the river.

Sunday 20th. I went up with one of the men to the villages. They treated us friendly and gave us victuals. After we were done eating they presented a bowlful to a buffaloe head, saying *"eat that."* Their superstitious credulity is so great, that they believe by using the head well the living buffaloe will come and that they will get a supply of meat.

Monday 21st. A clear cold day. Our hunters returned to the fort, and brought with them three horse load [*sic*] of venison and elk meat.

---

*It is presumed, no part of the great chain of rocky Mountains comes as near as 90 miles to fort Mandan; but it is not improbable that there may be a mountain, connected with them, which runs a considerable distance eastward along the great dividing ridge; and on some maps a mountain is laid down running east and west, south of the Assiniboin river and lake, which would appear to be not more than 90 or 100 miles from the Mandan villages.

The weather on the 22nd and 23rd. was warm, and we commenced cutting the ice from about our craft, in order to get them out of the river. The snow fell about three inches deep.

Thursday 24th. A cold day. Some of our hunters went out, but killed nothing.

Friday 25th. All hands were employed in cutting away the ice, which we find a tedious business.

Saturday 26th. A pleasant day and all hands employed in cutting wood, to make charcoal. We have a blacksmith with us, and a small set of blacksmith tools. The blacksmith makes war-axes, and other axes to cut wood; which are exchanged with the natives for corn, which is of great service to us as we could not bring much with us.[150]

On the 27th. and 28th. the weather became much more settled, warm and pleasant than it had been for some time.

Tuesday 29th. We attempted another plan for getting our water craft disengaged from the ice: which was to heat water in the boats, with hot stones; but in this project we failed, as the stones we found would not stand the fire, but broke to pieces.

Wednesday 30th. I went up the river and found another kind of stones, which broke in the same manner: so our batteaux and periogues remained fast in the ice.[151]

Thursday 31st. Some snow fell last night. Five hunters went out with two horses. In the morning the wind blew and was cold, towards the middle of the day the weather became moderate, and the afternoon was pleasant.

Friday 1st. Feb. 1805. A cold day. About 11 [of] our hunters came home, but had killed nothing. One of the men at the fort went out a short distance, and killed a small deer. On the next day he went out and killed another deer. This and the third were cold.

Monday 4th. A fine day. Captain Clarke and 18 more went down the river to hunt.[152] We proceeded on 20 miles and could see no game.

Tuesday 5th. We proceeded on to some Indian camps and there we killed three deer. The next day we went on to more Indian camps and killed some deer. On the 7th. we encamped in a bottom on the south side of the Missouri, and the next day turned out to hunt. We killed 10 elk and 18 deer, and remained there all night. On the 9th. we built a pen to secure our meat from the wolves, which are very numerous here; and in the evening went further down and encamped. The next morning we set out on our return towards the fort; and killed some elk and deer in our way. On the 12th. we arrived at the fort; and found that one of our interpreter's wives had in our absence made an ADDITION to our number.[153] On the 13th. we had three horses shod to bring home our meat.

Thursday 14th. Four men[154] set out early with the horse and sleds to bring home our meat; and had gone down about 25 miles when a party of Indians (they did not know of what nation) came upon them and robbed them of their horses one of which they gave back, and went off without doing the men any further injury. The same night the men came back and gave information of what had happened. At midnight Captain Lewis called for twenty volunteers who immediately turned out. Having made our arrangements, we set out early accompanied by some Indians; and having marched thirty miles encamped in some Indian huts.[155]

Saturday 16th. We renewed our pursuit early, and had a cold morning. Having proceeded twelve miles we discovered fresh smoke arrising [*sic*] at some old camps, where we had hid some meat before when Captain Clarke was down; and therefore advanced with caution. Having arrived at the place we found the savages were gone; had destroyed our meat, burnt the huts and fled into the plains. This morning the Indians, who had come down with us and one of our men whose feet had been a little frozen, returned home. We hunted the 17th and 18th and got a good deal of meat[156+] which we brought to a place where some more had been secured. The 19th we loaded our sleds very heavy, and fifteen men drew one and the horse the other, which was a small one. On the next day we arrived at the fort much fatigued,

Thursday 21st. Some rain fell to day, the first that has fallen since November. In the evening the weather became clear and pleasant.

Friday 22nd. Was a fine day and we again began to cut away the ice, and succeeded in getting out one of the periogues.

Saturday 23rd. We had fine pleasant weather, and all hands were engaged in cutting away the ice from the boat and the other periogue. At 4 o'clock in the afternoon we had the good fortune to get both free from the ice; and in the three following days succeeded in getting them all safe upon the bank. On the 27th we made preparations for making periogues to pursue our voyage in.

Thursday 28th. Sixteen of us went up the river about six miles, where we found and cut down trees for four canoes. While we were absent an express arrived from the Rickarees village with news that the Sioux had declared war against us, and also against the Mandans and Grossventers. They had boasted of the robbery of the 14th at the Rickarees village in their way home, and that they intended to massacre the whole of us in the spring. By this express we therefore found out that it was the Sioux who had taken the horses from our men.

Friday 1st. March, 1805. The same party encamped out to make the canoes, and continued until six were made.[157]

On the 20th. and 21st. we carried them to the river about a mile and an half distant: There I remained with two men to finish them, and to take care of them, until the 26th, when some men came up from the fort, and we put the canoes into the water. As the river had risen there was some water between the ice and the shore. We got three of them safe to the fort; but the ice breaking before the other three were got down, so filled the channel that we were obliged to carry them the rest of the way by land. On the 27th we put one of the canoes into the water to ascertain what weight they would carry. We found they would not carry as much as was expected, and Captain Lewis agreed to take a large periogue along. The remainder of the month we were employed in preparing our craft for a renewal of our voyage.[158]

Monday 1st April 1805. As our large boat was to return immediately to St. Louis, the whole of our craft was put into the water.[159] A considerable quantity of rain fell this day; the first of any consequence that had fallen here for six months. The 2nd, was a fair day but windy. On the 3rd the weather was fine and pleasant. Some boxes were made, in which it was intended to have packed skins of different animals, which had been procured in the country, to be sent down in the batteaux.

Thursday 4th. A fine clear day. We packed the boxes full of skins, buffaloe robes, and horns of the Mountain ram, of a great size for the president; and began to load the boat.

Friday 5th. This was a clear day and the wind blew hard and cold from the N.W. We took all our goods, stores and baggage out, divided and put them aboard our craft, that we might be ready to continue our voyage.

If this brief Journal should happen to be preserved, and be ever thought worthy of appearing in print: some readers will perhaps expect, that, after our long friendly intercourse with these Indians, among whom we have spent the winter; our acquaintance with those nations lower down the river and the information we received relative to several other nations, we ought to be prepared now, when we are about to renew our voyage, to give some account of the *fair sex* of the Missouri; and entertain them with narratives of feats of love as well as of arms. Though we could furnish a sufficient number of entertaining stories and pleasant anecdotes, we do not think it prudent to swell our Journal with them; as our views are directed to more useful information. Besides, as we are yet ignorant of the dangers, which may await us, and the difficulty of escape, should certain probable incidents occur, it may not be inconsistent with good policy to keep the Journal of as small and portable a size as circumstances will make practicable. It may be observed generally that chastity is not very highly esteemed by these people, and that the severe and loathsome effects *of certain French principles* are not uncommon among them. The fact is, that the women are generally considered an article of traffic and *indulgencies* are sold at a very moderate price. As a proof of this I will just mention, that for an old tobacco box, one of our men was granted the honour of passing a night with the daughter of the head chief of the Mandan nation. An old bawd with her punks, may also be found in some of the villages on the Missouri, as well as in the large cities of polished nations.[160]

CHAP. VII.

Saturday 6th [April 1805]. The day was clear and pleasant. This morning we heard that some of the Rickarees had come up to the Mandan villages. Our interpreter and some of the men were sent over to ascertain the truth of the report; and we were detained all day waiting their return.

Sunday 7th. The men returned and four of the Rickarees with them. The commanding officers held a conversation with these Indians; and they concluded that some of them would go down in the boat from their village to St. Louis. About 5 o'clock in the afternoon we left fort Mandans in good spirits. Thirty one men and a woman went up the river[161] and thirteen returned down it in the boat.[162] We had two periogues and six canoes, and proceeded about four miles, and encamped opposite the first Mandan village, on the North side.

Monday 8th. We set out early and had a clear day. The wind blew hard from the N.W. At 12 the word was passed from a canoe in the rear that it was sinking, when we halted in front and Captain Clarke went back to see what was the matter. This forenoon we passed two villages of the Grossventers, or Big-bellys nation of Indians on the South side and a small river on the same side called Cutteau or Knife river. The canoe which had been in distress, came up, and had received little damage except wetting some powder on board. The woman that is with us [Sacagawea] is a squaw of the Snake nation of Indians, and wife to our interpreter. We expect she will be of service to us, when passing through that nation. In the afternoon we passed very high bluffs on the South side; one of which had lately been a burning vulcano. The pumice stones lay very thick around it, and there was a strong smell of sulphur.*[163] We came about fourteen miles and encamped on the North side.[164]

Tuesday 9th. We set out early, and had a fine day; about 1 o'clock we passed a party of Grossventers hunting: made about twenty-two miles and encamped on the North side.

---

*"Mr. Mackay informed me, that in passing over the mountains, he observed several chasms in the earth that emitted heat and smoke, which diffused a strong sulphureous stench." Mackenzie's Voyage.

These appearances were near the eastern side of the Rocky mountains where they were crossed by Mr. Mackenzie's party; and in about lat. 56 North, and long. 120. West.

Wednesday 10th. We proceeded again early, and had rapid water and a great many sand-bars; but a fine pleasant day. Having proceeded about nineteen miles we encamped on the North side.

Friday 12th. Another fine day. We set out early as usual. About 8 we came to the mouth of the Little Missouri, a handsome small river that comes in on the South side where we halted and took breakfast. The river is very properly called the Little Missouri, for it exactly resembles the Missouri in colour, current and taste.[†] It was thought adviseable to remain here the remainder of the day, and air our loading. Some hunters went out and killed a deer, and Captain Clarke killed a hare, which was now changing its colour from white to grey.

Saturday 13th. We had a pleasant day and a fair wind; but our small canoes could not bear the sail. Some of the party caught some beaver, and some Frenchmen who were out trapping caught 7 of them. We passed a large creek on the South side, called Onion creek. We came 23 miles and encamped on the North side, where we found a wild goose nest on a tree about 60 feet high. One of the men climbed the tree and found one egg in the nest.

Sunday 14th. We started early as usual, and had a fine morning. As we were setting out a black dog came to us, and went along, supposed to have belonged to a band of the Assiniboins, who had been encamped near this place a few days ago. We passed a hill resembling a large haystack, all but about 10 feet of the top which was as white as chalk. The hills in general are much higher here than lower down the river; but the bottoms much the same. In the afternoon we passed a creek, called after our interpreter, Sharbons [Charbonneau's] creek. He had been, before, this far up the Missouri, and no white man any further, that we could discover. We made 16 miles and encamped in a handsome bottom on the North side.

Monday 15th. We had a pleasant day and a fair wind; set forward early as usual, and went on very well. Passed a large creek on the North side, called Goat-pen creek. We saw a number of buffaloe and two bears on the bank of the river. After going 23 miles we encamped on the South side.

Tuesday 16th. We had a clear pleasant day; and in the early part of it, a fair gentle wind. Captain Clarke went out and killed a Cabre or Antelope, the same kind of an animal, which we before called a goat.[165] The wind became flawy [gusty] and the sailing bad. After making 18 miles we encamped on the South side in a point of woods called the Grand point.

[†]The maps of Louisiana place the Mandan villages west of the little Missouri; whereas it is ascertained by this expedition to be 92 miles higher up the Missouri than the Mandans.

Wednesday 17th. We proceeded on early as usual with a fair wind. The day was fine and we made good way. Passed a beautiful plain and two large creeks on the North side, and another creek on the South. We saw a great many buffaloe and elk on the banks. At 1 o'clock we halted for dinner, when two men went out and in a few minutes killed 2 buffaloe.[+] We made 26 miles and encamped on the South side, and found that some rain had fallen during the day, where we encamped, though there was none where we had been.

Thursday 18th. The men caught some beaver, and killed a wild goose. The morning was fine and we went on very well until 1 o'clock, when the wind blew so hard down the river, we were obliged to lie to for 3 hours, after which we continued our voyage. This day Captain Clarke went by land and met us in the afternoon on the bank with an elk and a deer. We came about 14 miles and encamped in a good harbour on the North side, on account of the wind, which blew very hard all night accompanied with some drops of rain.

Friday 19th. A cloudy morning, with high wind. We did not set out until the next day. While we lay here, I went out to the hills, which I found very high, much washed by the rain, and without grass. I saw a part of a log quite petrified, and of which good whet-stones—or hones could be made.—I also saw where a hill had been on fire, and pumice stone around it. There is a great quantity of hysop in the vallies.[166] We killed an elk and some wild geese, and caught some beaver.

Saturday 20th. We set out again and had a cold disagreeable morning; rapid water and a strong wind. Some of the canoes took in a good deal of water; and we made but 6 miles, when we were obliged again to lie too, on account of the wind, and to dry our loading. While we lay here we killed three elk and got a number of Geese eggs out of their nests, which are generally built on trees.[167]

Sunday 21st. We proceeded on early; and had a fine clear morning, but cold: there was a sharp frost. We saw a great number of elk, buffaloe and deer on both sides of the river. About 12 the wind again rose and was disagreeable, but we continued our voyage. Two of our hunters went out this afternoon and caught three young buffaloe calves. We passed a small river called White Clay river on the North side and having gone 15 miles encamped on the South side.

Monday 22nd Before day light we continued our voyage; passed a beautiful bottom on the North side, covered with game of different kinds.[168] The wind as unfavourable to day, and the river here is very crooked. We came about 14 miles, then encamped on the South side and caught some beaver.[+]

Tuesday 23rd. We set out early and had a fine day; but the wind was ahead and we were obliged to lie too about three hours. We went 15 miles and encamped on the North side. Captain Clarke killed 3 blacktailed deer and a buffaloe calf.

Wednesday 24th. This was a clear day, but the wind blew so hard down the river we could not proceed.[169] While we lay here some of the men went to see some water at a distance which appeared like a river or small lake. In the afternoon they returned, and had found it only the water of the Missouri, which had run up a bottom. One of the men caught six young wolves and brought them in, and the other men killed some elk and deer.

Thursday 25th. We set out as usual and had a fine day; but about 11 were obliged to halt again the wind was so strong ahead. Captain Lewis and four men set off by land from this place to go to the river Jaune, or Yellow Stone river,[170] which it is believed is not very distant. I remarked, as a singular circumstance, that there is no dew in this Country, and very little rain. Can it be owing to the want of timber?[171] At 5 o'clock in the afternoon, we renewed our voyage; and having this day advanced about 13 miles, encamped on the South side.

Friday 26th. A fine day. We set out early, and having proceeded 10 miles came at 12 o'clock to the mouth of the Jaune and halted: Captain Lewis and his party had not arrived. I went up the point about 9 miles, where there are the most beautiful rich plains, I ever beheld. I saw a large pond or lake.—Captain Clarke while I was absent measured both rivers; and found the breadth of the Missouri to be 337 yards of water, and 190 of a sand beach; total 527 yards. That of the Yellow Stone river 297 yards of water and 561 of sand; total 858 yards. The mouth of this river is 1888 miles from the mouth of the Missouri; 278 from Fort Mandan and 186 from the mouth of Little Missouri.

The river Jaune is shallow, and Missouri deep and rapid. In the evening Captain Lewis with his party joined us; and had brought with them a buffaloe calf, which followed them 7 or 8 miles. We killed a number of calves, and found they made very good veal. There are a great many signs of beaver in this part of the country. We encamped on the point all night.[172]

Captain Clark and his men shooting Bears.

Saturday 27th. About 9 o'clock in the forenoon we renewed our voyage. The day was fine, but on account of a strong wind we were obliged at 1 to halt till 4, when we again went on; and having this day made 8 miles, encamped on the North side.[173]

Sunday 28th. We set out early, had a fine day and went on very well. About 9 we halted for breakfast under very high bluffs on the North side. About 15 miles above the Yellow Stone river, the banks on the Missouri are not so high as below it, and the sand bars are more in the middle of the river. We came 24 miles and encamped on the North side in a handsome bottom.[174] The bottoms here are not so large, and have less timber on them than those below the Jaune.

Monday 29th. We again set out early, had a clear morning and went on at a good rate. This forenoon we passed some of the highest bluffs I had ever seen; and on the top of the highest we saw some Mountain sheep, which the natives say are common about the Rocky mountains. These were the first we had seen, and we attemped to kill some of them but did not succeed. Captain Lewis, and one of the men, travelled some distance by land and killed a white bear. — The natives call them white, but they are more of a brown grey. They are longer than the common black bear, and have much larger feet and talons.[175] We went 25 miles and encamped on the bank of a small river, which comes in on the North side about 70 yards wide.

Tuesday 30th. We embarked at sunrise; had a fine morning and went on very well. We passed through a handsome Country, with a rich soil, and the prairies rising beautifully on both sides of the river. We went 24 miles and encamped on the North side. Captain Lewis killed a large elk here.

CHAP. VIII.

Wednesday 1st. May, 1805. We set out early in a cool morning; and went on till 12 o'clock, when the wind rose so high, that our small canoes could not stand the waves. We made only 10 miles this day.

Thursday 2nd. At day break it began to snow; and the wind continued so high, we could not proceed until the afternoon. While we lay here our hunters went out and killed some buffaloe and deer. They found some red cloth at an old Indian camp, which we suppose had been offered and left as a sacrifice; the Indians having some knowledge of a supreme being and this their mode of worship.[176] The snow did not fall more than an inch deep. At four we set out, went six miles, and encamped on the North side in a beautiful bottom.

Friday 3rd. We proceeded on our voyage this morning, though very cold and disagreeable, and a severe frost. The snow and green grass on the prairies exhibited an appearance somewhat uncommon. The cotton wood leaves are as large as dollars, notwithstanding the snow and such hard frost. We passed a small river on the north side called the 2000 mile river [an estimate of their mileage]. About a mile above we passed a large creek on the South side, called Porcupine creek. — We came this day about 20 miles and encamped on the North side.[177]

Saturday 4th. This day was more pleasant: in the forenoon we passed a creek on the South side, about 40 yards wide. The river has been more straight for two or three days than it was before; the bottoms larger and more timber on them. We went about eighteen miles and encamped on the North side. One of the men became sick this morning and has remained so all day.[178]

Sunday 5th. The morning was fine with some white frost. During this day the country appeared beautiful on both sides of the river. We went sixteen miles and encamped on the North side. The sick man has become better. Here we killed a very large brown bear, which measured three feet five inches round the head; three feet eleven inches round the neck; round the breast five feet 10½ inches; the length eight feet 7½ inches; round the middle of the fore leg 23 inches; and his talons four inches and three eights of an inch.[179]

Monday 6th. We set sail with a fair wind and pleasant weather. At 12 a few drops of rain fell, but it soon cleared up. We passed a river on the South side about 200 yards wide; but the water of this river sinks in the sand on the side of the Missouri. We went twenty-six miles and encamped on the South side.

Tuesday 7th. We again set out early and went on very well till 12 when it began to blow hard, and being all under sail one of our canoes turned over. Fortunately the accident happened near the shore; and after halting three hours we were able to go on again. Having this day made sixteen miles we encamped on the South side.

Wednesday 8th. We were again very early under way in a cloudy morning; about 12 some rain fell: at 2 we passed a handsome river on the North side about 200 yards wide called Milk river. There is a good deal of water in this river which is clear, and its banks beautiful. Our distance this day was about twenty-seven miles, and we encamped in a beautiful bottom on the South side.

Thursday 9th. We proceeded on early and had a fine day. The country on both sides begins to be more broken, and the river more crooked. At 1, we passed a creek on the South side, and having made about 25 miles we encamped at the mouth of a creek on the North side, called by the name of Warner's creek.[180]

Friday 10th. We set out early in a fair morning; but having gone five miles were obliged to halt and lye by during the day, on account of hard wind. Some small showers of rain occasionally fell. Here we killed some deer and buffaloe and took some beaver.

Saturday 11th. The morning was fine, we started at the usual hour: at 1 passed a small creek on the South side. This day we saw several great gangs of buffaloe, and other game in plenty. One of the men killed another large brown bear, about the size of the one lately killed.[181] We came seventeen miles and encamped on the South side.

Sunday 12th. We early renewed our voyage and had a pleasant morning; passed some hills on the North side, covered with pine and cedar, the first timber of any kind we have seen on the hills for a long time. At 1 we halted for dinner and a violent storm or wind then arose, which continued until night when some rain fell. Our distance this day only 13 1/2 miles.

Monday 13th. The weather continued stormy, and some few drops of rain fell. At 1 P.M. we embarked; passed three creeks, one on the North side and two on the South; went seven miles and encamped in a large bottom.

Tuesday 14th.[182] There was some white frost in the morning, we proceeded on early; passed black hills close to the river on the South side and some covered with pine timber at a distance. About 12 the day became warm. Banks of snow were seen lying on the hills on the North side. This forenoon we passed a large creek on the North side, and a small river on the South. About 4 in the afternoon we passed another small river on the South side near the mouth of which some of the men discovered a large brown bear, and six of them went out to kill it. They fired at it; but having only wounded it, it made battle and was near seizing some of them, but they all fortunately escaped, and at length succeeded in dispatching it.[183] These bears are very bold and ferocious; and very large and powerful. The natives say they have killed a number of their brave men. The periogues having gone ahead, while the people belonging to the canoes were dressing the bear, a sudden gust of wind arose, which overset one of the periogues before the sail could be got down. The men who had been on board, turned it again and got it to shore, full of water. It was immediately unloaded and the cargo opened, when we found a great part of the medicine, and other articles spoiled.[184] Here we encamped, having come to day 18 1/2 miles.

Wednesday 15th. We remained here all day to dry our baggage that had got wet. It was cloudy and unfavourable for the purpose, and some rain fell.

Thursday 16th. This was a fine day, and by 4 o'clock in the afternoon we had all our articles dry and on board again. At that time we proceeded on our voyage; passed high barren hills on both sides of the river, with only a few pine trees on them. We advanced seven miles and encamped in a handsome bottom on the South side where there are a number of old Indian huts.

Friday 17th. The morning was fine and we embarked early. The hills here come very close to the river on both sides, and have very little timber on them. They are very high and much washed. There are some of them, which at a distance resemble ancient steeples. We passed two rivers one on each side. During the whole of this day's voyage the Missouri was very handsome, and about 300 yards wide. We made 20½ miles and encamped on the South side.[185]

Saturday 18th. A cloudy morning. We proceeded as usual. The country much the same as yesterday: until about 12 o'clock, when the bottoms became more extensive on both sides of the river. There is still a small quantity of pine timber on the hills. We had some showers of rain in the forenoon; hail in the afternoon; and a fine clear evening. We went nineteen miles and encamped on the South side opposite an island.

Sunday 19th. The morning was foggy and there was some dew. The river is handsome and the country mountainous. We made 20 1/4 miles and encamped on the North side in a small bottom.[186]

Monday 20th. We set sail early and had a fine morning. Passed a creek on the south side and about 11 came to the mouth of the Muscle-shell river, a handsome river that comes in on the South side. The water of the Missouri is becoming more clear. We here spent the remainder of the day, having come seven miles. Captain Lewis had an observation here, which gave 47°. 00. 24. North latitude: and Captain Clarke measured the rivers. The Missouri here is 222 yards wide, and the Muscle-shell 110 yards. The water of the latter is of a pale colour, and the current is not rapid; its mouth is 660 miles above Fort Mandans.[187]

Tuesday 21st. We proceeded on early and had a fine morning; towards the middle of the day the wind blew hard; but we went on very well for 20 miles, and encamped on a sand-beach on the North side.

Wednesday 22nd. A cloudy morning. The wind blew so hard this morning, we did not get under way until 9 o'clock. The forenoon was cold and disagreeable, but the afternoon became more pleasant. We killed a brown bear and some other game on our way.+ Having gone 16 1/2 miles we encamped on the North side.[188]

Thursday 23rd. The morning was clear with a white frost, and ice as thick as window glass. We passed two creeks, one on each side of the river: and two islands which are not common. There are very few between these and fort Mandans, not more than six or eight. In the evening we killed a large bear in the river; but he sunk and we did not get him.* We went 28 1/2 miles and encamped.

Friday 24th. There was again some white frost this morning. We embarked early; passed a large creek on the North side and a beautiful island close on the southern shore. At the head of the island, came in another creek on the South side. The bottom of the river, and sand-bars have become much more gravelly than we found

---

*It is said that bears, beavers, otters and such animals will sink unless shot dead.

them at any place lower down. The water is high, rapid and more clear. At dinner time a party was sent out to bring the meat of some animals that had been killed at a distance. Here we left two canoes to wait for them and proceeded on. We passed a creek on the North side, and having made 24 1/4 miles encamped on the South side. The hills are near, on both sides of the river, and very high.[189]

Saturday 25th. We waited here in the morning until the canoes came up; and about 7 proceeded on our voyage. The forenoon was pleasant. We passed two creeks opposite to each other on the opposite sides of the river. About 12 we passed a bottom on the North side with one solitary tree on it, upon which there was an eagle's nest. The bottoms here are very small. As we went on this afternoon some of the party killed three of what the French and natives call mountain sheep; but they very little resemble sheep, except in the head, horns and feet.[190+] They are of a dun colour except on the belly and round the rump, where they are white. The horns of the male are very large; those of the female small. They have a fine soft hair. Captain Clarke calls them the Ibex, and says they resemble that animal more than any other. They are in size somewhat larger than a deer. The hills here are very high and steep. One of our men in an attempt to climb one had his shoulder dislocated;[191] it was however replaced without much difficulty. These hills are very much washed in general: they appear like great heaps of clay, washing away with every shower; with scarcely any herbs or grass on any of them. This evening we passed an island all prairie except a few trees on the upper end of it. We went 18 miles and encamped on the South side.

Sunday 26th. We set out early in a fine morning, and passed through a desert country; in which there is no timber on any part, except a few scattered pines on the hills. We saw few animals of any kind, but the Ibex or mountain sheep. One of our men killed a male, which had horns two feet long and four inches diameter at the root.* We passed two creeks this forenoon on the North side; and in the

---

*"The Ibex resembles the goat in the shape of it sbody [sic]; but differs in the horns which are much larger. They are bent backwards, full of knots; and it is generally asserted that there is a knot added every year. There are some of these found if we may believe Bellonius, at least two yards long. The Ibex has a large black beard, is of a brown colour, with a thick woven coat of hair. There is a streak of black runs along the top of the back; and the belly and back of the thighs are of a fawn colour. It is a native of the Alps, the Pyrenees, and mountains of Greece; extremely swift and capable of running with ease along the edges of precipices, where even the Wolf or the Fox, though instigated by hunger, dares not pursue it." *Goldsmith*

Such is the description given of the Ibex, but which to us does not appear to suit the animal found about the Rocky mountains called the mountain Ram. From what we have before heard of that animal, and from Mr. Gass's verbal description, we are led to believe, that it much more nearly resembles the wild sheep, called the Mufflon or Musmon, to be found in the uncultivated parts of Greece, Sardinia, Corsica and in the desart [sic] of Tartary; and which is thought to be the primitive race and the real sheep in its wild and

evening one of the men killed a buffaloe. At dark we came to large rapids, where we had to unite the crews of two or three canoes, to force them through.[192] It was sometime after night before we could encamp. We at length, after having gone twenty-one miles encamped on the South side in a small grove of timber, the first we had seen during the day.

Monday 27th. We have now got into a country which presents little to our view, but scenes of bareness and desolation; and see no encouraging prospects that it will terminate. Having proceeded (by the course of this river) about two thousand three hundred miles, it may therefore not be improper to make two or three general observations respecting the country we have passed.

From the mouth of the Missouri to that of the river Platte, a distance of more than six hundred miles, the land is generally of a good quality, with a sufficient quantity of timber; in many places very rich, and the country pleasant and beautiful.

From the confluence of the river Platte with the Missouri to the Sterile desert we lately entered a distance of upwards of fifteen hundred miles the soil is less rich, and except in the bottoms, the land of an inferior quality; but may in general be called good second rate land. The country is rather hilly than level, though not mountainous, rocky or stony. The hills in their unsheltered state are much exposed to be washed by heavy rains. This kind of country and soil which has fallen under our observation in our progress up the Missouri, extends it is understood, to a great distance on both sides of the river. Along the Missouri and the waters which flow into it, cotton wood and willows are frequent in the bottoms and islands; but the upland is almost entirely without timber, and consists of large prairies or plains the boundaries of which the eye cannot reach. The grass is generally short on these immense natural pastures, which

---

savage state. Perhaps it may be found to be exactly the same; of which we find the following description.

"The Mufflon, or Musmon, though covered with hair, bears a strong similitude to the Ram than to any other animal; like the Ram it has the eyes placed near the horns; and its ears are shorter than those of the goat: it also resembles the Ram in its horns, and in all the particular contours of its form. The horns also are alike; they are of a white or yellow colour; they have three sides as in the Ram, and bend backwards in the same manner behind the ears. The muzzle and inside of the ears are of a whitish colour tinctured with yellow; the other parts of the face are of a brownish grey . The general colour of the hair over the body is of a brown, approaching to that of the red deer. The inside of the thighs and belly are of a white tinctured with yellow. The form upon the whole seems more made for agility and strength than that of the common sheep; and the Mufflon is actually found to live in a savage state, and maintain itself either by force or swiftness against all the animals that live by rapine. Such is its extreme speed that many have been inclined rather to rank it among the deer kind, than the sheep. But in this they are deceived, as the Musmon has a mark that entirely distinguishes it from that species, being known never to shed its horns. In some these are seen to grow to a surprizing size; many of them measuring, in their convolutions, above two ells [an ell was about forty-five inches in England] long." *Goldsmith*

in the proper seasons are decorated with blossoms and flowers of various colours. The views from the hills are interesting and grand. Wide extended plains with their hills and vales, stretching away in lessening wavy ridges, until by their distance they fade from the sight; large rivers and streams in their rapid course, winding in various meanders; groves of cotton wood and willow along the waters intersecting the landscapes in different directions, dividing them into various forms, at length appearing like dark clouds and sinking in the horizon; these enlivened with the buffaloe, elk, deer, and other animals which in vast numbers feed upon the plains or pursue their prey, are the prominent objects, which compose the extensive prospects presented to the view and strike the attention of the beholder.[193]

The islands in the Missouri are of various sizes; in general not large and during high water mostly overflowed.

There are Indian paths along the Missouri and some in other parts of the country. Those along that river do not generally follow its windings but cut off points of land and pursue a direct course. There are also roads and paths made by the buffaloe and other animals; some of the buffaloe roads are at least ten feet wide. We did not embark this morning until 8 o'clock. The day was fine, but the wind ahead. We had difficult water, and passed through the most dismal country I ever beheld; nothing but barren mountains on both sides of the river, as far as our view could extend.[194] The bed of the river is rocky, and also the banks and hills in some places; but these are chiefly of earth. We went thirteen miles and encamped in a bottom, just large enough for the purpose, and made out to get enough of drift wood to cook with.

Tuesday 28th. We set sail early, had a fine morning, and proceeded on through this desert country untill about 4 o'clock P.M. when we came to a more pleasant part. We made twenty-one miles and encamped on the North side.

Wednesday 29th. We proceeded on early and had a fine morning; passed two rivers, one on each side. At 12 it became cloudy and began to rain. We went about eighteen miles and halted at a handsome grove of timber on the South side. It rained a little all the afternoon. Some of the men went out to hunt and killed an elk. Last night about 12 o'clock a buffaloe swiming the river happened to land at one of the periogues, crossed over it[195] and broke two guns, but not so as to render them useless. He then went straight on through the men where they were sleeping, but hurt none of them.[196] As we came along to day we passed a place where the Indians had driven above an hundred head of buffaloe down a precipice and killed them.[197]

Thursday 30th. The forenoon was cloudy, with some rain. We did not set out till late in the day. The hills came in close on the river again, but are not so high. Some of them are as black as coal and some white as chalk. We see a great many fresh Indian tracks or signs as we pass along. It rained a little all day; we went on slow and encamped early on the North side, in a small bottom with some cotton wood, having proceeded on eight miles. There are no pines to be seen on the hills.[198]

Friday 31st. We embarked early in a cloudy morning; passed through a mountainous country, but the game is more plenty, and we killed some buffaloe in our way.[+] About 11 o'clock it began to rain slowly, and continued raining two hours, when it cleared up. We passed some very curious cliffs and rocky peaks, in a long range. Some of them 200 feet high and not more than eight feet thick. They seem as if built by the hand of man, and are so numerous that they appear like the ruins of an antient [*sic*] city.[199] We went 17 1/2 miles and encamped at the mouth of a handsome creek on the North side.

Saturday 1st June, 1805. We embarked early. The morning was cloudy, but without rain. We passed through a more handsome country, than for some days past. It appears more level and there are some good bottoms on both sides of the river, but not large; also a number of beautiful small islands covered with cotton wood. We saw a number of mountain sheep. Yesterday our men killed three of them, that had remarkable large horns; one pair weighed 25 pounds. We passed a small river on the North side about 11 o'clock. The water is not so rapid to day as usual, but continues high. In the afternoon we passed a creek about 30 yards wide, and several small islands. We went 24 miles and encamped on a small island.

Sunday 2nd. We embarked early in a fine morning. The hills come close on the river, but are not so high nor so broken, as we found them a short distance lower down. This forenoon we passed two creeks, one on each side, and several islands covered with cotton wood; but there is not a stick of timber to be seen any where upon the hills. Some of the hunters killed a brown bear in a small bottom on the south side,[200+] and having come 18 miles we encamped just above the bottom on the same side, at the mouth of a large river.

Monday 3rd. We crossed over to the point between the two rivers and encamped there. The commanding officers could not determine which of these rivers or branches, it was proper to take; and therefore concluded to send a small party up each of them. Myself and two men went up the South branch,[201] and a serjeant[202] and two more up the North. The parties went up the two branches about 15 miles. We found the South branch rapid with a great many islands, and the general course South West. The other party reported the North branch as less rapid, and not so deep as the other. The North branch is 186 yards wide and the South 372 yards. The water of the South branch is clear, and that of the North muddy.[203] About a mile and an half up the point from the confluence, a handsome small river falls into the North branch, called Rose river.[204] Its water is muddy, and the current rapid. Captain Lewis took a meridian altitude at the point, which gave 47. 24. 12. North latitude. Captain Lewis and Captain Clarke were not yet satisfied with respect to the proper river to ascend.

Tuesday 4th. Captain Lewis with six men went up the North branch, to see if they could find any certain marks to determine whether that was the Missouri or not; and Captain Clarke myself and four others went up the South branch, for the same purpose with regard to that branch. About eight miles above the confluence, the South branch and the small river which falls into the North branch, are more than 200 yards apart. Near this place and close on the bank of the South branch is a beautiful spring where we refreshed ourselves with a good drink of grog; and proceeded on through the high plains. Here nothing grows but prickly pears, which are in abundance, and some short grass. We went on about thirty miles and found the river still extending in a South West direction. We saw a mountain to the South about 20 miles off, which appears to run East and West, and some spots on it resembing snow. In the evening we went towards the river to encamp, where one of the men having got down to a small point of woods on the bank, before the rest of the party, was attacked by a huge he-bear, and his gun missed fire.[205] We were about 200 yards from him, but the bank there was so steep we could not get down to his assistance: we, however, fired at the animal from the place where we stood and he went off without injuring the man. Having got down we all encamped in an old Indian lodge for the night.

Wednesday 5th. Some light showers of rain fell in the night, and the morning was cloudy. When preparing to set out we discovered three bears coming up the river towards us; we therefore halted a while and killed the whole of them. About 7 we set out along the plains again, and discovered the mountain South of us covered with snow, that had fallen last night. When we had gone about 11 miles we saw a large mountain to the West of us also covered with snow.

This mountain appeared to run from North to South, and to be very high. The bearing of the river is still South West. Captain Clarke thought this a good course for us to proceed on our voyage, and we turned back towards the camp again. We went about 15 miles and struck the small river about 20 miles from its mouth. Here we killed some elk and deer and encamped all night. There is a great deal of timber in the bottoms of this little river, and plenty of different kinds of game. In these bottoms I saw the stalks of a plant resembling flax in every particular.

Thursday 6th. We proceeded down the small river and killed some deer. About 1 o'clock we went on the plains again, which we kept on till we came to the point in the evening. Captain Lewis and his party had not returned. Some light rain fell this afternoon.

Friday 7th. It rained all day: Captain Lewis and party did not return.[206]

Saturday 8th. A fine cool morning. About 10 o'clock A.M. the water of the South river, or branch, became almost of the colour of claret, and remained so all day. The water of the other branch has the appearance of milk when contrasted with the water of this branch in its present state. About 4 in the afternoon Captain Lewis and his party came to camp. They had been up the North branch about 60 miles, and found it navigable that distance; not so full of islands as the other branch and a greater quantity of timber near it and plenty of game, which is not the case on the South branch. Its bearing something north of west a considerable distance, and then to the south of west. The party while out killed 18 deer and some elk.[+] From the appearance of the river where they left it to return, they supposed it might be navigable a considerable distance further. They saw no mountains ahead, but one off towards the north: it was not covered with snow like those we had seen. Both these rivers abound in fish; and we caught some of different kinds, but not large. About five o'clock in the afternoon the weather became cloudy and cold, and it began to rain. The officers concluded that the south branch was the most proper to ascend, which they think is the Missouri. The other they called Maria's river. At dark the rain ceased.

Sunday 9th. A fine morning. It was thought adviseable to leave the large periogue here and part of the stores and baggage, and some of the men were engaged in digging a case [cache] to bury them in. The water of the Missouri changed this morning to its former colour. The day was fine, but the wind blew hard from the northwest. One of the men killed an excellent fat buffaloe. There is a quantity of gooseberry and choak-cherry bushes on the point, and also some rabbit berries.[207]

Monday 10th. We hauled our large periogue[208] on an island in the mouth of Maria's river, and covered it over with brush. We then began to examine and assort our effects to see what would be least wanted and most proper to leave; but about two it began to rain and blow so hard, we were obliged to desist. The rain continued only an hour, and in the evening we loaded the rest of the craft, and left the remainder of our stores and baggage to be buried, consisting of corn, pork, flour, some powder and lead, and other articles amounting to about one thousand pounds weight.[209]

Tuesday 11th. A fine day. Captain Lewis and four men[210] set out this morning to go to the mountains, which we had discovered towards the west. The rest of the party were engaged in burying the baggage and goods which had been left,[211] and preparing to start the following morning.[212]

CHAP. IX.

Wednesday 12th [June 1805].[213] The morning was fine; we set out from the mouth of Maria's river, and went on very well. In the forenoon we passed 12 islands. At 1 o'clock the weather became cloudy and threatened rain; at 2 there was a light shower, and the day became clear. We passed three islands this afternoon and some handsome bluffs on both sides of the river. We went 18 miles and encamped in a small bottom on the north side, where we killed 2 elk and some deer.[+]

Thursday 13th. We set out early in a fine morning. Some dew fell last night. We passed a large creek on the south side, called Snow creek. The water of the river is very clear and the current very rapid. We passed a number of islands covered with timber; but there is none to be seen on the hills on either side. We went 14 miles and encamped on the south side.[214]

Friday 14th. We embarked early, and the morning was pleasant. About 7 o'clock A.M. we passed a place where Captain Lewis and his men had killed two bears, and had left a note directing us where to find them.[215] About 2 one of Captain Lewis's men met us, and informed us that the falls were about 20 miles above; and that Captain Lewis and the other three men, were gone on to examine what the distance was above the falls, before we could take the water again. We went 10 miles and encamped on a small bottom on the south side.[216]

Saturday 15th. We proceeded on as usual, but had the most rapid water, I ever saw any craft taken through.[217] At noon we stopped at the mouth of a creek on the south side called Strawberry creek, handsome rapid stream, but not large.[218] On a point above, there is a great quantity of strawberry, gooseberry and choak-cherry bushes; and there appears to be a good deal of small cotton-wood on the banks of this creek. In the afternoon we passed red bluffs on both sides of the river, and at night came to a large rapid which we did not venture to pass so late; and therefore encamped below on the north side, after going 12 miles.[219]

Sunday 16th. In the morning all hands were engaged in taking the canoes over the rapid about a mile in length, which having accomplished they returned and took up the periogue, where we halted to examine another great rapid close ahead. One man had been sent on last night to Captain Lewis, to find out what discoveries he had made. We remained here some time, and a few of the men went out to hunt. About noon Captain Lewis and the party with him joined us, and the hunters came in. Captain Lewis had been up the falls 15 miles above the first shoot or pitch, and found the falls continue all that distance, in which there were 5 different shoots 40 or 50 feet perpendicular each, and very rapid water between them.[220] As we found the south side the best to carry our canoes up, we crossed over and unloaded our craft. We then had to take the empty canoes to the side we had left, and to tow them up by a line about a mile, in order to get them up to the mouth of a small river on the south side, as a more convenient place to take them up the bank. This business was attended with great difficulty as well as danger, but we succeeded in getting them all over safe.

Monday 17th. Part of the men were employed in taking the canoes up the small river about a mile and an half; and some engaged in making small waggons to haul the canoes and loading above the falls. Captain Clarke and 4 men[221] went to view and survey our road to the place where we were to embark above the falls. Opposite the mouth of the small river, a beautiful sulphur spring rises out of the bank, of as strong sulphur water as I have ever seen. On the bottoms of this small river and also on the Missouri is a great quantity of flax growing, and at this time in bloom. Two men went out this morning to hunt for elk, in order to get their skins for covering to the iron frame of a boat, which we had with us. In the evening the men got the canoes to a proper place to take them upon land.

Tuesday 18th. The periogue was hauled out of the water and laid safe;[222] and some men went to dig a place for depositing more of our baggage. About 12 the two hunters came in, and could find no elk, but killed 10 deer. In the evening we compleated [*sic*] our waggons, which were made altogether of wood, and of a very ordinary quality; but it is expected they will answer the purpose.[223]

Wednesday 19th. A fine day, but the wind very high. Three hunters[224] set out for Medicine river, a large river above the falls, which comes in on the north side, to hunt for elk. We finished the burying place, so that we will be ready to start as soon as Capt. Clark returns. All our people are making mockasons to go through the prairie.

Thursday 20th. A cloudy morning: four hunters went out to kill some fat buffaloe. About 4 o'clock one of them came in for men to carry the meat to camp; as they had 14 down ready to butcher. We went out about a mile and an half, and brought in a load, leaving three men to dress the rest. Captain Clarke and his party returned, having found a tolerable good road except where some draughts crossed it. They had left their blankets and provision at the place where they expect we will again embark.

Friday 21st. This morning was also fine, but there was a high wind. The remainder of the meat was brought in, and one of the men killed 2 deer.[+]

Saturday 22nd. All hands, except two and the interpreter and his wife,[225] set out through the prairie with one canoe on a waggon loaded heavy with baggage. We went on slowly as our axletrees were weak; and about 12 o'clock one of them broke; when we had to halt and put in a new one. This accident happened at a draught where there was some willow, and we put in an axletree of that; which I believe is the best this country affords for the purpose. It was late in the evening before we got to the intended place of embarkation on the river.

Sunday 23rd. The morning was cloudy. When I awoke this morning I found a material difference between the river and country here and below the falls. Here the river is wide and the current gentle. There are three small islands at this place and some timber on the banks, but not much, and what is there is cotton-wood and willow. The banks are very low, and the country rising in plains a considerable distance on both sides of the river; and far off mountains covered with snow on both sides and ahead. Two of the men and myself remained with Captain Lewis here to assist him in putting together his iron boat, the rest went back for another load. The iron boat-frame is to be covered with skins and requires a quantity of thin shaved strips of wood for lining.[226] In the forenoon we put the frame together, which is 36 feet long, 4 1/2 wide, and 2 feet 2 inches deep. In the afternoon Capt. Lewis and one of the men went down to Medicine river, which is about two miles distant; to see whether the three men sent there to hunt had procured any elk skins. In the evening they found one of the hunters, and encamped with him all night.[227]

Monday 24th. In the morning Capt. Lewis came up to our camp. We found it very difficult to procure stuff for the boat.[228] The two men which Captain Lewis had left in the morning came to our camp in the afternoon,[229] but had seen nothing of the other two hunters.

In the evening there was a very heavy shower of rain; at night the weather cleared up, and the men arrived with two more canoes. The two hunters which Capt. Lewis could not find, had killed some buffaloe below the the mouth of the Medicine river,+ where one remained, and the other had gone across to the camp below the falls again, but had found no elk.[230]

Tuesday 25th. A cloudy morning. The men went back for more canoes and baggage; and one went down to the hunter's camp below Medicine river to bring him up in a canoe.[231] Another went up the river to look for elk. When he had gone about three miles, he was attacked by 3 brown bears, that were near devouring him; but he made his escape by running down a steep bank into the water. In this adventure he fell, injured his gun, and hurt one of his hands; therefore returned to camp.[232] One of the men and myself went over to an island to look for stuff for the canoe,[233] but could find nothing but bark, which perhaps will answer. We killed two elk on the island.+ There is in the bottoms a great quantity of spear-mint and currant bushes. Also multitudes of blackbirds. The musquitoes are very troublesome, though the snow is on the mountains so near. In the evening the two men came up the river with a quantity of good meat and 100 pounds of tallow.[234]

Wednesday 26th. A fine morning. Two hunters went up the river, and myself and another went over the river to collect bark;[235] where a great gang of buffaloe came near us, and we killed 7 of them.+ In the evening the men returned over the plains with two more canoes and baggage. One man fell very sick, and Captain Lewis had to bleed him with a penknife, having no other instrument at this camp.[236] Captain Clarke measured the length of this portage accurately and found it to be 18 miles. He also measured the height of the falls, and found them in a distance of 17 miles 362 feet 9 inches. The first great pitch 98 feet, the second 19 feet, the third 47 feet 8 inches, the fourth 26 feet; and a number of small pitches, amounting altogether to 362 feet 9 inches.

Thursday 27th. A fine day.[237] The men went back for the remaining canoe and baggage. The sick man is become better. This morning some elk came close to camp and we killed two of them. In the afternoon a dreadful hail storm came on, which lasted half an hour. Some of the lumps of ice that fell weighed 3 ounces, and measured 7 inches in circumference.[238] The ground was covered with them, as white as snow. It kept cloudy during the evening and some rain fell. At night the two hunters that went up the river returned. They had killed while out 9 elk and 3 bears.+

Friday 28th. A fine morning. There are but 6 persons now at this camp, but all busy about the boat; some shaving skins, some sewing them together; and some preparing the wood part.[239]

Saturday 29th. We had a very hard gust of wind and rain in the morning; but a fine forenoon after it. Captain Lewis and a hunter[240] went down the river about 7 miles, to see a very large spring which rises out of the bank of the Missouri on the south side. In the afternoon there was another heavy shower of rain, and after it a fine evening. Captain Lewis came to camp, but drenched with rain.[241]

Sunday 30th. A fine morning, and heavy dew, which is very rare in this country. The men with the canoe and baggage did not return, as we expected.

Monday 1st July, 1805. A fine day.[242] In the afternoon, Captain Clarke and the men came with all the baggage except some they had left six miles back. The hail that fell on the 27th hurt some of the men very badly. Captain Clarke, the interpreter, and the squaw and child, had gone to see the spring at the falls; and when the storm began, they took shelter under a bank at the mouth of a run; but in five minutes there was seven feet water in the run; and they were very near being swept away. They lost a gun, an umbrella and a Surveyor's compass, and barely escaped with their lives.[243]

Tuesday 2nd. A fine morning. The Surveyor's compass, which had been lost was found to day. The men went out for the baggage which had been left on the way, and got in with the whole of it, and canoes safe.[244]

In the evening, the most of the corps crossed over to an island, to attack and rout its monarch, a large brown bear, that held possession and seemed to defy all that would attempt to besiege him there. Our troops, however, stormed the place, gave no quarter, and its commander fell.+ Our army returned the same evening to camp without having suffered any loss on their side.[245]

Wednesday 3rd. A fine morning. I was so engaged with the boat, that I had not visited the falls. I therefore set out with one of the men to day for that purpose. I found the 2nd pitch the most beautiful, though not the highest. About a mile below the upper pitch, the largest and most beautiful spring rises out of the bank of the Missouri on the south side that I ever beheld. We had a light shower of rain. During this excursion I saw more buffalo than I had seen in any day previous: we killed 7 of them before we returned to camp. We also saw 25 wolves in one gang or pack.[246]

Thursday 4th. A fine day. A part of the men were busily engaged at the boat, and others in dressing skins for clothing, until about 4 o'clock in the afternoon, when we drank the last of our spirits in celebrating the day, and amused ourselves with dancing till 9 o'clock at night, when a shower of rain fell and we retired to rest.

Friday 5th. A fine morning. All the men, except five of us who were engaged at the boat, went to hunt; at night they came in and had killed several buffaloe and some cabres or antelopes.

Saturday 6th. As many of the hands as could find room to work were engaged at the boat; and four went down the river to hunt buffaloe, in order to get their skins to cover our craft. This was a beautiful and pleasant day.

Sunday 7th. The morning was fine. The hunters had remained out all night. In the evening some few drops of rain fell; and the hunters came in; but had not had good luck, the buffaloe being mostly out in the plains. At night we got our boat finished, all but greasing; and she was laid out to dry.[247]

Monday 8th. Again we had a fine morning, and a number of the party went out to hunt. In the evening they all came in, and had killed but three buffaloe, a deer and a cabre; and caught a small animal almost like a cat, of a light colour.[248] Yesterday one of the men caught a small squirrel, like a ground squirrel, but of a more dun colour, and more spotted.[249] We finished the boat this evening, having covered her with tallow and coal-dust. We called her the Experiment, and expect she will answer our purpose.[250]

Tuesday 9th. A fine morning, and heavy dew. In the forenoon we loaded our canoes, and put the Experiment into the water. She rides very light but leaks some. In the afternoon a storm of wind, with some rain came on from the north west, and we had again to unload some of our canoes, the waves ran so high. After the storm we had a fine evening. The tallow and coal were found not to answer the purpose; for as soon as dry, it cracked and scaled off, and the water came through the skins. Therefore for want of tar or pitch we had, after all our labour, to haul our new boat on shore, and leave it at this place.

Wednesday 10th. A fine cool morning. Captain Lewis and Captain Clarke thought it would be best to make two canoes more, if we could get timber large enough. So Captain Clarke and 10 men set out in search of it.[251] Some of the hunters having seen large timber about 20 miles up the river, the canoes were sent on loaded, and a party went by land; the distance that way being only 6 or 7 miles. If timber is found the canoes are to unload and return for the remainder of the baggage. Captain Lewis, myself and nine men staid to take the boat asunder and bury her; and deposited her safely under ground. Captain Lewis had an observation at 12 which gave 47° 3 10 N. Latitude. In the afternoon I went out to see if there were any buffaloe near, but found none: they appear to have all left the river. On the bank of a run where there are high rocks, I found a great quantity of sweet gooseberries, all ripe.

Thursday 11th. We continued here waiting for the return of the canoes until 2 o'clock; then four of us went out and killed a buffaloe and brought in part of the meat. The canoes did not come back this evening.[252]

Friday 12th. A fine morning. Myself and three of the men went up the river to assist Captain Clarke's party.[253] In our way we passed a small bottom on the north side of the river, in which there is an old Indian lodge 216 feet in circumference.[254] Here we saw some wild pigeons and turtle doves. Having gone about 7 miles we found Captain Clarke's party, who had cut down two trees and taken off logs for canoes, one 25 and the other 30 feet in length. The canoes had returned to our old camp, where Captain Lewis was.

Saturday 13th. A fine day, but high wind. Captain Lewis came up here, accompanied by the squaw.[255] He informed us that the canoes had started with all the baggage from the former encampment, which we had called White-bear camp. The musquitoes are very troublesome. This evening the canoes were finished except the putting in some knees.

Sunday 14th. A fine morning. About 11 o'clock the men came up with the canoes and baggage. The distance by water was found to be 22 miles, and by land only 6 miles. In the afternoon some rain fell but we continued to work at the canoes, and finished them ready for loading.

CHAP. X.

Monday 15th [July 1805]. After a night of heavy rain, we had a pleasant morning, and loaded the canoes. About 11 o'clock we set out from this place, which we had called Canoe camp; had fine still water, and passed some handsome small bottoms on both sides of the river. We also passed a handsome river on the south side about 100 yards wide, which seemed to have its source in a large mountain on the same side.[256] The snow appears to have melted from all the mountains in view. The country around is composed of dry plains, with short grass. We passed two small creeks, one on each side of the river; made 26 miles, and encamped on the north side.

Tuesday 16th. We embarked early and had a fine morning.[257] Captain Lewis and two men went on ahead to the mountain to take an observation. We passed the channel of a river on the south side without water, about 60 yards wide. We had fine water until about 1 o'clock, when we came within about two miles of the mountain; when the water became more rapid; but the current not so swift as below the falls. At this place there are a number of small islands. One of our men has been taken unwell.[258] In the afternoon we continued our voyage, and the water continued very rapid. We got about 3 miles into the first range of the Rock mountains, and encamped on the north side of the river on a sand beach. There is some fine timber on the mountains, but not much in this part. There are great hills of solid rock of a dark colour. This day we went about 20 miles.[259]

Wednesday 17th. We set out early, and the morning was fine and pleasant. At 8 o'clock we came to Captain Lewis's camp, at a very rapid place of the river, and took breakfast. We had here to join the crews of two canoes together, to go up the rapids which were about half a mile long.[260] The Missouri at this place is very narrow. At the head of these rapids a fine spring comes in on the south side, which rises about a quarter of a mile from the river; and has a good deal of small cotton-wood and willows on its banks. There is also another spring below the rapids, but it sinks before it reaches the river. We proceeded on through the mountains, a very desert looking part of the country. Some of the knobs or peaks of these mountains are 700 (perhaps some nearly 1200) feet high, all rock; and though they are almost perpendicular, we saw mountain sheep on the very tops of them. We saw few other animals to day. The general breadth of the river is 100 yards. We went 11 miles and encamped in a small bottom on the north side.

Thursday 18th. The morning was fair and we proceeded on early: passed Clear-water river on the north side about 50 yards wide, rapid and shallow. There are a great quantity of currants all along the river on both sides in the small bottoms. At breakfast time Captain Clarke with three men went on ahead.[261] About 11 we got through the higher part of the mountains, and to where there is less timber and the rocks not so large. In the forenoon we passed two small creeks on the north side, and in the afternoon a small river on the same side; above the mouth of which we got a deer skin, that Captain Clarke's man had hung up. The country continues much the same. We made 20 miles this day.

Friday 19th. A fine morning. At 9 we came to high parts of the mountains, which had a good deal of pine, spruce and cedar on them, and where there were not so many rocks; but no timber in the bottoms except some small willows. About 1 o'clock we had thunder, lightening and rain, which continued an hour or two, and then the weather became clear. This afternoon we passed parts of the mountains, that were very high, and mostly of solid rock of a light colour. The mountains are so close on the river on both sides that we scarcely could find room to encamp. We went about 20 miles and encamped on the south side. After night some rain fell.

Saturday 20th. We had a fine morning, and embarked early. About 8 we got out of the high part of the mountains, and came to where they are lower and not so rocky; and where there are the finest currants I ever saw of different kinds, red, yellow and black: the black are the most pleasant and palatable. There is also a good portion of timber on the mountains all along this part. We killed an elk in our way, and found the skin of one which Captain Clarke had left on the bank with a note, informing us he would pass the mountain he was then on, and wait for the canoes. We passed a small creek on the south side, and about 2 o'clock came to a level plain on the north side, from which we saw a strong smoke rising, and supposed it was from a fire made by Capt. Clarke. The river is very crooked in general, and here is a great bend to the southeast; and in the afternoon it turned so far that our course was north of east. We proceeded on through a valley between two mountains, one of which we passed, and the other is in view ahead. We went 15 miles and encamped at the mouth of a small run on the south side.[262]

Sunday 21st. We set out at sunrise and had a pleasant morning; passed some middling high hills on the river, and rocks of red purple colour; also two small creeks one on each side. There are a few pines on the hills. At noon our course began to change more to the southwest again; the wind blew very hard and some drops of rain fell. In the afternoon we passed through a ridge, where the river is very narrow; and close above a large cluster of small islands, where we had some difficulty to get along, the water being so much separated. We went 15 miles and an half and encamped on the south side, on a beautiful prairie bottom. One of our hunters killed a fine deer.[+]

Monday 22nd. We embarked early, the weather being pleasant: passed some fine springs on the southern shore, and a large island near the northern: On the south side the country is level to a good distance, but on the north the hills come close to the river. At breakfast our squaw informed us she had been at this place before when small.[263] Here we got a quantity of wild onions. At half past 9, we proceeded on again; passed a large island at noon; and in the afternoon, more islands: and came to a place where Captain Clarke and his party were encamped. They told us they had seen the same smoke, which we had discovered a few days ago, and found it had been made by the natives, who they supposed had seen some of us, and had fled, taking us for enemies. We went 17 miles and an half and encamped on an island; where we found the musquitoes very bad. We saw to day several banks of snow on a mountain west of us.

Tuesday 23rd. A cloudy morning. We embarked early, and at the same time Captain Clarke and four men[264] went on again to endeavour to meet with some of the natives. We had rapid water, and passed a great number of islands. Captain Clarke and his men killed four deer and a cabre, and left the skins and meat on the shore, where we could easily find them. The course of the river all day was nearly from the south, through a valley of 10 or 12 miles wide. The mountains are not so high nor so rocky, as those we passed. Large timber is not plenty, but there are a great quantity of small shrubs and willows. We passed a small river on the south side, and some banks of very white clay. We encamped on an island, having made 24 miles.

Wednesday 24th. The morning was fine, and we early prosecuted our voyage; passed a bank of very red earth, which our squaw told us the natives use for paint.[265] Deer are plenty among the bushes, and one of our men killed one on the bank. We continued through the valley all day: Went 19 miles and encamped on the north side.[266]

Thursday 25th. We embarked and proceeded on at the usual time, in a fine morning; we passed a beautiful plain on the north side, and at 2 o'clock we came to the entrance of another chain of mountains; where we took dinner and again went on. Passing through this chain we found some difficult rapids, but good water between them.[267] This chain of mountains are not so high, nor so rocky as those we passed before. Six very fine springs rise on the southern shore, about four miles above the entrance of this range. We went 16 miles and encamped on the north side.

Friday 26th. The morning was fine and we continued our course through the mountains. There are some cedar and spruce trees on the shores; but very little of any kind on the mountains. About 11 o'clock we got through this range into a valley: About 2 came to a large island and halted on it for dinner. A rattle-snake came among our canoes in the water, of a kind different from any I had seen. It was about two feet long, of a light colour, with small spots all over. One of our hunters went on ahead in the morning, and at this place killed 4 deer. While we remained here it became cloudy and some rain fell. At 4 o'clock we proceeded on through the valley; passed a creek on the south side, and having gone 18 miles and an half encamped on the same side, where a small mountain comes in to the river.

Saturday 27th. We continued our voyage early, and had a pleasant morning; proceeded on, and at 9 o'clock got through the small mountain. At the entrance of the valley, a branch of the Missouri comes in on the south side, about 60 yards wide; the current rapid but not very deep. Here we took breakfast, and having proceeded on a mile, came to another branch of the same size. There is very little difference in the size of the 3 branches.[268] On the bank of the north branch we found a note Captain Clarke had left informing us, he was ahead and had gone up the branch. We went on to the point, and, as the men were much fatigued, encamped in order to rest a day or two. After we halted here, it began to rain and continued three hours. About 12 o'clock Capt. Clarke and his men came to our encampment, and told us they had been up both branches a considerable distance, but could discover none of the natives. There is a beautiful valley at these forks; a good deal of timber on the branches, chiefly cotton-wood. Also currants, goose and service berries, and choak-cherries on the banks. The deer are plenty too; some of the men went out and killed several to day. Capt. Clarke was very un-well and had been so all last night. In the evening the weather be-came clear and we had a fine night.

Sunday 28th. As this was a fine day, the men were employed in airing the baggage, dressing skins and hunting. Capt. Clarke still continued unwell. Our squaw informed us that it was at this place she had been taken prisoner by the Grossventers 4 or 5 years ago.[269] From this valley we can discover a large mountain with snow on it, towards the southwest; and expect to pass by the northwest end of it. Capt. Lewis had a meridian altitude here, which gave 45° 22 34 .5 north latitude. We also remained here the 29th, which was a fine day, and the men chiefly employed in the same way. Capt. Clarke is getting better.

Tuesday 30th. We left our encampment at the forks, and pro-ceeded on about 7 o'clock A. M. up the north branch. This branch is about 60 yards wide and 6 feet deep, with a rapid current. We passed a number of islands. The valley continued on the south side all this day; but the spur of a mountain, about 5 or 6 miles from the forks came in close on the north side with very high cliffs of rocks. We encamped where it terminated, having made 13 miles and an half.

Wednesday 31st. We set out early, and had a fine cool morning with dew. Last night Capt. Lewis went on ahead, and the canoes being unable to get on to him, he was obliged to encamp out alone in this howling wilderness. We passed a small creek this morning on the south side, which empties into the river, through 2 or 3 mouths, on account of its being much dammed up by the beaver, which are very plenty. At breakfast time we came up to Capt. Lewis; and hav-ing made 17 miles and three quarters, encamped on an island.[270]

Thursday 1st August, 1805. We set out early in a fine morning and proceeded on till breakfast time;[271] when Capt. Lewis, myself and the two interpreters went on ahead to look for some of the Snake Indians.[272] Our course lay across a large mountain on the north side, over which we had a very fatiguing trip of about 11 miles. We then came to the river again, and found it ran through a handsome valley of from 6 to 8 miles wide. At the entrance of this valley, which is covered with small bushes, but has very little timber, we killed two elk[+] and left the meat for the canoes to take up, as the men stood much in need of it, having no fresh provisions on hand. We crossed a small creek on the north shore, and encamped on the same side.

Friday 2nd. The morning was fine and we went on at sunrise, proceeded 4 or 5 miles and crossed the river. In the middle of the day it was very warm in the valley, and at night very cold; so much so that two blankets were scarce a sufficient covering. On each side of the valley there is a high range of mountains, which run nearly parallel, with some spots of snow on their tops. We killed a deer; went about 24 miles and encamped on the south side.[273]

Saturday 3rd. A fine cool morning. We left a note for Capt. Clarke, continued our route along the valley; and passed several fine springs that issue from the mountains. Currants and service berries are in abundance along this valley, and we regaled ourselves with some of the best I had ever seen. We went about 22 miles and encamped. The night was disagreeably cold.[274]

Sunday 4th. At sunrise we continued our march, in a fine morning; went about 6 miles when we came to a fork of the river; crossed the south branch and from a high knob discovered that the river had forked below us, as we could see the timber on the north branch about 6 or 7 miles from the south and west branches. We therefore crossed to the north branch, and finding it not navigable for our canoes, went down to the confluence and left a note for Capt. Clarke directing him to take the left hand branch. We then went up the north branch about 10 miles and encamped on it.

Monday 5th. This morning Capt. Lewis thought it would be best for me and one of the interpreters[275] to go over to the west branch, and remain there, until he and the other should go higher up the north, cross over in search of Indians and then go down and join us. At night they came to our camp, but had not seen any of the natives, nor any fresh signs.

Tuesday 6th. We started early to go down to the point to see if the canoes had come up that far, and came upon the north branch about 2 miles above it. Here we discovered that the people in the canoes had not found the note, and with great difficulty, had proceeded 5 or 6 miles up the north branch.[276] In their return down one of the canoes was overturned; a knapsack, shot-pouch and powder-horn lost, and all the rest of the loading wet.[277] We got down to the forks about 12 o'clock, put all our baggage out to dry, and encamped for the night. Some hunters went out and killed 3 deer.[278]

Wednesday 7th. We remained here during the forenoon, which was fair and clear, and where Capt. Lewis took a meridian altitude, which made the latitude of this place 45° 2 53 north.[279] At 3 o'clock in the afternoon, we were ready to continue our voyage. In the evening a heavy cloud came up, and we had hard thunder with lightening and rain. We went on 7 miles and encamped on the north side, when the weather cleared, and we had a fine night. The canoes came 62 miles and three quarters while we were out.

' *Thursday 8th.* We proceeded on early and had a pleasant morning. The west branch which we went up is about 30 yards wide, and the south, which we passed, about 15 yards. Three hunters went by land to day, and at noon had killed 2 deer and a goat or cabre.⁺ The river is very crooked in this valley. The hunters again went out in the afternoon and killed 2 deer more. There are no buffaloe in this part of the country, and the other game is not plenty. We went this day 19 miles.[280]

We found out the reason why Capt. Clarke did not get the note left at the point, which was that a beaver had cut down and dragged off the pole, on which I had fixed it.[281]

Friday 9th. We set out at sunrise, and had a fine morning with some dew; proceeded on till 9 o'clock when we halted for breakfast. Here one of the hunters came to us who had been out since the morning the canoes went up the north branch by mistake, and who had that morning preceded them by land.[282] Here also Captain Lewis and three men[283] started to go on ahead;[284] and at 10 we proceeded on with the canoes. The river is narrow and very crooked, and the valley continues about the same breadth. There is some timber on the mountain on the south side, and white earth or rocks appearing through the pines. At noon we halted for dinner, and hauled out one of the canoes, which had sprung a leak and caulked her.

This morning our commanding officers thought proper that the Missouri should lose its name at the confluence of the three branches we had left on the 30th ultimo. The north branch, which we went up, they called JEFFERSON; the west or middle branch, MADISON; the south branch, about 2 miles up which a beautiful spring comes in, GALLATIN! and a small river above the forks they called *Philosophy*. Of the 3 branches we had just left, they called the north *Wisdom*, the south *Philanthropy*, and the west or middle fork, which we continued our voyage along, retained the name of JEFFERSON.[285] We went 14 miles and encamped on the south side. Our two hunters killed but one goat.

CHAP. XI.

Saturday, 10th [August 1805]. We set out early in a fine morning, and proceeded on through the valley, until breakfast time, when we came to a place where the river passes through a mountain. This narrow passage is not more than a quarter of a mile in length. At the upper end another valley commences, but not so wide as the one below. There is no timber in the lower end of this valley; and the river very crooked, narrow, and in some places so shallow, that we were obliged to get into the water and drag the canoes along. At 1 o'clock we halted to dine, when a shower of rain came on with thunder and lightening, and continued an hour, during which some hail fell. Two hunters were out to day and killed but one deer.⁺ We came 13 miles and encamped on the North side. Here the valley begins to be more extensive.

Sunday 11th. This morning was cloudy and we did not set out until after breakfast. Three hunters were sent out and we proceeded on about 3 miles, when we came to a large island, which is 3000 miles from the river Du Bois at the mouth of the Missouri. We therefore called it 3000 *mile Island.* We took up the South side of it, and had difficulty in passing the water being shallow. About 2 some rain fell.— Our hunters killed 3 deer and a goat. We went 14 miles and encamped on the North side.²⁸⁶

Monday 12th. We proceeded on at the usual time, and three hunters were again sent out. A few drops of rain fell to day. Our hunters killed 4 deer; and after making 12 miles we encamped on the North side.²⁸⁷

Tuesday 13th. A cloudy morning. We set out early, through rapid water; the river being crooked and narrow, and passed a small creek on the south side. The weather was cold during the whole of this day. We went 16 miles and encamped in a beautiful plain on the South side.²⁸⁸

Wednesday 14th. The morning was clear and cold. We embarked after breakfast; passed a small creek on the north side and a beautiful valley on the same side. Timber is very scarce, and only some few scattering trees along the river. Our hunters came in at noon, who had been out all day yesterday: they had killed 5 deer and a goat.[+] There are a few deer and goats in this part of the country; and otter and beaver in plenty along the river, but no other kind of game that we could discover. There are some fish in the river and trout of a large size, and of the black kind. We went 15 miles and encamped on the South side where we had great difficulty in procuring a sufficient quantity of wood to cook with.[289]

Thursday 15th.[290] We had a fine morning and proceeded on about 8 o'clock. Having gone 2 miles, we came to the entrance of a mountain, where Captain Lewis and his party on the second day after their departure had taken dinner; and had left 4 deer skins. At the entrance of the mountain there are two high pillars of rocks, resembling towers on each side of the river. The mountains are not very high and do not approach so near the river as some we have passed; they are about a quarter of a mile distant, and the river meanders along between them through the bushes and is not more the 20 yards wide, and about a foot and a half deep. The water is very cold, and severe and disagreeable to the men, who are frequently obliged to wade and drag the canoes. We went 15 miles and encamped on the South side.[291]

Friday 16th. We did not set out till after breakfast, and while here one of the men went out and killed a fine buck.[+] We proceeded through rapid water; the river is very narrow, crooked and shallow. This morning we passed a place where the hills come close to the river for a short distance, and then open on each side of a small valley, which, on account of the great quantity of service berries in it, we called Service-berry valley.[292] We passed over a rapid of about a quarter of a mile, and encamped on the South side, having come 15 miles.

Saturday 17th. A fine morning. We proceeded on about 2 miles and discovered a number of the natives, of the Snake nation, coming along the bank on the South side.[293] Captain Lewis had been as far as the waters of the Columbia river and met them there. We continued on about two miles further to a place where the river forks, and there halted and encamped, after much fatigue and difficulty. The water is so shallow that we had to drag the canoes, one at a time, almost all the way. The distance across from this place to the waters of the Columbia river is about 40 miles, and the road or way said to be good. There were about 20 of the natives came over with Captain Lewis and had the same number of horses. Here we unloaded the canoes, and had a talk with the Indians; and agreed with them that they should lend us some of their horses to carry our baggage to the Columbia river.[294]

Sunday 18th. A fine morning. We bought three horses of the Indians. Captain Clarke and 11 more, with our interpreter and his wife, and all the Indians set out at 11 o'clock to go over to the Columbia.[295] —The Indians went for horses to carry our baggage, and we to search for timber to make canoes for descending the Columbia. We proceeded up the north branch which is the largest and longest branch of Jefferson river, through a handsome valley about 5 miles wide. In this we found a number of springs and small branches, but no timber. There is plenty of grass and clover, and also some flax all along it. The Indians all except 5 went on ahead. We travelled 15 miles and encamped close on the branch which is about 5 yards wide. Here we killed two small deer. The country all around is very mountainous, with some few pine trees on the mountains. At three o'clock this afternoon there was a violent gust of wind, and some rain fell. In about an hour the weather became clear, and very cold, and continued cold all night.[296]

Monday 19th. A fine morning, but cold. We proceeded on at 8 o'clock along the valley for six miles, when the hills came more close on the branch, which here divides into three parts or other small branches, and two miles further the principal branch again forks, where the mountains commence with a thick grove of small pines on our left, and large rocks on our right. At 1 o'clock we dined at the head spring of the Missouri and Jefferson river, about 25 miles from the place, where we had left the canoes, and from which the course is nearly west. About 5 miles South of us we saw snow on the top of a mountain, and in the morning there was a severe white frost: but the sun shines very warm where we now are. At three o'clock we proceeded on, and at the foot of the dividing ridge, we met two Indians coming to meet us, and who appeared very glad to see us. The people of this nation instead of shaking hands as a token of friendship, put their arms round the neck of the person they salute. It is not more than a mile from the head spring of the Missouri to the head of one of the branches of the Columbia.[297] We proceeded on through the mountain; passed some fine springs and encamped about 36 miles from our camp, where the canoes are.[298] Here we were met by a number of the natives.[299]

Tuesday 20th. A fine cool frosty morning. We set out early and travelled about 4 miles, to a village of the Indians on the bank of a branch of the Columbia river, about ten yards wide and very rapid. At this place there are about 25 lodges made of willow bushes. They are the poorest and most miserable nation I ever beheld; having scarcely any thing to subsist on, except berries and a few fish, which they contrive by some means, to take. They have a great many fine horses, and nothing more; and on account of these they are much harassed by other nations. They move about in any direction where the berries are most plenty. We had a long talk with them, and they gave us very unfavourable accounts with respect to the rivers. From which we understood that they were not navigable down, and expect to perform the rout by land. Here we procured a guide, and left our interpreters to go on with the natives, and assist Captain Lewis and his party to bring on the baggage.

Captain Clarke and our party proceeded down the river with our guide, through a valley about 4 miles wide, of a rich soil, but almost without timber.—There are high mountains on both sides, with some pine trees on them. We went about 8 miles and encamped on a fine spring. One of our men remained behind at the village to buy a horse, and did not join us this evening.[300] Five of the Indians came and stayed with us during the night. They told us that they were sometimes reduced to such want, as to be obliged to eat their horses.

Wednesday 21st. About 7 o'clock in the morning we continued our journey down the valley, and came to a few lodges of Indians where our guide lives. We remained here about two hours, during which time a number of Indians passed us, going to fish. We proceeded on the way the Indians had gone; and one of our men went with them to the fishing place. The valley becomes very narrow here, and a large branch of the river comes in a short distance below.[301] Here we had to ascend high ground, the bottom is so narrow; and continued on the high ground about six miles when we came again to the river, where a fine branch flows in, the valley 4 or 5 miles wide. In this branch we shot a salmon about 6 pounds weight. We travelled 20 miles this day, and encamped at a place where the mountains come close to the river. In the valley through which we passed and all along the river, there are cherries, currants and other small fruit. The man who had remained behind at the first village and the other who had gone with the Indians to their fishing place, both joined us here. The Indians gave them five salmon to bring to us: and he that had stayed for a horse, brought one with him. At this place the river is about 70 yards wide.[302]

Thursday 22nd. The morning was fine, with a great white frost. We began our journey at 7 o'clock; and having travelled about a mile, crossed a branch of the river.[303] Here the mountains come so close on the river, we could not get through the narrows, and had to cross a very high mountain about 3 miles over, and then struck the river again, where there is a small bottom and one lodge of the natives in it, gathering berries, haws and cherries for winter food. We soon had to ascend another large mountain, and had to proceed in the same way until we crossed 4 of them, when we came to a large creek,[304] where there is a small bottom and 3 lodges of Indians. Three of our men having gone through the bottom to hunt, came first upon the lodges which greatly alarmed the unhappy natives, who all fell a weeping and began to run off; but the party coming up with the guide relieved them from their fears. They then received us kindly and gave us berries and fish to eat. We remained with them about two hours and gave them some presents. Those of the natives, who are detached in small parties, appear to live better, and to have a larger supply of provisions, than those who live in large villages. The people of these three lodges have gathered a quantity of sunflower seed, and also of the lambs-quarter, which they pound and mix with service berries, and make of the composition a kind of bread; which appears capable of sustaining life for some time. On this bread and the fish they take out of the river, these people, who appear to be the most wretched of the human species, chiefly subsist. They gave us some dried salmon, and we proceeded down the river; but with a great deal of difficulty: the mountains being so close, steep and rocky. The river here is about 80 yards wide, and a continual rapid, but not deep. We went about 15 miles to day, and encamped on a small island, as there was no other level place near. Game is scarce, and we killed nothing since the 18th but one deer; and our stock of provisions is exhausted.[305]

Friday 23rd. We proceeded down the river through dreadful narrows, where the rocks were in some places breast high, and no path or trail of any kind. This morning we killed a goose, and badly wounded a large buck in the water. One of our sergeants is very unwell.[306] We went on 3 miles, when Captain Clarke did not think proper to proceed further with the horses, until he should go forward and examine the pass. So we halted on a small flatt [*sic*] and breakfasted on some fish the natives had given us. Captain Clarke, our guide, and three men then went on. Another Indian who had come on from the last Indian camp remained with us. We had yet seen no timber large enough to make canoes. Two of the hunters went in search of the buck, which had been wounded; and the rest staid at the camp to fish. In the afternoon the men came in from hunting the wounded deer, but could not find him. They killed three prairie hens, or pheasants. At night the sergeant who had been sick, became better. We caught some small fish in the night. The natives take their fish by spearing them; their spears for this purpose are poles with bones fixed to the ends of them, with which they strike the fish. They have but four guns in the nation, and catch goats and some other animals by running them down with horses. The dresses of the women are a kind of shifts made of the skins of these goats and mountain sheep, which come down to the middle of the leg. Some of them have robes, but others none. Some of the men have shirts and some are without any. Some also have robes made of beaver and buffaloe skins; but there are few of the former. I saw one made of ground hog skins.[307]

Saturday 24th. We had a pleasant morning and some of the men went out to hunt. The river at this place is so confined by the mountains that it is not more than 20 yards wide, and very rapid. The mountains on the sides are not less than 1000 feet high and very steep. There are a few pines growing on them. We caught some small fish to day, and our hunters killed 5 prairie fowls. These were all we had to subsist on. At 1 o'clock Captain Clarke and his party returned, after having been down the river about 12 miles. They found it was not possible to go down either by land or water, without much risk and trouble. The water is so rapid and the bed of the river so rocky, that going by water appeared impracticable; and the mountains so amazingly high, steep and rocky, that it seemed impossible to go along the river by land. Our guide speaks of a way to sea, by going up the south fork of this river, getting on to the mountains that way, and then turning to the south west again. Captain Clarke therefore wrote a letter to Captain Lewis, and dispatched a man on horseback to meet him; and we all turned back up the river again, poor and uncomfortable enough, as we had nothing to eat, and there is no game. We proceeded up about 3 miles, and supperless went to rest for the night.

Sunday 25th. We set out early and had a fine morning; passed the Indian camp, where they gave us a little dried salmon, and proceeded back again over the mountains. Some hunters went on ahead and about 4 o'clock we got over the four mountains, and encamped in the valley. Two men went to hunt, and all the rest to fish. We soon caught as many small fish as made, with two salmon our guide got from some Indians, a comfortable supper. At dark our hunters came and had killed but one beaver.[308+]

Monday 26th. We had again a pleasant morning; and four hunters went on early ahead, and one man to look for horses. We breakfasted on the beaver and salmon, which had been saved from supper the preceding evening. The man, who had gone for the horses, having returned without finding them, 4 or 5 more went out, and our guide immediately found them. We then about 10 o'clock, proceeded on to the forks, where we found our hunters; but they had killed nothing. So we went up to a small village of the natives, got some fish from them, and lodged there all night.[309]

Tuesday 27th. A fine morning with frost; and eight of us went out to hunt. I observed some flax growing in the bottoms on this river, but saw no clover or timothy, as I had seen on the Missouri and Jefferson river. There is a kind of wild sage or hyssop, as high as a man's head, full of branches and leaves, which grows in these bottoms, with shrubs of different kinds. In the evening we all came in again and had killed nothing but a fish. We got some more from the natives, which we subsisted on. We lodged here again all night, but heard nothing from Captain Lewis.

Wednesday 28th. The morning again was pleasant, and I went on to the upper village, where I found Captain Lewis and his party buying horses.[310] They had got 23, which with 2 we had, made in the whole 25. I then returned to our camp, a distance of 15 miles, and arrived there late. I found the weather very cold for the season.

Thursday 29th. There was a severe white frost this morning. Captain Clarke and all the men except myself and another, who remained to keep camp and prepare packsaddles, went up to Captain Lewis's camp. While I lay here to day, one of the natives shewed me their method of producing fire, which is somewhat curious. They have two sticks ready for the operation, one about 9 and the other 18 inches long: the short stick they lay down flat and rub the end of the other upon it in a perpendicular direction for a few minutes; and the friction raises a kind of dust, which in a short time takes fire. These people make willow baskets so close and to such perfection as to hold water, for which purpose they make use of them. They make much use of the sunflower and lambs-quarter seed, as before mentioned; which with berries and wild cherries pounded together, compose the only bread they have any knowledge of, or in use. The fish they take in this river are of excellent kinds, especially the salmon, the roes of which when dried and pounded make the best of soup.[311]

Friday 30th. We remained here all day, and in the evening the whole of the corps came down with in [sic] a mile of our camp, and remained there all night, being a good place for grass.[312]

Saturday 31st. They all came down to our camp, and we proceeded on with 27 horses and one mule. Our old guide after consult-
ing with the rest of the Indians, thought it was better to go along the
north side of the Columbia, than on the south side.[313] We therefore
proceeded down, the same way Captain Clarke had been before, 30
miles, and then turned up a creek that comes in from the north,[314]
and encamped on it about 3 miles and an half from the mouth. Two
hunters had gone on ahead this morning, and at night joined us,
having killed one deer. The first cost of the articles, which had been
given for each horse, did not amount to more than from three to five
dollars; so that the whole of them only cost about one hundred
dollars.

CHAP. XII.

Sunday 1st Sept. 1805. We set out early in a fine morning, and travelled on nearly a west course. We found here the greatest quantity and best service berries, I had ever seen before; and abundance of choak-cherries. There is also a small bush grows in this part of the country, about 6 inches high, which bears a bunch of small purple berries. Some call it mountain holly; the fruit is of an acid taste. We are much better supplied with water than I expected; and cross several fine springs among the mountains through which we pass. At noon some rain fell, and the day continued cloudy. About the middle of the day Capt. Clarke's blackman's feet became so sore that he had to ride on horseback. At 3 o'clock we came to a creek, where there was fine grass and we halted to let our horses eat.[315] There are a great number of fish in this creek. After we halted the weather became cloudy, and a considerable quantity of rain fell. We therefore concluded to remain where we were all night, having come this day 18 miles. Our hunters killed a deer, and we caught 5 fish.[316]

Monday 2nd. The morning was cloudy. We set out early; proceeded up the creek, and passed some part closely timbered with spruce and pine. We went on with difficulty on account of the bushes, the narrowness of the way and stones that injured our horses feet, they being without shoes. In the forenoon we killed some pheasants and ducks, and a small squirrel. In the afternoon we had a good deal of rain, and the worst road (if road it can be called) that was ever travelled. The creek is become small and the hills come close in upon the banks of it, covered thick with standing timber and fallen trees; so that in some places we were obliged to go up the sides of the hills, which are very steep, and then down again in order to get along at all.[317] In going up these ascents the horses would sometimes fall backwards, which injured them very much; and one was so badly hurt that the driver was obliged to leave his load on the side of one of the hills.[318] In the low ground there are most beautiful tall strait pine trees of different kinds, except of white pine. Game is scarce; and a small quantity of dried salmon, which we got from the natives is almost our whole stock of provisions. A son of our guide joined us to day and is going on. We went 13 miles and encamped; but some of the men did not come up till late at night.

Tuesday 3rd. The morning of this day was cloudy and cool. Two men went back with a horse to bring on the load, which had been left behind last night; and we breakfasted on the last of our salmon and waited their return. Two hunters were sent on ahead, and on the return of the two men, who had been sent back, we pursued our journey up the creek, which still continued fatiguing almost beyond description. The country is very mountainous and thickly timbered; mostly with spruce pine. Having gone nine miles we halted for dinner, which was composed of a small portion of flour we had along and the last of our pork, which was but a trifle:— Our hunters had not killed any thing. We staid here about two hours, during which time some rain fell and the weather was extremely cold for the season. We then went on about 3 miles over a large mountain, to the head of another creek and encamped there for the night. This was not the creek our guide wished to have come upon; and to add to our misfortunes we had a cold evening with rain.[319]

Wednesday 4th. A considerable quantity of snow fell last night, and the morning was cloudy.[320] After eating a few grains of parched corn, we set out at 8 o'clock; crossed a large mountain and hit on the creek and small valley, which were wished for by our guide. We killed some pheasants on our way, and were about to make use of the last of our flour, when, to our great joy, one of our hunters killed a fine deer. So we dined upon that and proceeded down a small valley about a mile wide, with a rich black soil; in which there are a great quantity of sweet roots and herbs, such as sweet myrrh, angelica and several other, that the natives make use of, and of the names of which I am unacquainted. There is also timothy grass growing in it; and neither the valley nor the hills are so thickly timbered, as the mountains we had lately passed. What timber there is, is mostly pitch pine. We kept down the valley about 5 miles, and came to the Tussapa band of the Flathead nation of Indians, or a part of them.[321] We found them encamped on the creek and we encamped with them.*

Thursday 5th. This was a fine morning with a great white frost. The Indian dogs are so hungry and ravenous, that they eat 4 or 5 pair of our mockasons last night. We remained here all day, and recruited our horses to 40 and 3 colts;[322] and made 4 or 5 of this nation of Indians chiefs. They are a very friendly people; have plenty of robes and skins for covering, and a large stock of horses, some of which are very good; but they have nothing to eat, but berries, roots

---

*Captain Clarke in his letter to his brother, calls them the Oleachshoot band of the Tucksapax. It is of no very great importance, at present, to know by what names the several tribes and bands are distinguished; and Mr. Gass says that without an interpreter it was very difficult to ascertain them with any degree of certainty.

and such articles of food. This band is on its way over to the Missouri or Yellow-stone river to hunt buffaloe. They are the whitest Indians I ever saw.

Friday 6th. A cloudy morning. We exchanged some of our horses, that were fatigued, with the natives; about 12 o'clock some rain fell; and we prepared to move on. At 1 we started, when the Indians also set out. We proceeded over a mountain to a creek, and went down the creek, our course being northwest; found the country mountainous and poor; and the game scarce. Having travelled about 7 miles we encamped. Four hunters had been out to day, but killed nothing; we therefore supped upon a small quantity of corn we had yet left.

Saturday 7th. We set out early in a cloudy cool morning; and our hunters went on as usual. We proceeded down the creek, and in our way we were met by a hunter, who had not come in last night, and who had lost his horse. We halted at 12 o'clock, and one of the hunters killed 2 deer; which was a subject of much joy and congratulation.[323] Here we remained to dine, and some rain fell. On the south of this place there are very high mountains covered with snow and timber, and on the north prairie hills. After staying here 2 hours we proceeded on down the creek; found the country much the same as that which we had passed through in the forenoon; and having travelled about 20 miles since the morning, encamped for the night. The valley is become more extensive, and our creek has encreased [*sic*] to a considerable river. Some rain fell in the afternoon, and our hunters killed two cranes on our way.

Sunday 8th. The morning was wet, and we proceeded on over some beautiful plains. One of our hunters had remained out all night, at noon we halted and they all came in, having killed an elk and a deer. At 2 we proceeded on again, and had a cold, wet and disagreeable afternoon, but our road or way was level along the valley. Having travelled 20 miles, we encamped and our hunters came in, one of whom had killed a deer,[+] and another had caught two mares and a colt, which he brought with him.

Monday 9th. The morning was fair, but cool; and we continued our journey down the river. The soil of the valley is poor and gravelly; and the high snow-topped mountains are still in view on our left: Our course generally north a few degrees west. We halted at noon: on our way the hunters had killed 3 wild geese; so we have plenty of provisions at present.[324] At 2 o'clock we again went forward, and crossed over the Flathead river, about 100 yards wide, and which we called Clarke's river; passed through a close timbered bottom of about two miles, and again came into beautiful plains.[325] The timber on this bottom is pitch pine. We travelled 19 miles and encamped on a large creek, which comes in from the south. Our hunters this day killed 3 deer.[+]

Tuesday 10th. We remained here all this day, which was clear and pleasant, to let our horses rest, and to take an observation. At night our hunters came in, and had killed 5 deer.[+] With one of the hunters, 3 of the Flathead Indians came to our camp.[326] They informed us that the rest of their band was over on the Columbia river, about 5 or 6 days' journey distant, with pack-horses; that two of the Snake nation had stolen some of their horses, and that they were in pursuit of them. We gave them some presents, and one stayed to go over the mountains with us; the other two continued their pursuit.

Wednesday 11th. This was a fine morning, and we went out to collect our horses, in order to renew our journey, and found all but one. Capt. Lewis had a meridian altitude that gave 46° 48 28 .8 north latitude. In the bottoms here, there are a great quantity of cherries. The mountains are not so high, as at some distance back. At 4 o'clock in the afternoon the horse was found, and we proceeded on up the creek nearly a west course, through small bottoms.[327] We went about 6 miles and encamped; when our hunters came in but had killed nothing. The country is poor and mountainous.

Thursday 12th. We started early on our journey and had a fine morning. Having travelled 2 miles we reached the mountains which are very steep; but the road over them pretty good, as it is much travelled by the natives, who come across to the Flathead river to gather cherries and berries. Our hunters in a short time killed 4 deer. At noon we halted at a branch of the creek, on the banks of which are a number of strawberry vines, haws, and service berry bushes. At 2 we proceeded on over a large mountain, where there is no water, and we could find no place to encamp until late at night, when we arrived at a small branch, and encamped by it, in a very inconvenient place, having come 23 miles.[328]

Friday 13th. A cloudy morning. Capt. Lewis's horse could not be found; but some of the men were left to hunt for him and we proceeded on. When we had gone 2 miles, we came to a most beautiful warm spring, the water of which is considerably above blood-heat; and I could not bear my hand in it without uneasiness.[329] There are so many paths leading to and from this spring, that our guide took a wrong one for a mile or two, and we had bad travelling across till we got into the road again. At noon we halted. Game is scarce; and our hunters killed nothing since yesterday morning; though 4 of the best were constantly out, and every one of them furnished with a good horse. While we remained here, Captain Lewis and the men, who had been left with him, came up; but had not found the horse.[330] At 2 o'clock we proceeded on again over a mountain, and in our way found a deer, which our hunters had killed and hung up. In a short time we met with them, and Capt. Lewis sent two back to look for the horse. We passed over a dividing ridge to the waters of another creek, and after travelling 12 miles we encamped on the creek, up which there are some prairies or plains.

Saturday 14th. We set out early in a cloudy morning; passed over a large mountain, crossed Stony creek, about 30 yards wide, and then went over another large mountain, on which I saw service-berry bushes hanging full of fruit; but not yet ripe, owing to the coldness of the climate on these mountains: I also saw a number of other shrubs, which bear fruit, but for which I know no names. There are black elder and bore-tree, pitch and spruce pine all growing together on these mountains. Being here unable to find a place to halt at, where our horses could feed, we went on to the junction of Stony creek, with another large creek, which a short distance down becomes a considerable river, and encamped for the night, as it rained and was disagreeable travelling. The two hunters, that had gone back here joined us with Capt. Lewis's horse, but none of the hunters killed any thing except 2 or 3 pheasants; on which, without a miracle it was impossible to feed 30 hungry men and upwards, besides some Indians. So Capt. Lewis gave out some portable soup, which he had along, to be used in cases of necessity. Some of the men did not relish this soup, and agreed to kill a colt; which they immediately did, and set about roasting it; and which appeared to me to be good eating.[331] This day we travelled 17 miles.

CHAP. XIII.

Sunday 15th [September 1805]. Having breakfasted on colt, we moved on down the river 3 miles, and again took the mountains. In going up, one of the horses fell, and required 8 or 10 men to assist him in getting up again. We continued our march to 2 o'clock when we halted at a spring and dined on portable soup and a handful of parched corn. We then proceeded on our journey over the mountain to a high point, where, it being dark, we were obliged to encamp. There was here no water; but a bank of snow answered as a substitute; and we supped upon soup.

Monday 16th. Last night about 12 o'clock it began to snow. We renewed our march early, though the morning was very disagreeable, and proceeded over the most terrible mountains I ever beheld.[332] It continued snowing until 3 o'clock P.M. when we halted, took some more soup, and went on till we came to a small stream where we encamped for the night. Here we killed another colt[333] and supped on it. The snow fell so thick, and the day was so dark, that a person could not see to a distance of 200 yards. In the night and during the day the snow fell about 10 inches deep.

Tuesday 17th. Our horses scattered so much last night, that they were not collected until noon, at which time we began our march again.[334] It was a fine day with warm sunshine, which melted the snow very fast on the south sides of the hills, and made the travelling very fatiguing and uncomfortable. We continued over high desert mountains, where our hunters could find no game, nor signs of any except a bear's tract which they observed to day.—At dark we halted at a spring on the top of a mountain; killed another colt,[335] and encamped there all night.

Wednesday 18th. This was a clear cold frosty morning. All our horses except one were collected early: Six hunters went on ahead;[336] one man to look for the horse; and all the rest of us proceeded on our journey over the mountains, which are very high and rough. About 12 we passed a part where the snow was off, and no appearance that much had lately fallen. At 3 we came to snow again, and halted to take some soup, which we made with snow water, as no other could be found. Here the man, who had been sent for the horse came up,[337] but had not found him. Except on the sides of hills where it has fallen, the country is closely timbered with pitch and spruce pine, and what some call balsam-fir. We can see no prospect of getting off these desert mountains yet, except the appearance of a deep cove on each side of the ridge we are passing along. We remained here an hour and an half, and then proceeded on down a steep mountain, and encamped after travelling 18 miles. We had great difficulty in getting water, being obliged to go half a mile for it down a very steep precipice.

Thursday 19th. Our hunters did not join us last night, which was disagreeably cold. About 8 this morning we set out, and proceeded on in our way over the mountains; the sun shining warm and pleasant. We travelled a west course, and about 12 o'clock halted at a spring to take a little more soup. The snow is chiefly gone except on the north points of the high mountains. At 2 P.M. we again went on, and descended a steep mountain into a cove on our left hand, where there is a large creek, which here runs towards the east. The hills on each side, along which the trail or path passes, are very steep. One of our horses fell down the precipice about 100 feet, and was not killed, nor much hurt: the reason was, that there is no bottom below, and the precipice, the only bank, which the creek has; therefore the horse pitched into the water, without meeting with any intervening object, which could materially injure him.[338] We made 17 miles this day and encamped on a small branch of the creek. Having heard nothing from our hunters, we again supped upon some of our portable soup. The men are becoming lean and debilitated, on account of the scarcity and poor quality of the provisions on which we subsist: our horses' feet are also becoming very sore. We have, however, some hopes of getting soon out of this horrible mountainous desert, as we have discovered the appearance of a valley or level part of the country about 40 miles ahead. When this discovery was made there was as much joy and rejoicing among the corps, as happens among passengers at sea, who have experienced a dangerous and protracted voyage, when they first discover land on the long looked for coast.

Friday 20th. It was late before our horses were collected, but the day was fine; and at 9 o'clock we continued our march. Having proceeded about a mile, we came to a small glade, where our hunters had found a horse, and had killed, dressed and hung him up. Capt. Clarke, who had gone forward with the hunters, left a note inform-

ing us that he and they intended to go on to the valley or level country ahead, as there was no chance of killing any game in these desert
mountains. We loaded the meat and proceeded along the mountains.
At noon we stopped and dined, on our horse flesh: here we discovered that a horse, having Capt. Lewis's clothes and baggage on him,
had got into the bushes while we were loading the meat, and was
left behind.[339] One of the men therefore was sent back, but returned
without finding him. Two other men with a horse were then sent
back, and we continued our march along a ridge, where there are
rocks, that appear to be well calculated for making millstones; and
some beautiful tall cedars among the spruce pine. Night came on
before we got off this ridge, and we had much difficulty in finding
water. The soil on the western side of the mountains appears much
better than on the east; and not so rocky. We can see the valley ahead,
but a great way off.[340]

Saturday 21st. The morning was pleasant; but it was late before
we got our horses collected. About 10 o'clock we were ready to start;
and passed along the ridge with a great deal of difficulty and fatigue, our march being much impeded by the fallen timber. A great
portion of the timber through which we passed along this ridge is
dead, and a considerable part fallen; and our horses are weak and
much jaded. One of them got into a small swamp, and wet a bale of
merchandize. About 4 o'clock in the afternoon we got down the mountain to a creek, which runs nearly southwest. This course we suppose is a very good one for us. We went down this creek about a mile,
and encamped on it for the night in a small rich bottom. Here we
killed a duck and two or three pheasants; and supped upon them
and the last of our horse meat. We also killed a wolf and eat it.[+] The
hunters did not join us this evening, nor the two men who went to
look for the horse.

Sunday 22nd. This was a fine warm day. About 9 o'clock we continued our rout over a ridge about a west course, upon the top of
which there is a handsome small prairie; where we met one of our
hunters with a supply of roots, berries and some fish, which he procured from another band of the Flathead nation of Indians.[341] Captain Clarke and the hunters had arrived on the 20th at the encampment or lodges of these Indians which are in a beautiful prairie,
about 8 or 9 miles from this place. The roots they use are made into
a kind of bread; which is good and nourishing, and tastes like that
sometimes made of pumpkins. We remained here about an hour and
then proceeded on again, down the ridge along a very rough way:
and in the evening arrived in a fine large valley, clear of these dis-

mal and horrible mountains.[342] Here our two men overtook us; who had found the lost horse and clothing, but on their way to us lost both the horses.[343] The Indians belonging to this band, received us kindly, appeared pleased to see us, and gave us such provisions as they had. We were at a loss for an interpreter, none of our interpreters being able to understand them. Captain Clarke met us here: he had been over at the river, and found the distance 18 miles and a good road from this place. He thinks we will be able to take the water again at the place he had been at; and where he left 5 hunters, as there was some game about the river in that quarter.

Monday 23rd. The morning was warm and pleasant. We stayed here some time to procure provisions from the natives, for which we gave them in exchange a number of small articles. The provisions which we got consisted of roots, bread and fish.—Their bread is made of roots which they call comas, and which resemble onions in shape, but are of a sweet taste. This bread is manufactured by steaming, pounding and baking the roots on a kiln they have for the purpose.[344] About 4 o'clock we renewed our journey, and went 2 miles to another small village, through a beautiful rich plain, in which these roots grow in abundance. We halted at the second village all night and got some more provisions. About dark a shower of rain fell.

Tuesday 24th. The morning was fine, and about nine o'clock we set forward on our march towards the river, all but one man who had gone back to look for the horses and another that had remained at the first village. The men are generally unwell, owing to the change of diet. The valley is level and lightly timbered with pine and spruce trees. The soil is thin except in some small plains, where it is of the first quality. The adjacent country appears much the same; except that on the river it is broken with hills and some rocks. In the valley there are great quantities of service-berry bushes. In the evening we arrived at the camp of our hunters on a river about 100 yards broad, a branch of the Columbia.[345] The natives say it is two days march to the great river. We encamped on a small island with our hunters who had killed 5 deer, which was a very pleasing circumstance to us; as the Indian provisions did not agree with us. Captain Clarke gave all the sick a dose of Rush's Pills, to see what effect that would have. We found some of the natives here upon the river fishing.

Wednesday 25th. A fine, pleasant, warm morning. The hunters went out early and Captain Clarke rode out to see if there were any trees to be found large enough for canoes. The men in general appear to be getting much better; but Captain Lewis is very sick and taking medicine; and myself and two or three of the men are yet very unwell. The climate here is warm; and the heat to day was as great as we had experienced at any time during the summer. The water also is soft and warm, and perhaps causes our indisposition more than any thing else. In the evening Captain Clarke returned to camp, having discovered a place about 5 or 6 miles down the river, where a large branch comes in on the north side that will furnish timber large enough for our purpose. Our hunters also came in, and had killed nothing but a small panther[346] and a pheasant. The man who had remained at the first village came up.

Thursday 26th. The morning was fine; and at 9 o'clock we left our camp; proceeded down the river about 5 miles to the forks; and pitched our camp in a handsome small bottom opposite the point. A number of natives came down in small canoes, and encamped close to us, for the purpose of fishing; and while we were encamping we saw a small raft coming down the north fork loaded with fish. There appears to be a kind of sheep in this country, besides the Ibex or mountain sheep, and which have wool on.[347] I saw some of the skins, which the natives had, with wool four inches long, and as fine, white and soft as any I had ever seen. I also saw a buffaloe robe with its wool or fur on as fine and soft as that of beaver. Captain Lewis procured this, which we considered a curiosity, in exchange for another buffaloe robe.

This band of the Flatheads[348] have a great many beads and other articles, which they say they got from white men at the mouth of this river; or where the salt water is. They have a large stock of horses. Their buffaloe robes and other skins they chiefly procure on the Missouri, when they go over to hunt, as there are no buffaloe in this part of the country and very little other game.[349] The most of the men of this band are at present on a war expedition against some nation to the northwest, that had killed some of their people; as we understood in our imperfect communications with them. We arranged our camp and made preparations for making canoes.

Friday 27th. A fine warm morning. All the men, who were able were employed in making canoes.[350] About 10 o'clock the man came in who had gone to look for the horses, he had found one of them and killed a deer.[+] I feel much relieved from my indisposition.[351]

In the evening the greater part of the war party came in, and some of the principal men came down to our camp.[352] We could not understand what they had done, as we could only converse by signs. Medals were given by the Commanding Officers to 3 or 4 of them as leading men of their nation; and they remained about our camp.

The river below the fork is about 200 yards wide; the water is clear as chrystal, from 2 to 5 feet deep, and abounding with salmon of an excellent quality. The bottom of the river is stony and the banks chiefly composed of a round hard species of stone.

Saturday 28th. We had a pleasant morning and all hands, that were able, employed at the canoes.[353] —Game is very scarce, and our hunters unable to kill any meat. We are therefore obliged to live on fish and roots, that we procure from the natives; and which do not appear a suitable diet for us. Salt also is scarce without which fish is but poor and insipid. Our hunters killed nothing to day.[354]

Sunday 29th. A fine day; all our hunters went out, and all the men able to work, were employed at the Canoes. At noon two of our hunters came in with 3 deer;[+] a very welcome sight to the most of us. Five or six of the men continue unwell.

Monday 30th. The weather continued pleasant; and our hunters killed a deer.

Tuesday 1st Octr. 1805. This was a fine pleasant warm day. All the men are now able to work; but the greater number are very weak. To save them from hard labour, we have adopted the Indian method of burning out the canoes.[355]

Wednesday 2nd. Two men[356] were sent to the Indian village to purchase some provisions, as our hunters do not kill enough for us to subsist on. And least the Indian provisions should not agree with us, we killed one of our horses.

On the third, the men were employed as usual; on the morning of the fourth there was a white frost, after it a fine day. In the evening our two men returned, with a good supply of such provisions as the natives have.[357]

Saturday 5th. Having got pretty well forward in our canoe making, we collected all our horses and branded them, in order to leave them with the Indians, the old chief having promised that they should be well taken care of.[358] In the evening we got two of our canoes into the water.

During the sixth most of the hands were engaged at the other canoes; and we buried our saddles and some ammunition. The morning of the seventh was pleasant, and we put the last of our canoes into the water; loaded them, and found that they carried all our baggage with convenience. We had four large ones; and one small one, to look ahead. About 3 o'clock in the afternoon we began our

A Canoe striking on a Tree.

voyage down the river, and found the rapids in some places very dangerous. One of our canoes sprung a leak. We therefore halted and mended her, after going twenty miles. The hills come close on the river on both sides; where there are a few pine trees. Back from the river the tops of the hills, to a great distance are prairie land; and the country level.

Tuesday 8th. At 9 o'clock in a fine morning we continued our voyage down the river: passed three islands and several rapids; and at noon stopped at some Indian lodges, of which there are a great many along the river. At 2 we proceeded on again. In the evening, in passing through a rapid, I had my canoe stove, and she sunk. Fortunately the water was not more than waist deep, so our lives and baggage were saved, though the latter was wet.[359] We halted and encamped here to repair the canoe, after coming 18 miles. At this place there are some lodges of the natives on both sides of the river;[360] a number of whom keep about us, and we get some fish from them. Two chiefs of the upper village joined us here, and proposed to go on with us, until we should meet with white people; which they say will be at no great distance.[361]

Wednesday 9th. We stayed here during the whole of this day, which was very pleasant, and repaired our canoe.[362] In the evening we got her completed and all the baggage dry. Here our old Snake guide deserted and took his son with him. I suspect he was afraid of being cast away passing the rapids.[363] At dark one of the squaws, who keep about us, took a crazy fit, and cut her arms from the wrists to the shoulders, with a flint; and the natives had great trouble and difficulty in getting her pacified.[364] We have some Frenchmen, who prefer dog-flesh to fish; and they here got two or three dogs from the Indians. All the country around is high prairie, or open plains.

Thursday 10th. We had a fine morning; embarked early, and passed over some very bad rapids. In passing over one a canoe sprung a leak, but did not sink; though a greater part of the loading was wet; and we had to halt and dry it. We stopped a short distance above the junction of this with another large river. The natives call this eastern branch Koos-koos-ke,[365] and the western Ki-mo-ee-nem.[366] Yesterday evening I had a fit of the ague,[367] and have been very unwell to day; so much so that I am unable to steer my canoe. In about 2 hours we continued our voyage again; we found the southwest branch very large, and of a goslin-green colour. About a mile below the confluence we halted on the north side and encamped for the night, as the wind blew so hard we could not proceed. We came 20 miles to day.

Friday 11th. We set out early in a fine morning; proceeded on about 6 miles, and halted at some lodges of the natives, where we got fish and several dogs. We continued here about an hour and then went on. No accident happened to day though we passed some bad rapids. In the evening we stopped at some Indian camps and remained all night, having come 30 miles.[368] Here we got more fish and dogs. Most of our people having been accustomed to meat, do not relish the fish, but prefer dog meat; which, when well cooked, tastes very well. Here we met an Indian of another nation,[369] who informed us we could get to the falls in 4 days: which I presume are not very high as the salmon come above them in abundance. The country on both sides is high dry prairie plains without a stick of timber. There is no wood of any kind to be seen except a few small willows along the shore; so that it is with difficulty we can get enough to cook with. The hills on the river are not very high, but rocky; the rocks of a dark colour. The bed and shores of the river are very stony; and the stones of a round smooth kind.

Saturday 12th. We had a fine morning and proceeded on early.[370] Two of the Flathead chiefs remained on board with us, and two of their men went with the stranger in a small canoe, and acted as pilots or guides. We saw some ducks and a few geese, but did not kill any of them. There is no four-footed game of any kind near this part of the river, that we could discover; and we saw no birds of any kind, but a few hawks, eagles and crows. At noon we halted; cooked and eat some fish and then proceeded on. The country and river this day is much the same in appearance as what we passed yesterday. A little before sunset we came to a bad rapid, which we did not wish to pass at night, so we encamped above on the north side, having made 30 miles.

Some of the Flathead nation of Indians live all along the river this far down.[371] There are not more than 4 lodges in a place or village, and these small camps or villages are 8 or 10 miles apart: at each camp there are 5 or 6 small canoes. Their summer lodges are made of willows and flags, and their winter lodges of split pine, almost like rails, which they bring down on rafts to this part of the river where there is no timber.

Sunday 13th. This was a cloudy wet morning, and we did not set out till 11 o'clock: we then proceeded with two canoes at a time over the rapids, which are about 2 miles in length; and in about two hours got all over safe. We then went on again and passed more bad rapids, but got through safe. In the afternoon the weather cleared and we had a fine evening. Having gone 23 miles we encamped on the north side. The country continues much the same, all high dry prairie. One handsome creek comes in on the south side.[372]

Monday 14th. We embarked early in a fine clear cool morning; passed some rapids; and at 11 came to one very bad, but we got over without injury. We saw some geese and ducks this forenoon and killed some of the ducks. About 1 o'clock a canoe hit a rock,[373] and part of her sunk, and a number of the things floated out. With the assistance of the other canoes all the men got safe to shore; but the baggage was wet, and some articles were lost. We halted on an island to dry the baggage, having come 14 miles.

CHAP. XIV.

Tuesday 15th [October 1805]. This day was fine, clear and pleasant; and we continued here until the afternoon to dry our baggage that had been wet yesterday. The natives have great quantities of fish deposited on this island.* At 3 o'clock P.M. we got all our effects on board and proceeded on. Passed down a beautiful part of the river; and killed some geese and ducks. This river in general is very handsome, except at the rapids, where it is risking both life and property to pass; and even these rapids, when the bare view or prospect is considered distinct from the advantages of navigation, may add to its beauty, by interposing variety and scenes of romantick grandeur where there is so much uniformity in the appearance of the country. We went 18 miles this evening and halted at an old Indian camp on the north side, where we had great difficulty in procuring wood to cook with, as none at all grows in this part of the country.

Wednesday 16th. We had a fine morning and embarked early; proceeded on about 3 miles, when one of our canoes run upon some rocks in a rapid, but by unloading another canoe and sending it to her assistance, we go all safe to land, and then continued our voyage.[374] About 1 o'clock we came to another rapid, where all hands carried a load of the baggage by land about a mile, and then took the canoes over the rapids, two at a time, and in that way we got them all down safe and proceeded on. Having gone 21 miles we arrived at the great Columbia river, which comes in from the northwest.† We

---

* Immense numbers of salmon must ascend the western rivers every summer from the Pacific, and constitute a chief article in the food of the natives. Mr. M'Kenzie informs us that in the river, by which he arrived at the ocean, where it empties itself four or five hundred miles northwest of the mouth of the Columbia, the salmon are so abundant, that the natives have a constant and plentiful supply of that excellent fish. He also on his return states, under the date of the 6th and 7th of August, that the salmon in the waters of the Columbia were driving up the current in such large shoals, that the water seemed to be covered with fins of them.

†The size, course and appearance of this great river, seem to confirm beyond a doubt the opinion of Mr. M'Kenzie, who supposed that the large river, into which the branch he descended on the west side of the Rocky Mountains, having its source in these mountains near that of the Unjigah or Peace river, discharges its waters into the large river in latitude about 54° north, and longitude 122° west from London, or 47° west from Philadelphia, was the Columbia. The information he obtained from the Indians respecting this river before he left the Unjigah was, "that it was a large river and ran towards the midday sun; but did not empty itself into the sea." This opinion of these natives at a distance, with respect to its not emptying itself into the sea, must have arisen chiefly from what

found here a number of natives, of whose nations we have not yet found out the names.[375] We encamped on the point between the two rivers.[376] The country all round is level, rich and beautiful, but without timber.

Thursday 17th. We remained here all day for the purpose of taking an observation. We got a number of dogs from the natives. Salmon are very plenty but poor and dying, and therefore not fit for provisions. In the plains are a great many hares and a number of fowls, between the size of a pheasant and turkey, called heath hens or grous. We killed a great many of these fowls which are very good eating. The small river, which we called Flathead and afterwards Clarke's river, is a branch of the Great Columbia, and running a northwest course, falls into it a considerable distance above this place; we therefore never passed the mouth of that river.[377]

The Columbia here is 860 yards wide, and the Ki-moo-ee-nem[378] (called Lewis's river from its junction with the Koos-koos-ke[379]) 475 yards. They are both very low at this place. Our course since we took water has been a few degrees south of west: here the Columbia turns to the east of south.

Friday 18th. This was also a fine day and we remained here till after 12 o'clock. In the forenoon our Commanding Officers were employed in getting specimens of the language of the natives, there being three, or part of three, different nations here.[380] They are almost without clothing, having no covering of any account, except some deer skin robes and a few leggins of the same materials. The women have scarce sufficient to cover their nakedness.— Capt. Lewis had an observation at noon, which gave 46° 15 13 .9 north latitude. At one we proceeded on down the Great Columbia, which is a very

---

they had heard of its course, which is east of south and nearly parallel to the coast of the Pacific, and of the great distance it continued to run in that direction. The accounts he received after arriving at it, there called the *Great river,* or Tacoutche Tesse, also stated that it ran towards the mid-day sun; and that at its mouth, as the natives said they had been informed, white people were building houses. Mr. M'Kenzie having descended the river some distance, prevailed on a chief to delineate a sketch of the country on a large piece of bark; in which he described the river as running to the east of south, receiving many rivers, and every six or eight leagues, encumbered with falls and rapids, some of them very dangerous and six impracticable. He represented the carrying places as of great length, and passing over hills and mountains. He depicted the lands of three other tribes in succession who spoke different languages. Beyond them he knew nothing of the river or country, only that it was still a long way to the sea; and that, as he had heard, there was a lake before they reached the water, which the natives did not drink.

"The more I heard of the river," says Mr. M'Kenzie, "the more I was convinced it could not empty itself into the ocean to the north of what is called the river of the West, so that with its windings the distance must be very great." It is not improbable that the distance by water, from the place Mr. M'Kenzie struck this river, to its mouth (supposing it to be the Columbia, Oregon or Great river of the West) is upwards of 1000 miles and its whole course from its source 1500. By the lake mentioned by the Indian chief is no doubt meant the bay at the mouth of the Columbia, and wide part of the river where the tide water ascends and renders the whole unfit to drink.

beautiful river. The course is something to the east of south for about 12 miles and then winds round to almost a west course. We passed some islands and a number of the camps of the natives, which appear to be very shy and distant. We went 21 miles and halted close below an Indian camp; where they have thirty canoes; and a great quantity of dried fish.[381]

Saturday 19th. The morning was clear and pleasant, with some white frost. A number of the natives came to our camp, and our Commanding Officers presented one of them with a medal[382] and other small articles. At 8 o'clock we proceeded on; passed some islands and bad rapids, but no accident happened. We also passed a great many Indian camps. In the whole country around there are only level plains, except a few hills on some parts of the river. We went 36 miles and halted opposite a large Indian camp;[383] and about thirty-six canoe loads of them came over to see us; some of whom remained all night; but we could not have much conversation with them as we did not understand their language. They are clothed much in the same manner with those at the forks above. The custom prevails among these Indians of burying all the property of the deceased, with the body. Amongst these savages when any of them die, his baskets, bags, clothing, horses and other property are all interred: even his canoe is split into pieces and set up round his grave.[384]

Sunday 20th. A fine clear frosty morning. We set out early; passed along a handsome part of the river; saw some pelicans and gulls. And as the shores are lined with dead salmon, there are abundance of crows and ravens. Vast quantities of these fish die at this time of the year. At noon we came to an Indian camp on the point of a large island, where we stopped and got some fish and other provisions. We here saw some articles which shewed that white people had been here or not far distant during the summer. They have a hempen seine and some ash paddles which they did not make themselves.[385] At 1 o'clock we proceeded on again, went 42 miles, and encamped without any of the natives being along, which is unusual on this river. We could not get a single stick of wood to cook with; and had only a few small green willows.

Monday 21st. We continued our voyage at an early hour, and had a fine morning. At 10, we came to the lodges of some of the natives,[386] and halted with them about 2 hours. Here we got some bread, made of a small white root, which grows in this part of the country. We saw among them some small robes made of the skins of grey squirrels, some racoon skins, and acorns, which are signs of a timbered country not far distant. Having proceeded on again, we passed several more lodges of Indians; and through two very rocky rapid parts of the river with great difficulty. We went 32 miles and encamped at some Indian lodges, where we procured wood from the natives to cook with.

Tuesday 22nd. The morning was fine and we went on early, and saw a great number of ducks, geese and gulls. At 10 o'clock we came to a large island, where the river has cut its way through the point of a high hill. Opposite to this island a large river comes in on the south side, called by the natives the Sho-Sho-ne or Snake-Indian river;[387] and which has large rapids close to its mouth. This, or the Ki-moo-ee-nem, is the same river, whose head waters we saw at the Snake nation.[388]

The natives are very numerous on the island and all along the river. Their lodges are of bulrushes and flags, made into a kind of mats, and formed into a hut or lodge.[389]

About 3 miles lower down we came to the first falls or great rapids; and had 1300 yards of a portage over bad ground. All our baggage was got over this evening and we encamped with it; but are not certain whether we can take our canoes by water. Our voyage to day, to the head of the rapids or falls was 18 miles.

Wednesday 23rd. A pleasant day. At 9 o'clock in the forenoon all hands, but three left to keep camp, went up and took the canoes over to the south side; as the natives said that was the best side of the river to take them down. Here we had to drag them 450 yards round the first pitch which is 20 feet perpendicular. We then put them into the water and let them down the rest of the way by cords. The whole height of the falls is 37 feet 8 inches, in a distance of 1200 yards.[390] In the evening we got all our canoes safe down to the encampment on the north side. The natives are very numerous about these falls, as it is a great fishing place in the spring of the year. The country on both sides of the river here is high, and the bluffs rocky. Captain Lewis had an observation, which made the latitude of this place 45° 42 57. 3. North. We got several dogs from these Indians, which we find strong wholesome diet. The high water mark below the falls is 48 feet, and above only 10 feet four inches from the surface of the water: so that in high water there is nothing but a rapid, and the salmon can pass up without difficulty. The reason of this rise in the water below the falls is, that for three miles down, the river is so confined by rocks (being not more than than 70 yards wide) that it cannot discharge the water, as fast as it comes over the falls, until what is deficient in breadth is made up in depth. About the great pitch the appearance of the place is terrifying, with vast rocks, and the river below the pitch, foaming through different channels.[391]

Thursday 24th. We had a fine morning and proceeded on early; found the water very rapid below the falls; and having gone 4 miles below the narrows, came to other narrows still more confined and the rocks higher. At the head of these narrows we halted about 2 o'clock at a great Indian village,[392] and remained there all night. We got fish and dogs from the natives, and some berries, different from any we got before, some call them cranberries; whether of the real kind or not I am not certain. In our way down to day we saw a great many sea otters swimming in the river, and killed some, but could not get them as they sunk to the bottom. This village has better lodges than any on the river above; one story of which is sunk under ground and lined with flags mats: The upper part about 4 feet above ground is covered over with cedar bark, and they are tolerably comfortable houses.

Friday 25th. We found there were bad rapids in the narrows and therefore carried over part of our baggage by land, about three quarters of a mile; and then took the canoes over, one at a time. In going over one of them filled with water, on account of which we were detained three hours. The rapids continued 3 or 4 miles, when the river became more placid. At night we came to a place where there is a considerable quantity of timber on the hills; both oak and pine, and encamped at the mouth of a creek on the south side. The natives about here are, or pretend to be, very uneasy, and say the Indians below will kill us. We purchased from them a quantity of dried pounded fish, which they had prepared in that way for sale. They have six scaffolds of a great size for the purpose of drying their fish on.

Saturday 26th. A fine morning. We hauled up all our canoes to dress and repair them, as they had been injured in passing over the portage, round the falls. Some hunters went out and killed 6 deer and some squirrels. In the afternoon about 20 of the natives came to our camp (among whom were the head chiefs of the two villages about the falls) who had been out hunting when we passed down. The Commanding Officers gave medals to the chiefs, and some other small articles; and they appeared satisfied and some remained with us all night.

Sunday 27th. This was a fine clear morning, but the wind blew very hard up the river, and we remained here all day. This is the first hunting ground we have had for a long time, and some of our men went out. Part of the natives remained with us; but we cannot find out to what nation they belong. We suppose them to be a band of the Flathead nation, as all their heads are compressed into the same form;[393] though they do not speak exactly the same language, but there is no great difference, and this may be a dialect of the same. This singular and deforming operation is performed in infancy in the following manner. A piece of board is placed against the back of the head extending from the shoulders some distance above it; another shorter piece extends from the eye brows to the top of the first, and they are then bound together with thongs or cords made of skins, so as to press back the forehead, make the head rise at the top, and force it out above the ears. In the evening our hunters came in and had killed 4 deer and some squirrels. The wind blew hard all this day.

Monday 28th. Just before day light there was a shower of rain; but at sun rise the morning was fine and clear. At 8 o'clock we embarked, went about 4 miles, and halted at a small village of the natives and got some dogs from them.[394] Here we stayed about an hour and proceeded on again for about a mile, when we were compelled to stop on account of the wind, which blew so hard ahead that we were unable to continue our voyage. In the course of the day there were some showers of rain. In the evening one of the men went out and killed a fine deer. We were in a good safe harbour and remained there all night, accompanied by the natives.

Tuesday 29th. We embarked early in a cloudy morning; passed high hills on both sides of the river, on which there was pine timber; and some birch on the banks of the river. At breakfast time we stopt at a small village of the natives and purchased some more dogs: then proceeded on; passed a number more Indian camps, and a high mountainous country on both sides. In the evening we discovered a high mountain to the south, not more than five miles off, covered with snow. We have here still water; and the breadth of the river is from three quarters to a mile. We went 23 miles and encamped at a small village on the north side.

Wednesday 30th. The morning was cloudy; the river and country we found much the same as yesterday. At noon we stopped to dine and one of the men went out and killed a large buck. A number of fine springs come down the hills on the South side; and we passed a small river on the north. In the evening we came to the head of falls, where there is a large Indian village.[395] On our way down we saw a great many swans, geese and ducks;[396] and a number of sea otter.

There are some small bottoms along the river, with cotton wood on them, and on the banks of the river some white oak, ash and hazlenut.[397] At a distance there are ponds which abound with geese and ducks. It rained hard all day, and we came only 15 miles.

Thursday 31st. The morning was cloudy. We unloaded our canoes and took them past the rapids, some part of the way by water, and some over rocks 8 or 10 feet high. It was the most fatiguing business we have been engaged in for a long time, and we got but two over all day, the distance about a mile, and the fall of the water about 25 feet in that distance.[398]

Friday 1st Nov. 1805. We had a cool frosty morning. We carried down our baggage before breakfast as we could not go into the water, without uneasiness on account of the cold. In the forenoon we took down the other two canoes. A number of the natives with 4 canoes joined us here from above. Their canoes were loaded with pounded salmon, which they were taking down the river to barter for beads and other articles.[399]

Saturday 2nd. There is here a small rapid below the falls, where the men had to carry part of the baggage across a portage of two miles and an half, while the rest took down the canoes. At 12 o'clock we proceeded on again; passed a narrow rapid part of the river of about 8 miles, the hills on both sides are very high, and a number of fine springs flowing out of them, some of which fall 200 feet perpendicular. The hills are mostly solid rock. On our way we passed two Indian lodges. At the end of eight miles, the river opens to the breadth of a mile, with a gentle current. We came 23 miles, and encamped at a high peak resembling a tower on the south side. The country here becomes level, and the river broader. One of the Indian canoes remained with us and the other three went on. On our way and at camp we killed 17 geese and brants.[400+]

Sunday 3rd. The morning was foggy: one of the men went out and killed a fine buck.[+] At 9 we proceeded on, but could not see the country we were passing, on account of the fog, which was very thick till noon when it disappeared, and we had a beautiful day. We at that time came to the mouth of a river on the south side, a quarter of a mile broad, but not more than 6 or 8 inches deep, running over a bar of quicksand.[401] At this place we dined on venison and goose; and from which we can see the high point of a mountain covered with snow, in about a southeast direction from us. Our Commanding Officers are of opinion that it is Mount Hood, discovered by a Lieutenant of Vancoover, who was up this river 75 miles. The river that falls in here has two mouths, through which it drives out a considerable quantity of sand into the Columbia. Opposite the lower mouth there is a handsome island.[402] At 2 o'clock we proceeded on, and passed another island. The country on both sides appears level and closely timbered: on the river the timber is cotton wood, maple and some ash; and back from it mostly spruce pine. We made 13 miles and encamped on a large island, in which is a large pond full of swans, geese and ducks. On our way and here we killed some of each kind. At night, Captain Lewis had a small canoe carried over to the pond in order to hunt by moon light, but the party did not happen to have good luck, having killed only a swan and three ducks.[+]

CHAP. XV.

Monday 4th [November 1805]. A fine morning. We embarked early; passed two large islands, and a beautiful part of the river. The tide raised the water last night 2 feet. We went about 7 miles and came to a large Indian village,[403] where they informed us that in two days we would come to two ships with white people in them.[404] The Indians here have a great deal of new cloth among them, and other articles which they got from these ships. We got some dogs and roots from the natives. The roots are of a superior quality to any I had before seen: they are called whapto; resemble a potatoe when cooked, and are about as big as a hen egg. Game is more plenty here than up the river, and one of the men killed a deer this morning. At this camp of the natives they have 52 canoes, well calculated for riding waves. We proceeded on, and passed some handsome islands, and down a beautiful part of the river. We also passed a number of Indian lodges; and saw a great many swans, geese, ducks, cranes, and gulls. We went 28 miles and encamped on the north side. In the evening we saw Mount Rainy[405] on the same side. It is a handsome point of a mountain with little or no timber on it, very high, and a considerable distance off this place.

Tuesday 5th. We embarked very early. Some rain fell last night about 2 o'clock, and the morning was cloudy. We passed several handsome islands, generally near the shore, on the one side or the other of the river. The country on both sides is somewhat higher than what we passed yesterday, and closely covered with spruce timber. The bottoms are large, covered with cotton wood, maple, and the like kinds of wood. We passed a great many Indian camps,[406] their lodges made chiefly of poles and cedar bark. At noon we stopped about an hour at an island, and some of the men went out and killed nine brants and a swan. Three of the brants were quite white except the points of their wings, which were black. We proceeded on in the afternoon, during which some rain and a little hail fell; went 31 miles and encamped on the north side. Here the tide rises and falls 4 feet.[407]

Wednesday 6th. We set out early in a cloudy morning after a disagreeable night of rain. Saw a number of natives, going up and down the river in canoes. Also passed some of their lodges. The Indians in this part of the country have but few horses, their intercourse and business being chiefly by water. The high land comes more close on the river in this part. Having gone 29 miles we encamped on the south side.[408]

Thursday 7th. We set out again early in a foggy morning; went about 6 miles and came to an Indian camp, where we got some fresh fish and dogs. The dress of the squaws here is different from that of those up the river; it consists of a long fringe made of soft bark, which they tie round the waist, and which comes down almost to their knees; and of a small robe, made out of small skins cut into thongs and wove somewhat like carpetting.[409] We remained here about 2 hours and then proceeded on. At this place the river is about 3 miles wide, with a number of small islands, and the country broken. In the evening we came to a part of the river, where it is 5 miles broad. We went 34 miles and encamped on the south side at the mouth of a fine spring.[410]

Friday 8th. We embarked early. The morning was cloudy, and there was a hard wind from the east. We went about 5 miles and came to a bay 12 or 14 miles wide. We had to coast round it, as the wind raised the waves so high we could go no other way. We halted and dined at a point on the north side of the bay where a small river comes in. We again proceeded on coasting, till we came to a point of land where the bay becomes much narrower; and the water quite salt. The waves here ran so high we were obliged to lie to, and let the tide leave our canoes on dry ground. This point we called Cape Swell; and the bay above, Shallow Bay,[411] as there is no great depth of water. In crossing the bay when the tide was out, some of our men got sea sick, the swells were so great.[412] In it there are a great many swans, geese, ducks and other water fowls. The whole of this day was wet and disagreeable; and the distance we made, in a straight line, was not more than 9 miles; though the distance we coasted was above 20 miles.

Saturday 9th. The morning was windy, rainy and disagreeable, and we were obliged to remain at Cape Swell all day and unload our canoes to prevent them from sinking; notwithstanding some of them did sink when the tide came in at noon. We had no fresh water, except what rain we caught by putting out our vessels.[413] We remained here all night, and the rain continued.

Sunday 10th. We had a rainy morning, but the wind was not so high as it had been yesterday; and we set out from Cape Swell, coasted along for 8 miles, passed some high cliffs of sandy rocks, and then came to a point; where we found the swells so high, the wind having risen, that we could not proceed: so we had to return back about a mile to get a safe harbour. Here we dined on some pounded salmon, that we had procured from the Indians; and unloaded our canoes. After we had been here about 2 hours, it became more calm and we loaded the canoes again, but could not get round the point, the swells were still so high; we therefore put too at a branch of fresh water, under high cliffs of rocks and unloaded again. Here we scarcely had room to lie between the rocks and water; but we made shift to do it among some drift wood that had been beat up by the tide. It rained hard all night and was very disagreeable. While on our way down to day we saw some porpoises, sea otter and a great many sea gulls. The water is become very salt [*sic*].

Monday 11th. The morning was wet and the wind still blowing, so that we could not proceed; we therefore built large fires and made our situation as comfortable as possible, but still bad enough, as we have no tents, or covering to defend us, except our blankets and some mats we got from the Indians,[414] which we put on poles to keep off the rain. It continued raining and blowing all day; and at 4 o'clock in the afternoon the tide was so high that we had to leave our lodges, until it got lower in the evening. Some of the men went about 40 perches[415] up the river and caught 15 fine large fish.[416]

Tuesday 12th. A cloudy wet morning, after a terrible night of rain, hail, thunder and lightening. We thought it best to move our camp, and fixed our canoes and loaded them with stones to keep them down. We went about the eighth of a mile from this place, and fixed ourselves as well as we could, and remained all night. The rain still continued, and the river remained very rough.[417]

Wednesday 13th. This was another disagreeable rainy day, and we remained at camp being unable to get away. At 9 o'clock in the forenoon it became a little more calm than usual; and 3 men took a canoe, which we got from the Indians of a kind excellent for riding swells, and set out to go to the point on the sea shore, to ascertain whether there were any white people there, or if they were gone.[418]

Thursday 14th. We expected last night to have been able to proceed on this morning, but the rain continued, and the river still remained rough; and are therefore obliged to lie by. About noon one of the 3 men who had gone in the canoe, returned having broke the lock of his gun:[419] but the other two went on by land, as the swells ran so high that they could not possibly get the canoe along. About the same time some Indians in a canoe came up the river, and had stolen a gig from the men; but the one who returned got it from them again when he came up. In the evening Captain Lewis with 4 men started by land to see if any white people were to be found.[420] The rest remained in camp; and the weather continued wet, and the most disagreeable I had ever seen.[421]

Friday 15th. This morning the weather appeared to settle and clear off, but the river remained still rough. So we were obliged to continue here until about 1 o'clock, when the weather became more calm, and we loaded and set out from our disagreeable camp;[422] went about 3 miles, when we came to the mouth of the [Columbia] river, where it empties into a handsome bay. Here we halted on a sand beach, formed a comfortable camp, and remained in full view of the ocean, at this time more raging than pacific. One of the two men who first went out came to us here,[423] the other had joined Captain Lewis's party.[424] Last night the Indians[425] had stolen their arms and accoutrements, but restored them on the arrival of Captain Lewis and his men in the morning.

Saturday 16th. This was a clear morning and the wind pretty high. We could see the waves, like small mountains, rolling out in the ocean, and pretty bad in the bay.

CHAP. XVI.

WE are now at the end of our voyage, which has been completely accomplished according to the intention of the expedition, the object of which was to discover a passage by the way of the Missouri and Columbia rivers to the Pacific ocean; notwithstanding the difficulties, privations and dangers, which we had to encounter, endure and surmount.[426]

This morning 5 of the men went out to hunt; and about 3 o'clock all came in but one. They had killed 2 deer, 9 brants, 2 geese, 1 crane, and 3 ducks.[427+] The day being clear we got all our baggage dried, and in good order; and quietly rested until Capt. Lewis and his party should return.

Sunday 17th [November 1805]. We had a fine pleasant clear morning, and 6 hunters went out. About noon they all came in; but the hunter who remained out last night did not return. He had killed 2 deer and the other men brought them in with some brants and a deer they had killed. About the same time Capt. Lewis, and his party returned. They had been round the bay, and seen where white people had been in the course of the summer: but they had all sailed away. Captain Lewis and his party killed a deer and some brants. In the evening the remaining hunter came in and had killed another deer.

There are but few Indians settled down about the seashore; their dress is similar to that of some of those above. The women have a kind of fringe petticoats, made of filaments or tassels of the white cedar bark wrought with a string at the upper part, which is tied round the waist. These tassels or fringe are of some use as a covering, while the ladies are standing erect and the weather calm; but in any other position, or when the wind blows, their charms have but a precarious defence.

A number of both sexes keep about our camp; some have robes made of muskrat skins sewed together, and I saw some of loon-skins. Their diet is chiefly fish and roots.

MEMORANDUM

Of the computed distance in miles to the furthest point of discovery on the Pacific ocean, from the place where the canoes were deposited near the head of the Missouri, which from its mouth

	is 3096
From place of deposit to head spring	24
To first fork of the Sho-sho-ne river	14
To first large fork down the river	18
To forks of the road at mouth of Tour creek	14
To fishing creek, after leaving the river	23
To Flathead, or Clarke's river at Fish camp	41
To the mouth of Travellers-rest creek	76
To the foot of the great range of Mountains, east side	12
To ditto ditto ditto west side	130
To the Flathead village in a plain	3
To the Koos-koos-ke river	18
To the Canoe camp, at the forks	6
To the Ki-moo-ee-nem	60
To the Great Columbia, by Lewis's river	140
To the mouth of the Sho-sho-ne, or Snake River	162
To the Great Falls of Columbia	6
To the Short Narrows	3
To the Long ditto	3
To the mouth of Catarack river, north side	23
To the Grand Shoot, or Rapids	42
To the Last Rapids, or Strawberry island	6
To the mouth of Quicksand river, south side	56
To Shallow Bay, at salt water	136
To Blustry Point, on north side	13
To Point Open-slope, below encampment	3
To Chin-Ook river at bottom of Haley's Bay	12
To Cape Disappointment on Western ocean	13
To Capt. Clarke's tour N. W. along coast	10

miles 4133[428]

Monday 18th. The morning was cloudy. Capt. Clarke and 10 men went down to Cape Disappointment,[429] to get a more full view of the ocean;[430] and 3 went out to hunt. In the course of the day we got some dried salmon and roots from the natives. In the evening our hunters came in with a deer, 2 brants, a squirrel, a hawk, and a flounder, which the tide had thrown on a sand-bar.[+] The Indians still remained with us and Capt. Lewis got a specimen of their language. Those, who live about the seashore, and on Rogue's-harbour creek, a large creek that comes in on the north side of the bay, call themselves the Chin-ook nation.[431]

Tuesday 19th. We had a cloudy, rainy morning; but some of the hunters went out. About 1 o'clock the natives, who, had been with us some time, went away; and at 4 another party of the same nation came, and encamped close by us. They consisted of 15 men and one squaw. The dress of the squaw was the same with those of the others. Several of the men have robes made of brant skins: one of them had a hat made of the bark of white cedar and beargrass, very handsomely wrought and water proof.—One of our party purchased it for an old razor. Our hunters killed 3 deer to day.

Wednesday 20th. We had a fine clear morning; the Indians remained at our camp; and Capt. Lewis gave one of them a medal, as he ranked as a chief in the nation. One of the men went out to hunt in the morning, and in a short time killed 2 deer.[+] This day continued clear and pleasant throughout. At 4 o'clock in the afternoon Capt. Clarke and his party returned to camp, and had killed a deer and some brants.[+] They had been about 10 miles north of the cape, and found the country along the seashore level, with spruce-pine timber, and some prairies and ponds of water. They killed a remarkably large buzzard, of a species different from any I had seen. It was 9 feet across the wings, and 3 feet 10 inches from the bill to the tail.[432] They found some pumice stones, which had been thrown out by the waves, of a quality superior to those on the Missouri;[433] also a number of shells of different kinds.

Thursday 21st. A cloudy morning. About 8 o'clock all the natives left us. The wind blew so violent to day, and the waves ran so high, that we could not set out on our return, which is our intention to do as soon as weather and water will permit. The season being so far advanced, we wish to establish our winter quarters as soon as possible. One of the natives here had a robe of sea-otter skins, of the finest fur I ever saw; which the Commanding Officers wanted very much, and offered two blankets for it, which the owner refused, and said he would not take five. He wanted beads of a blue colour, of which we had none, but some that were on a belt belonging to our interpreter's squaw; so they gave him the belt for the skins.[434] In the evening more of the natives[435] came to our camp, and the night was very wet and disagreeable.[436]

Friday 22nd. This was a rainy and stormy morning; and we were not yet able to set out: the wind blew very hard from the south, and the river was rougher than it has been since we came here. At noon the tide was higher than common, and one of our canoes got among some logs, and was split. The rain and wind continued all day violent.

Saturday 23rd. The weather was somewhat cloudy but more calm. Some of the men went out to hunt and some to mend the canoe which had been split in the storm yesterday. The natives still stay with us, and have a few roots and berries to subsist on at present; but I cannot conjecture how they live during the winter. They have no mockasons or leggins of any kind; and scarce any other covering than the small robes, which were mentioned before.

In the afternoon 10 of the Clat-sop nation,[437] that live on the south side of the river came over to our camp. These are also naked, except the small robes which hardly cover their shoulders. One of these men had the reddest hair I ever saw, and a fair skin much freckled.[438] In the evening our hunters came in, and had killed 3 deer, 8 brants and 12 ducks.—In the evening the weather cleared and we had a fine night.

Sunday 24th. The morning was fine with some white frost. As this was a fine clear day, it was thought proper to remain here in order to take some observations, which the bad weather had before rendered impossible. The latitude of this bay was found to be 46° 19 11 .7 north;* and at our camp at the head of the bay the river is 3 miles and 660 yards wide. The natives stayed with us all day. At night the party were consulted by the Commanding Officers, as to the place most proper for winter quarters; and the most of them were of opinion, that it would be best, in the first place, to go over to the south side of the river, and ascertain whether good hunting ground could be found there. Should that be the case, it would be more eligible place than higher up the river, on account of getting salt, as that is a very scarce article with us.[439]

---

*Geographers have stated that the Columbia enters the ocean in latitude 46° 18 north. The difference is therefore only 1 minute 11 seconds and 7 tenths. The longitude by mistake they have made 236° 34 west; but which is the east longitude, leaving 123° 26 for the west longitude. Mr. M'Kenzie arrived at the ocean in latitude 52° 23 43 or 6° 4 31 north of the mouth of the Columbia; and in longitude 128° 2 or 4° 36 west of the mouth of the Columbia. This will shew the general course of the western coast between those places, to which the river and great chain of the Rocky Mountains are nearly parallel.

Monday 25th. The morning was pleasant, though cloudy, with a white frost. We loaded our canoes and proceeded on: went about 9 miles and made an attempt to cross the river, but failed; we therefore kept up the north side, round Shallow-bay, and encamped about 4 miles above it.

Tuesday 26th. The morning of this day was cloudy and wet; but we set out early, went about a mile and then crossed the river; passing in our way several islands. Immediately after we crossed we came to a small village of the natives, and procured a few roots, called Wapto, from them, and then proceeded on, coasting down the bay on the south side. The whole of the day was wet and unpleasant, and in the evening we encamped for the night.

Wednesday 27th. We set out early in a wet morning; coasted round, and turned a sharp cape about a mile; when we found the swells running so high that we had to halt, unload our canoes and haul them out on the shore. Here we remained the afternoon and had a very wet night.[440]

Thursday 28th. We had a wet windy morning; some of the hunters went out, but had no luck. It rained all day; and we had here no fresh water, but what was taken out of the canoes as the rain fell.[441]

Friday 29th. The weather continues cloudy and wet. Capt. Lewis and 4 men started, to go down and examine whether there is good hunting and whether we can winter near the salt water.[442] Some of the hunters went out and in the evening returned without killing any game, which appears scarce. The hunting is also difficult, the country being full of thickets and fallen timber. There were some showers of rain and hail during the day.

Saturday 30th. This was a fair day; and some hunters went round the cape and killed two or three ducks. This is all the supply of fresh provisions, that we have had since we have been at this camp. We live almost altogether on pounded salmon. The whole of the day was fair, pleasant and warm for the season.

Sunday 1st Decr. 1805. The whole of this day was cloudy. Some of the hunters went out but had not the fortune to kill any thing, not even a duck.

Monday 2nd. The day was again cloudy and wet. Some of the hunters went out in the morning; and in the afternoon one of them came in, after killing a fine elk.[443+] A party of the men went out to bring in the meat, which is a very seasonable supply, a number complaining of the bad effects of the fish diet. Neither the hunters nor the men, who went for the meat returned. In the evening the weather became clear, and we had a fine night.

Tuesday 3rd. The morning was foggy. About 9 o'clock the men came in with the meat of the elk.—They had a disagreeable trip, it being dark before they arrived at the place where the elk had been killed; and the darkness, fallen timber and underbrush prevented their return; so that they had to encamp out all night. Six of the natives came to our camp, the first who have appeared since our arrival, and after staying an hour proceeded down the river. The greater part of the day was fair, but in the evening it clouded over and rained again. At dark our other two hunters came in, and had killed 6 elk some distance from the river.[444+]

Wednesday 4th. We had a cloudy rainy morning. The river was so rough, we could not set out with the canoes, and six or seven men were sent to dress the elk that had been killed and take care of the meat. The rain continued all day.

Thursday 5th. Again we had a wet stormy day, so that the men were unable to proceed with the canoes. About 11 o'clock Capt. Lewis and three of his party came back to camp; the other two were left to take care of some meat they had killed. They have found a place about 15 miles from this camp, up a small river which puts into a large bay on the south side of the Columbia, that will answer very well for winter quarters, as game is very plenty, which is the main object with us; and we intend to move there as soon as circumstances will admit. There is more wet weather on this coast, than I ever knew in any other place; during a month we have had but 3 fair days; and there is no prospect of a change.

Friday 6th. We had another wet morning, and were not able to set out. At noon it rained very hard, and the tide flowed so high, that in some part of our camp the water was a foot deep: we had therefore to remove to higher ground. In the afternoon it still continued to rain hard.

Saturday 7th. About 12 last night the rain ceased and we had a fine clear morning. We put our canoes into the water, loaded them, and started for our intended wintering place. We coasted down the south side about a mile, and then met with the six men, who had gone for meat.[445] They had brought 4 of the skins but no meat, the distance being great and the weather very bad. The swells being too high here to land we went two miles further and took the men in. We then proceeded round the bay[446] until we came to the mouth of a river about 100 yards broad, which we went up about 2 miles to the place fixed upon for winter quarters, unloaded our canoes, and carried our baggage about 200 yards to a spring, where we encamped.[447]

Sunday 8th. We had a fine fair morning with some white frost. Capt. Clarke with 5 men set out to go to the ocean, and myself with 11 more to bring in the meat, which the two men left by Captain Lewis were taking care of. We went up the small river in our canoes about two miles, then up a branch of it on the west side two miles, then by land about two miles more, where we found the men and the meat, of which we all carried two large loads to our canoes, and proceeded down to camp. In the evening it began to rain again. The country towards the south is mountainous at some distance off; and there is some snow on the mountains. Near our camp, the country is closely timbered with spruce-pine, the soil rich, but not deep; and there are numerous springs of running water.[448]

Monday 9th. The morning was cloudy and wet. A serjeant and 8 men were sent to bring in the remainder of the meat we left yesterday;[449] some were employed in making our camp comfortable, and others in clearing a place for huts and a small fort. In the evening some of the natives came to our camp, the first we have seen for some days. It continued cloudy and wet all day.[450]

Tuesday 10th. We had another wet cloudy morning; and all hands were employed at work notwithstanding the rain. About 2 o'clock Capt. Clarke and 3 of his party returned to camp; the other two remained out to hunt.[451] They found the ocean to be about 7 miles from our camp; for 4 miles the land high and closely timbered: the remainder prairie cut with some streams of water. They killed an elk and saw about 50 in one gang.[+] They also saw three lodges of Indians on the seashore. The natives which were at our our [*sic*] camp, went away this morning after receiving some presents. In the evening we laid the foundation of our huts.

Wednesday 11th. This day was also cloudy and wet; but we continued at our hut-building.[452]

Thursday 12th. This morning was cloudy without rain. In the forenoon we finished 3 rooms of our cabins, all but the covering; which I expect will be a difficult part of the business, as we have not yet found any timber which splits well; two men went out to make some boards, if possible, for our roofs. About 3 o'clock in the afternoon a number of the natives from the seashore came to our camp, and remained all night. Some rain fell in the evening.

Friday 13th. We had a cloudy, but fine morning; and all hands were engaged at work. The party of Indians who came yesterday went away, and another party came about the middle of the day. Two hunters came in, and had killed 18 elk,[+] not more than 4 miles distant. The day continued cloudy and some rain fell in the evening.

Saturday 14th. The two hunters that had killed the elk, went back with two other men to take care of the meat. In the course of the day a good deal of rain fell; the weather here still continues warm, and there has been no freezing except a little white frost. In the afternoon the savages all went away. We completed the building of our huts, 7 in number, all but the covering, which I now find will not be so difficult as I expected; as we have found a kind of timber in plenty, which splits freely and makes the finest puncheons I have ever seen. They can be split 10 feet long and 2 broad, not more than an inch and an half thick.[453]

Sunday 15th. The morning was cloudy. Captain Clarke with 16 of the party started to bring in the meat the 4 men were taking care of; myself and 2 others were employed in fixing and finishing the quarters of the Commanding Officers, and 2 more preparing puncheons for covering the huts. Some light showers fell during the day; and at night 3 Indians came to our camp, and brought us two large salmon.

Monday 16th. This was a wet morning with high wind. About 8 Capt. Clarke and 15 men came in loaded with meat; they left a canoe with 7 men to bring in the remainder. They had a very bad night, as the weather was stormy and a great deal of rain fell. Notwithstanding this, a serjeant and four men, who had got lost, lay out all night without fire.[454] As soon as they arrived all hands were set to carrying up the meat, and putting it in a house we had prepared for the purpose. The whole of the day was stormy and wet.[455]

Tuesday 17th. This was another cloudy day, with some light showers of rain and hail. About 11 o'clock the 7 men came with the canoe and the remainder of the meat. We still continued working at our huts.

Wednesday 18th. Snow fell last night about an inch deep, and the morning was stormy. In the middle of the day the weather became clear, and we had a fine afternoon.

Thursday 19th. This was a fine clear cool morning, and we expected to have some fair pleasant weather, but at noon it became cloudy again and began to rain.[456]

Friday 20th. The morning was cloudy and wet.—We collected all the puncheons or slabs we had made, and some which we got from some Indian huts up the bay, but found we had not enough to cover all our huts. About 10 o'clock the weather became clear; but before night it rained as fast as before. From this day to the 25th we had occasionally rain and high winds, but the weather still continued warm.[457] On the evening of the 24th we got all our huts covered and daubed.

Wednesday 25th. Was another cloudy wet day.—This morning we left our camp and moved into our huts. At daybreak all the men paraded and fired a round of small arms, wishing the Commanding Officers a merry Christmas. In the course of the day Capt. Lewis and Capt. Clarke collected what tobacco remained and divided it among those who used tobacco as a Christmas-gift; to the others they gave handkerchiefs in lieu of it.[458] We had no spirituous liquors to elevate our spirits this Christmas; but of this we had but little need, as we were all in very good health. Our living is not very good; meat is plenty, but of an ordinary quality, as the elk are poor in this part of the country. We have no kind of provisions but meat, and we are without salt to season that.

The 26th, 27th and 28th, were cloudy with rain. We found our huts smoked; there being no chimnies in them except in the officers' rooms. The men were therefore employed, except some hunters who went out, in making chimnies to the huts. In the evening of the 27th we were informed that a large fish, answering to the description of a whale, was driven upon shore.[459] In the forenoon of the 28th six men started for the seashore to make salt, as we have none in the fort. Two hunters returned, having killed a deer,+ and three went out to hunt.

Sunday 29th. This was a cloudy morning; but a fair day succeeded; and three more hunters went out. In the afternoon several of the Chin-ook nation came to our fort with Wapto roots and dried salmon to trade.[460] We purchased some from them and found the supply seasonable as our meat on hand is somewhat spoiled. The men about the fort are engaged in finishing our small fortification.

Monday 30th. Heavy showers of rain fell last night, but the morning was fair, and we had some sunshine, which happens very seldom; light showers of rain fell during the day. About 2 o'clock the 3 hunters that first went out came in; and had killed four elk.+ Seven men went out immediately and brought them into the fort safe, which was a pleasing sight, the meat we had on hand being spoiled.[461] This evening we completely finished our fortification.

Tuesday 31st. Another cloudy morning. Some more of the natives came to trade with Wapto roots and salmon: the first party had gone off in the morning.[462]

CHAP. XVII.

Wednesday 1st Jan. 1806. The year commenced with a wet day; but the weather still continues warm; and the ticks, flies and other insects are in abundance, which appears to us very extraordinary at this season of the year, in a latitude so far north. Two hunters went out this morning. We gave our Fortification the name of Fort Clatsop.[463] In the evening our two hunters, that went out this morning, returned and had killed two large elk about three miles from the Fort.[464]

Thursday 2nd. This also was a cloudy wet day. Fourteen men went out in the morning and brought the meat of the elk into the Fort.

Friday 3rd. The weather is still cloudy and wet. I set out this morning with one of the men[465] to go to the salt works, to see what progress those engaged in that business had made; and why some of them had not returned, as they had been expected for some time.[466] We proceeded along a dividing ridge, expecting to pass the heads of some creeks, which intervened. We travelled all day and could see no game; and the rain still continued. In the evening we arrived at a place where two of the men had killed an elk some time ago. Here we struck up a fire, supped upon the marrow bones and remained all night.[467]

Saturday 4th. The morning was wet; but we proceeded on, and passed the head of a creek which we supposed was the last in our rout to the salt works. Immediately after passing the creek, the man with me killed an elk;+ when we halted and took breakfast of it, and then went on. We got into low ground, passed through a marsh about 1/2 a mile in breadth, where the water was knee deep; then got into a beautiful prairie about five miles wide, and which runs along the sea shore about 30 miles from Point Adams on the south side of Hayley's Bay, in nearly a southwest course and ends at a high point of a mountain, called Clarke's view on the sea shore. Through this plain or prairie runs another creek, or small river which we could not pass without some craft: so we encamped on a creek and supped on the elk's tongue, which we had brought with us.

Sunday 5th. This was a very wet day. We killed a squirrel and eat it; made a raft to cross the creek; but when it was tried we found it would carry only one person at a time; the man with me was therefore sent over first, who thought he could shove the raft across again, but when he attempted, it only went halfway: so that there was one of us on each side and the raft in the middle. I, however notwithstanding the cold, stript and swam to the raft, brought it over and then crossed on it in safety;[468] when we pursued our journey, and in a short time came to some Indian camps on the sea shore. The rain and wind continued so violent that we agreed to stay at these camps all night.[469]

Monday 6th. We had a fair morning and the weather cleared up, after two months of rain, except 4 days. We therefore set out from these lodges; passed the mouth of a considerable river; went about two miles up the shore, and found our salt makers at work. Two of their detachment had set out for the fort on the 4th and the man that had come with me and two more went to hunt.

Tuesday 7th. Another fine day. About noon Captain Clarke with 14 men came to the salt-makers camp,[470] in their way to the place where the large fish had been driven on shore, some distance beyond this camp. The Indians about our fort had procured a considerable quantity of the meat, which we found very good.[471] The 8th was a fine day and I remained at camp. The 9th was also fair and pleasant; and about noon Captain Clarke and his party returned here; the distance being about 17 miles. They found the skeleton of the whale which measured 105 feet in length and the head 12. The natives had taken all the meat off its bones, by scalding and the other means, for the purpose of trade.[472] The Indians, who live up there are another of nation, and call themselves the Callemex nation.[473] They are a ferocious nation: one of them was going to kill one of our men, for his blanket; but was prevented by a squaw of the Chinook nation, who lives among them, and who raised an alarm.[474] There is a small river comes into the sea at that place. Captain Clarke and his party remained at the camp all night, during which some rain fell.

Friday 10th. The morning was fine and Captain Clarke and his party started, and I remained at this camp to wait the return of the man who had come with me and who was out hunting.[475] The 11th was also pleasant, and I proceeded with a party for the fort; where about 9 o'clock we arrived the next day. Two hunters had gone out from the fort in the morning, and killed 7 elk about two miles from it.[+]

Monday 13th. The weather changed and we had a cloudy wet day; and all the hands, who could be spared were engaged in bringing the meat of the elk, killed yesterday to camp.

Tuesday 14th. The morning was pleasant; and two men were sent to the salt works to assist in making salt. The rest of our people were employed in drying and taking care of the meat; and in dressing elk skins for mokasins, which is a laborious business,[476] but we have no alternative in this part of the country.

The 15th. and 16th. were both wet throughout, and the men employed as on the 14th. In the morning of the 17th there were some clouds; but about 10 o'clock they disappeared and we had a fine day.— About the same time 8 of the natives of the Clatsop nation came to our fort, and stayed till the evening. A hunter went out in the morning and killed a deer.[+]

Saturday 18th. Last night was very dark; and early in it rain came on and continued all night. This day is also wet. Some of the natives visited us and went away in the evening.

Sunday 19th. Four hunters went out this morning, which was fair with flying clouds; but in the evening it began to rain again. We had another visit from some of the natives.[477]

Monday 20th. It rained hard all day. Some of the natives again came to see us, whom we suffered, contrary to our usual practice, to remain in the fort all night; the evening was so wet and stormy. It also rained on the 21st and 22nd. Our hunters killed three elk.[+] On my way with a party to bring in the meat of these, I saw some amazingly large trees of the fir kind; they are from 12 to 15 feet in diameter.

Thursday 23rd. We had a fine clear cool morning, and two men were sent on to the salt works.[478] The day continued pleasant until about 4 o'clock in the afternoon, when the weather became cloudy, and it began to rain.

Friday 24th. At daylight some snow fell, and there were several snow showers during the day. In the afternoon two of our hunters and some of the natives came to the fort in an Indian canoe with the meat of two deer and an elk they had killed.[+] The Indians were bare-footed notwithstanding the snow on the ground; and the evening was so bad we permitted them to stay in the fort all night.[479]

Saturday 25th. The morning was cloudy and some showers of snow fell in the course of the day; and in the night it fell to the depth of 8 inches. On the 26th there were some light showers during the day; but in the evening the weather cleared up, and it began to freeze hard. This is the first freezing weather of any consequence we have had during the winter.

Monday 27th. This was a clear cold frosty morning; and the snow about 9 inches deep. Where the sun shone on it during the day, a considerable quantity of it melted; but these places were few, as the whole face of the country near this is closely covered with fir timber. In the afternoon a hunter came in[480] and informed us that the party he had been with had killed 10 elk.[481+]

Tuesday 28th. A clear cold morning, and the weather continued cold all day. About half of our men were employed bringing home meat; and it was found a very cold uncomfortable business. The two men who lately went to the salt works returned with a small supply.[482]

Wednesday 29th. We had a cold clear morning; and the day continued clear throughout. On the 30th the weather was cloudy; and not so cold as the day before; and some snow fell.

Friday 31st. This was a clear cold morning.—Seven of us went up the small river in a canoe to hunt; but after we had gone a mile, we were stopped by the ice and had to return to the fort. One of the men at the salt works had been out hunting, and killed an elk;[483+] and called at the fort for men to assist him in taking the meat to their camp.[484]

Saturday 1st Feb. 1806. We had a fine clear cold morning. A number of the men[485] went out to bring meat to the fort, and to take some to the salt works.[486]

Sunday 2nd. The morning was pleasant and the weather more moderate. About the middle of the day it began to thaw and in the evening to rain. Some of our men were engaged to day bringing in more meat.

Monday 3rd. Some light showers of rain fell in the course of last night; and this day is still somewhat wet and cloudy. One of our hunters came in, who had killed seven elk,+ and returned with a party and a canoe to bring in the meat. We are fortunate in getting as much meat as we can eat; but we have no other kind of provisions.

Tuesday 4th. This was a fine clear morning. Last night the men, who had gone to carry the meat to the salt works, returned and brought us a bushel of salt. This day continued throughout clear and pleasant; and the 5th was a clear cool day. One of our hunters came in, who had killed 6 elk.[487+]

Thursday 6th. We had a cool fair morning. Ten of us started with a canoe to bring in the meat of the elk, killed yesterday; and had to encamp out all night but with the assistance of the elk skins and our blankets, we lodged pretty comfortable, though the snow was 4 or 5 inches deep.

Friday 7th. The morning was fair, and all hands engaged bringing in the meat; we got some to the fort; but myself and part of the men had again to encamp out. It rained hard and we had a disagreeable night.

Saturday 8th. About noon there were showers of rain and hail. Some of the hunters killed 4 more elk[+] and we got all the meat safe to camp in the evening.

Sunday 9th. We had a fine morning; but in the course of the day we had sometimes sunshine, and and sometimes showers of rain. One of our hunters caught a beaver.[+]

Monday 10th. A light snow fell last night, and the morning was pleasant. In the afternoon two men came from the salt works, with information that two others were sick[488] and a third had cut his knee so badly he could scarcely walk.[489]

Tuesday 11th. This was a fine morning. A serjeant[490] and six men were sent to bring the sick men to the fort. At the same time myself and two men went out to hunt,[491] and remained out to the 17th during which time there was a great deal of heavy rain, and the weather changeable and disagreeable.—While we were out we killed 8 elk.[+] During one of the most disagreeable nights, myself and another lay out in our shirts and overalls, with only one elk skin to defend us from a violent night's rain. We had started a gang of elk, and in order to be light in the pursuit left our clothes where the first was killed, and could not get back before dark. Our shirts and overalls being all of leather made it the more disagreeable.[492]

Monday 17th. The day was stormy; we set out for the fort and arrived there in the afternoon.[493] We found the sick men at the fort, and still very bad. One of the men brought word from the salt works, that they had made about 4 bushels of salt; and the Commanding Officers throught that would be sufficient to serve the party, until we should arrive at the Missouri where there is some deposited.

Tuesday 18th. The morning of this day was cloudy. A sergeant and six men set out to go to the salt works, to bring the salt and kettles to the fort. At the same time I started with 10 more to bring in meat; but the weather was so stormy we could not get round the bay, and we all returned to the fort.⁴⁹⁴

Wednesday 19th. We were employed in bringing in meat, and the sergeant and 7 men again set out for the salt works by land, to bring the salt and kettles to the fort. The day was very wet and stormy.⁴⁹⁵

Thursday 20th. This was a cloudy morning. A member of the Chinook Indians came to the fort with hats to trade. They are made of the cedar bark and silk grass, look handsome and keep out the rain. But little rain fell to day, and in the evening we turned out the natives as usual, and they all went home.⁴⁹⁶

Friday 21st. About 1 o'clock, our salt makers came home, with the salt and baggage. They had a very unpleasant day, as it rained hard during the whole of it.

Saturday 22nd. This was a fine clear day; and some of the natives again visited us, and brought some hats which we purchased at a moderate price. The 23rd was also clear and pleasant;⁴⁹⁷ but the morning of the 24th was cloudy, and at 10 o'clock it began to rain hard. About noon a number of the natives came to the fort to trade. The rain continued with high stormy wind; and we suffered the Indians to remain in the fort all night.

Tuesday 25th. The rain continued and the weather was stormy. About 10 o'clock the natives went away, though it continued to rain very fast. They brought us yesterday a number of small fish,⁴⁹⁸ of a very excellent kind, resembling a herring, and about half the size.

Wednesday 26th. We had a fair morning; some of the hunters went out,⁴⁹⁹ as our store of provisions was getting small, and three men went in search of these small fish,⁵⁰⁰ which we had found very good eating.—The 27th was a cloudy wet day.⁵⁰¹ Three of our hunters came in, and had killed an elk.⁺

Friday 28th. This was a foggy morning, and the forenoon cloudy. A sergeant⁵⁰² and six men went out to bring in the meat, and returned about noon. The greater part of this day was fair and pleasant; and in the evening three hunters came in, and had killed five elk.⁵⁰³⁺

CHAP. XVIII.

Saturday 1st March, 1806. We had a cloudy wet morning. I set out with 8 men and 4 hunters to bring the meat of the elk that had been killed, which was at a greater distance from the fort than any we had yet brought in. There is a large river that flows into the southeast part of Hailey's Bay; upon which about 20 miles from its mouth, our hunters discovered falls, which had about 60 feet of a perpendicular pitch.[504]

Sunday 2nd. This day was also wet. The fishing party returned at night, and brought with them some thousands of the same kind of small fish,[505] we got from the natives a few days ago, and also some sturgeon.

The Indian name of the river we were up yesterday is Kil-hou-a-nak-kle,[506] and that of the small river, which passes the fort Ne-tul.[507]

Monday 3rd. It rained all this day and the following. Our sick men are getting better, but slowly, as they have little or no suitable nourishment.[508]

Wednesday 5th. About 12 o'clock last night the rains ceased, and we had a fine morning. A number of the natives visited us; and at night our hunters returned, but had killed nothing.[509]

Thursday 6th. Our stock of provisions being nearly exhausted, 6 men were sent out in different directions to hunt; and three more were sent to endeavour to procure some fish, as the natives take a great number of small fish about 20 miles distant from the fort by water. Some men were also employed in repairing the canoes that we may be able to set out on our return immediately, should our hunters be unsuccessful. The elk, almost the only game in this part of the country, are chiefly gone to the mountains. This day continued fair throughout.

Friday 7th. This was a wet morning, and some showers fell occasionally during the day. Among our other difficulties we now experience the want of tobacco, and out of 33 persons composing our party, there are but 7 who do not make use of it: we use crab-tree bark as a substitute.[510] In the evening one of our hunters came in and had killed an elk a considerable distance off.[+]

Saturday 8th. Some snow fell last night, and the morning was stormy and disagreeable. About 9 o'clock another of our hunters came in, who had killed 2 elk;[+] and later some time the remaining three, having killed but one deer,[+] and lost their canoe.[511]

Sunday 9th. This morning 10 men[512] went out to hunt. There were some light showers of snow this forenoon, but during the greater part of it the sun shone clear and warm. In the afternoon some of the natives came to visit us, and brought some of the small fish, which they call Ulken. Two hunters came in in the evening, but had not killed any thing. The men sent to fish are still absent, owing perhaps to the high swells in the bay. The Indians remained in the fort all night.

On the 10th we had changeable weather, with snow showers. At noon two more hunters went out.

Tuesday 11th. The weather was nearly the same as yesterday. Three men went across the bay in a canoe to hunt. Two other hunters came in but had killed nothing. At noon our fishermen returned with some ulken and sturgeon.[513] The morning of the 12th was pleasant; but towards the evening the day became cloudy. Another hunter went out.[514]

Thursday 13th. The morning was fine and two more hunters went out early. About 10 the hunters who had gone across the bay returned, and had killed 2 elk and 2 deer.[+]

I this day took an account of the number of pairs of mockasons each man in the party had; and found the whole to be 338 pair. This stock was not provided without great labour, as the most of them are made of the skins of elk. Each man has also a sufficient quantity of patch-leather.[515] Some of the men went out to look for the lost canoe,[516] and killed 2 elk.[+]

Friday 14th. We had a fine morning; and four hunters set out early.[517] I went with a party and brought in the meat of 2 elk which were killed last evening.[518] Two hunters, who had gone out yesterday morning returned very much fatigued, and had killed nothing but a goose and a raven which they eat last night.[+] While out to day I saw a number of musquitoes flying about. I also saw a great quantity of sheep-sorrel growing in the woods of a very large size.[519]

Saturday 15th. There was a fine pleasant morning. About noon our hunters came in and had killed four elk. A number of the natives came to the fort to day.[520]

Sunday 16th. Last night it became cloudy and began to rain; and the rain has continued all day.—The Indians stayed about the fort the whole of this day. Yesterday while I was absent, getting our meat home, one of the hunters killed two vultures, the largest fowls I had ever seen. I never saw any such as these except on the Columbia river and the seacoast.

On the 17th it rained occasionally during the whole of the day. We got a canoe from the natives, for which we gave an officer's uniform coat.[521]

Tuesday 18th. The weather was much like that of yesterday, and some hail fell in the course of the day. Some of the men are repairing the small canoes, and making preparations to return up the river, as soon as the weather will permit.[522] One of the hunters killed an elk.[+]

The morning of the 19th was stormy, some hard showers of hail fell and it continued cloudy through the day.[523]

Thursday 20th. The whole of this day was wet and disagreeable. We intended to have set out to day on our return, but the weather was too bad. I made a calculation of the number of elk and deer killed by the party from the 1st of Dec. 1805 to the 20th March 1806, which gave 131 elk and 20 deer. There were a few smaller quadrupeds killed such as otter and beaver; and one racoon. The meat of some of the elk was not brought to the fort.[524]

Friday 21st. We had a cloudy wet morning. Two of the hunters went out this morning and about 10 o'clock we were visited by some of the Clat-sop Indians. These and the Chin-ook, Cath-la-mas, Cal-a-mex and Chiltz nations, who inhabit the seacoast, all dress in the same manner. The men are wholly naked except a small robe; the women have only the the [*sic*] addition of the short petticoat. Their language also is nearly the same; and they all observe the same ceremony of depositing with the remains of the dead all their property, or placing it at their graves. I believe I saw as many as an hundred canoes at one burying-place of the Chin-ooks, on the north side of the Columbia, at its entrance into Hailey's Bay: and there are a great many at the burying-place of every village. These Indians on the coast have no horses, and very little property of any kind, except their canoes. The women are much inclined to venery, and like those on the Missouri are sold to prostitution at an easy rate.

An old Chin-ook squaw frequently visited our quarters with nine girls which she kept as prostitutes.[525] To the honour of the Flatheads, who live on the west side of the Rocky Mountains, and extend some distance down the Columbia, we must mention them as an exception; as they do not exhibit those loose feelings of carnal desire, nor appear addicted to the common customs of prostitution: and they are the only nation on the whole route where any thing like chastity is regarded.[526] In the evening our two hunters returned, but had killed nothing.

Saturday 22nd. We had a cloudy wet morning. Three hunters were sent on ahead to remain at some good hunting ground until we should all come up; and six others to hunt near the fort. In the evening all these came in, except one, without any success.

Sunday 23rd. There was a cloudy wet morning.—The hunter who remained out last night, came in early, and had killed an elk.[527+] We were employed this forenoon in dividing and packing up our loading; and distributing it among the canoes, which were five in number, three large and two small. At noon we put it on board; and at 1 o'clock left fort Clatsop. The afternoon was fair, we proceeded round Point William, went about 19 miles, and encamped at the mouth of a creek, where we found the three hunters, that had been sent on ahead; and who had killed two elk[+] about a mile and an half distant.

Monday 24th. After a bad night's rest, on account of the rain 15 men went out and brought the meat of the two elk to our camp. The morning was fair and after breakfast they all embarked, except the men belonging to my canoe which the tide had left aground. The hunters went on in the small canoe ahead, and I had to wait for the rising of the tide. In about two hours I was able to follow the other canoes, and proceeded on about 12 miles to a village of the Cath-la-mas where the rest of the party had halted.[528] When I arrived we all proceeded on again, and in the evening encamped at an old village, which had been vacated.

Tuesday 25th. We set out after breakfast and had a fair morning; proceeded on to 12 o'clock, when we again halted, the wind and tide being both against us. When the tide began to rise we went on again, saw some of the natives in canoes descending the river,[529] and in the afternoon passed an Indian lodge, where one of the men purchased an otter skin.—At this time the wind rose and blew very hard accompanied with rain; notwith-standing we proceeded on till night, when we came to the mouth of a small creek which formed a good harbour for our canoes. Here we found several of the natives encamped and catching sturgeon, of which they had taken 14 large ones.

Wednesday 26th. After a disagreeable night's rain, and wind, we continued our voyage. As we passed along I saw a great many flowers full blown of different colours; and grass and other herbage growing fast: I saw nettles two feet high of this spring's growth.

Thursday 27th. There was a cloudy wet morning. We embarked early and went about 6 miles, when we came to a small Indian village,[530] where the natives received us very kindly. They belong to the Chil-ook nation, and differ something in their language from the Chin-ooks. We got some Wapto roots and fish from them and then proceeded on, though it rained very hard. Two small canoes went on ahead to Deer island, in order to kill some game by the time we should come up. We passed several Indian lodges where the natives were fishing for sturgeon, and got a large one out of a small canoe; a number of which followed us with 2 Indians in each of them. At night we encamped where we had plenty of good wood, oak and ash.

Friday 28th. The morning was cloudy. We set out early, and at 10 o'clock came to Deer island; where those who had gone ahead in the small canoes had encamped, and all gone out to hunt except one. In a short time a hunter returned with a large deer, and we concluded to stay here all day and repair two of our canoes, that leaked. It rained at intervals during the day. Our hunters came in and had killed 7 deer in all.[+] Some of the men went to bring in the meat, and others went out and killed some geese and ducks. At the last village we passed I took notice of a difference in the dress of the females, from that of those below, about the coast and Hailey's Bay. Instead of the short petticoat, they have a piece of thin dressed skin tied tight round their loins, with a narrow slip coming up between their thighs.[531] On this island there are a greater number of snakes, than I had ever seen in any other place; they appeared almost as numerous as the blades of grass; and are a species of Garter snake. When our men went for the deer, they found that the fowls had devoured four of the carcases entirely, except the bones. So they brought in the other two; and we finished our canoes and put them in the water. The Columbia river is now very high, which makes it more difficult to ascend.

Saturday 29th. The morning was pleasant with some white frost and we proceeded on early; passed some old Indian lodges, and in the afternoon came to a large village, where we were received with great kindness, and got fish and wapto roots to eat. Here we bought some dogs[532] and waptos, and then went on agian [*sic*], about a mile, and encamped. One of the sick men is quite recovered and the other two are getting better.[533]

Sunday 30th. The morning was fair with some dew. We set out early accompanied by several of the natives in canoes. The river is very high, over-flowing all its banks. We passed some villages of the natives on Wapto island,[534] which is about 20 miles long and one broad, but did not halt at any of them. The natives of this country ought to have the credit of making the finest canoes, perhaps in the world, both as to service and beauty; and are no less expert in working them when made.*[535] We had a beautiful day throughout, and in the evening encamped on a handsome prairie in sight of a large pond on the north side of the river.

Monday 31st. This was a beautiful clear morning, and we proceeded on early. One of the men went along shore, and in a short time killed a deer: the deer are very plenty on this part of the river.— We proceeded on, and passed a large village which was full of people as we went down, but is now all deserted except one lodge.[536] In the evening we came to a small prairie opposite the mouth of Quicksand river, where we encamped.

Tuesday 1st April, 1806. We had a cloudy morning; and we agreed to stay here all day, for the purpose of hunting. So 9 hunters set out early; 3 of whom went up Quicksand river[537] and killed a deer:+ the other six killed 4 elk and a deer. In the evening nine of us went to bring in the meat of the elk; but it being late we were obliged to encamp out all night.

Wednesday 2nd. We returned in the morning to camp; and it was agreed to stay here some time longer to hunt and dry meat.[538] Therefore 3 parties went out to hunt. Myself and 4 men went below the mouth of Sandy river, and killed an elk, some deer and a black bear.+

Thursday 3rd. We went out and killed some deer; and then to bring in the meat of the bear and dry that of the elk; but it rained so hard we could not dry the meat; and therefore brought in the carcase of the bear. On our way we saw 3 small cubs in a den, but the old bear was not with them. In the evening we returned to our camp, and remained there all night.

Friday 4th. After a cloudy morning, we turned out and killed a deer and some geese, and then went to the camp. A party that went

---

*"I had imagined that the Canadians, who accompanied me were the most expert canoemen in the world, but they are very inferior to these people [the natives near the coast] as they themselves acknowledged, in conducting those vessels." *M'Kenzie*

out on the upper side of Sandy river, killed 4 elk,[+] and some of the men were out drying the meat.

While I was out hunting, Capt. Clarke got information that a large river came in on the south side of the Columbia, about 40 miles below this place, opposite a large island, which had concealed it from our view; and went down with six men to view it. He found it to be a very large river, 500 yards wide, with several nations of Indians living on it; and its source supposed to be near the head waters of some of the rivers, which fall into the gulph of California.[539] On their return they bought some dogs at an Indian village; and last night arrived at camp. Four men were sent on ahead this forenoon in a canoe to hunt; and I went out with two more to the den where we saw the cubs, to watch for the old bear; we stayed there until dark and then encamped about a quarter of a mile off, and went back early in the morning; but the old one was not returned: so we took the cubs and returned to camp.[540]

Saturday 5th. The weather was pleasant. There is a beautiful prairie and a number of ponds below the mouth of Sandy river; and about two miles from the Columbia the soil is rich with white cedar timber, which is very much stripped of its bark, the natives making use of it both for food and clothing.[†] A number of the Indians visit us daily; and the females in general have that leather covering round their loins, which is somewhat in the form of a truss.

Sunday 6th. We had a fine morning with some fog; about 10 o'clock we set out; passed a beautiful prairie on the north side, which we could not see for the fog as we went down; proceeded on about 9 miles and came to our hunters' camp. They had killed 5 elk;[+] so we halted, sent out for the meat and began to dry it.[541] We are now at the head of the Columbia valley; which is a fine valley about 70 miles long, abounding with roots of different kinds, which the natives use for food, especially the Wapto roots which they gather out of the ponds. The timber is mostly of the fir kind, with some cherry, dogwood, soft maple and ash; and a variety of shrubs which bear fruit of a fine flavour, that the natives make use of for food.[542]

Monday 7th. This was a pleasant day, but cloudy. Three hunters went on ahead again and the rest of the party remained drying meat to subsist on while we passed the Columbia plains, as there is no game in that part of the country, according to the accounts given by

---

[†]Mr. M'Kenzie also mentions that the western Indians make use of the inner tegument of the bark of trees for food; and that it is generally considered by the more interior Indians as a delicacy, rather than an article of common food; that on this and herbs they are used to sustain themselves on their journies. He likewise states that of the inner rind of the hemlock, taken off early in the spring they make a kind of cakes, which they eat with salmon oil, and of which they appear very fond.

the natives, who are daily coming down; and say that those remaining in the plains are in a starving condition, and will continue so
until the salmon begin to run, which is very soon expected. We continued here all day; and one of our hunters killed a beautiful small
bird of the quail kind.[+]

Tuesday 8th. This was a fine morning, but the wind blew so hard
from the northeast that it was impossible to go on; and about 8 o'clock
the swells ran so high that we had to unload our canoes, and haul
some of them out of the water to prevent their being injured. Some
of the men are complaining of rheumatick pains; which are to be
expected from the wet and cold we suffered last winter, during which
from the 4th of November 1805 to the 25th of March 1806, there
were not more than twelve days in which it did not rain, and of
these but six were clear.[543] Two hunters, who had gone out in the
morning returned, but had killed nothing, except a beautiful small
duck.[+544]

CHAP. XIX.

Wednesday 9th [April 1806]. The morning was pleasant; we therefore loaded our canoes and proceeded on till 11 o'clock when we stopped at a large Indian village on the north side; but a number of the huts were unoccupied. They are of the Al-e-is nation. At the time we halted 3 canoe loads of them were setting out for the falls to fish. We took breakfast here and bought 5 dogs from them.[545] The women all wear the small leather bandage, but are quite naked otherwise, except what is covered by the small robe they wear round their shoulders.[546] In the afternoon the weather became cloudy and some rain fell. In the evening we came to a large rapid at the lower end of Strawberry island; where there are a number of the natives about settling on the north side. Here we crossed over, after buying two dogs from them, and encamped behind the island.[547] Some rain continued falling.

Thursday 10th. A party of men went out to collect pitch to repair one of our canoes, which was split; and the rest went round the point of the island, and took the canoes over the rapid, one at a time, with the assistance of a line. When we got over the rapids we crossed to another village of the natives on the north side, where I saw the skin of a wild sheep,[548] which had fine beautiful wool on it. Here we took breakfast and waited the arrival of the other canoe, which in about an hour came up; and the men when out for pitch killed 3 deer.[549+] We proceeded on, and the water was so rapid, that we had to tow the canoes up by the line almost all the way to the landing at the lower end of the portage, a distance of about six miles. In passing a bad place the tow-line of the small canoe, which the hunters had on ahead, broke; but fortunately there was nothing in her, as the three hunters were on shore dragging her up, and had taken out all the loading. As she passed by us Capt. Lewis got some of the natives to bring her to shore.[550] In the evening we got to the end of the portage, which is about two miles. We took our baggage to the top of the hill and remained with it all night; during which some showers of rain fell.

Friday 11th. We had a cloudy morning. All our men, who were able set out to take the canoes through the grand shoot. About 1 o'clock we got two over; and then proceeded to take two more, which we succeeded in after great toil and danger; and 3 hunters went on ahead in the least.[551]

Saturday 12th. This morning was wet. We all set out to take the other canoe over; but after we had fastened the rope to her she swung out into the current, which was so strong, that it pulled the rope out of the men's hands and went down the river.—We then went to carry our baggage across the portage, which was a very fatiguing business; but about sunset we got all over. It rained at intervals all day; and upon the very high mountains on the south side of the river, snow fell and continued on the trees and rocks during the whole of the day. We had a number of the natives about us in the day time; but they left us at night. We encamped, all excessively fatigued, at the upper end of the portage.

Sunday 13th. There was a cloudy morning. Having divided the load of the lost canoe among the 4 that were left, we renewed our voyage and passed a large deserted village on the north side. Captain Lewis with the two small canoes, crossed to the south side, where there is a large village inhabited, to endeavour to purchase a small canoe or two, as we were very much crowded in the four we had. Capt. Clarke with the two large canoes continued on along the northern shore, till we passed Crusatte's river, when the wind rose so high we could not go on, so we halted and waited for Capt. Lewis. Two hunters went out about 3 hours, but killed nothing. By this time the wind fell and we went on 3 miles to a better harbour, where we halted on the north side of the river. Capt. Clarke and 3 men went out to hunt; and Capt. Lewis having come up and crossed over to us, we fixed our camp for the night. He got 2 canoes and 3 dogs from the inhabitants of the large village.—They are of the Wey-eh-hoo nation[552] and have twelve lodges here. At dark Capt. Clarke and party returned, and had killed two deer.+

Monday 14th. The morning was fine with some fog. About 9 o'clock our 3 hunters, who had gone ahead and proceeded up Crusatte's river some distance returned, having killed 4 deer.+ At 10 o'clock we continued our voyage, and at 1 came to a new settlement of the natives on the north side, where we saw some horses, the first we have seen since October last. These horses appeared in good case. The wind blew hard from the southwest and the weather was clear and cool, but there has been no frost lately, except on the tops of the high hills. We stayed here three hours and then proceeded on; passed several Indian camps, and halted at a small creek on the north side, where there are a number of Indian lodges.

Tuesday 15th. The morning was fair. The Commanding Officers attempted to purchase some horses, but could not agree with the Indians on the price; so we proceeded on about 4 miles to another village, at the mouth of the Catarack river. Here we got some Shape-e-leel, a kind of bread the natives make of roots, and bake in the sun; and which is strong and palatable. Here another trial was made to get some horses, but without success; and we again proceeded on; passed a place where there was a village in good order last fall when we went down; but has been lately torn down, and again erected at a short distance from the old ground where it formerly stood. The reason of this removal I cannot conjecture, unless to avoid the fleas, which are more numerous in this country than any insects I ever saw.*

About three o'clock in the afternoon we came to Rock Camp, where we stayed two days as we went down. Some hunters went out in the evening and killed a deer.[553+]

Wednesday 16th This was a pleasant day.[554] As we did not expect to be able to navigate the Columbia river much farther, Captain Clarke, with some of the men and some goods went over the river to endeavour to procure some horses. I was out hunting this morning and killed a rattlesnake among the rocks. Some hunters that went out in the morning returned in the evening and had killed two deer,[+] some ducks and four squirrels, three of a beautiful speckled kind, and as large as a common grey squirrel, but the tail not so bushy.[+]

Thursday 17th. This was a fine morning. Some hunters went out and we remained at this camp all day; in the evening our hunters came in and had killed a deer.[+] We made 12 packsaddles. Captain Clarke still remains over the river.[555]

Friday 18th. We had fine weather and all set out from this place, and proceeded on with great difficulty and danger to the foot of the long narrows; and expect to be able to take the canoes no further.— Here we met one of the men from Captain Clarke with 4 horses. In coming up, one of our small canoes got split so that we were obliged to carry the load two miles by land to this place. Wood here is very scarce, as the Columbia plains have commenced. Several of the men

---

*"We had however the curiosity to visit the houses (of a deserted village) which were erected upon posts; and we suffered very severely from the indulgence of it; for the floors were covered with fleas, and we were immediately in the same condition, for which we had no remedy but to take to the water. There was not a spot round the houses, free from grass, that was not alive, as it were, with this vermin." *M'Kenzie.*

went up to the village with their buffaloe robes, to dispose of them for horses. Could we get about 12 horses we would be able to go by land.

Saturday 19th. The morning was cloudy and all hands were engaged in carrying the baggage and canoes over the portage, which is two miles in length. Five more horses were got in the course of the day. Some light showers of rain fell in the afternoon, and about 4 o'clock, we got all our baggage and canoes across except the two large ones, of which we made firewood. At the same time Captain Clarke and four men went on ahead to the village at the great falls[556] to endeavour to get some more horses, by the time we arrive there, a distance of about 8 miles from this village. In the evening the weather cleared up and we had a fine night.

Sunday 20th. This was a pleasant morning with some white frost. We got two more horses and lost one; remained here all day and had a great deal of trouble with our horses, as they are all studs, and break almost every rope we can raise. We had to tie them up at night, and one broke away notwithstanding all our care and attention. We have also much trouble with the Indians as they are disposed to steal whenever they have an opportunity. With all our care they stole 4 or 5 tomakawks [*sic*].[557]

Monday 21st. This was another pleasant morning with some white frost. We found the horse, which had broke away last night, and made preparations for setting out from this place. While we were making preparations to start, an Indian stole some iron articles from among the men's hands; which so irritated Captain Lewis, that he struck him; which was the first act of the kind, that had happened during the expedition. The Indians however did not resent it, otherwise it is probable we would have had a skirmish with them. This morning we disposed of two canoes and used another for firewood.[558] At 10 o'clock we set out from the first narrows with 9 horses of our own and one we borrowed, and 2 canoes all loaded heavy. I went with three other men in the canoes, and had some difficulty in passing the short narrows. About 3 in the afternoon we arrived at the great falls of Columbia, where we met with Captain Clarke and the men that were with him. Here we got another horse; carried our canoes and baggage round the falls and halted for dinner. We also got some dogs here and shapeleel,[559] which we subsist on chiefly at present. We halted here two hours and then proceeded on again. The party that went by land had to leave the river, and take out to the hill a part of the way. I crossed with my canoe to the south side where there is the best water, and passed a large rock island, opposite to which the Sho-sho-ne river[560] flows in from the south. We went on till dark, and then run our small canoe among some willows, and laid down to sleep. We did not make any fire for fear the savages, who are very numerous along this part of the river, might come and rob us.

Tuesday 22nd. This was a pleasant morning and high wind. We proceeded on about 3 miles, when the wind became so violent, that we could not proceed any further, and halted and unloaded our canoes. Having remained here two hours, the other canoe came up, and we proceeded on though the wind was high and river rough. At sunset I crossed over, where the party going by land came in sight, and halted at a small village on the north side; but the other canoe kept on along the southern shore. In the course of this day two more horses were procured, and at this small village we got some more dogs and shapaleel [*sic*].[561]

Wednesday 23rd. We had a cloudy morning. I went also by water to day, and we had very laborious work in getting along. In the evening we met the party at a large village of the Wal-la-waltz nation on the north side of the river; where the other canoe had also arrived. Here we halted, unloaded the canoes and encamped. A horse had got away last night and could not be found.[562]

Thursday 24th. The weather was pleasant. We lost another horse last night, and were detained here this morning, looking for him. We got six horses at this place, three of which were borrowed from an Indian who was going with his family along with us. We sold our two small canoes; and at noon an Indian who had gone to look for the lost horse returned with him.[563] At 2 o'clock we all started by land on the north side of the river, accompanied by several of the natives with their families and horses. We entered the low country, the great and beautiful plains of Columbia, and proceeded on till evening when we encamped at two mat-lodges of the natives, and got two dogs and some shapaleel. The natives who were travelling in our party encamped with us.

Friday 25th. The morning was pleasant, and we set out early. At 10 o'clock we met a great many of the natives on horseback, who turned back with us. At noon we came to a very large band of the Wal-a-waltz nation,[564] the most numerous we had seen on the Columbia; I suppose it consisted of 500 persons, men, women, and children; and all of them tolerably well clothed with robes of the skins of the deer, the ibex or big horned animal and buffaloe. They have a great many horses and lately came to the river to fish for salmon.

We halted here two hours and then went on. The men in general complain of their feet being sore; and the officers have to go on foot to permit some of them to ride.[565] We went 13 miles and encamped at a small grove of willows. There being no other wood for a considerable distance.

Saturday 26th. Last night Capt. Lewis and Capt. Clarke got each a horse, and we set out early, had a fine morning, and proceeded on very well, most of the men having their knapsacks carried on the horses. At noon we halted and took a little of our dried meat, which is the only food we have. At 2 o'clock we continued our journey, and the officers were obliged to go on foot again, to let some of the men ride whose feet were very sore. The country is level and has a most beautiful appearance. On these plains there is a species of clover, as large as any I have seen, and has a large red handsome blossom. The leaves are not quite so large as those of the red clover cultivated in the Atlantic States, but has seven and eight leaves on a branch. We were overtaken and passed by a great number of the natives, with large droves of horses, that look well and are in good order. We travelled about 25 miles and encamped at a small grove of willows.

Sunday 27th. The morning was cloudy with some light showers of rain; and about 9 o'clock we proceeded on through the plains, accompanied by a great many of the natives. Some light showers of rain fell at intervals during the day; and after halting about 2 hours we continued our journey to sunset, when we came to a large village of mat-lodges, belonging to a band of the Wal-la-wal-las, who have encamped here on the north side of the river. Here we remained all night, and the natives were good enough to supply us with some faggots of brush, they had gathered in the plains from the sage bushes, which grow in great abundance on some parts of these plains and are very large.

Monday 28th. The morning was pleasant, and we spent it with the Indians, and got dogs, fish, shap-a-leel and roots from them. At 10 o'clock we began to take our horses over the river at this place, as we can lessen our journey considerably by crossing: We borrowed canoes from the natives, and swam the horses along side, and at 2 o'clock in the afternoon had them all landed safe, after a good deal of trouble. From this place we can discover a range of mountains, covered with snow, in a southeast direction and about fifty miles distant. In the evening the weather was cloudy, and it thundered and threatened rain, a few drops of which fell. We remained here all night, and about dark above and [sic] hundred of the natives came down from the forks to see us. They joined with those at this place and performed a great dance. We were a very interesting sight to the surrounding crowd, as nine-tenths of them had never before seen a white man.[566]

Tuesday 29th. The natives remained about our camp all night; and we bought some dogs and a horse from them. The day was fair, and we got all our baggage transported to the south side of the river. Here are a great many of the natives encamped on a large creek, which comes in from the south, and those on the north side are moving over as fast as they can. We encamped on the creek, and got three horses, some dogs, shap-a-leel, some roots call com-mas and other small roots, which were good to eat and nourishing.[567]

Wednesday 30th. This was a cloudy morning, and we stayed here till about 11 o'clock to collect our horses, and got two more; and have now altogether twenty-three horses. We then set out from Wal-la-wal-la river and nation; proceeded on about fourteen miles through an extensive plain, when we struck a branch of the Wal-la-wal-la river, and halted for the night. We saw no animals or birds of any kind, except two pheasants, one of which Capt. Clarke killed. The whole of this plain is of a sandy surface and affords but thin grass, with some branches of shrubs which resemble sage or hyssop. On the south side of this branch the soil is of earth and rich, covered with grass, and very handsome. We are still accompanied by several of the natives.

Thursday 1st of May, 1806. Some rain fell during the night, and the morning continues cloudy. We set out early and travelled up the branch, which is a fine stream about twenty yards wide, with some cotton-wood, birch and willows on its banks. One of the four hunters, who went forward very early this morning, returned at noon with a beaver he had killed; other game is scarce. We then halted to dine, where the road forks, one going up the branch an east course, and the other north towards the large river. Here our Indians differed in opinion with respect to the best road to be taken. The man with the family and gang of horses said he would go across to the Great river to-morrow; but we followed the opinion of the young man our guide, and proceeded on up the creek. We travelled about twenty-five miles, and encamped without any of the natives, except our guide, who generally keeps with the hunters, one of whom killed a deer this evening.+ The higher we go up the creek the cotton-wood is more large and plenty; and the plains beautiful.

Friday 2nd. A fine morning. Last night about 9 o'clock, three of the Wal-la-wal-las came up with us, and brought a steel trap that had been left at our camp on the north side of the Columbia, opposite the mouth of the Wal-la-wal-la river; perhaps one of the greatest instances of honesty ever known among Indians.[568] Some hunters went on ahead, and having collected our horses, we found one missing; some of the men went to look for him, and brought him back. We then continued our journey up this branch; and saw to our right a range of high hills covered with timber and snow, not more than ten miles distant. We went fifteen miles and encamped on the north fork, the creek having forked about two miles below our encampment. The south fork is the largest, and from its course is supposed to issue from those snow-topped hills on our right. In the evening our hunters joined us, and had killed only one beaver and an otter. The three Indians remained with us all day; and at night we set three steel traps, there being a great many beaver signs on this branch.

Saturday 3rd. We had a wet uncomfortable morning, and when the horses were collected one was found missing, and one of our hunters went back after him, while the rest of us continued our journey. This morning our guide and three other Indians went on ahead. We continued our rout about ten miles, when we struck a creek, having left the other entirely to our right; and halted. Our hunter came up with the horse. The wind was very high this forenoon, and rather cold for the season; with some rain. We continued about two hours and eat the last of our dried meat; and are altogether without other provisions, as our stock of dogs is exhausted, and we can kill no game in these plains. In the evening we met a chief and nine of his men, who appeared glad to see us.[569] We encamped on a small branch or spring, as it was too far to go over the hills. The Indians say we can get over to-morrow by noon. The wind continued to blow hard and some snow showers fell in the afternoon.

Sunday 4th. We had a severe frost last night; and the morning was cold and clear. We were early on our march over a handsome plain; and came to another creek, which we kept down until we came to Lewis's river, some distance below the forks of Koos-koos-ke;[570] where we halted at an Indian lodge, and could get nothing to eat, except some bread made of a kind of roots I was unacquainted with. We had, however, a dog, which we bought from the Indians, who met us last night; but this was a scanty allowance for thirty odd hungry men. We remained here about two hours, got a dog, and proceeded up the south side of Lewis's river, about three miles, when we met with one of our old chiefs,[571] who had come down with us last fall; and who advised us to cross the river, as the best road is on the north side. We therefore were occupied in crossing, during the remainder of the day as we could raise but four small canoes from the natives at this place. We, however, by dark got all safe over, and encamped on the north side, accompanied by a great many of the natives, who appear a friendly and well disposed people.

CHAP. XX.

Monday 5th [May 1806]. We had a fine morning, and proceeded on early, accompanied by our old chief and a number of the natives. About 10 o'clock we passed the forks, and kept along the north side of Koos-koos-ke;[572] at noon we halted at three lodges of Indians, where we got three dogs and some roots.— We also got one of our horses, which we had left here last fall in the care of the old chief who is now with us;[573] and says that the Snake guide, who deserted us last fall, stole and took two of our horses with him.[574] We remained here about an hour, and then continued our journey; came to a large lodge of the natives, at the mouth of a creek, where we encamped. This lodge is built much after the form of the Virginia fodder houses;[575] is about fifty yards long, and contains twenty families. We here could get no provisions but shap-a-leel and roots.

Tuesday 6th. There was a cloudy wet morning; and we stayed in our camp. Capt. Lewis and Capt. Clarke acted as physicians to the sick of the village or lodge, for which they gave us a small horse, that we killed and eat, as we had no other meat of any kind. We continued here until about 3 o'clock, when we started and went on about nine miles, and encamped close to a lodge of the natives.

Wednesday 7th. This was a fine morning, and we continued here till after breakfast, when we proceeded on about four miles to another Indian lodge, at the mouth of a small creek, where we had to cross the river again, in order to get to a better road. At this lodge the natives found two canisters of ammunition, which we had buried last fall on our way down, and which they took care of and returned to us safe. All the Indians from the Rocky Mountains to the falls of Columbia, are an honest, ingenuous and well disposed people; but from the falls to the seacoast, and along it, they are a rascally, thieving set. We were here detained about three hours in crossing, as we had but one canoe to transport ourselves and baggage. We then proceeded over a large hill and struck a small creek, about five miles below the place, where we made our canoes in October last. Here we encamped for the night, accompanied by two Indians, one of which can speak the Sho-sho-ne or Snake language. We will therefore be able to hold some conversation with the natives in this part of the country, as our squaw is of the Snake nation.[576]

Thursday 8th. The morning of this day was pleasant; and we remained here some time, to endeavour to kill some deer; and the hunters were sent out.— Here some of the natives came to our camp, and informed us, that we could not cross the mountains for a moon and an half; as the snow was too deep, and no grass for our horses to subsist on. We have the mountains in view from this place, all covered white with snow. At noon our hunters came in and had killed four deer and some pheasants.[+] About 3 o'clock we continued our journey; passed over a very high hill, and encamped on a small run; where we met our other old chief,[577] who had gone down the river with us last fall. He told us that his men had found our saddles, where we had hid them, and that he had them safe. He also gave us an account of thirty-six of our horses, and where they were.[578]

Friday 9th. There was a cloudy morning; some hunters went out, and we proceeded on for about six miles, when we came to the old chief's lodge, where his family is encamped to gather roots. We are now got into a part of the country where timber is plenty, chiefly pitch pine.

Between the great falls of the Columbia and this place, we saw more horses, than I ever before saw in the same space of country. They are not of the largest size of horses, but very good and active.[579] At noon two of the Indians went to look for our horses, and the old chief with one of our men who knew where some powder and ball was buried, went to bring our packsaddles. In the evening they all returned with 21 horses and about as many packsaddles. Our horses are generally in good order. Our hunters also returned but had killed nothing.

Saturday 10th. At dark last night the weather became cloudy and it rained about an hour when the rain turned to snow, and it continued snowing all night. In the morning the weather became clear. Where we are lying in the plains the snow is about five inches deep; and amidst snow and frost we have nothing whatever to eat. Without breakfast we started to go to a village of the natives, who live on a branch of the river, about a south course from this place. We travelled through the snow about 12 miles, and then went down a long steep descent to the branch where the village is situated. When we were about half way down the hill there was not a particle of snow nor the least appearance of it. It was about 3 o'clock when we arrived at the village,[580] and the Commanding Officers held a conversation with the natives, who informed them that they had not more provisions and roots, than they wanted for themselves. They, however, divided their stock with us; and told us what they had given was all they could spare; but drove up some horses and told us to shoot one, which we did.[581] They then offered another, but that was reserved for another time, and we dressed the one we had killed; and in our situation find it very good eating. We remained here all night. One of the hunters who had gone on before the party did not join us yet.[582]

Sunday 11th. This was a fine clear morning; and we lay here all day. The natives treat us very well; the Officers practice as physicians among their sick, and they gave them a very handsome mare and colt. About 12 o'clock our hunter came in and brought two deer with him.[+] We now find a great many more men among the Indians than when we went down last fall; and several chiefs, which had then been out at war.[583] In the evening the natives brought in six more of our horses.

Monday 12th. We had another fine morning and remained here also to day. The natives in the course of the day gave us four horses, one of which we killed to eat. We also got bread made of roots, which the natives call Co-was, and sweet roots which they call Com-mas. In the afternoon they brought three more of our old stock of horses.*

---

*The information yet acquired, furnishing but few certain data, on which a correct general view of the country west of the Rocky Mountains could be founded, especially on the south side of the Kooskooske, Lewis's river, and the Columbia after its confluence with that river, it would only be attempting imposture to pretend to be able to give it. A few observations, however, may be of some use to such readers, as have paid but little attention to the Geography of our country, and prompt to further inquiry.

Between the Rocky Mountains, which running a northwest course, are said to enter the North Sea in latitude 70° north, and longitude 135° west from London or 60° west from Philadelphia (about 11° west of the mouth of the Columbia) and another range of high mountains, running nearly in the same direction along the coast of the Pacific, there is a large tract of open country extending along the above rivers and towards the north, in breadth from east to west 350 or 400 miles; but which, by Mr. M'Kenzie's account, appears to be contracted in the latitude of his rout near the 53rd degree to the breadth of about 200 miles, where the country is rough and covered with timber. Mr. M'Kenzie represents some parts of these mountains to be of an amazing height, with their snow-clad summits lost in the clouds. Describing the situation of his party "sitting round a blazing fire" the first evening of the day, which they had begun to ascend these mountains on their return, and which was that of the 26th of July; he observes "even at this place, which is only, as it were, the first step towards gaining the summit of the mountains, the climate was very sensibly changed. The air that fanned the village which we left at noon, was mild and cheering; the grass was verdant, and the wild fruits ripe around it. But here the snow was not yet dissolved, the ground was still bound by the frost, the herbage had scarce begun to spring, and the crowberry bushes were just beginning to blossom." This range of lofty mountains prevents the Tacoutche or Columbia river from finding a direct course to the ocean, and forces it in a direction somewhat east of south, to traverse by various windings that large tract of country, until it arrives near the 46th degree of latitude, when it turns to the west, and at length finds its way to the Ocean through the Columbia valley.

From the information gained by the late expedition, by M'Kenzie's voyage, the discoveries of Captain Cooke and others, it appears there are great quantities of timber, chiefly of the pine or fir kind, between the shore of the Pacific and the chain of mountains which run near it; but between these and the Rocky Mountains, expecially south of M'Kenzie's

Tuesday 13th. We had a fine morning with white frost. Having collected our horses we found we had 60 and all pretty good except 4, which were studs and had sore backs.[584] At noon we proceeded down the branch, which has a good deal of cotton wood, willow and cherry tree on its banks; and is a bold rapid stream about 15 yards wide. We kept down the branch about four miles; and then came to the river where it passes through a beautiful plain.—Here we halted to wait for a canoe, which we expected that some of the natives would bring up the river, to assist us in crossing; when we intend to encamp until the snow shall have sufficiently melted to admit of our crossing the mountains. At dark the canoe came, but it being too late to cross we encamped on the south side.

Wednesday 14th. The morning was pleasant with some white frost. Three hunters went over very early to the north side of the river. All the rest of the men were employed in collecting our horses and taking over the baggage. About noon we got all the horses and baggage over safe; and met with one of our hunters, who had killed two bears, some distance off. So two men were dispatched with him to bring in the meat; and we set about forming a camp at the remains of an ancient village on the north side of the Koos-koos-ke river.[585] We were accompanied by a number of natives, one of whom gave us a horse; and three more of our old stock were brought in by them. In the afternoon we had an operation performed on seven of our horses, to render them more peaceable; which was done by one of the natives upon all but one.[586] In the evening the men came in with the meat of the two bears; and also our other hunters who had killed three more, all of the grizly kind.[587+] We gave some of the meat to the natives at our camp, who cooked it in their own way; which was done in the following manner. They first collected some stones and heated them, upon which they placed a part of the meat, and upon the meat some small brush, and so alternately brush, until all the meat was on; when the whole was covered with brush and lastly with earth; so that the heap or mass had something of the appearance of a small coalpit on fire. An hour and an half was necessary to cook it in this way. The natives remained at our camp all night.[588]

---

rout, a great part is open prairie or plains almost totally without timber. Mr. M'Kenzie says of the information of the chief, who delineated for him a sketch of the river and country on a piece of bark, "As far as his knowledge of the river extended, the country on either side was level, in many places without wood, and abounding in red deer, and some of a small fallow kind."

According to the verbal relation of Mr Gass, the land on the Columbia is generally of a better quality than on the Missouri; and where a greater number of roots grow, such as the natives subsit [sic] on. The Missouri in its general course is deeper, more crooked and rapid than the Columbia; but the latter has more rapids or cataracts; and its water is clear.

Thursday 15th. This was a fine morning, and some hunters went out early. The rest of the party were engaged making places of shelter, to defend them from the stormy weather. Some had small sails to cover their little hovels, and others had to make frames and cover them with grass. Around our camp the plains have the appearance of a meadow before it is mowed, and affords abundance of food for our horses. Here we expect to remain a month before we can cross the mountains. The natives staid all day at our camp; and one of them had round his neck a scalp of an Indian, with six thumbs and four fingers of other Indians he had killed in battle, of the Sho-sho-ne, or Snake nation.[589] The nation here the Cho-co-nish, is very numerous, as well as the other. These nations have been long at war and destroyed a great many of each other in a few years past.

From the Mandan nation to the Pacific ocean, the arms of the Indians are generally bows and arrows, and the war-mallet. The war-mallet is a club with a large head of wood or stone; those of stone are generally covered with leather, and fastened to the end of the club with thongs or straps of leather and the sinews of animals.*

In the afternoon two of our hunters came in and had killed nothing but some grous; four more continued out.

Friday 16th. The morning was cloudy and some rain fell; but in about two hours it cleared away and we had a fine day. An Indian performed the quieting operation on two more of our horses. In the evening two of our hunters came in, and brought with them two deer and some ducks.[590+] Two of the hunters still remained out. The natives all left our camp this evening.[591]

Thursday [Saturday] 17th. We had a cloudy wet morning and some light rain all day. Our other two hunters came in and had killed two large bears.+ They said it snowed on the hills, when it rained at our camp in the valley.

Sunday 18th. The morning was cloudy, but without rain; and ten of the party turned out to hunt.—None of the natives visited us yesterday, or to day; until about 2 o'clock in the afternoon, when five came that had not I seen [*sic*] before. They remained about an hour and had some eye water put into their eyes which were sore; after which they went away, and an old man and his wife came for some medicine, as the old woman was sick. In the evening four hunters came in and had killed nothing, but some grous.+

---

* The publisher has seen one of these stone heads, lately found at *Hatfield*, the farm of Mr David Davis, three miles from Pittsburgh on the Allegheny river. It is of a hard species of stone and weighs seven ounces. It is nearly spherical with a groove cut round to hold, as is supposed, the strap by which it is fastened to the club. Mr Gass says it is exactly like those he had seen to the westward. There is perhaps nothing which in form it so much resembles as a common round pincushion. In close combat the war-mallet, when skilfully wielded, must be a destructive and deadly weapon.

Monday 19th. We had a cloudy wet morning. The old Indian and his wife staid all night and got more medicine. A party of the men went to some Indian lodges about four miles up the river to buy roots; and in the afternoon returned with a good many of them. Several of the natives came to our camp[592] with the men and in the evening all went away. We got another of our old stock of horses; and have now all we left except three; two of which the old Snake guide took with him. At dark two of our hunters came in but had not killed any thing.[593] The day was fair during the whole of the afternoon.

Tuesday 20th. We again had a very wet morning.[594] Two more of our hunters came in, but had killed nothing. It continued raining till about noon, when we had fair weather with some sunshine. The hunters said it also snowed on the hills to day, where they were hunting, while it rained at our camp. About 2 o'clock in the afternoon, another hunter came in and brought a deer that he had killed.[+] In the afternoon four of our hunters again went out. In the evening there were some light showers.

Wednesday 21st. There was a cloudy morning. Two more hunters went out; and some men set about making a canoe to fish in, when the salmon come up, as we do not expect to leave this place before the middle of June. To day we made a small lodge of poles and covered it with grass, for Captain Lewis and Captain Clarke, as their tent is not sufficient to defend them from the rain.[595] At 10 o'clock the weather became clear, and in the evening, was cold.

Thursday 22nd. We had a fine clear morning with some white frost. At three o'clock five of our hunters came in with five deer;[+] previous to which we had killed a fine colt. In the afternoon we saw a great number of the natives on horseback pursuing a deer on the opposite side of the river. They drove it so hard that it was obliged to take the water, when some of our men went down the bank and shot it,[+] and the natives got on a raft and caught it. These Indians are the most active horsemen I ever saw: They will gallop their horses over precipices, that I should not think of riding over at all.[596]

The frames of their saddles are made of wood nicely jointed, and then covered with raw skins, which when they become dry, bind every part tight, and keep the joints in their places. The saddles rise very high before and behind, in the manner of the saddles of the Spaniards, from whom they no doubt received the form; and also obtained their breed of horses. When the Indians are going to mount they throw their buffaloe robes over the saddles and ride on them, as the saddles would otherwise be too hard.[597]

CHAP. XXI.

Friday 23rd [May 1806]. We again had a fine morning.–One of our sergeants shot a deer at a lick close to our camp, and wounded it very bad, but it got to the river and swam over. Two young Indians who had been at our camp all night, then mounted their horses, swam over and drove it back; and we killed it and gave them half of it.[+] The river is about two hundred yards wide and cold and rapid. In the afternoon all the hunters came in but had killed nothing more.

Saturday 24th. This was another fine morning, and two hunters went out. One of the men that were sick, still keeps unwell, with a bad pain in his back; and is in a helpless state. Yesterday we gave him an Indian sweat and he is some better to day.[598]

Sunday 25th. There was a cloudy morning, and some light showers of rain fell. Five more hunters went out to day. In the evening yesterday two of the natives brought an Indian to our camp, who had lost the use of his limbs, to see if the officers could cure him, and to day we gave him a sweat.—Our interpreter's child has been very sick, but is getting better.[599] In the afternoon the two hunters who went out yesterday returned; but had not killed any thing. The weather became clear and we had a fine evening, and three more hunters went out.

Monday 26th. This day was fine and pleasant, and we finished our canoe and put her into the water.[600]—In the afternoon two hunters came in, but had not killed any thing: they had procured some roots at a village about fourteen miles up the river. Our stock of provisions is exhausted, and we have nothing to eat but some roots, which we get from the natives at a very dear rate.

Tuesday 27th. The morning was fair and pleasant, and several of our men went to the villages around us to procure roots. These roots are a good diet, but in general we do not relish them so well as meat. We therefore killed another horse to day, which one of the natives gave us sometime ago for that purpose. He was so wild and vicious that we could not manage him, or do any thing with him.

Our sick man is getting some better, and the interpreter's child is recovering fast. The Indian, that we have under cure, had another sweat to day;[601] and our horses, that have had the quieting operation performed on them are all mending. In the afternoon some rain fell, and three of our hunters came in, and brought with them five deer, they had killed:[+] three men also came in from the villages and brought a good supply of roots; six yet remained out.[602]

Wednesday 28th. There was a cloudy foggy morning. Some hunters went out this morning, and in the afternoon three of them came in with eight deer;[+] at the same time three more of our men returned from the villages.[603]

Thursday 29th. The morning was cloudy and wet, and the river is rising very fast; which gives us hopes that the snow is leaving the mountains. At 10 o'clock the river ceased rising and the weather became clear.[604]

Friday 30th. The morning was fine, with a little fog. Two of our men in a canoe attempting to swim their horses over the river, struck the canoe against a tree, and she immediately sunk; but they got on shore, with the loss of three blankets, a blanket-coat, and some articles of merchandize they had with them to exchange for roots.[605] The loss of these blankets is the greatest which hath [*sic*] happened to any individuals since we began our voyage, as there are only three men in the party, who have more than a blanket a piece. The river is so high that the trees stand some distance in the water. In the afternoon one of our hunters came in, who with another had killed three deer, which one of them stayed to take care of as their horses had left them.[606+]

Saturday 31st. We had a fine clear morning with a heavy dew. The hunters went out with two horses for the venison; and two men went over the river to the villages. About noon a deer was seen swimming the river and some of our men killed it. Our canoe still lies under water at the opposite shore, but we have a small Indian canoe, that serves to cross in. In the afternoon the two men came from the village with some of the natives, and one of our old stock of horses, which is the last, except the two which they assure us the old Snake guide took. In the evening the weather became cloudy, and we had some rain with sharp thunder and lightening. The two hunters came in with the venison.[+]

Sunday 1st June, 1806. We had a fine morning after some light showers of rain during the night.—Since last evening the river rose eighteen inches. Two hunters went out this morning, and some of the natives came to see us.[607] The sick Indian is getting much better. The officers got some bear-skins from the Indians, that are almost as white as a blanket. They say that the bears from which they get these skins are a harmless kind, and not so bold and ferocious as the grizly and brown bear.

Monday 2nd. The morning was cloudy, and six of the men went out to hunt. About noon three men, who had gone over to Lewis's river, about two and an half days' journey distant, to get some fish, returned with a few very good salmon, and some roots which they bought at the different villages of the natives, which they passed.[608] One of these men[609] got two Spanish dollars from an Indian for an old razor.—They said they got the dollars from about a Snake Indian's neck, they had killed some time ago. There are several dollars among these people which they get in some way. We suppose the Snake Indians, some of whom do not live very far from New Mexico, get them from the Spaniards in that quarter. The Snake Indians also get horses from the Spaniards.—The men had a very disagreeable trip as the roads were mountainous and slippery. They saw a number of deer, and of the ibex or big-horn.

Tuesday 3rd. This was a cloudy morning with a few drops of rain; and there were some light showers during the forenoon at intervals. The river rises in the night and falls in the day time; which is occasioned by the snow melting by the heat of the sun on the mountains, which are too distant for the snow water to reach this place until after night. In the evening three hunters came in with the meat of five deer and a small bear.⁺ Several of the natives continued at our camp.

Wednesday 4th. It rained slowly almost all last night, and for some time this morning. The river fell considerably yesterday, and in the night rose only an inch and an half. At noon one of our hunters came in with two deer he had killed.⁺ The afternoon was clear and pleasant.

Thursday 5th. There was a fine pleasant morning with heavy dew. In the afternoon four hunters came in with the meat of five more deer, and a bear.⁺ An Indian came with them, who had been part of the way over the mountains; but found the road too bad and the snow too deep to cross; so we are obliged to remain where we are sometime longer.

Friday 6th. The morning was pleasant, and Capt. Clarke and five of the party went over the river to buy some roots at the villages, and in the evening returned with a good supply accompanied by some of the natives.

Saturday 7th. We had a cloudy morning with a few drops of rain. I went over with five of our party to the village, on the other side of the river;[610] and while we were going some snow fell. The greater part of the natives were out hunting. In the evening we all returned to camp, except two, who remained at the village. Some of the natives again came to visit us, one of whom gave a horse to one of our men, who is very fond of conversing with them and of learning their language.[611]

Sunday 8th. There was a pleasant morning; and our two men came over from the village, and a hunter, who had been out, returned without killing any thing. Several of the natives still stay about our camp, and are of opinion we cannot cross the mountains for some time yet. We, however, mean to remove a short distance to where the hunting is better.[612]

Monday 9th. This was a fine pleasant day. We caught all our horses and hoppled them, so that we might get them easily to-morrow. We also exchanged some mares with young colts, and some of the horses who had not got quite well, for others more capable of bearing the fatigue of crossing the mountains.

Tuesday 10th. We collected all our horses, but one,[613] and set out accompanied by several of the natives, travelled about twelve miles and arrived at what we call the Com-mas flat, where we first met the natives after crossing the Rocky Mountains last fall. Here we encamped and some hunters went out. The com-mas grows in great abundance on this plain; and at this time looks beautiful, being in full bloom with flowers of a pale blue colour.[614]—At night our hunters came in and had killed one deer.⁺

Wednesday 11th. We had a fine morning with some white frost. Several of the men turned out to hunt; and returned at noon, having killed a bear and two deer.⁺ In this plain there are the most strawberry vines I ever saw, and now all in blossom. This plain contains about two thousand acres, and is surrounded with beautiful pine timber of different kinds. The soil is very good; the underwood among the timber chiefly service-berry and gooseberry bushes. In the evening several of the men started, with an intention of encamping out to hunt; and one went back to our late camp to look for the horse, which had been left behind. The natives all left us and we remained in quietness by ourselves.

Thursday 12th.[615] We had a fine lovely morning with a heavy dew. I went out with some of the party to hunt; about 8 o'clock the musquitoes became very troublesome; and at 10 we all came in without any success. About the same time the man, who had gone back for the horse returned with him.[616] About an hour after four hunters, who had been out during the night came in; three of them had been without success, but the other brought in two deer.[+] There are a good many deer here, and some bears, but they are very wild, as they are much pursued by the natives. There is no game of any other kind, except squirrels and some other small animals. The squirrels are about the size of our common grey squirrels, and very handsome. They are of a brown grey colour, beautifully speckled with small brown spots, and burrow in the ground. We killed several of them since we came to this camp. The magpie is also plenty here, and woodpeckers of a different kind from any I had before seen. They are about the size of a common red-headed woodpecker; but are all black except the belly and neck, where the ends of the feathers are tipped with a deep red, but this tipping extends to so short a distance on the feathers, that at a distance the bird looks wholly black. In the afternoon one of the natives came to our camp,[617] and one of the two hunters that were out, returned but had killed nothing. In the evening some hunters went out with intention to stay all night. The Indian who came to our camp said he had a notion to cross the mountains with us.

Friday 13th. There was a fine morning, and a hunter or two went out. The Indian exchanged horses with one of our men, whose horse had not recovered, and was unable to cross the mountains; and then went home to the village. At noon two of our men took their loads and went on ahead about eight miles to a small prairie to hunt until we should come up. During the afternoon the men who went out yesterday to hunt returned with eight deer.[+] In the evening the weather became cloudy. The musquitoes are very troublesome.

Saturday 14th. We had a cloudy morning. Some hunters again went out; at 10 o'clock one came in with a deer;[+] and in the evening the rest of them, but they had not killed any thing.

Sunday 15th. This was a cloudy wet morning with some thunder. We left Com-mas flat to attempt to cross the mountains; and had sixty-six horses, all very good. We ascended a high mount with a good deal of difficulty, as the path was very slippery, but got over safe to a small prairie, where the two men, who had gone on ahead had killed two deer and hung them up.[+] We took the meat, proceeded down the hill and found the hunters who had killed another deer.[+] We halted at a creek and took dinner; then proceeded over a very difficult road on account of the fallen timber. We had rain at intervals during the forenoon, but the afternoon was clear. We encamped in a small glade where there was plenty of grass for the horses.

Monday 16th. We had a pleasant morning, and renewed our journey; went up a handsome creek about three miles, and then took to the hills which are very rough with a great many banks of snow, some of them four or five feet deep.[618] These banks are so closely packed and condensed, that they carry our horses, and are all in a thawing state. We halted for dinner at a handsome stream where there was some grass for our horses; and in about two hours proceeded on again, and had some rain. In the afternoon we found the snow banks more numerous, extensive and deep: in some of them the snow was as much as eight feet deep. In the evening we came to Hungry creek (where Capt. Clarke killed a horse last fall and left it for the party) and encamped, that our horses might get some grass as we do not expect they will get any soon again; and there is not much here.

Tuesday 17th. There was a cloudy morning, but without rain. We early continued our march; took down Hungry creek about six miles, and then took up a large mountain. When we got about half way up the mountain the ground was entirely covered with snow three feet deep; and as we ascended it still became deeper, until we arrived at the top, where it was twelve or fifteen feet deep; but it in general carried our horses. Here there was not the appearance of a green shrub, or any thing for our horses to subsist on; and we know it cannot be better for four days march even could we find the road or course, which appears almost impossible, without a guide perfectly acquainted with the mountains. We therefore halted to determine what was best to be done, as it appeared not only imprudent but highly dangerous to proceed without a guide of any kind. After remaining about two hours we concluded it would be most adviseable to go back to some place where there was food for our horses. We therefore hung up our loading on poles, tied to and extended between trees, covered it all safe with deer skins, and turned back melancholy and disappointed.[619] At this time it began to rain; and we proceeded down to Hungry creek again; went up it about two miles, and encamped for the night where our horses could get something to eat. The grass and plants here are just putting out, and the shrubs budding. It rained hard during the afternoon.

Wednesday 18th. The morning was cloudy and several showers of rain fell during the day. We started about 8 o'clock, and found the road very slippery and bad. Two men[620] went on ahead to the village to enquire for a guide, and two more remained to look for two horses that could not be found. We proceeded on with four men in front to cut some bushes out of the path; but did not go far till one of the men cut himself very badly with a large knife;[621] when we had to halt and bind up his wound. We again went forward, and in crossing the creek the horse of one of our men fell with him, threw him off, hurt his leg and lost his blanket.[622] We halted for dinner at the same place where we dined on the 16th and had a gust of rain, hail, thunder and light-ening, which lasted an hour, when the weather cleared and we had a fine afternoon. We continued our march till we came to a small glade on the branch of a creek, where we encamped, and some hunters went out in the evening, we had left two men to hunt at the place where we dined. We found the musquitoes very troublesome on the creek, notwithstanding the snow is at so short a distance up the mountains. At night our hunters came to camp, having killed noth-ing; but saw some large fish in the creek, which they supposed were salmon.

Thursday 19th. This was a fine morning; some hunters went out and we agreed to stay here all day that our horses might rest and feed. At 10 o'clock our hunters came in and had killed a deer.[+] Two men are trying to take some of the fish with a gig. At noon the two men who had been left at Hungry creek to look for the horses came up, but had not found them: and with them the two hunters, who were left at the place we dined yesterday, and had killed two deer.[+] In the evening one of the large fish was caught, which we found to be a salmon-trout.

Friday 20th. There was a fine morning; we caught six of the salmon-trout; and some hunters went out. About 9 o'clock one of them returned and had killed a brown bear.[+] The musquitoes and gnats are very troublesome. In the evening the other hunters came in and had killed only one deer.[+]

CHAP. XXII.

Saturday 21st [June 1806]. We had again a fine morning; and we collected our horses in order to return to the Com-mas flat. We proceeded on to a creek, where we met two young Indians, who said they were come [*sic*] to go over the mountains with us. We halted here for dinner; after which, all our party proceeded on to Com-mas flat, except myself and two men who remained here to hunt.[623] We wish to kill as much meat as will serve the party, until we get back where our loading was left, as we have plenty of roots there to serve us over the mountains. One of our best horses got snagged to day, and was left here.[624] The two Indians remained with us, and in the evening one of the men killed a deer.[+]

Sunday 22nd. We had a pleasant day. The two hunters went out early and the Indians remained with me at the camp. At noon the hunters came in, but had killed nothing but one small pheasant.[625] In the evening they made another excursion, but were unsuccessful.

Monday 23rd. We had again a fine morning; and the men went out to hunt. While they were out the two Indians went on. About 10 o'clock the hunters came in without having killed any thing; and at noon two men came to our camp with orders for four of us to follow the Indians, if they were gone, until we should overtake them, and get them to halt if possible, till the party should come up; but if not, to follow them on and blaze the way after them; as the man who had gone to inquire for a guide had not returned, and it was not known whether he would get one or not.[626] The men said they had had good luck at the Com-mas flat, having killed ten deer and three bears. I immediately started with three of the men after the Indians, leaving one to take care of the camp, and the lame horse and some more that were there. We proceeded on till we came to the creek where we had stayed the 19th and 20th, and overtook the Indians encamped there, and encamped with them.

They had caught two salmon-trout since they came to this camp; and shortly after we came one of our men killed a duck; and we remained together during the night.

Tuesday 24th. There was a cloudy morning. We gave each of the Indians a pair of mockasons, and they agreed to stay to day and wait for the party.—One of our hunters went out, but had no success. The day keeps cloudy, and the musquitoes are very troublesome. There is also a small black fly in this country, that so torments our horses, that they can get no rest, but when we make small fires to keep them off. At noon two hunters went on ahead to a small creek, to endeavour to kill some provision, as we cannot kill any here; and unless the party come up to night, I intend to go on with the Indians tomorrow morning.[627] In the evening the party arrived with three more Indians, and we all encamped together for the night.[628]

Wednesday 25th. There was light shower of rain this morning. We proceeded forward early; and two men and an Indian were sent ahead to look for the horses we left behind when we were here before.[629] At noon we halted at the creek where the two men were hunting, but they had killed nothing. We here took dinner, and proceeded on to Hungry creek, where we met the men with the horses, and encamped for the night. A considerable quantity of rain had fallen during the afternoon.

Thursday 26th We had a foggy morning; proceeded on early; and found the banks of snow much decreased: at noon we arrived at the place where we had left our baggage and stores. The snow here had sunk twenty inches. We took some dinner, but there was nothing for our horses to eat. We measured the depth of the snow here and found it ten feet ten inches. We proceeded over some very steep tops of the mountains and deep snow; but the snow was not so deep in the drafts between them; and fortunately we got in the evening to the side of the hill where the snow was gone; and there was very good grass for our horses. So we encamped there all night. Some heavy showers of rain had fallen in the afternoon.

Friday 27th. We had a cloudy morning and at 8 o'clock we renewed our march, proceeding over some of the steepest mountains I ever passed. The snow is so deep that we cannot wind along the sides of these steeps, but must slide straight down. The horses generally do not sink more than three inches in the snow; but sometimes they break through to their bellies. We kept on without halting to about 5 o'clock in the evening, when we stopped at the side of a hill where the snow was off, and where there was a little grass; and we here encamped for the night. The day was pleasant throughout; but it appeared to me somewhat extraordinary, to be travelling over snow six or eight feet deep in the latter end of June. The most of us, however, had saved our socks as we expected to find snow on these mountains.

Saturday 28th. The morning was pleasant, we set out early, and passed the place where we had encamped on the 15th Sept. last when the snow fell on us. After passing this place about a mile, we took a left hand path, and travelled along high ridges till noon, when we came to a good place of grass; where we halted and remained all the afternoon to let our horses feed, as they had but little grass last night. Some hunters went out, as we saw some elk signs here, and our meat is exhausted. We still have a good stock of roots, which we pound and make thick soup of, that eats very well. In the evening our hunters came in but had not killed any thing. On the south side of this ridge there is summer with grass and other herbage in abundance; and on the north side, winter with snow six or eight feet deep.

Sunday 29th. There was a foggy morning. We set out early, proceeded over some bad hills, and came to the old path; at which time there was a shower of rain, with hail, thunder and lightening, that lasted about an hour. At 10 o'clock we left the snow, and in the evening we arrived at the warm spring; where we encamped for the night, and most of us bathed in its water.[630] One of our hunters killed a deer where we dined at the glades or plains on Glade creek; and where there is good grass, and com-mas also grows. Two other hunters went on ahead and killed another deer on the way.[631+]

Monday 30th. We continued our march early and had a fine morning. When we were ready to set out, we saw a deer coming to a lick at the hot spring, and one of our hunters shot it.[+] Two hunters went on ahead. At noon another went out a short time, and killed a fine deer.[+] We halted for dinner at the same place, where we dined on the 12th of Sept. 1805, as we passed over to the Western ocean. After dinner we proceeded on, and on our way found three deer that one of the hunters had killed and left for us.[+] In the evening we arrived at Travellers'-rest creek, where the party rested two days last fall, and where it empties into Flathead (called Clarke's) river, a beautiful river about one hundred yards wide at this place; but there is no fish of any consequence in it; and according to the Indian account, there are falls on it, between this place and its mouth, where it empties into the Columbia, six or seven hundred feet high; and which probably prevent the fish from coming up. Here we encamped and met with the hunters.

Tuesday 1st July, 1806. We had a fine morning, and remained here[632] to rest ourselves and horses after the severe fatigue of coming over the mountains, and some hunters went out. The Indians still continue with us.[633] Here the party is to be separated; some of us are to go straight across to the falls of the Missouri and some to the head waters of Jefferson river, where we left the canoes. At the falls we expect to be subdivided, as Capt. Lewis, myself and four or five men intend to go up Maria's river as far as the 50th degree of latitude; and a party to remain at the falls to prepare harness and other things necessary for hauling our canoes and baggage over the portage.—Perhaps Capt. Clarke, who goes up the river here, may also take a party and go down the Riviere Jaune, or Yellow-stone river.[634] In the afternoon our hunters came in, and had killed twelve deer, most of them in good order.

Wednesday 2nd. We continued here during this day, which was fine and pleasant, fixing our loading and making other arrangements for our separation. One of our hunters went out and killed two deer.[+]— The musquitoes are very troublesome at this place.[635]

CHAP. XXIII.

Thursday 3rd [July 1806]. We had again a fine morning, collected our horses and set out. Captain Lewis and his party went down Clarke's river,[636] and Captain Clarke with the rest of the party went up it. All the natives accompanied Captain Lewis. We proceeded on down Clarke's river about 12 miles, when we came to the forks; and made three rafts to carry ourselves and baggage over. The river here is about 150 yards wide, and very beautiful. We had to make three trips with our rafts, and in the evening got all over safe; when we moved on up the north branch, which is our way over the falls of the Missouri, and after travelling a mile and an half encamped for the night. Two hunters went out and killed three deer. The musketoes are worse here than I have known them at any place, since we left the old Maha village on the Missouri. This north branch of the river is called by the natives Isquet-co-qual-la, which means, the road to the buffaloe.*

Friday 4th. We had a beautiful morning and waited here some time in order to have a morning hunt, as our guides intend to return, and we wish to give them a plentiful supply of provisions to carry them back over the mountains. While our hunters were out a young Indian came to our camp, who had crossed the mountains after us. At 10 o'clock our hunters came in, but had not killed any thing. We were, however, able to furnish them with two deer and an half, from those that were killed yesterday. We then gave them some presents and took a friendly leave of them: and it is but justice to say, that the whole nation to which they belong, are the most friendly, honest and ingenuous people that we have seen in the course of our voyage and travels. After taking our farewell of these good hearted, hospitable and obliging sons of the west,[637] we proceeded on up Isquet-co-qual-la through a handsome prairie of about 10 miles, after which the hills come close on the river, on both sides, and we had a rough

---

*The rout taken by Captain Lewis and his party is the direct road to the falls of the Missouri, mentioned in Captain Clarke's letter [in Donald Jackson, *Letters of the Lewis and Clark Expedition*, vol. 2, Urbana: University of Illinois Press, 1962, letter 208]; that taken by Captain Clarke and his party leads to the head waters of the main branch of the Missouri, which they ascended in their outward bound voyage, and which is a considerable distance south of the direct course from the falls to the crossing place of the great chain of Rocky Mountains.

road to pass. Having made 18 miles we encamped for the night; where the country is very mountainous on both sides of the river, which runs nearly east and west, and is a deep rapid stream about 80 yards wide.[638]

Saturday 5th. We had another beautiful morning, set out early and proceeded on the same course as yesterday through a rough country, with a number of branches or small streams flowing from the hills. We killed one deer⁺and about 11 o'clock came to a valley three quarters of a mile wide, all plains, where we halted to dine and to let our horses feed. The hills upon each side are handsomely covered with timber of the fir kind. While we rested here one of our hunters killed a cabre or antelope. At 1 o'clock we proceeded on again up the valley. When we had gone about nine miles we came to and crossed a river, about 35 yards wide, which flows in with a rapid current from some snow topped mountains on the north, where the valley is two or three miles wide.[639] Having gone about four miles further we came to the head of the valley, where the hills come close upon the river for two miles. After we had passed these narrows we came to another large and beautiful valley four or fives miles wide, and all plains, except some timber on the river banks. In the evening we encamped on the bank of a handsome creek which comes in from the north, a bold stream of 15 yards wide.

Sunday 6th. We had a fine clear morning with some white frost, and renewed our journey early; saw a great many service berries, not yet ripe, and some flax which grows on these plains. Having gone about seven miles we crossed a north branch of the Co-qual-la-isquet, which is 40 yards wide and was mid-rib deep on our horses, with a rapid current. About seven miles up the valley we passed a beautiful small lake; where the river and road leaves the valley, and bears towards the northeast between two hills not very large. We kept up the river, through a small brushy valley about the [*sic*] eighth of a mile wide, for a mile and an half, and then halted for dinner. Here our two hunters came to us, and had killed a deer. We keep two men out every day hunting. In this small valley there is a considerable quantity of cotton wood timber; and the musketoes are very troublesome. At 1 o'clock we proceeded on, passed a number of handsome streams which fall into the river, and a number of old Indian lodges. As we advance the valley becomes more extensive, and is all plain. At night we encamped on a beautiful creek, having travelled twenty five miles. Our hunters killed four deer to day.[640]

Monday 7th. We had a wet night, and a cloudy morning. Continued our journey early along the valley, which is very beautiful with a great deal of clover in its plains. Having gone about five miles, we crossed the main branch of the river, which comes in from the north; and up which the road goes about five miles further and then takes over a hill towards the east. On the top of this hill there are two beautiful ponds, of about three acres in size. We passed over the ridge and struck a small stream, which we at first thought was of the head waters of the Missouri, but found it was not. Here we halted for dinner, and after staying three hours, proceeded on four miles up the branch, when we came to the dividing ridge between the waters of the Missouri and Columbia; passed over the ridge and came to a fine spring the waters of which run into the Missouri.[641] We then kept down this stream or branch about a mile; then turned a north course along the side of the dividing ridge for eight miles, passing a number of small streams or branches, and at 9 o'clock at night en- camped after coming thirty two miles.[642]

Tuesday 8th. The morning was pleasant with some white frost. We started early and proceeded on nearly north; saw several deer, cabre and wolves in the plains, and after going three miles and an half passed torrent creek, a large creek that runs into Medicine river. Shortly after we passed this creek we went off the path or trail, travelled straight across the plains, and in about fifteen miles struck Medicine river, close above the forks where we halted for dinner; and one of our hunters killed a deer and a cabre.[+] In the afternoon we proceeded down Medicine river nine miles; and having come in the whole to day twenty eight miles encamped for the night; and found the musketoes very troublesome.[643]

Wednesday 9th. A cloudy morning. We set out early to go down the river; but had not proceeded far until it began to rain, and we halted at some old Indian lodges, where we took shelter. In an hours time the rain slackened, and we proceeded on; but had not gone far before it began to rain again, and the weather was very cold for the season. At noon we came up with our hunters, who had killed a large buffaloe;[+] so we halted and some of us went and dressed it, and brought in the best of the meat which was very good. We encamped here and lay by during the afternoon as the rain continued during the whole of it.[644]

Thursday 10th. At dark last evening the weather cleared up, and was cold all night. This morning was clear and cold, and all the mountains in sight were covered with snow, which fell yesterday and last night.[*] At 8 o'clock we started down the river, and in the

---

[*] It will not be a subject of surprize that snow should fall here in the middle of summer, when the elevation of this part of the country, which divides the eastern from the western waters, is taken into view. Every person will be able to comprehend, that no small degree of elevation, above its mouth, will be sufficient to give so rapid a course to the Missouri for upwards of 3000 miles, even supposing there were no great falls or cataracts.

course of the day our hunters killed five deer, two elk and a bear.[645+]
The road was a very muddy [sic] after the rain. The country on both
sides is composed of beautiful plains; the river about 80 yards wide
and tolerably straight, with some cotton wood timber on its banks;
and plenty of game of different kinds ranging through the plains.
Having made 24 miles we encamped for the night.[646]

Friday 11th. This was a fine morning and we set out early to
cross the point, and having gone eight miles, came to the Missouri
at the Bear islands, nearly opposite our old encampment. Here our
hunters, in a short time, killed five buffaloe; and we saved the best
of the meat; and of the skinsmade [sic] two canoes to transport ourselves and baggage across the river. The buffaloe are in large droves
about this place.

Saturday 12th. Again a fine morning. We went out to collect our
horses and found that ten of them were missing. I then set out to
look for them, went seven miles up Medicine river, where I found
three of them and returned to camp. Two more went to hunt for
them, and the rest of us crossed the river in our new craft which we
find answer [sic] the purpose very well. At night one of the men
returned without finding the lost horses.[647]

Sunday 13th. The morning was pleasant, and we moved about a
mile up to our old encampment; opened a deposit we had made here
and found some things spoiled; and the other man that went to look
for the horses not being returned we remained here all day airing
and sunning the baggage and stores. The musketoes torment us very
much, and the wolves continually howl night and day around our
camp.[648]

Monday 14th. There was a pleasant morning.—We staid here
also to day; and the musketoes continued to torment us until about
noon, when a fine breeze of wind arose and drove them, for a while
away. We deposited the most valuable part of our baggage and stores
on a large island so that if the Indians came they would not get it.

Tuesday 15th. We had pleasant weather. One of our men started
to go down to the other end of the portage, to see if the periogue was
safe, which we had left there; and in the afternoon the man who had
gone after the horses returned unsuccessful; but as he saw some
fresh Indian signs he supposes they were stolen and taken back over
the dividing ridge. Capt. Lewis therefore concluded to take fewer
men and horses with him than he had intended on his excursion up
Maria's river.[649] In the evening the man who had started to go to the

An American having struck a Bear but not killed him, escapes into a Tree.

other end of the portage, returned without being there. A white bear met him at Willow creek, that so frightened his horse, that he threw him off among the feet of the animal; but he fortunately (being too near to shoot) had sufficient presence of mind to hit the bear on the head with his gun; and the stroke so stunned it, that it gave him time to get up a tree close by before it could seize him. The blow, however, broke the gun and rendered it useless; and the bear watched him about three hours and went away; when he came down, caught his horse about two miles distant and returned to camp.[650] These bears are very numerous in this part of the country and very dangerous, as they will attack a man every opportunity.

Wednesday 16th. There was a fine morning. We collected our horses, of which Capt. Lewis took six and left four to haul the canoes and baggage over the portage; and then started to go up Maria's river with only three hunters.[651] We continued here to repair our waggons or truckles to transport the baggage and canoes on when the men with them should arrive.—The musquitoes are still very troublesome.

When Capt. Lewis left us,[652] he gave orders that we should wait at the mouth of Maria's river to the 1st of Sept. at which time, should he not arrive, we were to proceed on and join Capt. Clarke at the mouth of the Yellow-stone river, and then to return home: but informed us, that should his life and health be preserved he would meet us at the mouth of Maria's river on the 5th of August.

Thursday 17th. We had a pleasant day, and high wind; which drives away the musquitoes and relieves us from those tormenting insects.

Friday 18th. There was another pleasant day, and I went down with three of the men to the lower end of the portage to examine the periogue and deposit there, and found all safe. We took some tobacco out of the deposit, covered up all again, until the party should arrive with the canoes, and returned to camp.[653]

Saturday 19th. The weather continues pleasant and most of the men are employed in dressing skins, as we have got all ready for crossing the portage as soon as the canoes arrive.[654] The musquitoes were very troublesome to day. At 3 o'clock in the afternoon a sergeant and nine men arrived at our camp with the canoes and some baggage.[655] They informed me that they had a good passage over the mountains to the Missouri; and on their way saw a boiling-hot spring, which in twenty-five minutes would boil meat put into it quite well and fit for eating.—This spring is on the head waters of Wisdom river. They had got to the canoe-deposit on the 8th instant and found every thing safe: the whole party then came down to the forks at the mouth of Jefferson river; where Capt. Clarke with ten men and the interpreter left them and went up Gallatin's river in order to cross over to the Jaune, or Yellow-stone river. They had plenty of provisions all the way. In the evening we hauled the canoes out to dry.

Sunday 20th. We had a fine day; but the musquitoes were very bad. We concluded to stay here all day, as the men, who had come with the canoes, were fatigued; and in the evening tried our horses in harness and found they would draw very well.[656]

Monday 21st. A pleasant morning. One of the men went out for the horses; and the rest of us put two canoes on the waggons, and moved them forward by hand some distance, when the man returned without finding the horses. Two more then went out to look for them, and at noon came back without finding them. In the afternoon some more men went to look for them, who at night returned also without seeing any thing of them; and we lay where the canoes were all night.

Tuesday 22nd. We had a fine morning. Eight of us started in various directions to look for the horses, and in a short time two of the men found them; harnessed them in the waggons and moved on about four miles, when one of the axletrees broke; and they returned to the river to mend it. Myself and one of the men did not return till dark, and then came to the place where the canoes were upon the plains, with some of the men. Here a heavy shower of rain came on with thunder and lightening; and we remained at this place all night.[657]

Wednesday 23rd. There was a pleasant morning after the rain; and I went with the man who came with me last night, and joined the party at the river. They had repaired the waggons and put on two more canoes; one of which was very large and gave us a great deal of trouble, as we could not make axletrees out of the willow that would stand more than six or eight miles. At 5 o'clock we got to Willow creek, and encamped for the night; and made a new axletree. In our way to day one of the men cut his leg very bad with a knife,[658] which so lamed him that he had to ride in one of the canoes.

Thursday 24th. This was a cloudy morning. I was very much indisposed last night and am yet very unwell. I therefore staid at this camp, and the party went back for two more canoes. About 3 o'clock one of the waggons with a canoe arrived; and the party with it; having let the horses feed a while, and taken dinner, they proceeded on to Portage river. About an hour after they started a very heavy shower of rain, accompanied with thunder and lightning, came on, and lasted about an hour and an half. After this we had a fine evening, and a little before sunset the other waggon with a canoe arrived; when we encamped for the night. The man who cut his leg is still very lame and continues at this camp.[659]

Friday 25th. This was a fine morning with very heavy dew. The party set out early to Portage river with the canoe; and in a short time the men with the other waggon came back; I was by this time so much recovered as to be able to return with the party for another canoe; which is all we will bring over, as the other is very heavy and injured; and we expect that the five small ones with the periogues will be sufficient to carry ourselves and baggage down the Missouri. About 2 o'clock the waggons met at Willow creek, when we had another very heavy shower of rain accompanied with thunder and lightning. At 3 o'clock we set out with both the waggons and 2 canoes to Portage river; it rained on us hard all the way, and the road was so muddy that the horses were not able to haul the loads, without

Captain Lewis shooting an Indian.

the assistance of every man at the waggons. At night we arrived at Portage river, and then had four canoes there safe.

Saturday 26th. The morning was cloudy. Eight of us went back to Willow creek for the other canoe, and the rest of the party were employed in taking down the canoes and baggage to the lower end of the portage, where the periogue had been left.[660] It rained very hard all night, which has made the plains so muddy, that it is with the greatest difficulty we can get along with the canoe; though in the evening, after a hard day's labour, we got her safe to Portage river, and the men run her down to the lower landing place, where we encamped. A few drops of rain fell in the course of the day.[661]

CHAP. XXIV.

Sunday 27th [July 1806]. In a fine clear pleasant morning, myself and one of the men crossed the river with the horses,[662] in order to go by land to the mouth of Maria's river: the rest of the party here are to go by water. We proceeded on through the plains about twenty miles, and in our way saw a great many buffaloe. We then struck Tansy or Rose river, which we kept down about ten miles and encamped. The land along this river is handsomely covered with Cotton wood timber and there is an abundance of game of different kinds. In our way we killed a buffaloe and a goat.[663+] The wolves in packs occasionally hunt these goats, which are too swift to be run down and taken by a single wolf. The wolves having fixed upon their intended prey and taken their stations, a part of the pack commence the chace [*sic*], and running it in a circle, are at certain intervals relieved by others. In this manner they are able to run a goat down. At the falls where the wolves are plenty, I had an opportunity of seeing one of these hunts.[664]

Monday 28th. The morning was fine and pleasant, and at an early hour we proceeded down the river. In our way we killed six goats or antelopes and seven buffaloe;+ and about one o'clock came to the point at the mouth of Maria's river, where we met with the party who had come down from the falls by water, and who had just arrived; and also unexpectedly with Captain Lewis and the three men who had gone with him.[665] They had joined the party descending the river this forenoon, after riding one hundred and twenty miles since yesterday morning, when they had a skirmish with a party of the Prairie Grossventres, or Bigbellied Indians who inhabit the plains up Maria's river;[666] of which they gave the following account. On the evening of the 26th Captain Lewis and his party met with eight of those Indians, who seemed very friendly and gave them two robes. In return Captain Lewis gave one of them, who was a chief, a medal; and they all continued together during the night; but after break of day the next morning, the Indians snatched up three of our men's guns and ran off with them. One Indian had the guns of two men, who pursued and caught him, and one of them killed him with his knife; and they got back the guns. Another had Captain Lewis's gun, but immediately gave it up. The Party then went to catch their horses, and found the Indians driving them off; when Captain Lewis shot one of them, and gave him a mortal wound; who notwithstanding returned the fire, but without hurting the Captain.[667] So our men got all their own horses, but one, and a number of those belonging to the Indians, as they ran off in confusion and left every thing they had. Our men then saddled their horses, and made towards the Missouri as fast as possible; after Captain Lewis had satisfied himself with respect to the geography of the country up Maria's river.

We this day took the articles out of the place of deposit, and examined the large red periogue we left here, and found it too rotten to take down the river. We therefore took what nails out of it we could, left our horses on the plains and proceeded down the river. About the time we started, a heavy gust of rain and hail accompanied with thunder and lightning came on and lasted about an hour, after which we had a cloudy wet afternoon, and in the evening we encamped about twenty five miles below the forks.[668]

Tuesday 29th. Early in a cloudy morning we commenced our voy age [*sic*] from the mouth of Maria's river; and the current of the Missouri being very swift, we went down rapidly. At noon we saw some Ibex or Bighorns at the entrance of a range of high rough hills; and we halted and killed two of them.[+] Having dined we proceeded on again, and in our way, during the afternoon, killed seven more of these mountain sheep.[+] There are few other animals in this range of high country. In the evening we encamped opposite the mouth of Slaughter river, and Captain Lewis had four of those animals skeletonized, to take with him to the seat of Government of the United States. A considerable quantity of rain fell in the course of the day.[669]

Wednesday 30th. We embarked early in a cloudy morning with some rain. In our way through this high range of mountains, we killed four more of the large horned animals, two buffaloe, two beaver and a bear.[+]

The water of the river is very thick and muddy, on account of the late falls of rain, which wash those clay hills very much. We went down the river upwards of 70 miles to day, and encamped on a prairie island. Heavy rain fell at intervals during the day.

Thursday 31st. We set out early, though it continued at intervals to rain hard; about 10 o'clock we saw a great gang of elk on a small island, where we halted and in a short time killed fifteen of them.[670] We took the skins and the best parts of the meat, and proceeded. At noon we halted to dine, and had then a very heavy shower of rain. We also killed another of the Large horned animals or mountain sheep.⁺—We remained here about an hour, then proceeded on, and will soon be clear of this range of high rough country. In our way this afternoon, we killed two mule and twelve other deer, and two beaver. Though the afternoon was wet and disagreeable, we came 70 miles to day.

Friday 1st Aug. 1806. We embarked early in a wet disagreeable morning, and in a short time saw a large brown or grizly bear swimming in the river, which we killed, and took on board;⁺ passed the mouth of Muscle shoal river; and at noon halted to dine at some old Indian lodges. Captain Lewis being afraid, from the dampness of the weather, that the skins he had procured of these big-horned animals would spoil, thought it adviseable to stay here this afternoon and dry them by a fire in these old lodges: and some of the men went out to hunt. About an hour after we landed here, a large bear came so close to our camp, that one of the men shot and killed it from our fire. In the evening our hunters came in and had killed several deer. The afternoon was cloudy with some rain; and having made a fire and put the skins to dry with two men to attend them, made our arrangements for the night.

Saturday 2nd. This was a fine clear morning, and Captain Lewis thought it best to stay here to day also and dry all our baggage, as it was become damp and wet. Two hunters were sent on in a canoe to hunt; and in the course of the day we got every thing dry and ready to set out the next morning.

Sunday 3rd. We had a fine morning, and at 6 o'clock got under way and proceeded on. Having gone ten miles we came up with the hunters who had killed twenty four deer.⁺ We went on very rapidly and saw great gangs of elk feeding on the shores, but few buffaloe. At sunset we encamped having gone 73 miles.[671]

Monday 4th. This was another pleasant day and we proceeded on early.[672] One of the small canoes with two hunters did not come up last night. We left another small canoe with some hunters behind and proceeded on.[673] We went very rapidly, and in our way killed a buffaloe, an elk and some deer.⁺ At five o'clock we passed the mouth of Milk river, which was very high and the current strong. Having proceeded 88 miles we encamped for the night.[674]

Tuesday 5th. Last night was cloudy and thunder was heard at a distance. About midnight the small canoe we left yesterday came floating down with the current, and would have passsd [*sic*] us if our centinel had not hailed it: the hunters in it killed a bear and two deer.[+] This morning was also cloudy, and we halted here till noon in expectation that the other canoe would come down; but there was then no appearance of it; and we began to suspect it had passed in the night. The forenoon had become clear and pleasant, and at noon we got under way. As we went on we killed a very fat buffaloe and some deer; and two hunters who went on ahead in the morning killed two very large brown bears.[+] At sunset we encamped and at dark a violent gust of wind and rain came on with thunder and lightening, which lasted about an hour; after which we had a fine clear night.

Wednesdny [sic] 6th. We embarked early, and had a fine morning, but high wind. At 12 o'clock the wind blew so violent that it became dangerous to go on, and we halted; and some of the men went out and shot a large buck, but not dead and he got into the river; when two of them pursued in a canoe and caught him. Having remained here three hours, we again went on until night and encamped. We have yet seen nothing of the two hunters who had been left behind in the small canoe.

Thursday 7th. The morning was cloudy, and we set out early, after a very heavy shower of rain which fell before day light. We proceeded on very well, and about 4 o'clock arrived at the mouth of the Yellow Stone river. We found that Captain Clarke had been encamped on the point some time ago, and had left it. We discovered nothing to inform us where he was gone, except a few words written or traced in the sand, which were *"W. C. a few miles further down on the right hand side."* Captain Lewis having left a few lines for the two men in the canoe, to inform them, if they are still behind, where we were gone, we continued our voyage. At night we encamped after coming above 100 miles; and though dark, killed a fat buffaloe at the place of our encampment.

Friday 8th. We had a fine clear cool morning with some white frost; proceeded on early and in a short time past one of Captain Clarke's camps. At nine o'clock we halted to repair the periogue, and to dress some skins to make ourselves clothing. The musquitoes are more troublesome here than at any place since we left the falls of the Missouri. A party of men went out to hunt and killed some elk and deer;[+] the rest were employed in dressing deer and cabre skins.[675]

Saturday 9th. This was another fine day; and most of the men were employed as yesterday; and in making small oars for our canoes. Two of them went over the river and killed an elk aud [sic] a deer.[+]

Sunday 10th. We had a fine morning and were employed in repairing the periogue and dressing skins, until 3 o'clock in the afternoon, when we got the periogue completed, loaded our craft, and at four o'clock proceeded on to the mouth of White-earth river, and encamped opposite it on the same bottom, where we encamped on the 21st April 1805. In the afternoon some drops of rain fell; and the musquitoes here were very bad indeed.

Monday 11th. The morning was pleasant; and we set out early; passed Captain Clarke's encampment of the night of the 8th Instant, and proceeded on to the burnt bluffs, where we saw a gang of elk feeding. The canoes were then sent to shore with a party of men to endeavour to kill some of them; and we proceeded on with the periogue. In about a half a mile further we saw another gang; when we halted and Captain Lewis and one of the men went out after them. In a short time Captain Lewis returned wounded and very much alarmed; and ordered us to our arms, supposing he had been shot at by Indians. Having prepared for an attack, I went out with three men to reconnoitre and examine the bushes, which are very thick at this place, and could see no Indians; but after some time met with the man who went out with Captain Lewis, and found on inquiry that he had shot him by accident through the hips, and without knowing it pursued the game.—[676] Having made this discovery we returned to the periouge [*sic*]; examined and dressed Captain Lewis's wound; and found the ball, which had lodged in his overalls. The canoes having come down, we proceeded on, after dressing two elk that had been killed at this place, and passed an encampment which Captain Clarke had left in the morning. We found a note here informing us, that the Indians had stolen all the horses which he had sent with a serjeant[677] and party, from Yellow Stone river, and that the serjeant with the party came down in skin canoes and met him at this place. We then proceeded on some distance and encamped.

Tuesday 12th. The morning was pleasant and we proceeded on. Captain Lewis is in good spirits; but his wound stiff and sore. Having gone about nine miles we met with two men on the river trapping and hunting.[678] Captain Lewis gave them some ammunition, and directions with respect to the river above. They informed us that Captain Clarke and party had passed them yesterday at noon. We proceeded on and at 10 o'clock overtook Captain Clarke and his party, all in good health. The two men with the small canoe, who had been some time absent, came down and joined at the place where we met with the two strangers: and now, (thanks to God)[679] we are all together again in good health, except Captain Lewis, and his wound is not dangerous.

After the Corps were seperated [*sic*] among the mountains, as before mentioned, Captain Clarke's party proceeded on to the Canoe deposit, near the head of the main branch of the Missouri (called Jefferson's river) and having descended with the canoes to the mouth of the branch, which they called Gallatin, Captain Clarke with ten men left those, who were to take down the canoes to the falls; travelled three days up Gallatin's river towards the south, when they crossed a ridge and came upon the waters of the Jaune or Yellowstone river. Having gone about 100 miles down this river by land they made two canoes, and Captain Clarke having sent off a sergeant and three men with the horses to the Mandan villages, went down himself with six other men by water.[680] On the second day after the sergeant and his party had started for the Mandan villages, the Indians stole the whole of the horses, and the party were obliged to descend the river in skin canoes.[681] Captain Clarke's party in their rout had found game plenty of different kinds, buffaloe, elk, deer, beaver, otter and some other animals. They also found the Yellow-Stone river a pleasant and navigable stream, with a rich soil along it; but timber scarce.

We here took the men on board, and left the buffaloe canoes. At night we encamped on a sand beach, as the musketoes are not so bad there as in the woods.

Wednesday 13th. After a stormy night of wind and rain we set out early in a fine morning; about nine o'clock passed the Little Missouri and went on very well during the whole of the day. In the evening those in some of the small canoes, which were ahead, saw Indians, who fled before they could speak to them. At night we encamped opposite an old wintering village of the Grossventres, which had been deserted some time ago.

Thursday 14th. The morning of this day was pleasant, and we embarked early. In a short time we arrived near to our old friends the Grossventres and Mandans; and fixed our encam pment [*sic*] in a central position, so as to be most convenient to the different villages. The inhabitants of all the villages appeared very glad to see us, and sent us presents of corn, beans and squashes.[682]

Friday 15th. We had a fine clear pleasant morning, and continued here all day, to ascertain whether any of the chiefs would go down with us or not.—They had to hold councils among themselves, and we had to wait for their answers. The two hunters we left up the river came down, staid with us here, and got one of our party to join in partnership with them, and to return up the rivers Missouri and Jaune to hunt.[683]

Saturday 16th. There was a fine cool day; and we yet remained here, waiting an answer from the natives. Some of these Indians are very kind and obliging; furnishing us with corn, beans and squashes; but there are others very troublesome, and steal whenever they have an opportunity. Yesterday and to-day, they stole several knives and spoons; and three powder horns, and two pouches, filled with ammunition.

In the afternoon the chief, called the Big-White, concluded to go down with us, and we agreed to stay until 12 o'clock to-morrow; that he might have an opportunity to get ready for his voyage and mission.[684] The Commanding Officers gave discharges to the man who agreed to return with the hunters up the river, and the interpreter;[685] who intends settling among these Indians, and to whom they gave the blacksmith's tools; supposing they might be useful to the nation. They also gave a small piece of ordnance to the Grossventers, which they appeared very fond of.[686]

Sunday 17th. There were some flying clouds this morning, and the weather was cold for the season. The two strange hunters, with the man who had received his discharge and was to go up the river with them, went on early. We lashed our small canoes together, two and two, as we expect they will be more steady this way and carry larger loads. At noon we dropped down to the village of the Big-White: and he, his wife and a child, with Geesem the interpreter for the Big-White, his wife and two children embarked in two of our canoes to go to the United States. We proceeded on at two o'clock; the wind was high, and river rough; and in the evening we encamped having descended about twenty miles.

Monday 18th. We set out early in a cloudy morning, and the wind high. At 10 o'clock we killed two deer, when we halted for an hour and cooked some venison. In the evening we encamped, and some of the men went out and killed five or six more deer.

Tuesday 19th. This was a cloudy windy morning; and the water so rough, that our small canoes could not safely ride the waves: so we remained here and several of the men went out to hunt. We do not go on so rapidly as we did higher up the river: but having lashed our small canoes together, we go on very safe and can make fifty or sixty miles a day Captain Lewis is getting much better and we are all in good spirits. At 3 o'clock in the afternoon the wind ceased, and we proceeded on, and met with our hunters on the bank, who had killed six elk and eleven deer. We took the meat on board, proceeded on, and encamped on a sand-beach.

Wednesday 20th. We embarked early after a heavy gust of wind and rain, and proceeded on very well. The forenoon was cloudy, without rain; and in the afternoon the weather became clear and pleasant.—We went about seventy miles, and encamped; where we found the musketoes very troublesome.

Thursday 21st. We proceeded on early and had a fine morning. At 10 o'clock we arrived at the first village of the Rickarees, and halted. In our way here we met three Frenchmen in a canoe;[687] one of them a young man, who formerly belonged to the North West Company of traders, wished to go with us to the United States; which our Commanding Officers consented to and he was taken on board one of our canoes. When we halted and landed at the villages, the natives generally assembled, and Captain Clarke held a council with them; when they declared they would live in peace with all nations; but that their chiefs and warriors would not go to the United States at present, as they had sent one chief already, and he had not returned.[688] There are also a great many of the Chien, or Dog nation encamped here, in large handsome leather lodges; and who have come to trade with the Rickarees for corn and beans, for which they give in exchange buffaloe meat and robes.[689] They are a very silly superstitious people. Captain Clarke gave one of their chiefs a medal, which he gave back with a buffaloe robe, and said he was afraid of white people, and did not like to take any thing from them: but after some persuasion he accepted the medal, and we left them.* Here a Frenchman joined us to go to St. Louis, who was in the service of the Commanding Officers;[690] and we dropped down to the village on the island, and encamped for the night.

---

*We think that some further proof is necessary to establish the weakness and superstition of these Indians. Had the chief persevered in his rejection of the medal, we, instead of thinking him silly and superstitious, would have been inclined to the opinion, that he was the wisest Indian on the Missouri.

CHAP. XXV.

Friday 22nd [August 1806]. There was a cloudy wet morning, after a night of hard rain, and we stayed at this village to 12 o'clock. The natives used us friendly and with kindness; gave us corn and beans with other articles;[691] but none of them would go down with us. At noon we got under way; and having proceeded twelve miles the weather became clear, and we halted to dry our baggage, which got very wet last night. At four o'clock we again went on, and had a fine passage till night when we encamped.[692]

Saturday 23rd. We set out early in a fine morning, but the wind was high; and we went on very well till near noon, when the wind blew so hard that we had to halt, and were detained about four hours. Three hunters went on ahead by land, and when we had overtaken them they had killed two elk and some deer,[+] and we halted to take in the meat. Here we had a very heavy shower of rain, which detained us another hour. We encamped at night and found the musketoes very troublesome.

Sunday 24th. We had a fine morning, and went on very well till noon, when the wind rose and blew so strong that we were obliged to halt. Having lain by three hours we again proceeded, but did not go far before we were obliged on account of the wind, again to stop, and encamp for the night.

Monday 25th. The morning was again pleasant, and we proceeded on early, having sent forward two small canoes with five men to hunt. When we had gone twelve miles, we came to the mouth of the Chien river, where we halted and staid till noon, for the purpose of taking an observation. Some of the men went out to hunt, and while we remained here, killed three small deer.[+] At half past 12 o'clock we proceeded on again, and in a short time overtook our canoes with the hunters, that had gone on ahead, and killed three deer. In the evening we encamped in a handsome bottom, and a hunter killed another deer.[+]

Tuesday 26th. We set out early, and had a pleasant morning; passed Teeton river, but saw no signs of the Teeton band of the Sioux nation. In the evening we passed Landselle's fort; but found no persons inhabiting it.[693] At dark we encamped after coming about sixty miles.

Wednesday 27th. We again had a pleasant day and embarked early: proceeded on till we came to the upper end of the Great-bend, and there stopped to hunt.* As our hunters saw no game, we in a short time continued our voyage round the bend; at the lower end of which we killed an elk. As we were passing an island we saw a gang of buffaloe feeding on it; when we halted and killed three of them, and encamped on the island for the night.

Thursday 28th. We had another pleasant day; embarked early, and proceeded on till about 11 o'clock, when we arrived at Pleasant camp, and halted.[694] We left this camp on the 18th September 1804. The Commanding Officers wishing to procure and take down with them the skeletons of some mule deer, and cabre; and knowing that there were but few of those animals lower down the river, continued here the remainder of the day, and sent out six or eight hunters; who returned at night without finding any of the wished for animals, but killed some fat buffaloe and common deer.[+]

Friday 29th. The morning was cloudy and some hunters went on ahead very early; while we amused ourselves till 10 o'clock gathering plumbs, of which there is great abundance at this place. We then went on, and passed White river on the south side. The Missouri here is very full of sand bars and shoals, and we find difficulty in getting along. About 2 o'clock we halted to kill some buffaloe, but were unsuccessful, and we proceeded, till evening, and encamped.[695]

Saturday 30th. We had a pleasant morning, and went on early, three hunters starting ahead. We killed some buffaloe and elk in our way, and about 2 o'clock met a band of the Teetons, fifty or sixty in number, and halted on the opposite side of the river as we did not wish to have any intercourse with them. Here we waited for three hunters, who were behind; and during our stay eight or nine of the

---

*In a former geographical note (pa. 62) we stated that the place where Mr. Thompson, Astronomer to the North West Company, took his observations in the year 1798 to ascertain the latitude and longitude of the northern bend of the Missouri, was near the longitude of the Mandan villages. If what Mr Thompson called the northern bend is the same with what Mr. Gass calls the great bend (of which there appears little doubt) the longitude of the Mandan villages will be between two and three degrees west of the northern, or great bend; or in about longitude 104 degrees west of London, 29 degrees west of Philadelphia, 11 1-2 degrees west of the mouth of the Missouri, and nearly 20 degrees east of the mouth of the Columbia. This will still shew the great errors of those maps of Louisiana, which place the Mandan villages 20 degrees west of the longitude of the confluence of the Missouri and Mississippi; and less than 12 degrees east of that of the mouth of the Columbia.

Indians swam to a sand bar about sixty yards from us, and we found that they were the same rascals, who had given us trouble as went went up. We could not converse with them, but one of our men understanding the language of the Ponis, of which they understood some words; we through him let them know that we wanted to have nothing to do with them; and that if they troubled us, we would kill every one of them. They then withdrew, and the whole party left the river and went off to the hills.[696] Our three hunters returned, and we proceeded on, and in the evening encamped on a sand bar in the river.

Sunday 31st. There was a cloudy morning, after a disagreeable night of wind and hard rain. We set out early; went on very well all day, and in the evening encamped, where we found the Musketoes very troublesome.

Monday 1st Sept. 1806. This was a fine pleasant day and we set out early, and about 10 o'clock met nine of the Yonktin band of the Sioux nation of Indians on the south side of the river.[697] We halted and gave them some corn, and then proceeded on with an unfavourable wind. At night we arrived at our encampment of the 31st of August 1804, where we held a treaty with a band of the Sioux nation, and encamped for the night.

Tuesday 2nd. We had a fine morning, but high wind; set out early, and went on till noon, when we halted, and some men went out and killed two fine fat buffaloe cows;+ and brought in the best of the meat. The musketoes are very troublesome. We again started and went on about two miles, when the wind blew so violent that we had to encamp for the night, on a large sand bar, where the musketoes are not so bad, as where there are woods or bushes.[698]

Wednesday 3rd. In a pleasant morning we got early under way, and went very well all day. About 5 o'clock in the afternoon, we met a Mr. Aird, a trader, who was going up the Missouri, and we encamped with him.[699] At sunset a violent gust of wind and rain, with thunder and lightning came on and lasted two hours.

Thursday 4th. There was a cloudy morning. We exchanged some corn with Mr. Aird for tobacco, which our party stood much in need of; and his party, having lost a boat load of provisions in their way up, wanted the corn. We then proceeded on till we came to our old camp near the Maha village, where we halted to dry our baggage, which got very wet last night, and remained all night. The natives are all out in the plains.[700]

Friday 5th. This was a fine morning, and we early embarked, and went on very well, till night, when we encamped on a sand bar, where the musketoes were very troublesome.

Saturday 6th. We set out early, in a fine morning, saw a number of pelicans, and about 8 o'clock a gang of elk, when some hunters went out but returned without killing any. At 11 o'clock we met a barge belonging to a Mr. Shotto, of St. Louis, loaded with merchandize, for the purpose of trading with the Sioux nation of Indians.[701] We got some spirituous liquors from this party the first we had tasted since the 4th of July 1805, and remained with them about three hours; sent some hunters a head and proceeded on till about 3 o'clock in the afternoon, when we halted and waited for the hunters at the place agreed on to meet them, but they did not come in and we encamped for the night.

Sunday 7th. We had a pleasant morning. The hunters not having come in we left a canoe, with directions to wait till 12 o'clock for them; and proceeded on. About 9 o'clock we met with our hunters, but they had not killed any thing; and at 11 halted to hunt and wait for the canoe. In a short time we killed three elk and brought in the meat; and the canoe having come up we proceeded on, and at sunset encamped. The musquitoes are not so troublesome as they were some time ago.

Monday 8th. We again had a pleasant morning; and proceeded on early; at 10 o'clock we passed council bluffs where we held the first council with the Ottos on the 1st, 2nd, and 3rd of August 1804, and in the evening encamped on a small island, having gone on very well during the day.

Tuesday 9th. We embarked early and in a short time passed the mouth of the great river Platte; went on very well all day, and at night encamped on a sand beach opposite the Bald-pated prairie.

Wednesday 10th. We had a pleasant morning, embarked early and went on very well. At 4 o'clock P. M. we met a periogue with four men, going to trade with the Loups or Wolf Indians, who live up the river Platte. We remained with these men about an hour, got some whisky from them, and then continued our voyage.[702] In a short time we met another periogue and seven men, going to trade with the Mahas, who live on the Missouri.[703] We staid some time with these men, then proceeded and at night encamped on a willow island.

Thursday 11th. We set out early; and had a cloudy morning, and light showers of rain during the forenoon. At two in the afternoon we stopped to hunt, and soon killed two deer and a turkey:[+] then proceeded on and at sunset encamped on an island.

Friday 12th. The morning was fine and we again embarked early. In half an hour we met two periogues going up to trade; staid with them a short time and went on. About an hour after we met with a Mr. M'Clelland in a large boat with twelve men going up to trade with the Mahas. Our commanding officers were acquainted with Mr. M'Clelland, and we halted and remained with him all day, in order to get some satisfactory information from him, after our long absence from the United States. He, and two Frenchmen who were with him had severally instructions from the government to make inquiry after our party; as they were beginning to be uneasy about us.[704]

Saturday 13th. We had a pleasant morning after some rain that fell yesterday, and again proceeded on early with unfavourable wind. At 10 we halted to hunt, staid about three hours and killed four deer. We then continued our voyage to sunset and encamped. We had a few musketoes, but they were not so bad as we had found them higher up the river.

Sunday 14th. In a fine morning we proceeded on early and went very well, until 3 o'clock when we met three large batteaux loaded with merchandize, going up to different nations of Indians for the purpose of trade. The people in them were very glad to see us, and gave us some whiskey, pork, and biscuit.[705] We remained with them two hours and again went on. We killed five deer on the bank to day as we floated down; and saw a fine young horse. At sunset we encamped on a small island.

Monday 15th. The morning was pleasant and we embarked early. In a short time we killed a fine large elk;[+] at 11 o'clock passed the Kanzon river, and encamped at sunset.

Tuesday 16th. This was another pleasant day. We proceeded on early, and at 9'clock [*sic*] met a large periogue with eight men, going to trade with the Ponis nation of Indians on the river Platte about seventy or eight miles from its mouth.[706] At 11 we met a batteaux and two canoes going up to the Kanowas nation, who live on a river of the same name. We halted with them a while, then proceeded on, and at sunset encamped on an island.

Wednesday 17th. We went on early and had a pleasant day, but very warm. One of our party last night caught a large catfish, supposed to weight 100 pounds. We got a great many papaws on our way to day: a kind of fruit in great abundance on the Missouri from the river Platte to its mouth; and also down the Mississippi. About 11 o'clock we passed through a bad part of the river, where it was so filled with sawyers that we could hardly find room to pass through safe. About two in the afternoon we meet a large keel-boat, commanded by a Captain M'Clanen,[707] loaded with merchandize and bound to the Spanish country by the way of the river Platte. He intended to go by land across the mountain, and get the Spaniards to bring their gold and silver on this side, where he could take his goods and trade with them. He had fifteen hands, an interpreter and a black. He intends to discharge his men on this side of the mountain, and to get some of the Ponis, who live on the river Plate to accompany him to the Spanish country. Mr. M'Clanen gave all our party as much whiskey as they could drink, and a bag of biscuit. Some of the men were sent on ahead in two small canoes to hunt, and we encamped here for the night.

Thursday 18th. We gave Mr. McClanen a keg of corn; took our leave of him and proceeded on. In a short time, passed the mouth of the river Grand, and soon after overtook the hunters, who had not killed any thing. We continued our voyage all day without waiting to hunt; gathering some papaws on the shores, and in the evening encamped on an island.[708]

The 19th, was a fine day, and at day light we continued our voyage; passed the mouth of Mine river; Saw several turkeys on the shores, but did not delay a moment to hunt;[709] being so anxious to reach St. Louis, where, without any important occurrence, we arrived on the 23rd[710] and were received with great kindness and marks of friendship by the inhabitants, after an absence of two years, four months and ten days.

ENDNOTES

Introduction

1. Roy E. Appleman, *Lewis and Clark* (Washington, D.C.: U.S. Department of the Interior, National Park Service, 1975), 17–23.
2. Robert Lange, "$2,500.00 Vs. $38,722.25—The Financial Outlay for the Historic Enterprise," *We Proceeded On* 1:2 (February 1975), 17–18.
3. Mary P. Adams, "Jefferson's Reaction to the Treaty of San Ildefonso," *Journal of Southern History* 21:2 (1955), 173–88.
4. William H. Goetzmann, *Exploration and Empire: The Explorer and the Scientist in the Winning of the American West* (New York: W. W. Norton & Company, 1978), xi.
5. Moulton's first volume beautifully reproduces all of the maps created during the expedition. Gary Moulton, ed., The Journals of the Lewis and Clark Expedition, Vol. 1: Atlas *of the Lewis and Clark Expedition* (Lincoln: University of Nebraska Press, 1983).
6. Edward Thornton to Lord Hawkesbury, March 1803, in Donald Jackson, ed., *Letters of the Lewis and Clark Expedition with Related Documents, 1783–1854* 2nd edition revised (Urbana: University of Ilinois Press, 1978; 1962), 25–27.
7. Jackson, *Letters of the Lewis and Clark Expedition*, 61–66.
8. Ibid., 1–2.
9. Ibid., 58.
10. J. G. Jacob, *The Life and Times of Patrick Gass, Now Sole Survivor of the Overland Expedition to the Pacific, under Lewis and Clark, in 1804–5–6* (Wellsburg, Va.: Jacob & Smith, 1859), 36–37.
11. For biographical references, see Charles G. Clarke, *The Men of the Lewis and Clark Expedition, a Biographical Roster of the Fifty-one Members and a Composite Diary of Their Activities from All Known Sources* (Glendale, Calif.: The Arthur H. Clark Company, 1970), 37–72. Bernard DeVoto, ed., *The Journals of Lewis and Clark* (Boston: Houghton Mifflin Company, 1953), 489–91.
12. Clarke, *Men of the Lewis and Clark Expediton*, 71.
13. Moulton, *The Journals of the Lewis and Clark Expedition*, 2:214, 215 n. 2.
14. Olin D. Wheeler, *The Trail of Lewis and Clark*, (New York: G. P. Putnam's Sons, 1904), 2:311-14.
15. Clarke, *Men of the Lewis and Clark Expediton*, 37–72.
16. Eldon G. Chuinard,"Sergeant Patrick Gass: Irishman? Scotsman?" *We Proceeded On* 8:1 (February 1982), 5.
17. Jacob, *The Life and Times of Patrick Gass*, 12.
18. Ibid., 14.
19. Clarke, *Men of the Lewis and Clark Expediton*, 53, 147.
20. Thwaites, *Original Journals*, 1:125.
21. Jacob, *The Life and Times of Patrick Gass*, 10.
22. Ibid., 148.
23. Earle E. Forrest, ed., *A Journal of the Voyages and Travels of a Corps of Discovery, under the Command of Capt. Lewis and Capt. Clarke of the Army of the United States, from the Mouth of the River Missouri through the Interior Parts of North America to the Pacific Ocean, During the Years 1804, 1805, and 1806. Containing an authentic relation of the most interesting transactions during the expedition,—A description of the country,—And an account of its inhabitants, soil, climate, curiosities, and vegetable and animal productions. By Patrick Gass, One of the Persons Employed in the Expedition. With Geographical and Explanatory Notes* (Minneapolis: Ross & Haines, 1958), xiv.

24. Jackson, *Letters of the Lewis and Clark Expedition,* 650–51 n. 2.
25. Gass's military record states that "in Fort Independence on the Mississippi in September, 1813, Gass lost the use of his left eye." National Archives Record Group A, file 24097.
26. *The 1830 Virginia Census* (Brooke County) cites one young female in John Hamilton's house between ten and fifteen years of age, so the oldest Maria could have been in 1831 was sixteen. National Archives, series M19, reel 189:150.
27. Earle E. Forrest, "Patrick Gass, Carpenter of the Lewis and Clark Expedition," *Bulletin of the Missouri Historical Society* 4 (July 1948), 221.
28. Newton, Nicholas, and Sprankle, *History of the Panhandle* (Wheeling, W. Va.: J. A. Caldwell, 1879), 349. J. G. Jacob confirms Gass's interment date as April 3, 1870, in the *Brooke County Record* (Wellsburg, W. Va.: Wellsburg Herald Office, 1882), 188–90.
29. Jackson, *Letters of the Lewis and Clark Expedition,* 385–86, 399–408. See Appendix C.
30. John Rickman, *Journal of Captain Cook's Last Voyage to the Pacific Ocean Discovery: Performed in the Years 1776, 1777, 1778, 1779* (rpt., Ann Arbor, Mich: University Microfilms, 1966; London: E. Newbery, 1781); and John Ledyard, *Journal of Captain Cook's Last Voyage to the Pacific Ocean, and in Quest of a Northwest Passage, Between Asia and America Performed in the Years 1776, 1777, 1778, and 1779,* ed. James Kenneth Munford (rpt., Corvallis: Oregon State University Press, 1963; Hartford: Nathaniel Patten, 1783).
31. In "Sedulous Sergeant, Patrick Gass: An Original Biography by Direct Descendents," *Montana The Magazine of Western History* 5 (Summer 1955), James Smith and Kathryn Smith assert that the unedited Gass manuscript "must have exceeded that of Captain Clark for uniqueness of spelling and punctuation" (p. 22). But discovery of Gass's account book proves this not to be the case.
32. Paul Russell Cutright, *A History of the Lewis and Clark Journals* (Norman: University of Oklahoma Press, 1976), 31.
33. Smith and Smith, "Sedulous Sergeant," 22.

Chapter 1: May 14, 1804–July 23, 1804

34. Gass missed five days in his journal at St. Charles. The corps's activities are described by Private Joseph Whitehouse, who noted on May 18 that they had "passed the evening verry agreeable dancing with the french ladies, & c." On the 20th, Whitehouse noted, "Several of the party went to church, which the French call mass, and sore [saw] their way of performing & c." Reuben Gold Thwaites, ed., *Original Journals of the Lewis and Clark Expedition, 1804–1806,* 8 vols. (New York: Arno Press, 1969), 7:31.
35. Captain William Clark identified these Indians as Kickapoos and stated that they brought four deer to the party and received two quarts of whiskey. Moulton, *Journals of the Lewis and Clark Expedition,* 2:245.
36. Captain Clark called it "Osage Womans R.," deriving from the French appellation, *Rivière Femme Osage.* Ibid., 2:248.
37. Gass did not mention on the 26th that the troops were reorganized from two into three messes, or smaller details, within the corps. Captain Lewis assigned Private Gass to the group under Sergeant Floyd. Moulton, *Journals of the Lewis and Clark Expedition,* 2:255.
38. Ordway identified this man as Private George Shannon. Milo M. Quaife, ed., *The Journals of Captain Meriwether Lewis and Sergeant John Ordway* (Madison: State Historical Society of Wisconsin, 1916), 81. Hunters identified in other journals, but not by Gass, are indicated with a superscript plus sign ([+]); see Appendix B. There are many instances where no one identifies hunters.
39. Whitehouse had not returned and was considered lost. Ibid.
40. This is the first of many rich descriptions Gass added to the expedition journals by his identification of trees. See also June 1, 1804.
41. Whitehouse was the man who was found. See note 39.
42. This is the Moreau River in Cole County, Missouri. Moulton, *Journals of the Lewis and Clark Expedition,* 2:274.
43. Gass did not mention Manitou Indian drawings on a rock (ibid., 284), which Ordway described as "a Pickture of the Devil." Quaife, *Journals of Lewis and Ordway,* 83.
44. This is now Bonne Femme Creek in Boone County, Missouri. Quaife, *Journals of Lewis and Ordway,* 281.

45. Whitehouse said that on the 7th, the party killed three rattlesnakes and George Drouillard killed a female and two cub bears. Thwaites, *Original Journals*, 7:34. The men killed for protection, not food, as game abounded in this region.

46. This is probably Pierre Fresne Creek in Saline County, Missouri. Moulton, *Journals of the Lewis and Clark Expedition*, 2:290.

47. Quaife identified this stream as Hurrricane Creek in Missouri. Quaife, *Journals of Lewis and Ordway*, 84.

48. The Little Chariton meets the main Chariton a little above the mouth of the latter in Chariton County, Missouri, near present-day Glasgow. They were named for Jean Chariton, an early trader. Moulton, *Journals of the Lewis and Clark Expedtion*, 2:293.

49. Whitehouse noted that they swam horses and ferried men across the Missouri River on the 10th. Thwaites, *Original Journals*, 7:35.

50. Patrick Gass had his 33rd birthday on June 12, 1804.

51. The Frenchman was Pierre Dorion, Senior, who was married to a Yankton Sioux; he lived with that tribe and knew its language. Moulton, *Journals of the Lewis and Clark Expedition*, 2:295. Whitehouse reported that one of the men of Stoddard's company on the white pirogue was sent back. Thwaites, *Original Journals*, 7:35. It could have been Ebenezer Tuttle or Isaac White. Arlen J. Large, "Additions to the Party," *We Proceeded On* 16 (February 1990), 9. The decision to bring Dorion aboard and send another man back would facilitate communication with Indians upstream.

52. The men used the tow rope to pull the boats upstream when they could not be rowed, poled, or sailed.

53. Fort de Cavagnial was used between 1744 and 1764, when the French had jurisdiction over the area. It is located in Leavenworth County, Kansas. Moulton, *Journals of the Lewis and Clark Expedition*, 2:343.

54. A rattlesnake bit Joseph Field on the outer part of his foot, according to Ordway. Quaife, *Journals of Lewis and Ordway*, 92.

55. Ordway noted that Alexander Willard was court-martialed on the 12th for falling asleep while on sentinel duty. Gass neglected to mention another significant event on July 12: the party passed Indian mounds in present-day Missouri. Moulton, *Journals of the Lewis and Clark Expedition*, 2:370.

56. Drouillard and Floyd went ashore, said Ordway, while he and Clark went on the south side. Quaife, *Journals of Lewis and Ordway*, 97.

57. These hunters included R. Field, who was in charge of the horses, according to Ordway's notes. Ibid., 96, 98.

58. George Drouillard and Peter Cruzatte were dispatched with tobacco to the Otoes and Pawnees, Whitehouse wrote. Moulton, *Journals of the Lewis and Clark Expedition*, 2:415. Quaife, *Journals of Lewis and Ordway*, 101. Their visit furthered the diplomatic mission of the expedition to explain the change of government. President Jefferson asked Lewis and Clark to inform native people that the territory was now under the jurisdiction of the United States of America, which desired peace among them as well as to protect them.

59. The expedition used U.S. flags to announce the change of territorial government, presenting them to American Indians as a symbol of their supposed new allegiance to it. Bob Saindon, "The Flags of the Lewis and Clark Expedition," *We Proceeded On* 7 (November 1981), 22–26.

Chapter 2: July 27, 1804–August 31,1804

60. Sergeant Charles Floyd noted that they swam the horses to the south side, where traveling was better. Thwaites, *Original Journals*, 7:21.

61. Clark called it Indian Knob Creek north of Council Bluffs, Iowa; it is now known as Pigeon Creek. Moulton, *Journals of the Lewis and Clark Expedition*, 2:423, 425.

62. Clark identified the man as a Missouri Indian who lived with the "Otteauze" (Otoes). Ibid., 2:424.

63. "Prarow" is an anglicized form of the French word *blaireau*, or "badger."

64. George Drouillard brought in the young live beaver. Thwaites, *Original Journals*, 7:47.

65. Drouillard and Colter went to look for horses and G. Gibson went to search for Private Joseph Barter, always referred to in the journals as "La Liberté," a Frenchman of the party who left on the 29th and did not return. Thwaites, *Original Journals*, 7:46–47.

La Liberté, whose name may have ironically matched his bent against discipline and constriction, became the only deserter.

66. Fourteen Oto Indians arrived to spend the night. Quaife, *Journals of Lewis and Ordway*, 104. The Otoes and Missouris had merged in the late eighteenth century. Their camp on the Platte River, above the mouth of Elkhorn, is now in Saunders County, Nebraska. Moulton, *Journals of the Lewis and Clark Expedition*, 2:447 n. 1.

67. Gass's reference to latitude shows evidence of "campfire editing." He copied this and other such references from Lewis, who had the instruments to ascertain latitude and regularly noted the same in his journal.

68. "Making Chiefs" symbolized the bestowal of authority on certain Indians Lewis and Clark perceived as leaders in the European sense of political leadership, a concept not applicable to Native American civilizations.

69. Private Moses B. Reed supposedly went back for his knife on the 4th. Examining his knapsack, the party discovered that he took his clothes, powder, and balls. Floyd wrote on August 7 that Reed intended "to Desarte from us with out aney Jest Case." Thwaites, *Original Journals*, 7:24.

70. G. Drouillard, W. Bratton, R. Field, and W. Labiche were dispatched to recover Reed, according to Ordway. Quaife, *Journals of Lewis and Ordway,* 107. Nicholas Biddle, the first editor of the journals of Lewis and Clark in 1814, crossed out the order to take Reed "dead or alive," but Gass's journal had already printed the story in 1807. Moulton, *Journals of the Lewis and Clark Expedition*, 2:456

71. This description of the pelican exemplifies Gass's succinct verbiage, not that of the editor David McKeehan.

72. Floyd stated that the hill on which Blackbird, the Omaha chief, was buried was 300 feet high; natives went "2 or 3 times a year to Cryes [cry] over him." About 300 native people had died of smallpox, including the chief. Thwaites, *Original Journals,* 7:25.

73. Ordway wrote that he and four men, Peter Cruzatte, George Shannon, William Werner, and Alexander Carson, found 300 cabins in the Mahar [Omaha Indian] village. It had been burned four years before when half of the village had died of smallpox. The current inhabitants were absent, hunting buffalo. Quaife, *Journals of Lewis and Ordway,* 110.

74. The fish story varies slightly: Clark said 318 fish. Moulton, *Journals of the Lewis and Clark Expedition,* 2:483. Floyd stated that he was there with Captain Clark, and they counted 317 fish of different kinds. Thwaites, *Original Journals,* 7:26. Whitehouse reported 386. Thwaites, *Original Journals,* 7:50. Ordway settled for a round 300. Quaife, *Journals of Lewis and Ordway,* 111. Gass tells us that the fish were caught "with trails or brush nets."

75. Whitehouse wrote that Labiche left the rest of party and returned on the 17th; Drouillard, Bratton, and Field returned with Reed. Thwaites, *Original Journals,* 7:50. James Ronda said Labiche came to camp a day early. *Lewis and Clark among the Indians* (Lincoln: University of Nebraska Press, 1984), 20.

76. Floyd probably died of appendicitis. Ordway said, "We buried him with the honours of war." Quaife, *Journals of Lewis and Ordway,* 112. The earliest manual on U. S. Army procedure, printed in 1820, states that military funeral rites then included gun salutes. There is no mention of religion.

77. Gass omitted recording a fact very important to him: on the 22nd, the corps held an election to replace Sergeant Floyd. Patrick Gass received nineteen votes, showing the men's preference to promote him to sergeant in charge of Floyd's mess. Bratton was runner-up, and Gibson received some votes. Moulton, *Journals of the Lewis and Clark Expedition*, 2:501.

Lewis wrote in his orderly book on August, 26, 1804 (from Thwaites, *Original Journals,* 1:125):

The commanding officers have thought proper to appoint Patric Gass, a Sergeant in *the corps of volunteers for North Western Discovery;* he is therefore to be obeyed and respected accordingly.

Serg.^t Gass is directed to take charge of the late Serg.^t Floyd's mess, and immediately to enter on the discharge of such other duties, as have by their previous orders been prescribed for the government of the Sergeants of this corps.

The Commanding officers have every reason to hope from the previous faithfull services of Serg.^t Gass,that this expression of their approbation will be still further confirmed by his vigilent attention in future to his duties as a Sergeant. the Commanding officers are still further confirmed in the high opinion they had previously formed of the capacity, deligence and integrety of Serg.ᵗ Gass, from the wish expressed by a large majority of his comrades for his appointment as Sergeant.

MERIWETHER LEWIS,
Cap.ᵗ U.S. Reg.ᵗ Infty.
Wᴹ CLARK Cp.ᵗ &c.

78. Lewis, Ordway, and ten others went to bring back the buffalo meat. Ibid., 118.
79. Besides the two captains, ten men (including Ordway) went in search of the little people the Indians feared. Ibid., 119.
80. Sergeant Pryor went with two Indians, one an Omaha, the other a Sioux, and a Frenchman. Ibid., 126. James Ronda identified the three Indians mentioned by Gass as two Yankton Sioux and one Omaha, and the old Frenchman as Dorion. Pierre Dorion stayed with the Yankton Sioux to promote peace between that tribe and the Omahas. Ronda, *Lewis and Clark among the Indians*, 23, 31.
81. On this day Shannon and the horses walked ahead and became lost. On the 29th Colter went to look for him. Quaife, *Journals of Lewis and Ordway*, 118.
82. These Native Americans were Yankton Sioux. Ronda, *Journals of the Lewis and Clark Expedition*, 24.
83. Whitehouse added to Gass's description of this celebration that Indian boys shot bows and arrows for beads. Lewis shot the air gun for them, exciting the Indians with its ball holes in a tree. Young Yankton men painted themselves at nightfall, dancing and giving "whoops" as they started. Warriors bragged about warring and stealing horses. Thwaites, *Original Journals*, 7:54–55. Gass's is the only account that noted the absence of females.
84. See Ordway's diary for an enriched account of five Indian speeches given on the 31st. Quaife, *Journals of Lewis and Ordway*, 120–23. Dorion, the old Frenchman, stayed with the Sioux to promote peace and to accompany one of the chiefs to the United States Capitol.

Chapter 3: September 1, 1804–September 28, 1804

85. Colter left the meat. He was looking for Shannon, who was searching for the horses when he became lost. Quaife, *Journals of Lewis and Ordway*, 126.
86. The reason they got only one prairie dog after filling all the holes is because these animals dig labyrinthine tunnels with numerous exits.
87. This story is not repeated in other journals of the expedition.
88. Pryor and Drouillard discovered the spring, according to Lewis. Moulton, *Journals of the Lewis and Clark Expedition*, 3:63.
89. They found Shannon, only nineteen, who had been lost for more than two weeks. Ordway wrote that Shannon said he followed tracks he took for those of the expedition but that must have instead belonged to Indians. He subsisted only on grapes since he had shot all of his bullets. Quaife, *Journals of Lewis and Ordway*, 129.
90. Newman went with Gass and Clark, noted Whitehouse. Ibid., 58.
91. Ordway wrote that he, Pryor, and Shannon went out to gather plums. Ibid., 130.
92. George Drouillard was setting a beaver trap every night during this part of the trip. Ibid.
93. The large white hare that John Shields killed and the dark reddish pronghorn sheep that Clark killed were stuffed to be sent to Washington, "skin. . . bones and all," according to Ordway. Ibid., 131.
94. R. Field went with Gass to explore the White River, reported Whitehouse. Thwaites, *Original Journals*, 7:58. The White River is in South Dakota.
95. A "bottom" is a rich land bordering a river, usually protected, such as a small valley with trees. Gass loved this kind of land.
96. This rich description is nearly verbatim with Ordway's account, proof of "campfire editing."
97. This "prairie wolf" is a coyote, contrasted by Clark with "large wolves," or gray wolves. Moulton, *Journals of the Lewis and Clark Expedition*, 3:87 n. 1, 4.
98. This is the crossing of Crow, Elm, and Campbell creeks in South Dakota. Moulton, *Journals of the Lewis and Clark Expedition*, 3:91, and Thwaites, *Original Journals*, 1:157.

99. Régis Loisel, born in Montreal and running fur trading operations from St. Louis by the turn of the century, had met the Corps of Discovery on May 25, 1804. A valuable source for the party regarding the Missouri tribes, Loisel had spent the winter of 1803–1804 at his fort on Cedar Island. On September 22 when the explorers visited the site, the fort was abandoned. Moulton, *Journals of the Lewis and Clark Expedition*, 2:253 n. 9. Also see Bernard DeVoto, *The Course of Empire* (Boston: Houghton Mifflin Company, 1952), 439.

100. Gass's descriptions are almost exactly like Whitehouse's version. Clark put notes in the margin about these construction details the next day. It is reasonable to assume that Gass was the leader of the "campfire editors" on these and other building descriptions because he was the only sergeant who was a qualified carpenter.

101. Drouillard and Shields came with the horse. Quaife, *Journals of Lewis and Ordway*, 135.

102. Here Gass described a travois, which the Indians harnessed to dogs to transport belongings from one camp to another.

103. Colter had gone to kill an elk when the horse was stolen. Quaife, *Journals of Lewis and Ordway*, 135.

104. These are the Brulé band of the Teton Sioux now called Lakota. The Frenchman was Cruzatte, who knew very little of the Sioux language. Ronda, *Lewis and Clark among the Indians*, 30–31.

105. Lewis noted on the 25th, "This day the Tetons and ourselves had nearly come to an open ruptr." Moulton, *Journals of the Lewis and Clark Expedition*, 3:131.

106. Ordway wrote of the Brulé village on the 27th, "Sgt. Gass informed me. . . he counted 80 lodges. . . 10 persons each. . . which were built round with poles about 15 or 20 feet high and covered with dressed buffalo hides painted red. they draw them. . . with their dogs." Quaife, *Journals of Lewis and Ordway*, 141. Whitehouse used almost Gass's exact words for his entry. Thwaites, *Original Journals*, 7:64. Lewis did not write about the village; Clark did not go into the Indian camp until evening and did not discuss lodges, work, food, or water.

107. Here is an excellent example of "Jeffersonian Enlightenment theory" at work on the trail, accepted by the corps. This notion held that civilization can progress through education, that Native Americans needed to advance from their "uncivilized" society toward the ideals of the Euro-American "civilized" society. In this case, Lewis urged a band of Brulés to give lip service to the idea that skills of negotiation versus war would yield peace.

108. Whitehouse reported that the Indians "whipped off" their women and children (from the many who were observing the whites depart from the shore) and left only sixty warriors. Some had guns and others bows and arrows ready for war. The chiefs spoke to them to draw back their weapons, and then requested tobacco. Thwaites, *Original Journals*, 7:65.

109. A "carrot of tobacco" depicted a quantity bunched together, the way it was transported and traded at the time, not an exact weight. Men used tobacco for chewing and smoking and as an item of high value for trade with Native Americans.

Chapter 4: September 29–October 23, 1804

110. Ordway said 200 Indians (Teton Sioux of the Brulé band, see note 99) followed on shore, and the party anchored 100 yards from shore opposite them. Quaife, *Journals of Lewis and Ordway*, 144.

111. *Chien* means "dog" in French.

112. Ordway said the guest was a young Frenchman who lived with the man Clark called Mr. Jon Vallie [Jean Vallé]. Quaife, *Journals of Lewis and Ordway*, 145; Moulton, *Journals of the Lewis and Clark Expedition*, 3:135 and 136 n. 3.

113. This South Dakota river is now called the Grand River. Quaife, *Journals of the Lewis and Clark Expedition*, 148. This passage is an interesting example of campfire editing. Ordway and Gass agreed, but Clark called this river "Wetarhoo." The next creek mentioned is called the Maropa by Clark. See Moulton, *Journals of the Lewis and Clark Expedition*, 3:150, 153 n. 2, 5.

114. Two Frenchmen came with Lewis in his pirogue. They were Joseph Gravelines and Pierre-Antoine Tabeau, both employees of Régis Loisel. Moulton, *Journals of the Lewis and Clark Expedition*, 3:152, 154, 155.

115. Here Gass's rich description of the Arikara lodges seems to serve as the basis for Clark's entry on October 12th. Ibid., 3:161.

116. Clark noted on the 10th, and Gass did not, that York "makes himself turrible" to the Arikaras who are fascinated by Clark's black servant. Ibid., 3:157.

117. Clark did not mention a squaw accompanying the party until the 16th, after Gass had noted her presence.

118. The court-martial trial of John Newman on the 13th for "mutinous expression" featured Gass, Ordway, and eight privates as the jury. They sentenced Newman to 75 lashes and expulsion from the permanent party. When the Arikara chief witnessed the corporal punishment, he wept with pity until the crime and the trial were explained to him. The Arikaras punished by death but never by the humiliation of whipping. Moulton, *Journals of the Lewis and Clark Expedition,* 3:170, 172.

119. Ordway reported that York, Clark's black servant, became the greatest curiosity to the Arikaras: "All the nation made a great deal of him the children would follow after him, & if he turned towards them they would run from him & hollow as if they were terrefied, & afraid of him." Quaife, *Journals of Lewis and Ordway,* 154.

120. Ordway wrote, "We Saw Some of the Goats floating down with the arrows Sticking up in them." Ibid.

121. The canoe belonged to Gravellin, who had been with the party since the 8th. Ibid., 155.

122. The name derived from round stones found at the bottom of this river. The party had lost its anchor during the encounter with the Teton Sioux days earlier and now took one of the stones to use for an anchor. Ibid.

123. This was the party's first encounter with a grizzly bear.

124. Clark thought these men were warlike and maybe stealing horses from the Mandans. Moulton, *Journals of the Lewis and Clark Expedition,* 3:191. Lewis identified these Indians as Teton Sioux in Nicholas Biddle's *Journals of the Expedition under the Command of Capts. Lewis and Clark* (New York: Heritage Press, 1962), 1:71.

Chapter 5: October 24–December 25, 1804

125. Gass was specific here, saying that five Indians came to the party and "our Indian" (the Arikara chief who had been with the party) joined the other Indians. Clark described it as a group including the son of a Mandan chief whose missing fingers and scars symbolized his grief from losing loved ones. Clark added that the customs and manners of the Mandans were similar to the Arikaras, but the Mandans were milder in gestures and language. Moulton, *Journals of the Lewis and Clark Expedition,* 3:196.

126. The Irishman was Hugh McCracken. Ibid., 3:199, 201 n. 4.

127. Ordway noted there were two or three Frenchmen, one with an Indian woman and a child, who was "tolerable white." Quaife, *Journals of Lewis and Ordway,* 159. identifies him as René Jessaume.

128. The iron mill to grind corn would have been a very useful tool for the Mandan people, but they later broke it up for arrows. See Moulton, *Journals of the Lewis and Clark Expedition,* 3:213 n. 3.

129. The corps built Fort Mandan in present-day McLean County, seven or eight miles below the mouth of the Knife River. Quaife, *Journals of Lewis and Ordway,* 162.

130. Ordway noted that they used cottonwood for the split planks. Ibid.

131. Gass here offered the best description of the construction of the corps' headquarters at the Mandan village for the winter of 1804–1805.

132. Gass wrote sparingly at this time because he was busy building the fort at Mandan, where the corps stayed for the winter. During this period, Clark noted that the weather was very cold. On the 22nd, Clark counseled an Indian who nearly murdered his wife because she slept with Ordway. Eight days earlier, when the first confrontation between the couple occurred, the wife had fled to Charbonneau's squaws (one of whom was Sacagawea) near the fort. When she returned home, her furious husband beat her; she then went back to the fort with three stab wounds. Clark also spoke to Ordway, prohibited the corps from touching the woman, and assured the husband that no one would knowingly sleep with an Indian woman whom they knew to be anyone's wife. Moulton, *Journals of the Lewis and Clark Expedition,* 3:239. Ordway does not mention the episode in his journal.

133. Pryor hurt himself taking down the mast, an injury that plagued him throughout the journey. Ibid., 2:243

134. This man was George Henderson of the Hudson's Bay Company. Ibid., 3:251.

135. Whitehouse wrote that "the Big white a Cheif of the mandans Came to Our fort in the Morning to Inform Us that the Buffelow was Close to us a Comeing in." Thwaites, *Original Journals,* 7:70. The chief was Sheheke, who later went to Washington, D.C. Gass later told his biographer that Sheheke was the best-looking Indian he ever saw. A drawing of the chief appears in Jacob, *Life and Times of Patrick Gass,* 108–9.

136. Clark wrote that his servant York's feet and penis were frostbitten. Moulton, *Journals of the Lewis and Clark Expedition,* 3:255.

137. Ordway wrote that though the rooms were warm the sentinel on duty had to be relieved from the cold every hour. Quaife, *Journals of Lewis and Ordway,* 171. Only Gass mentioned the sleds he and others built to haul the meat.

138. Hugh Heney or Hené, Régis Loisel's employee on the Missouri River, brought a letter from Charles Chaboillez, an official of the North West Company. Moulton, *Journals of the Lewis and Clark Expedition,* 3:258. This letter responded to one sent to Chaboillez by Lewis and Clark from the Mandan village on October 31, 1804, apprising him of their presence, their British passport, and their intention to explore western North America. They asked Chaboillez about his knowledge of the area. Elliot Coues, ed., *History of the Lewis and Clark Expedition* (New York: Frances P. Harper, 1893), 1:187–88.

139. Whitehouse credited Gass with building the sled. Thwaites, *Original Journals,* 7:71.

140. The labor/management view is clear by this passage. Clark, who was making maps, did not mention the work until the next day.

141. Ordway wrote of the Christmas celebration, "Continued firing dancing & frolicking dureing the whole day. the Savages did not Trouble as we had requested them not to come as it was a Great medicine day with us." Quaife, *Journals of Lewis and Ordway,* 174.

142. In the Christmas accounts, nothing religious was mentioned. Gass's wording was almost identical to Whitehouse's, another example of campfire editing. Gass's mention of the "three squaws, wives of our interpreter" (Charbonneau and Jessaume) was his first reference to Sacagawea. She had been won in a card game or purchased by Charbonneau from Gros Ventre Indians who had held her captive. She was one of three Indian women staying with Charbonneau as wives the winter of 1803–1804 at the Mandan village.

143. Whitehouse skipped this period also. Ordway noted seven men went to the Indian village on the 26th. On the 27th, the men finished the floor in Charbonneau's hut and the blacksmith shop. On the 29th, Mandan women brought iron objects to fix in the new shop and gave the party corn, beans, squash, and Indian bread. Quaife, *Journals of Lewis and Ordway,* 174. Clark said the Indians were "much Surprised at the Bellos & method of makeing Sundery ariticles of Iron." Moulton, *Journals of the Lewis and Clark Expedition,* 3:262.

Chapter 6: January 1–April 5, 1805

144. Ordway was among these men. He wrote that they took along a "fiddle, Tambereen & a Sounden horn." Quaife, *Journals of Lewis and Ordway,* 175. Clark said, "I ordered my black Servent to Dance which amused the Croud verry much, and Some what astonished them, that So large a man Should be active." Moulton, *Journals of the Lewis and Clark Expedition,* 3:267.

145. This is another example of the enlisted men copying from each other. The wording almost exactly matches that of Whitehouse's journal.

146. The reason for sparse entries from the third to the thirteenth is not clear. On the 5th, Clark described a "Buffalow Dance" custom: for three nights the young men offered their wives to older men as presents, believing that sexual intercourse transferred power from the old men to the young men via the women. The concept of power transference through intercourse explained why some Native Americans offered their wives to white visitors, whom they considered "big medicine" or powerful. Moulton, *Journals of the Lewis and Clark Expedition,* 3:268; Ronda, *Lewis and Clark among the Indians,* 65, 107.

It was 18 degrees below zero at 4 P.M. on the 5th and 28 degrees below zero on January 10. Moulton, *Journals of the Lewis and Clark Expedition,* 3:281–82.

147. The travelers were Charbonneau and another Frenchman, who returned from the Minetarees (also called Gros Ventres or Big Bellies) with frostbite. Moulton, *Journals of the Lewis and Clark Expedition,* 3:272. Ordway said that "Sharbinow arived in the evening with the horses loaded with Grees fat meat &. C." Quaife, *Journals of Lewis and Ordway,* 177.

148. The man with the frozen feet was Whitehouse. Lewis mentioned an eclipse of the moon the night of the 14th. Clark noted that several men had caught venereal disease from the Mandan women. Moulton, *Journals of the Lewis and Clark Expedition,* 3:273.

149. Francois Larocque and Charles McKenzie worked for the Northwest Fur Company at Fort Assinoboine. Quaife, *Journals of Lewis and Ordway,* 177 n. 1.

150. Gass's descriptions of the work done on the 25th and 26th contrast with the entries of Clark, who was visiting the Indians and treating one for pleurisy. Thwaites, *Original Journals,* 1:251.

151. From the 22nd through the 30th, Gass focused on getting the boats out of the ice. Clark finally mentioned this on February 3. Ibid., 1:253.

152. On February 4, Clark took out a hunting party that included Gass. They returned on the 12th. Ibid., 1:253, 259.

153. Sacagawea, Charbonneau's wife, gave birth on February 11, 1805, to a boy named Jean Baptiste Charbonneau, nicknamed "Pomp" by Clark.

154. Clark dispatched Drouillard, Frazer, Goodrich, and Newman with two horse-drawn sleighs to get the meat that was killed on the hunt. Moulton, *Journals of the Lewis and Clark Expedition,* 3:296.

155. Gass and Ordway were among the volunteers who accompanied Lewis in pursuit of 106 Sioux who had stolen two of the party's horses. Quaife, *Journals of Lewis and Ordway,* 184.

156. Clark wrote that Lewis and his party brought back about 3,000 pounds of meat from thirty-six deer and fourteen elk. Thwaites, *Original Journals,* 1:264.

157. Gass was busy freeing boats from the ice February 23–27 and making canoes with a party of sixteen from February 28 through March 20, in preparation for their departure upstream. The large batteaux would return downstream with information, so additional smaller craft were needed for the trip upstream. On Tuesday the 19th, Ordway wrote that Gass came down to the fort and informed the corps that the pirogues were finished and that he needed more men to take them to the river. Quaife, *Journals of Lewis and Ordway,* 187.

On March 14, Charbonneau moved out of the fort, pitching his tent outside. Ordway stated that Gravelines was to take his place. Ibid., 186. Clark wrote that Charbonneau had rejected the terms of employment on the 11th, but returned with apologies on the 17th, wanting to rejoin. Clark rehired him. Moulton, *Journals of the Lewis and Clark Expedition,* 3:312, 316.

158. Ordway noted that there was an ice run on the river on the 28th. Quaife, *Journals of Lewis and Ordway,* 188. This meant the river would soon be clear to ascend, although the current must have been strong with the spring runoff.

159. The whole of their craft comprised the large bateau (or keelboat), two pirogues (larger than canoes), and six newly made canoes.

160. This passage is one of the more frequently quoted ones in Gass's journal. The style is too pompous for Gass, except the phrase "old bawd and her punks," which does not reflect McKeehan's writing style. This section on prostitution on the Missouri makes us wonder what the original manuscript might have said: Did Gass include more narratives of "entertaining stories and pleasant anecdotes" than McKeehan printed? Did McKeehan decide not "to swell the journal" with them, judging them not "useful information" for a "small and portable" journal, as he noted in his preface? Only discovery of the long-lost Gass manuscript could ultimately answer these questions.

Chapter 7: April 6–April 30, 1805

161. There were two captains, three sergeants, twenty-three privates, two interpreters, one black servant, one Indian woman, and her child. See Appendix A

162. Thirteen men returned to St. Louis in the large keelboat, or "bateau." These included pilot Gravelines, Corporal Warfington, six privates, two Frenchmen, two engagés, and one Arikara Indian. Only two of the returning men had expected to be permanent members: Privates John Newman and Moses Reed, who had been discharged for misconduct and desertion. The returning group carried treasures acquired on the trip thus far, which the captains sent back to the States for President Jefferson, including writings and curious animals and birds. Quaife, *Journals of Lewis and Ordway*, 191.

163. In *Voyages from Montreal* (1801), Alexander Mackenzie wrote about chasms in the earth emitting heat and smoke (which are noted here by McKeehan), "I should certainly have visited this phaenomenon, if I had been sufficiently qualified as a naturalist, to have offered scientific conjectures or observations therein" (p. 176).

164. Lewis wrote that a Mandan woman came to accompany a man of the party on the 8th and was sent back. Moulton, *Journals of the Lewis and Clark Expedition*, 4:13–14. A Mandan man also joined them April 8 and 9. Thwaites, *Original Journals*, 1:287–91.

165. Gass showed the changing nomenclature for new species with this comment. Lewis called it an antelope. Moulton, *Journals of the Lewis and Clark Expedition*, 4:45.

166. This Gass entry offers unique and beautiful descriptions of the hills, the petrified log, and its potential uses. Lewis noted whetstone on April 22. Ibid., 4:60.

167. Geese build their large nests in trees if they can find mature trees with wide forks. Otherwise, geese build their nests on the ground. Fish and game departments today construct wooden platforms for geese, to protect their eggs from predators.

168. Ordway thought they saw a thousand animals at once. Quaife, *Journals of Lewis and Ordway*, 200.

169. Lewis and Clark noted that the men complained of sore eyes, perhaps due to blowing sand. Dr. Eldon G. Chuinard, *Only One Man Died: The Medical Aspects of the Lewis and Clark Expedition* (Glendale, Calif.: The Arthur H. Clark Company, 1979), 158, 279, surmised that the sore eyes could have been caused by the glare of the sun on the water or by venereal disease.

170. *Roche jaune* means "yellow stone" in French.

171. Gass's observation about the relationship of dew and want of timber shows his eye for trees.

172. Gass did not mention the festivity that the corps enjoyed here, drinking a "dram" (technically eight drams is but an ounce, but colloquially it probably signified a "swig" or gulp) of whiskey, playing the fiddle, and dancing. Moulton, *Journals of the Lewis and Clark Expedition,* 4:70.

173. Lewis noted that there was an abundance of bald eagles in this area, where the Yellowstone and the Missouri merge. Ibid., 4:78.

174. Ordway said they stopped at 3 P.M., made a fire, and dined. Quaife, *Journals of Lewis and Ordway,* 203.

175. This was the first grizzly bear to be killed by the party. It chased Lewis and his companion 70–80 yards, according to his journal. Moulton, *Journals of the Lewis and Clark Expedition,* 4:84.

Chapter 8: May 1–June 11, 1805

176. In this first mention of religion in his journal, Gass acknowledges "a supreme being," commenting that Indians paid homage to same by offering red cloth "as a sacrifice." The journals by Lewis, Ordway, and Whitehouse all mentioned the finding in the same terms. Lewis said Joseph Field found it "suspended on the bough of a tree near an old indian hunting cam[p]." Thwaites, *Original Journals,* 1:360.

177. Whitehouse noted that they broke the irons off the red pirogue on which the rudder hung. They mended it before leaving the next morning at nine o'clock. Thwaites, *Original Journals,* 7:77.

178. The sick man was Joseph Field, who had dysentery and fever. Lewis gave him "a doze of Glauber salts" to flush him and "30 drops of laudnum" (tincture of opium) to help him sleep. Moulton, *Journals of the Lewis and Clark Expedition,* 4:109, 111 n. 4.

179. Clark and Drouillard killed the largest bear they had seen, estimated to weigh 500–600 pounds. Lewis said it took ten balls, five through his "lights" (lungs) to kill him. Ibid., 4:114, 115). Ordway reported that they found a catfish in the bear's stomach. Quaife, *Journals of Lewis and Ordway,* 207.

180. Lewis described on May 9 the delicious "harvest of white puddings" (*boudin blanc)* that Charbonneau, apparently their top cook, had been recently preparing from buffalo entrails. See Moulton, *Journals of the Lewis and Clark Expedition,* 4:131.
181. Bratton shot the grizzly through the lungs. It had chased him a half mile, then went double that distance before making a bed in which to lie and bleed. Lewis and party shot him again in the head, ending his misery. Ibid., 4:141.
182. This was the first anniversary of the party's departure from Camp DuBois near St. Louis. Whitehouse said that Gass saw banks of snow on the north side of some hills. Thwaites, *Original Journals,* 7:82. Ordway noted, "Our mocassions froze near the fire." Quaife, *Journals of Lewis and Ordway,* 211.
183. Six concealed, skilled hunters shot eight balls into this bear. The grizzly ran at them with his mouth open, nearly catching two of them, who escaped by jumping over a twenty-foot precipice into the river. The bear jumped in also, and was then shot in the head. Moulton, *Journals of the Lewis and Clark Expedition,* 4:151.
184. A squall of wind struck the white pirogue about 6 P.M., threatening to overturn it. Charbonneau, whom Lewis described as "perhaps the most timid waterman in the world," and who could not swim, sat at the helm of this canoe, helplessly calling for God's mercy. Cruzatte, the master boatman, threatened to shoot him if he would not take hold of the rudder. Doing so, the pirogue was righted and rowed to shore. The men removed all articles from the craft to dry. Two other men aboard could not swim. After the drama, Lewis wrote, "to console ourselves and cheer the sperits of our men and accordingly took a drink of grog and gave each man a gill of sperits." Clark added that Sacagawea caught many of the floating articles before they were lost. Ibid., 4:152–53, 154. Both captains watched this exasperating event from the shore.
185. Clark mentioned the outcrops of coal of the Fort Union Formation, which flank what is now known as Seven Blackfoot Creek. Ibid., 4:163 n. 8.

     The captains both noted that Clark saw a fortified but abandoned camp of a Minetaree war party that had probably set out in March to war against the Blackfoot Indians. Ibid., 4:159, 161. The party had not encountered any Native Americans since leaving the Mandans.
186. Ordway reported that a beaver bit Lewis's Newfoundland dog, Seaman. Ordway had previously told of Seaman swimming for ducks, but Gass did not mention him. Quaife, *Journals of Lewis and Ordway,* 214.
187. Lewis recorded that right up the Musselshell River, another stream discharged. They called it the "sahcagarmeah or bird woman's River, after our interpreter the Snake woman." Moulton, *Journals of the Lewis and Clark Expedition,* 4:171.
188. Ordway complained of the great amount of prickly pear. The men killed a bear and rendered oil from it. Quaife, *Journals of Lewis and Ordway,* 216.
189. These "high" hills, or those about thirty miles south of the river, are now called the Judith Mountains in Fergus County, Montana. Ibid., 217.
190. Drouillard shot this mountain sheep, which had a head and horns that weighed twenty-seven pounds. Moulton, *Journals of the Lewis and Clark Expedition,* 4:193.
191. Gibson, one of the hunters, dislocated his shoulder but got it back in place again, said Whitehouse. Thwaites, *Original Journals,* 7:88.
192. These were Elk Fawn Rapids, now Bird Rapids, Montana. Moulton, *Journals of the Lewis and Clark Expedition,* 4:207 n. 6.
193. Gass's observations in this section preceded those of Walter Prescott Webb by a century and a quarter, but Gass clearly articulated the division between the humid, timbered, green East and the "second-rate" land of the barren, arid West at about the 98th meridian. Gass, not Lewis or Clark, contributed this perceptive delineation. Webb's thesis on the physical basis for the economy of the West was appears in *The Great Plains* (Boston: Ginn, 1931).
194. This is present-day Missouri River Breaks in Fergus County, Montana. Obviously, the barren landscape did not appeal to Gass, who loved timber and verdure.
195. Lewis reflected that the white pirogue, which had almost sunk some weeks earlier, seemed to be attended by an "evil genii." Moulton, *Journals of the Lewis and Clark Expedition,* 4:215.
196. Lewis said that a bull buffalo approached within eighteen inches of the heads of sleeping men before the sentinel sounded the alarm. Lewis's dog, Seaman, chased the buffalo away. York ruined his rifle by "negligently" leaving it in the pirogue. Ibid.

197. Whitehouse noted that about one hundred Indian lodges had been here recently, probably those of Blackfeet. Thwaites, *Original Journals,* 7:90–91. Ordway said that Sacagawea examined the moccasins left behind and ascertained they belonged to Indians who lived north of the river, below the Rocky Mountains. Her tribe made moccasins differently. Around the dead buffalo roamed numerous gentle wolves, unafraid of the men. Clark killed one with his spear. Quaife, *Journals of Lewis and Ordway,* 221.

198. The party had to use a tow rope. The banks were slippery and the men could scarcely walk. A tow cord on the white pirogue broke in a river rapid, without harming the boat, according to Ordway's journal. Ibid., 221–22.

199. Gass's descriptions of the white cliffs along the Missouri River in present-day Chouteau County, Montana, parallel Lewis's remarkable passage about this area: "... a most romantic appearance... a thousand grotesque figures... eligant ranges of lofty freestone buildings... collumns of various sculpture both grooved and plain... long galleries in front of those buildings... with the help of less immigiation we see the remains or ruins of eligant buildings." Moulton, *Journals of the Lewis and Clark Expedition,* 4:225.

200. This bear was very near to catching Drouillard and Charbonneau when it was shot in the head. Ibid., 4:242.

201. Gass, Whitehouse, and one other man went south up the Missouri branch.

202. Sergeant Pryor and two others went north up the Marias branch.

203. Ascertaining the correct branch to ascend was very important so as not to lose a season—they had to get over the mountains before autumn. It was a confusing decision because the Missouri was the clear branch and the Marias was muddy like the Missouri River below the confluence, so most men thought the Marias was the correct branch. The captains did not agree with the majority and fortunately selected the correct branch. Moulton, *Journals of the Lewis and Clark Expedition,* 4:252–64.

204. This is now Teton River in Montana. Quaife, *Journals of Lewis and Ordway,* 225.

205. Joseph Field could not fire because his gun was wet. Other companions yelled and shot at the bear, who fortunately turned to the river. Clark said the bear moved close enough to strike Field's foot. Moulton, *Journals of the Lewis and Clark Expedition,* 4:256.

206. Lewis slipped at a narrow pass on the wet gumbo mud and saved himself from falling into the river ninety feet below with his espontoon (a short pike carried by infantry officers in the eighteenth and nineteenth century), when Windsor cried, "God, God! Captain What shall I do?" Lewis said Windsor's right arm and leg were over the edge and he was clinging on by his left hand. Lewis calmly advised him to get his knife from his belt with his free hand and dig a hole in the bank for his right foot. Windsor thus saved himself. Ibid., 4:262–63.

207. The officers gave the party each a dram of whiskey on June 9. They played the fiddle and danced, Whitehouse wrote. Thwaites, *Original Journals,* 7:98. Rabbit berries are also known as buffalo berries, or *Sheperdia argentea.* Ibid., 7:437.

208. The red pirogue was the larger.

209. Sacagawea was very sick. Clark bled her in accordance with the medical practice of Benjamin Rush, a friend of President Jefferson who tutored Lewis prior to the journey. Moulton, *Journals of the Lewis and Clark Expedition,* 4:275–76.

210. Lewis, Drouillard, Gibson, Joseph Field, and Goodrich set out for the snowy southern mountains, Ordway reported. Quaife, Journals of *Lewis and Ordway,* 229.

211. Ordway listed the buried items: one keg of powder, one bar of lead, one keg of flour, one keg of pork, two kegs of parched meal, a bellows and tolls, an auger, planes, saws, axes, tin cups, dutch ovens, bearskins, packs of beaver skins, buffalo robes, and a number of other articles such as ram's horns. Ibid., 229–30.

212. Clark bled Sacagawea again. Moulton, *Journals of the Lewis and Clark Expedition,* 4:279.

Chapter 9: June 12–July 14, 1805

213. Patrick Gass was thirty-four on June 12, 1805.

214. Lewis's party, including J. Field, Drouillard, Gibson, and Goodrich, discovered the Great Falls on June 13. Moulton, *Journals of the Lewis and Clark Expedition,* 4:283.

215. Lewis had been walking alone to "see where the rappids termineated [sic] above" and was going to return to camp for dinner. He had just shot a buffalo when a grizzly chased him before he had a chance to reload his gun. (He swore never to let this happen again.) He ran into the water and the bear fortunately turned away. Then he ran into a "tyger cat" (cougar), which disappeared in its burrow when he shot at it. Three hundred yards from this, he was charged by three bull buffalo! So many misadventures made Lewis wonder if he might be dreaming, but the prickly pear biting his feet through his moccasins convinced him that he was not. To read Lewis's own version of this adventure story, see ibid., 4:292–94.

216. Clark noted that Sacagawea was very gravely ill. Ibid., 4:294. Ordway mentioned it. Quaife, *Journals of Lewis and Ordway,* 231. So did Whitehouse. Thwaites, *Original Journals,* 7:100. Gass is the only journalist who did not.

217. This wording is identical to that in Ordway's journal. Quaife, *Journals of Lewis and Ordway,* 231.

218. Strawberry Creek is now Highwood Creek, Montana. Ibid., 231, n. 3.

219. Rattlesnakes were thick in this country and are mentioned by both captains on this date. Moulton, *Journals of the Lewis and Clark Expedition,* 4:297–98.

220. This passage describes the Great Falls of the Missouri, in Montana.

221. This party included Alexander Willard, John Colter, and perhaps Joseph Field. Moulton, *Journals of the Lewis and Clark Expedition,* 4:305 n. 1. Gass wrote that Clark took four men; all other journalists say five.

222. This was the white pirogue. The red pirogue had already been hidden.

223. On June 18, Sacagawea was finally better. All sources but Gass noted her recovery. Chuinard, *Only One Man Died,* 289, refers to Drake W. Will, who thinks that her grave illness from June 12 through June 17 may have been chronic pelvic inflammatory disease, due to gonorrheal infection. The twitching she exhibited could have been due to the loss of minerals from being bled. Bleeding, a cure Lewis learned from Benjamin Rush, fortunately fell out of vogue soon after this era.

224. The three hunters were George Drouillard, Reuben Field, and George Shannon. Moulton, *Journals of the Lewis and Clark Expedition,* 4:309.

225. Lewis said that all except Ordway, Charbonneau, Goodrich, York, and the Indian woman (Sacagawea) set out. Ibid., 4:325. Whitehouse stated that York stayed at the lower camp, where he shot a fat buffalo. Thwaites, *Original Journals,* 7:105.

226. Gass, Joseph Field, and John Shields were chosen by Lewis to make his iron boat. Moulton, *Journals of the Lewis and Clark Expedition,* 4:323. Lewis had toted the frame all this way and expected to cover it with leather. The men worked on it from June 24 to July 9, when it sank.

227. Lewis and J. Field met Shannon. Ibid., 4:327.

228. Lewis noted that Gass and Shields were making slow progress in finding willow and box elder to cut four and one-half–foot lengths for the boat. He instructed Frazer to stay to sew hides together. Ibid., 4:330.

229. Shannon and Joseph Field returned. Lewis had returned earlier. Ibid.

230. Lewis said Drouillard and Reuben Field had been hunting. Ibid., 4:329–30.

231. Lewis sent Frazer to Drouillard's camp to get the hunter and gather the meat he had killed. Ibid., 4:331.

232. Joseph Field leaped down the river bank and escaped the bears but hurt his hand. Ibid.

233. Gass and Shields were sent to the island to look for wood. Ibid.

234. Drouillard and Frazer brought back 800 pounds of meat. Ibid.

235. Gass's companion was still Shields. Ibid.

236. Whitehouse was very sick from drinking too much water while he was hot. He was bled. Thwaites, *Original Journals,* 7:108.

237. Lewis noted that Gass and Shields were making little progress in the operation of shaving and fitting horizontal bars of wood in sections of the iron boat because the timber was so crooked. Moulton, *Journals of the Lewis and Clark Expedition,* 4:336.

238. Clark mentioned the hail in his notes on weather at the end of the month. Ibid., 4:348. Ordway added that the hail was seven inches in circumference at Lewis's camp. The men at his own camp, "being naked," would have been bruised by such hailstones with the wind so high and violent. Apparently it was so hot, and the work was so hard, that the men were mostly naked and without hats. Quaife, *Journals of Lewis and Ordway,* 241.

239. The people at Gass's camp were Frazer, Whitehouse, Gass, Shields, Lewis, J. Field, and Drouillard. Moulton, *Journals of Lewis and Clark,* 4:337.

240. The hunter with Lewis was Drouillard. Ibid., 4:339.

241. This was the day that Clark, Charbonneau, Sacagawea, and the infant Jean Baptiste nearly perished getting out of a ravine that quickly filled with water during a downpour. Ibid., 4:342–33.

242. Lewis wrote that he set Gass to work making strips of willow limbs, which were not good but the best available. Ibid., 4:349.

243. The Lewis and Clark parties rejoined on July 1, so Gass and Whitehouse were two days late in reporting this event.

244. The portage was now complete.

245. This account is not like those in other journals, nor is it Gass's perfunctory style. McKeehan's editing hand must have played a part here.

246. Gass, McNeal, and several others visited the falls and the big spring, viewing an immense number of buffalo and wolves. These events are not noted in other journals. Moulton, *Journals of the Lewis and Clark Expedition,* 4:359.

247. On July 7, Whitehouse was employed in making leather clothes for the men. Thwaites, *Original Journals,* 7:111.

248. This was a kit fox, sometimes called a swift fox. Moulton, *Journals of the Lewis and Clark Expedition,* 4:367, 368 n. 2.

249. This was a thirteen-striped ground squirrel. Paul Russell Cutright, *Lewis and Clark: Pioneering Naturalists* (Urbana: University of Illinois Press, 1969; Lincoln: Bison Books, 1989), 166.

250. Gass is the first and only journalist to refer to the iron boat by name. He had spent two weeks working on it. As the boat was taking shape, it would have been natural for the builders to think of christening it.

251. The ten men included Pryor and four woodchoppers, two invalids (York was sick on the 7th, and Bratton had an infected finger), and one hunter (Drouillard?). The two invalids could have been Potts and LePage. Moulton, *Journals of the Lewis and Clark Expedition,* 4:366, 374, 373. See note 254.

252. On the 11th, a rattlesnake bit Whitehouse's legging. He shot it. The snake measured four feet, two inches long and five and one half inches around. Thwaites, *Original Journals,* 7:113.

253. Lewis sent Gass and three others to Clark's camp to build the canoes after the failure of the iron boat, the *Experiment.* Moulton, *Journals of the Lewis and Clark Expedition,* 4:376.

254. The old Indian lodge was probably of the Piegan Blackfeet tribe. Ibid., 4:378.

255. Whitehouse wrote that Lewis, a sick Frenchman, and the interpreter's wife went across by land. Thwaites, *Original Journals,* 7:113. The Frenchman was Baptiste LePage. Moulton, *Journals of the Lewis and Clark Expedition,* 4:378.

Chapter 10: July 15–August 9, 1805

256. This river, west of Great Falls in present-day Montana, was named Smith's River in honor of Robert Smith, Secretary of the Navy. It still bears the same name. Moulton, *Journals of the Lewis and Clark Expedition,* 4:382.

257. Ordway forgot an axe and was sent back for it. Quaife, *Journals of Lewis and Ordway,* 247; Thwaites, *Original Journals,* 7:115.

258. Lewis said he set out with the two invalids, whom he identified as Potts and LePage. Moulton, *Journals of the Lewis and Clark Expedition,* 4:386.

259. Whitehouse wrote that they camped at the entrance of the Rocky Mountains. Thwaites, *Original Journals,* 7:115.

260. Ordway explained that they emptied some articles and double-manned the tow lines to bring the canoes up the half-mile-long rapids. They sent back for baggage. Quaife, *Journals of Lewis and Ordway,* 248.

261. The three men were J. Field, Potts, and York. Moulton, *Journals of the Lewis and Clark Expedition,* 4:398.

262. Prickly pear, a ground-covering cactus, was so thick that the men could hardly find a place to lie in camp. Ibid., 4:407.

263. Here Sacagawea encouraged the party by saying the Three Forks of the Missouri were not far away. The party then understood they were near her people. Lewis was

very eager to meet with the Snake Indians because they had horses that might be used to transport the party over the mountains. Clearly, the corps could not continue on foot up these rocky rapid rivers. For a discussion of subsequent journalistic stretching of the verb *guide* in regard to Sacagawea's role, see Arlen J. Large and Edrie L. Vinson, "Sacagawea: The Guide vs. The Purists," *We Proceeded On* 19 (February 1993), 4–10.

264. The four men who asked to go were Joseph and Reuben Field, Frazer, and Charbonneau. Moulton, *Journals of the Lewis and Clark Expedition,* 4:418.

265. Gass's recording here is interesting compared to that of Lewis, who mentioned the red earth but didn't note Sacagawea's comment that Indians used it for paint.

266. Lewis lamented the decline of buffalo as they proceeded, "from the appearance of bones and excrement of old date the buffaloe sometimes straggle into this valley; but there is no fresh sighn of them and I begin [*sic*] think that our harrvest of white puddings is at an end, at least untill our return to the buffaloe country. our trio of pests still invade and obstruct us on all occasions, these are the Musqetoes eye knats and prickley pears, equal to any three curses that ever poor Egypt laiboured under, except the *Mahometant yoke.* the men complain of being much fortiegued, their labour is excessively great. I occasionly encourage them by assisting in the labour of navigating the canoes, and have learned to *push a tolerable good pole* in their fraize." Moulton, *Journals of the Lewis and Clark Expedition,* 4:423.

267. Lewis named Gass's Creek after Sergeant Gass (Moulton, *Journals of the Lewis and Clark Expedition,* 4:426):

> we passed a large Crk. today in the plain country, 25 yds. wide, which discharges itself on the Stard. side; it is composed of five streams which unite in the plain at no great distance from the river and have their souces [*sic*] in the Mts. this stream we called Gass's Creek. after Sergt. Patric Gass one of our party.

Moulton says this stream, in Broadwater County, Montana, is now called Crow Creek. Ibid., 4:429 n. 2.

268. This is present-day Three Forks, Montana.

269. Sacagawea had been taken prisoner here five years before by the Gros Ventres (also known as Minatarees or Big Bellies). This tribe killed four men, four women, and a number of boys of the Snake (Shoshone) nation and took females as prisoners. Moulton, *Journals of the Lewis and Clark Expedition,* 5:9.

270. Gass was injured, wrote Lewis. He strained his back when he slipped and fell backwards on the gunwale of the canoe. It was painful for him to work in the canoe but he could walk, so he accompanied Lewis to go "in quest of the Snake Indians." Ibid., 5:18.

271. The men's daily schedule seems to have been to arise at sunrise and work a few hours, pausing for a cold breakfast, then proceeding on until afternoon, when they set up camp and cooked the kill of the day.

272. Gass, Lewis, Charbonneau, and Drouillard searched for Snake (Shoshone) Indians, as reported by Whitehouse. Thwaites, *Original Journals,* 7:125.

273. Gass lost Captain Lewis's tomahawk in the thick brush soon after passing the river, and they could not find it. Lewis wrote, "I regret the loss of this usefull implement, however accidents will happen in the best families, and I consoled myself with the recollection that it was not the only one we had with us." Moulton, *Journals of the Lewis and Clark Expedition,* 5:32.

274. R. Field killed a "panther" (cougar) on an island. It was seven and a half feet in length and differed from those in the States, being of a reddish brown color. This was the first killed by the expedition. Quaife, *Journals of Lewis and Ordway,* 257.

275. Lewis wrote that Charbonneau complained of not being able to "march far," so he sent him with Gass to pass the rapid river near the camp and go at their leisure through a level bottom to a point of high timber about seven miles distant on the middle fork, which was in view. Lewis and Drouillard continued up the river. Moulton, *Journals of the Lewis and Clark Expedition,* 5:44.

276. The main corps went with Captain Clark up the right-hand fork of the Missouri, or the Big Hole (Wisdom), River. The current was very swift, and the men had trouble hauling the canoes over the rapids. George Drouillard informed them on the 6th that this appeared to be the wrong fork. The mistake occurred because a beaver had chewed down the tree on which Gass had placed a message directing Clark's group, making

it impossible for the men to follow the advance party. Quaife, *Journals of Lewis and Ordway,* 259.

277. Gass erroneously described this accident. Whitehouse nearly lost his life and hurt his leg. Ibid., 260.

278. Whitehouse mentioned that George Shannon was lost; Gass did not. He was scouting up the Wisdom River ahead of Clark's party, which had reversed directions to pursue the other fork, without Shannon's knowledge. Thwaites, *Original Journals,* 7:129; Quaife, *Journals of Lewis and Ordway,* 260.

279. Lewis said Gass helped him with the "observation of equal altitudes" of the sun, a measurement used to establish local time. Gass apparently errs in his record of latitude: Lewis records it as 45° 2' 43.8s. Moulton, *Journals of the Lewis and Clark Expedition,* 5:56.

The group waited here until 3:00 P.M. to dry their goods. Lewis sent R. Field to look for Shannon. Ibid., 5:55.

280. R. Field rejoined the group. He had been looking unsuccessfully for Shannon. Thwaites, *Original Journals,* 7:130.

281. Gass noted why Clark missed the fork—a beaver cut down the tree where Gass had posted a notice. Moulton, *Journals of the Lewis and Clark Expedition,* 5:59.

282. Here Gass finally mentioned Shannon's three-day absence. Whitehouse wrote that Shannon rejoined the group after being gone three days. Thwaites, *Original Journals,* 7:130.

283. Drouillard, Hugh McNeal, and John Shields were the three men who went ahead. Ibid.

284. Lewis was becoming desperate to find Indians and horses. However, on August 10, he was still dreaming of the Northwest Passage when he wrote, "I do not beleive that the world can furnish an example of a river runing to the extent which the Missouri and Jefferson's rivers do through such a mountainous country and at the same time so navigable as they are. if the Columbia furnishes us such another example, a communication across the continent by water will be practicable and safe." Moulton, *Journals of the Lewis and Clark Expedition,* 5:65.

285. Thomas Jefferson was president, James Madison was secretary of state, and Albert Gallatin was secretary of the treasury of the United States in 1805.

Chapter 11: August 1—August 31, 1805

286. On the 11th, Lewis, who had gone ahead to look for Indians, finally saw a Shoshone and approached him, but Drouillard and Shields inadvertently scared him away. Moulton, *Journals of the Lewis and Clark Expedition,* 5:68–70.

287. On the 12th, Lewis and his small scouting party crossed the Continental Divide at Lemhi Pass (on what is now the Idaho-Montana border) while they were tracking Indians. Lewis wrote that two miles short of Lemhi Pass, "McNeal had exultingly stood with a foot on each side of this little rivulet and thanked his god that he had lived to bestride the mighty & heretofore deemed endless Missouri." Ibid., 5:74. Just over Lemhi Pass are the headwaters of rivers that eventually flow into the Columbia.

288. Whitehouse noted seeing otter, bald eagles, and ducks and that the men caught a number of trout on August 13. Thwaites, *Original Journals,* 7:133.

Lewis's entry for the 13th is very rich. His small party came upon two women, a man, and some dogs who saw them and disappeared. Then they approached three women. One fled. An old woman and a twelve-year-old girl stayed, waiting to die. Through Drouillard's art of gesticulation, Lewis asked the old woman to call the young one back, and gave trinkets to all, asking in sign language to be taken to their leaders. When they met about sixty warriors on horses, those women spoke to their men and showed the white men's gifts. When the Indian men approached the strangers, they put their left arms over the right shoulders of their guests, clasping their backs and placing their left cheeks to the newcomers', saying "*âh-hí-e, âh-hí-e,* I am much rejoiced." Lewis wrote, "We wer all carresed and besmeared with their grease and paint till I was heartily tired of the national hug. . . and [they] pulled of [*sic*] their mockersons before they would receive or smoke the pipe. . . of friendship [showing their sincerity that] they may always go bearfoot if they are not sincere." Moulton, *Journals of the Lewis and Clark Expedition,* 5:79.

289. Clark wrote on the 14th, "I checked our interpreter [Charbonneau] for Strikeing his woman at their Dinner." Ibid., 5:93.

290. Lewis, in the advance party, was talking with Cameawait, Sacagawea's "brother." (She called him "brother," but he could have been a cousin.) Lewis was convincing him of friendship, prior to his crucial need to buy horses from his tribe for the overland trip west. Ibid., 5:96–97.

291. While Clark's party was fishing, a rattlesnake on the ground between Clark's feet nearly bit him. He killed it and several more, according to Whitehouse. Thwaites, *Original Journals*, 7:134.

292. Clark, Charbonneau, and Sacagawea walked on the shore and picked berries. Whitehouse said the Indian woman, "gethered a pale full & gave them to the party at noon." Ibid., 7:134–35.

293. Whitehouse noted that the party first heard the Indians singing. Ibid., 136.

294. Gass's account of this agreement is really an oversimplification of Lewis's trip, meeting with the Shoshones, and attempts to buy horses. Negotiations for horses lasted days. By the 17th, Lewis had been told by Cameahwait, the chief, that the Salmon River was impassable. Lewis waited anxiously for Clark's party to arrive while the Shoshones went to meet him.

   Gass failed to mention a significant event for the 17th: Sacagawea recognized Cameahwait, the chief, as her "brother" (see note 290). Clark described it thusly, "The Great Chief of this nation proved to be the brother of the *Woman* with us and is a man of Influence Sence & easey & reserved manners, appears to possess a great deel of Cincerity." Moulton, *Journals of the Lewis and Clark Expedition*, 5:114.

295. This party under Clark was going to check on the possibility of a passage through the Salmon River. It included Sergeants Gass and Pryor, Privates Collins, Colter, Cruzatte, Shannon, Windsor, and four others unidentified. Charbonneau and Sacagawea went as far as the Indian village. Moulton, *Journals of the Lewis and Clark Expedition*, 5:116 n. 4.

296. On August 18, Lewis had his thirty-first birthday and waxed philosophically about wanting to improve his contribution to humanity, "to live for *mankind*, as I have heretofore lived *for myself*." Ibid., 5:118.

297. This branch of the Columbia has been identified as Horseshoe Bend Creek. John Peebles, "Rugged Waters: Trails and Campsites of Lewis and Clark in the Salmon River Country," *Idaho Yesterdays* 8 (Summer 1964), 7.

298. Peebles placed this encampment on Pattee Creek. Ibid.

299. Back at the Indian village, the majority of the party were engaged in dressing skins, making pack saddles, fishing, and packing baggage for an overland trip. Lewis was bargaining for more horses. Quaife, *Journals of Lewis and Ordway*, 270. Lewis found that the value of one mule equaled that of two to four horses. Moulton, *Journals of the Lewis and Clark Expedition*, 5:123

300. Cruzatte stayed at the Shoshone camp to buy a horse. Ibid., 5:137.

301. This was Carmen Creek. Peebles, "Rugged Waters," 9.

   Collins went to the fishing place, returning with Cruzatte later on the 21st. Moulton, *Journals of the Lewis and Clark Expedition*, 5:137–38.

302. This August morning Ordway wrote, "The ink freezes in my pen now," as the sun rose. Lewis hid baggage left behind for their overland horseback journey. Quaife, *Journals of Lewis and Ordway*, 271.

303. This was Boyle Creek. Peebles, "Rugged Waters," 9.

304. This was the North Fork of the Salmon River, where Gass went with Clark's party to scout a westward river passage. Ibid.

305. Whitehouse said that, at this time, he was employed making leather shirts and overalls. Also at the main camp, Lewis bought three horses and two mules. The party caught 520 fish and divided them with the Shoshones. Charbonneau, Sacagawea, and party arrived. Lewis "made two of the Indians chiefs," presenting them with presents. Thwaites, *Original Journals*, 7:140. During this time, Gass was with Clark on the present-day Salmon River in Idaho.

306. This man was Sergeant Pryor. Moulton, *Journals of the Lewis and Clark Expedition*, 5:157 n. 5.

307. Whitehouse reported from the main camp on the east side of the divide that they had sunk the canoes for safekeeping until the party's return. Thwaites, *Original Journals*, 7:141.

308. On the 25th, Lewis discovered from Charbonneau that the Shoshone tribe planned to go to the Missouri country to hunt. Lewis confronted Cameahwait about his promise to trade horses and assist the corps in getting to the west side of the mountains. Cameahwait hesitated and apologized, saying his people were hungry. When the hunters returned on the 25th, Lewis gave the day's kill to the Shoshone women and children, remaining "supperless" himself. Moulton, *Journals of the Lewis and Clark Expedition*, 5:166.

309. On the 26th, Ordway told the story of the birth that occurred while Shoshone women were helping to transport baggage for the Corps of Discovery across the Lemhi Pass: "one of our Indian women was taken sick rideing a long & halted a fiew minutes & had hir child without detaining us." Quaife, *Journals of Lewis and Ordway*, 274. Moulton, *Journals of the Lewis and Clark Expedition*, 5:171.

310. Whitehouse wrote that Gass joined Lewis's group about 2 o'clock and told them Clark and the rest of the men were waiting about twelve miles downriver. Lewis sent Gass back to get Clark's help in packing the horses. Thwaites, *Original Journals*, 7:144.

311. Gass's observation of Lemhi Shoshones' fire building, salmon drying, and basket-making stands as a rare contribution to ethnology for him, significant because the exploration party comprised the first white men to visit them.

312. On August 30, in the high mountain area where game was scarce, Clark said the hunters killed two deer; it was the first time he had eaten meat in eight days. Moulton, *Journals of the Lewis and Clark Expedition*, 5:178.

313. They continued to buy horses. Clark gave a musket for a horse to bring the total to twenty-nine. Moulton, *Journals of the Lewis and Clark Expedition*, 5:178. Toby, the old guide (who is not named until Ordway's entry of May 4, 1806; Quaife, *Journals of Lewis and Ordway*, 352) said there were two ways to go: south of the river in the desert, where there was no game or water; or north through the rough mountains, which in ten days would bring them to a fork that in fifteen days would take them to the "salt water." Ibid., 277.

314. This is Boyles Creek again. Ibid., 279. Peebles, "Rugged Waters," 9.

Chapter 12: September 1–September 14, 1805

315. On September 1, Clark noted that all the Lemhi Shoshone left the combined party except for their guide, Toby. The party was traveling to the North Fork of the Salmon River and camped on its bank south of present-day Gibbonsville, Idaho. Moulton, *Journals of the Lewis and Clark Expedition*, 5:183 n.1.

316. Whitehouse wrote that they descended a mountain "nearly as Steep as the roof of a house." Thwaites, *Original Journals*, 7:147.

317. Whitehouse bemoaned, "We Call this place dismal Swamp, and it is a lonsom rough part of the Country." Thwaites, *Original Journals*, 7:147. Ordway also described a "dismal Swamp. . . very rough and rockey." Quaife, *Journals of Lewis and Ordway*, 279.

318. Whitehouse told of three or four horses falling backwards and rolling to the foot of the hills. Thwaites, *Original Journals*, 7:147.

319. Gass's language here defied his usual sanguine tone. Ordway confirmed the sentiment, saying the men were wet, hungry, cold, and fatigued. Quaife, *Journals of Lewis and Ordway*, 280.

320. Whitehouse was graphic on the 6th, when he wrote, "Our mockersons froze hard." Thwaites, *Original Journals*, 7:148. So was Ordway when he recorded, "Our fingers aked with the cold." Quaife, *Journals of Lewis and Ordway*, 280.

321. About thirty Flathead Indians at Ross's Hole (Montana) had 400–500 horses. Ordway said they received the corps in a friendly manner. Giving each officer a white robe of dressed skins, the Flatheads put their arms around the necks of the members of the Lewis and Clark party. Sergeant Ordway described them as well-dressed, decent-looking, light-complexioned "Welch Indians," with a "bur" on their tongue. Quaife, *Journals of Lewis and Ordway*, 281. Whitehouse described their language by saying it sounded like they had a speech impediment and the interpreters had to go through six languages to be understood, but they were the "likelyest and honestst Savages we have ever yet Seen." Thwaites, *Original Journals*, 7:150. Lewis noted they were "a very light coloured people of large stature and comely form," in his entry for September 10, 1805. Moulton, *Journals of the Lewis and Clark Expedition*, 5:197.

James Ronda, *Lewis and Clark among the Indians,* 155–56, identifies these Indians as Flatheads, who did not practice the custom of flattening heads, and identifies their language as Salishan. They were Ootlashoots of the Tushepaw nation who joined the Shoshones for the annual buffalo hunt on the Missouri, camped at Ross's Hole when they met Lewis and Clark.

The chain of translation was from Lewis's English, to Labiche's French to Charbonneau's Hidatsa, to Sacagawea's Shoshone, to a Shoshone boy's Salish. (This was a boy freed by these Flatheads from another tribe that had taken him slave. He apparently had remained with the Flatheads.)

322. Clark exchanged seven horses and purchased eleven more. "those people possess ellegant horses," he wrote. Moulton, *Journals of the Lewis and Clark Expedition,* 5:188.

323. One must contrast the elation of the hungry corps over two deer with their complaisance on the Missouri plains, where profuse kills were made, waste occurred, and they finally had decided to kill only what they needed for the day.

324. Clark tallied the kill at four deer, four ducks, and three prairie fowls. Moulton, *Journals of the Lewis and Clark Expedition,* 5:193.

325. On September 9, they arrived at Travellers Rest, near the present-day Idaho-Montana border.

326. These three Indians are not identifed by Ronda. Ralph Space, *The Lolo Trail: A History of Events Connected with the Lolo Trail Since Lewis and Clark* (Lewiston, Idaho: Princraft Printing, 1984), 5, wrote that they were Nez Perce; Moulton agreed, *Journals of the Lewis and Clark Expedition,* 5:198 n. 3. The Flatheads had gone hunting with the Snakes.

327. At this point the men were starting west on the Lolo Trail (named subsequent to the expedition) along Lolo Creek. Nez Perce followed this route to buffalo country in Montana from their homes, located from the Weippe Prairie westward in Idaho to the present Washington-Oregon border. Moulton, *Journals of the Lewis and Clark Expedition,* 199 n. 4.

328. Ordway wrote that it was 10:00 P.M. before they found a place to camp. Quaife, *Journals of Lewis and Ordway,* 285.

329. This was Lolo Hot Springs. Moulton, *Journals of the Lewis and Clark Expedition,* 5:203.

330. Captain Lewis's horse was missing. Quaife, *Journals of Lewis and Ordway,* 285.

331. This occurred on Colt Killed (now White Sand) Creek, on the Lochsa River, near the present-day Powell Ranger Station.

Chapter 13: September 15–October 14, 1805

332. Whitehouse reported that some of the men without socks wrapped rags on their feet. Thwaites, *Original Journals,* 7:157.

333. This was the second colt killed. Whitehouse and Ordway agreed. Ibid.; Quaife, *Journals of Lewis and Ordway,* 287.

334. Whitehouse noted, "The mare which owned the colt, which we killed, went back & led 4 more horses back to where we took dinner yesterday." Thwaites, *Original Journals,* 7:157. Following her instincts, the mare went back looking for her colt where she last saw it.

335. This was the third colt killed. Whitehouse said it was a "Sucking colt." Thwaites, *Original Journals,* 7:158. Ordway noted it was their last colt. Quaife, *Journals of Lewis and Ordway,* 287. Clark missed reporting this.

336. These six men, led by Clark, included R. Field and Shields. They were sent ahead to find the main party. Moulton, *Journals of the Lewis and Clark Expedition,* 5:211, 214 n. 2.

337. Willard had been sent for the horse. Ibid., 5:211.

338. Frazer's horse fell, Lewis reported. Ibid., 5:215.

339. Baptiste LePage had been in charge of the lost pack horse with all of Captain Lewis's belongings and was sent back to search for it. Ibid., 5:218.

340. On the 20th, Clark met the Nez Perce at the Weippe Prairie, Idaho. Sahaptian speakers, they were called "Choppunish" or "Pierced Noses." Ronda, *Lewis and Clark among the Indians,* 158.

341. Clark had sent R. Field with an Indian and some salmon to meet Lewis and his group. Moulton, *Journals of the Lewis and Clark Expedition,* 5:226. The "Savages was verry glad to See us," said Whitehouse. Thwaites, *Original Journals,* 7:161.

342. Gass's usual positive tone reappears as he contrasts the "handsome small prairie" of modern-day Weippe to the "dismal and horrible mountains" they had just crossed on the Lolo Trail.

343. Ordway reported that they found the horse carrying Lewis's things, but they lost the horse they took with them. Quaife, *Journals of Lewis and Ordway,* 289. Whitehouse added that they brought the baggage on their own backs after losing both horses. Thwaites, *Original Journals,* 7:161.

344. Gass's identification of camas roots and the way they are cooked into bread is informative, as is his description of its bloom later in the text.

345. The north fork of the Clearwater River, on which the group camped, flows into the Snake River at present-day Lewiston, Idaho; the Snake flows into the Columbia near Kennewick and Pasco, Washington.

346. The small panther was a bobcat.

347. These must be mountain goats, which have a beautiful white "wool," not mountain sheep, which have a sleek dun colored hide.

348. These were Nez Perce. See note 340.

349. Although Nez Perce traveled widely to The Dalles to trade with Columbian tribes and to the Plains to hunt buffalo, the Corps of Discovery brought the first known white people to their homeland. One of their women, Watkuweis, who was befriended by whites in Canada, assured the party's safety by her admonition to her tribespeople to "do them no hurt." Ronda, *Lewis and Clark among the Indians,* 159.

350. Whitehouse wrote that they prepared their axes for building canoes and divided the party into five groups to cut down pitch pine trees. Thwaites, *Original Journals,* 7:164.

351. One of three times when Gass fell ill, this time he, like nearly all of the corps, probably was suffering the gastronomical effects of changing to a diet of camas roots and dried salmon. On the 24th, Clark was treating this ailment with Rush's pills.

352. This camp was at the junction of the north fork and the main fork of the Clearwater River in Idaho. They stayed here from September 26 until October 7 to make canoes, and called it "Canoe Camp."

353. They were making paddles as well as canoes.

354. Lewis was very sick from the diet, as were Drouillard and most of the men, Clark said. Moulton, *Journals of the Lewis and Clark Expedition,* 5:235.

355. Instead of chipping the wood out to hollow the center of the canoes, the Nez Perce burned out the center, saving much labor for the tired, weak, and ill men.

356. These men were Frazer and Goodrich. Ibid., 5:244.

357. On the 4th, Whitehouse wrote that some of the men ate a fat dog. Thwaites, *Original Journals,* 7:166. The Frenchmen in the party were particularly fond of dog. Captain Clark was one of the few who could not eat it.

358. Whitehouse said they collected their horses, cropped the fore manes, and branded them with a stirrup iron on the near fore shoulder, to identify them on the return of the corps. They intended to leave the horses with Twisted Hair, but he wished to accompany them; in that event, the corps would leave the horses in the care of his two sons. There were thirty-eight horses. Thwaites, *Original Journals,* 7:166. Moulton, *Journals of the Lewis and Clark Expedition,* 5:250. Nez Perce oral tradition.

359. In his journal, Whitehouse gave a good description of the canoe accident. One of the canoes struck a rock and wheeled around, nearly splitting the craft in two. It threw its steerman, Gass, overboard. But he reached the sinking canoe that hung on the rocks "in a doeful Situation. Some of the men on board could not swim and them that could had no chance for the waves and rocks." An Indian went out in a small canoe to rescue them. The little canoe from which Whitehouse was watching paddled out to rescue some of the baggage. Thompson was injured in the accident. Men emptied the canoe to repair it. Thwaites, *Original Journals,* 7:168; Moulton, *Journals of the Lewis and Clark Expedition,* 5:251.

360. They bought two dogs to eat from the natives at an Indian village on shore. Thwaites, *Original Journals,* 7:167.

361. These chiefs were Nez Perce, Twisted Hair, and Tetoharsky. Moulton, *Journals of the Lewis and Clark Expedition,* 5:250 n. 2.

362. Clark said four men were put to work on the canoe: Sergeant Pryor, Sergeant Gass, and Privates Joseph Field and George Gibson. Ibid., 252.

363. Toby and his son left without pay. Quaife, *Journals of Lewis and Ordway*, 296. It was later discovered that they had taken two horses, less than fair compensation for their services as guides from the Lemhi mountains to the Palouse plains. Undoubtedly, the two Shoshone were terrified after witnessing the canoe wreck, as Gass contended. Ronda, *Lewis and Clark among the Indians*, 162, suspects that they also feared potentially hostile tribes as they approached less familiar territory.

364. While the corps was enjoying fiddle music, an Indian woman began singing and gave all her audience some roots. Whitehouse wrote that she hysterically took a flint from her husband and cut her arms "so that the blood gushed out. She wiped up the blood and eat it. then tore off Some beeds and peaces of copper &c. which hung about hir and gave out to them that were round hir a little to each one. Still kept her Singing and makeing a hishing noise. She then ran around went to the water Some of her kindred went after hir and brought hir back She then fell in to a fit and continued Stiff and Speechless Some time they pored water on hir face untill She came too. Cap. Clark gave hir Some Small things which pleased hir." Thwaites, *Original Journals,* 7:168–69.

365. Gass used the Nez Perce word for the modern-day Clearwater River.

366. Gass referred to the modern-day Snake River, named "Lewis's River" by the corps. The Snake and Clearwater meet where Lewiston, Idaho, and Clarkston, Washington, sit on opposite sides of the Snake River, the boundary between Idaho and Washington.

367. It is unlikely that Gass suffered a fit of the ague, a fever like malaria, especially in view of his long and healthy life. After his canoe accident, he probably was exhausted with fever and cold. Chuinard, *Only One Man Died,* 175 n. 19, missed Gass's reference to ague.

368. They camped below Almota Creek near present-day Almota, Washington. Moulton, *Journals of the Lewis and Clark Expedition,* 5:264 n. 9.

369. Since the party traveled with two Nez Perce on the 11th, the Indian of another nation was not Nez Perce and remains unidentified. Ordway said they bought salmon and eight or ten fat dogs. He also noted that the Indians along the river had copper trade items, including kettles and trinkets. Quaife, *Journals of Lewis and Ordway,* 297.

370. "Early" was 7:00 A.M., according to Clark. Moulton, *Journals of the Lewis and Clark Expedition,* 5:264. According to the calculations of Ludd A. Trozpek, of Claremont, California, this was about an hour after sunrise, which occurred at 6:04 A.M. at that longitude on October 12, 1805. The corps was then on the Snake River near present-day Penawawa Creek, Washington. Ibid., 5:264–66.

371. Tribes in this area were Sahaptian speakers, not Flatheads.

372. On the 13th, Whitehouse wrote that the Indians were riding horses rapidly along the side of the river to keep up with the party. Thwaites, *Original Journals,* 7:171–72.

373. This canoe was under the command of Ordway. It left four men standing on a rock until another canoe came to rescue them. Ibid., 172.

Chapter 14: October 15–November 3, 1805

374. Whitehouse was aboard the canoe under Sgt. Pryor's command that ran into rocks. Thwaites, *Original Journals,* 7:173; Moulton, *Journals of the Lewis and Clark Expedition,* 5:276.

375. Yakimas and Wanapams sold the party eight dogs and salmon. Moulton, *Journals of the Lewis and Clark Expedition,* 5:184 n. 8. Two hundred Wanapam men came with Chief Cutssahnem, singing and beating on drums. The captains smoked with them and relied on Teotarsky and Twisted Hair to translate the Sahaptian tongue of the newcomers. Ronda, *Lewis and Clark among the Indians,* 165.

376. The point between two rivers is just southeast of Pasco, Washington, at present-day Sacajawea State Park.

377. The Yakima River is a northwest tributary of the Columbia near this site, at the present-day town of Richland, Benton County, Washington.

378. The Kimooeenum is the Snake River.

379. The Kooskooske is the Clearwater River.

380. Three nations lived near each other in this general area: the Palouse (who used boards to flatten their heads), the Yakimas, and the Wanapams, who were in the same language group as the Nez Perce. Moulton, *Journals of the Lewis and Clark Expedition,* 5:284. The two Nez Perce chiefs were still with the corps, so communication was possible.

381. Clark thought the fish offered them had been taken dead from the shore, so he bought forty dogs to eat. Moulton, *Journals of the Lewis and Clark Expedition,* 5:294.

382. Yellepit, chief of the Walla Wallas, was the Indian to whom they presented a medal. Clark described him as "a bold handsom Indian, with a dignified countenance about 35 years of age, about 5 feet 8 inches high and well perpotiond." Moulton, *Journals of the Lewis and Clark Expedition,* 5:303.

383. This large Indian camp was probably the Umatilla Indian village. Ronda, *Lewis and Clark among the Indians,* 167–68.

384. This passage parallels the account in Whitehouse. Thwaites, *Original Journals,* 7:176. Clark did not include the description until the 20th.

385. Interestingly, each journal noted different articles as proof of the white man's presence: Clark noted a "salors jacket" (Moulton, *Journals of the Lewis and Clark Expedition,* 5:309); Whitehouse mentioned "red cloth" (Thwaites, *Original Journals,* 7:176); Ordway saw "copper kittles, and scarlet" (Quaife, *Journals of Lewis and Ordway,* 301). Gass is the only one to note hempen seine. Both he and Whitehouse noted ash paddles, another example of Gass's "working-man's eye."

Ronda, *Lewis and Clark among the Indians,* 169, points out that The Dalles was a great trading center joining the Chinookan- and Sahaptian-speaking peoples.

386. These natives were probably related to the Indians at the falls below, a Salishan language people. Moulton, *Journals of the Lewis and Clark Expedition,* 5:319 n. 3.

387. This is probably the present-day Deschutes River. Ibid., 325 n. 1.

388. Gass's conclusion was erroneous. The Deschutes is not the same as the Salmon River. Clark believed the Salmon to be the river in the Snake nation that joined the Columbia, but the Salmon River dumps into the Snake just above Hells Canyon on the Idaho-Oregon border.

389. Whitehouse said that some of these Native Americans had cabins of white cedar bark. These people possessed small canoes and good-looking horses. Thwaites, *Original Journals,* 7:178.

390. Celilo Falls, a magnificent landmark and fishing area, used to be located between Wasco County, Oregon, and Klickitat County, Washington. The falls were covered completely by floodwaters of the Dalles Dam, completed in 1957.

391. At this point, the corps heard the rumor from one of the Nez Perce chiefs traveling with them that the Wishram-Wasco Indians, an upper Chinookan-speaking tribe had threatened to kill them. Ronda, *Lewis and Clark among the Indians,* 172–73. Whitehouse's response was, "we were not afraid of them for we think we can drive three times our nomber." Thwaites, *Original Journals,* 7:179.

392. The "great Indian village" at The Dalles was the Wishram village of Nixluidix on the north side of the river. Wascoes lived on the south side of the river at The Dalles and were part of the great trading center that dealt in European cloth and ironware from the coast, salmon at The Dalles, and buffalo products (dried meat and hides), dried salmon and buffalo grasses for weaving from the plateau tribes to the east. This great trading center was the boundary between Sahaptian and Chinookan speakers. Ronda, *Lewis and Clark among the Indians,* 170–73.

393. Clark noted that all the female babies and many of the male babies had this apparatus to flatten their heads. Moulton, *Journals of the Lewis and Clark Expedition,* 5:345.

394. Whitehouse reported seeing a British musket, a sword, and copper tea kettles in this village. Thwaites, *Original Journals,* 7:182. These people were one of several groups of eastern Chinookan-speaking people living in present-day Wasco County, Oregon, and Klickitat County, Washington. Moulton, *Journals of the Lewis and Clark Expedition,* 5:346 n. 3.

395. The Yehuh, a Chinookan-speaking people, lived here in eight houses. Ibid., 356, 357 n. 4.

396. Gass did not mention, as Clark did, the sighting of a "large Buzzard," later identified as a California condor on the 30th. Ibid., 5:356.

397. This description is representative of Gass's perspective and writing style. It also shows what he liked: "There are some small bottoms. . . oak, ash and hazelnut."

398. Clark told of Indian burial practices he observed while walking around the island: "the bones in Some of those vaults wer 4 feet thick, in others the Dead was yet layed Side of each other nearly East & west, raped up & bound Securley in robes, great numbers of trinkets Brass Kittle, Sea Shells, Iron, Pan Hare &c. &c. was hung about the vaults and great many wooden gods, or Imags of men Cut in wood, Set up round the vaults, Some of those So old and worn by time that they were nearly worn out of Shape, and Some of those vaults So old that they were roted entirely to the ground." He also saw where natives dug for roots to eat. Moulton, *Journals of the Lewis and Clark Expedition,* 5:359. This description is quite a contrast from the "fatiguing business" Gass described for the day, portaging canoes around the rapids of the Columbia.

399. All of the Indians including the Snakes (Shoshones), Nez Perce (Chopunnish), and the various tribes of the Columbia River valued blue beads far above the rest. To have known that fact would have helped the corps immensely when preparing provisions to trade with the Indians before they left St. Louis.

400. A brant is a waterfowl of the genus *Branta,* which breed in arctic regions and migrate southward chiefly along the coast.

401. This is the Sandy River. Notes of J. Nielson Barry, Special Collections, Boise State University Library.

402. This is Government Island. Ibid.

The Indians were following along the water on November 3, telling the corps in sign language that they were two days from seeing ocean vessels with white people aboard. Thwaites, *Original Journals,* 7:186.

Chapter 15: November 4–November 16, 1805

403. This village was "a large Skilloot village" inhabited by a Chinookan-speaking people located near the mouth of the Willamette River. Ronda, *Lewis and Clark among the Indians,* 176. Clark observed that both the men and the women had flattened heads. They lived mainly on fish and wapato roots (an egg-shaped root extracted from underwater by native women of the area, and a good source of carbohydrates.) These Indians stole Clark's pipe tomahawk. Thwaites, *Original Journals,* 3:197–99.

404. They met no white men, but Whitehouse noted upon meeting a large canoe loaded with Indians that one of them could curse a little in English. Thwaites, *Original Journals,* 7:187.

405. Ordway identified the mountain as "mount rainy." Clark wrote that it was Mount Helen, after striking "Mt Rainier." Ordway and Gass collaborated here. Quaife, *Journals of Lewis and Ordway,* 308; Moulton, *Journals of the Lewis and Clark Expedition,* 6:16.

406. These camps provided shelter for the Cathlapotle tribe of Chinookan Indian group. Thwaites, *Original Journals,* 3:201 n. 1.

407. Whitehouse wrote on the 5th that some Indians got in their canoes and came to see the corps, wanting to trade elk skins for muskets. Ibid., 7:188.

Clark noted on the 5th that it was the first night "clear of Indians" since they reached the Columbia. Moulton, *Journals of the Lewis and Clark Expedition,* 6:24.

408. The 6th was the last entry of Whitehouse's journal except for a mileage chart.

409. These Indians were the Warkiacum, a Chinookan people. Clark reported that their houses were built five feet above the ground. Thwaites, *Original Journals,* 3:208. Gass's description of the way thongs of skin for women's dresses were woven into a king of "carpetting" is the best among the journalists. But Clark's description (from Thwaites, *Original Journals,* 3:208–9) of the Indian women's dress in this village comprises an interesting anecdote of the journals:

> their robes are Smaller only covering their Sholders & falling down to near the hip. and Sometims when it is cold a piec of fur curiously plated and connected so as to meet around the body from the arms to the hips. "The garment which occupies the Waist and thence as low as the knee before and mid leg behind, cannot properly be called a petticoat, in the common accep[ta]tion of the word; it is a *Tissue* formed of white cedar bark bruised or broken into Small Strans, which are interwoven in their center by means of Several cords of the same Materials which Serves as well for a girdle as to hold in place the Strans of bark which forms the tissue, and which Strans, confined in the middle, hang withe

their ends pendulous from the waist, the whole being of Suff[i]cent thickness when the female Stands erect to conceal those parts useally covered from familiar view, but when she stoops or places herself in any other attitude this battery of Venus is not altogether impervious to the penetrating eye of the amorite."

Clark later copied the passage in quotations from Lewis's Codex J entry for March 19, 1806. Moulton, *Journals of the Lewis and Clark Expedition*, 6:34 n. 6.

410. This camp was at Pillar Rock. Clark wrote, "Great joy in camp. We are in view of the *Ocian* [*sic*], this great Pacific Octean [*sic*] which we have been so long anxious to See. and the roreing or noise made by the waves brakeing on the rockey Shores." Thwaites, *Original Journals*, 3:210. Thwaites noted that it was not possible to see the ocean from this point, but in a storm, waves would break on shore and perhaps ocean breakers might have been heard.

411. This is the site of present-day Grays Bay, Washington. Quaife, *Journals of Lewis and Ordway*, 309; Moulton, *Journals of the Lewis and Clark Expedition*, 6:37 n. 5.

412. Clark said the swells were so high and the canoes rolled in such a manner as to cause several to become ill, including Reuben Field, Weiser, McNeal, and Sacagawea. Thwaites, *Original Journals*, 3:211.

413. There was no fresh water because the Columbia at this point is brackish.

414. These Indians are the Cathlahma, a Chinookan tribe. The Indians, the best canoesmen the corps had ever seen, crossed the river where it was five miles wide in the highest waves the men had ever seen small crafts ride. Thwaites, *Original Journals*, 3:217.

415. A "perch" is a unit of length equal to a rod, or about five and a half yards; forty perches is about 220 yards.

416. Ordway said that on the 11th, the Indians saw vessels in the mouth of the Columbia, and one man, Mr. Haily, who traded with them. But the ships were gone. Quaife, *Journals of Lewis and Ordway*, 310.

417. On the 12th, three men, Bratton, Willard, and Gibson, tried to descend the river in canoes. After going a mile, they returned for fear of capsizing. Thwaites, *Original Journals*, 3:218.

418. Shannon, Willard, and Colter were sent in an Indian canoe to find a bay good for harboring canoes. Ibid., 3:221.

419. Colter returned and said there were no white men. Ibid.

420. Clark reported that Lewis and four men, Drouillard, J. and R. Field, and Frazer, set out by land. Ibid.

421. This marked a second low point for Gass, after the Lolo Trail. Clark also said that the rain rotted over half of the men's clothing. Ibid., 3:223.

422. Clark wrote, "About 3 oClock the wind luled, and the river became calm, I had the canoes loaded in great haste and Set Out, from this dismal nitich where we have been confined for 6 days passed, without the possibility of proceeding on, returning to a better Situation, or get out to hunt; Scerce of Provisions, and torents of rain poreing on us all the time." Ibid., 3:225.

423. This man was Shannon. Moulton, *Journals of the Lewis and Clark Expedition*, 6:48.

424. The other man was Willard. Ibid.

425. These were Chinooks proper (sometimes called Tsinuks), from which came the Chinookan family of Indians. Thwaites, *Original Journals*, 3:226 n. 3. Clark described them as four hundred souls, well-armed, with a "craveing disposition" for trading. Ibid., 3:230.

Chapter 16: November 17–December 31, 1805

426. The writing style at this point of summary reveals David McKeehan's hand, found both in this introductory statement and in the wording of the November 17th description of Indian dress. Goetzmann's theory that exploration meeting expectation unfolds in the statement that the voyage's goal of finding a passage between the Missouri and Columbia rivers had been accomplished. This attitude ignored the difficulties Gass described as the party crossed the Idaho mountains.

427. Clark credited York with bringing in two geese and eight black, white, and speckled brants. Thwaites, *Original Journals*, 3:227. York's success at hunting points out that he experienced an unusual life for a black American at the turn of the nineteenth century: carrying a gun, establishing fairly egalitarian rela-

tionships with his fellow travelers (besides favors he probably bestowed on Clark), and enjoying the enthusiastic admiration of native peoples for his dancing and the color of his skin. (Black denoted power: black paint was applied for war dances among some tribes.)

428. Clark calculated 4,162 miles from the mouth of the Missouri to the Pacific Ocean. Ibid., Thwaites, *Original Journals*, 3:233 n. 2.

429. Cape Disappointment is now the site of Fort Canby in Washington, where the Gass account book resides, thanks to the generosity of its owners, descendants of Patrick Gass.

430. Clark reported that the following men expressed a desire to go with him to the ocean: Pryor, Ordway, Joseph and Reuben Field, Shannon, Colter, Labiche, Bratton, Weiser, Charbonneau, and York. Ibid., Thwaites, *Original Journals*, 3:229.

431. The Chinook nation had been a center of trading networks on the Pacific coast since the mid 1790s. Chinooks traded sea otter and beaver pelts for copper and iron items, bolts of cloth, blue beads, needles, and other manufactured goods. The expedition's scanty supply of goods perplexed the Chinooks, who were accustomed to brisk trade with personnel from amply stocked English and American ships. See Ronda, *Lewis and Clark among the Indians*, 181-184. Hence Lewis noted that they had become "great higlers in trade." Thwaites, *Original Journals*, 3:311.

Sexual relations accompanied commercial intercourse between Europeans and Chinooks. Clark noted that some Chinook women and children were in "a desperate Situation covered with sores scabs & ulsers no doubt the effects of venereal disorders which Several of this nation which I have Seen appears to have." Ibid., 3:232.

432. This was really a California condor, as large as an Andean condor. While with Clark's party on the 19th near Cape Disappointment, Reuben Field killed it. Ibid., 3:232–33.

433. Gass is the only writer to mention the pumice stone.

434. The value of blue beads was already well established, but unfortunately it was not known when Lewis prepared the journey's provisions. Sacagawea's sacrifice of her own belt for the sake of the corps seems to have been taken for granted. But the next day, Clark noted, "We gave the Squar a Coate of Blue Cloth for the belt of Blue Beeds we gave for the Sea otter skins purchased of an Indian." Thwaites, *Original Journals,* 7:239. At the end of her service to the corps at Fort Mandan, the captains did not pay Sacagawea.

435. These natives came from the Chiltz nation and the Clatsops. Ibid., 3:241.

436. Clark wrote on this night that several Indians and squaws came "for the purpose of gratifying the passions of our men, These people view sensuality as a necessary evill, & do not appear to abhore this as crime in the unmarried females." The captains gave the men ribbon to "bestow on their favourite Lasses," hoping thereby to save more important utensils and tools that might have been donated. These Indians wore their hair loose and put trinkets in their ears, mostly blue beads. They tattooed their legs for personal embellishment. Ibid., 3:239–40.

437. Clark explained that these Clatsop Indians were the survivors of a larger nation destroyed by smallpox. They spoke the language of the Chinooks and resembled them in all respects except thievery, at which "we have not cought them at as yet." Ibid., 3:245.

438. This Indian, more than most of the half-breeds, showed his Celtic parentage, gained from a crew member of one of many British voyages on the West Coast prior to the Lewis and Clark expedition.

439. This democratic process of ascertaining their winter headquarters included York and Sacagawea. For a breakdown of the voting, see Thwaites, *Original Journals,* 3:246–47.

440. From November 27 through December 7, 1805, the men stayed at this site due to wet weather.

441. On the 28th, a Clatsop Indian traveling with them stole an axe. Clark shamed him on finding it and informed him that the Indians could not proceed with the party. Ibid., 3:253.

442. Clark noted that they had nothing to eat except a little pounded fish that they had bought at Celilo Falls. The five men who went with Lewis to look for winter quarters on the south side of the river were George Drouillard, Reuben Field, George Shan-

non, Francois Labiche, and John Colter. All others were employed in hunting or drying leather and preparing it for use. Ibid., 3: 255, 256.

443. This is the first elk to have been shot by the corps west of the Rocky Mountains. Ibid., 3:263.

444. The corps was tired of dried fish. They bought roots and ate them with elk soup. Sacagawea took the bones after the marrow was eaten to chop them and render a pint of grease. Ibid., 3:265.

445. York went on a hunting trip without Clark. He lost his way from Pryor's group, and later rejoined them. Ibid., 3:270.

446. Subsequently called Young's Bay, Clark named this bay after Lewis. Quaife, *Journals of Lewis and Ordway,* 315.

447. Fort Clatsop sat on a high point on the west side, three miles above the mouth, on the present-day Lewis and Clark River. Ibid., 316.

448. On the 8th, Clark pursued elk through bogs that the weight of a man would shake for a half acre. He sank up to his hips. Thwaites, *Original Journals,* 3:272.

449. Sergeant Ordway led the party of men to get meat. Quaife, *Journals of Lewis and Ordway,* 316.

450. Clark spent this night with the chief and his wife, noting, "I had not been long on my mats before I was attacked most Violently by the flees and they kept up a close Siege dureing the night." He described two games that the Indians played. One featured the passing of a bone the size of a bean among them while they sang, occasionally holding out their hands for someone to choose who had the property. They risked all their beads and valuable effects on this game, which occupied about three hours. Ibid., 274–75.

451. Drouillard and Shannon remained out to hunt. Ibid., 273.

452. Since Gass was the head carpenter, he was extremely busy at this time, however, Ordway's journal noted that four men were sick on the 11th, and that George Gibson had dysentery. Quaife, *Journals of Lewis and Ordway,* 316. Clark's journal identifies them further: Pryor again had a dislocated shoulder; Joseph Field had boils on his legs; and Werner had a strained knee. Thwaites, *Original Journals,* 3:277; Chuinard, *Only One Man Died,* 337.

453. Gass's description of how his crew built Fort Clatsop by splitting puncheons (upright framing timbers) into boards adds an important detail to the literature on Fort Clatsop. Probably the timber that readily split into long boards was cedar.
   On the 14th, Clark noted York's illness with "Cholick," acute abdominal pain, and "gripeing" [grippe], a contagious virus similar to influenza. Thwaites, *Original Journals,* 3:280.

454. Part of the group bringing in the meat missed their way and stayed out in the cold and wet with no fire. They included Ordway, and Privates Collins, Colter, Whitehouse, and McNeal. Ibid., 3:281; Quaife, *Journals of Lewis and Ordway,* 317.

455. Clark described the 16th was "one of the worst days that ever was!" Thwaites, *Original Journals,* 3:281.

456. Clark sent Pryor and eight men in two canoes to get boards from an abandoned Indian village for the roof. Ibid., 3:285.

457. Gass took a hiatus from journal writing again due to his role in the construction of Fort Clatsop. By December 24th the huts were done.

458. Clark noted that for Christmas, Sacagawea gave him two dozen white weasel tails. Lewis gave him fleece hosiery, a vest, drawers, and socks. Whitehouse gave him moccasins, and Goodrich, an Indian basket. The Indians also gave Clark some black root before they left the fort. No other Christmas exchanges were mentioned in the diaries. Thwaites, *Original Journals,* 3:290.
   Gass and Ordway had a cheerful tone this Christmas, but Clark wrote, "We would have Spent this day the nativity of Christ in feasting, had we any thing either to raise our Sperits or even gratify our appetites, our Diner concisted of pore Elk, so much Spoiled that we eate it thro' mear necessity, Some Spoiled pounded fish and a fiew roots." Ibid., 3: 290–91.

459. On the 27th, the men completed chimneys and bunks. J. Field finished a table and two chairs for the captains. Ibid., 3:291.
   Clark also noted that many men had wet gun powder and the smoke in the huts was very bad. He added that each time the Indians visited, they left swarms of fleas. Ibid., 3:291, 297.

On the 27th, Clark chose J. Field, Bratton, and Gibson to make salt at Point Adams; they left on the 28th. On the 27th Clark also sent R. Field and Collins to hunt, and ordered Drouillard, Shannon, and Labiche to leave the morning of the 28th to hunt. Ibid., 3:291.

460. Indians told the corps on the 29th that a whale was beached on the Northwest coast, and Indians were collecting fat from it. Ibid., 3:293.

Clark said that the chief, four men, and two women of the Warciacum tribe visited in the evening, giving them some roots. The corps, in return, gave medals, beads, red ribbon, and pieces of brass wire. Ibid., 3:293–94.

461. One of the worst hardships of the coastal weather was that the wet climate with warm nights, never below freezing, mildewed and rotted food quickly. Therefore, hunting for fresh meat became a constant challenge. The process of making jerky of meat, which the party practiced on the plains, could not be accomplished without dry weather.

462. On the 31st, Clark wrote that they had dug sinks (probably for toilet drainage) and erected a sentinel box for the fort. With the party of the Clatsops on the 31st came a man of about 25 years who was much lighter than other natives. He had long, red, dusky hair and was five feet ten inches tall. He understood English but could not speak it. Thwaites, *Original Journals*, 3:301.

Ross Cox's journal of his adventures at Astoria, *Adventures on the Columbia* (New York, 1832) told about this red-haired Indian, Jack Ramsey, who had his father's name tattooed on his arm. The father had deserted an English ship to live with the Indians. Later, at Fort Astoria, Ramsey wore trousers when he visited Fort Astoria.

Chapter 17: January 1–February 28, 1806

463. Gass is the only journalist to note the naming of the fort. Lewis and Clark use the name to head their journal entries. Moulton, *Journals of the Lewis and Clark Expedition*, 6:151, 153.

464. On January 1, 1806, Lewis wrote an "Orderly Book" appropriate for the regular army living under military rule at the new fort. The frontier customs of egalitarian rule and fraternization with the Indians made it necessary for him to clarify the way the corps would maintain discipline and continue cooperation. No Indians were allowed in the fort overnight. None of the party were to sell articles of iron, ammunition, or tools. Thwaites, *Original Journals,* 3:302–4.

On January 1, Clark made a list of thirteen trading ships with which the Indians were familiar. Ibid., 3:306–7.

Ronda, *Lewis and Clark among the Indians,* 201, noted that more than a hundred ships had been engaged in the fur trade on the Northwest Coast between 1788 and 1803.

465. Shannon was the other man. Thwaites, *Original Journals,* 3:309.

466. Gass and Shannon were to seek the whereabouts of Weiser and Willard, who had not returned from the saltworks that the men built on at a site now called Cannon Beach. Ibid.

467. Clark wrote on the 3rd that the party had purchased dogs from the Indians. He noted that the men were healthier while eating dog than any time since they were in buffalo country, although he himself could not reconcile eating it. Ibid., 3:310.

468. This passage reveals Gass's humor and resourcefulness.

469. On January 5, Lewis reported that the salt makers, Weiser and Willard, returned and said that they had erected a camp and could get three quarts to a gallon of salt a day. Lewis noted that it was "excellent, fine, strong & white." He and many of the corps considered salt a treat, but Clark was indifferent to it. Ibid., 3:313–14.

470. Clark wrote that twelve men and two canoes went. One of the party, Sacagawea, asserted her wish to see the ocean and "the monstrous fish" (the whale) after coming so far. Ibid., 3:314–15.

471. Clark wrote that they got whale blubber from Willard and Weiser, and it tasted like beaver (Lewis added dog, but Clark did not). Ibid., 3:312–14.

472. Clark was not able to get more than three hundred pounds of blubber and a few gallons of oil from these "pernurious" Indians. Ibid., 3:333. Coues identified the "fish" as a great gray whale of the Pacific and thought the length was exaggerated. Ibid., 3:324 n. 1. Gass is the only journalist who mentioned the whale's head was twelve feet long, although he was not at the site with Clark's party.

473. Ronda, *Lewis and Clark among the Indians,* 186, identified these Indians as Tillamooks. Clark called them Kilamox. Thwaites, *Original Journals,* 3:324; Moulton, *Journals of the Lewis and Clark Expedition,* 6:202 n. 2.

474. The man was McNeal, who was warned by a Chinook woman who had befriended him. She knew of the plot and held McNeal by the blanket the intended assassin (a member of another band) hoped to steal, meanwhile alarming other men of the village who came to save him. Thwaites, *Original Journals,* 3:329.

475. Clark wrote that he directed Sergeant Gass to continue making salt until Shannon returned from hunting, and then for the two of them to come to the fort. Ibid., 3:335.

476. In this entry, as in most at Fort Clatsop, Clark copied Lewis's entries. Both said that the men were still making elkskin clothing and needed more brains to work into the skins in order to tan them. Ibid., 4:7–8.

477. Lewis wrote that visiting Clatsops brought hats of woven cedar bark and bear grass with various colors and figures. Nearly waterproof, these hats were a popular trade item. He noted that Clatsops communally shared their provisions and "the greatest harmoney seems to exist among them." Moulton, *Journals of the Lewis and Clark Expedition,* 6:221, 222.

478. The two men dispatched to the salt-makers camp were Howard and Werner. Thwaites, *Original Journals,* 4:7.

479. Lewis described the events of the day with these Indians, saying they were in awe of the air gun. When the Clatsops saw Drouillard shoot an elk with the gun, it gave them "a very exalted opinion of us as marksmen and the superior excellence of our rifles compared with their guns; this may be of service to us, as it will deter them from any acts of hostility if they have ever meditated any such. My Air-gun also astonishes them very much; they cannot comprehend it's shooting so often and without powder; and think that it is *great medicine* which comprehends every thing that is to them incomprehensible." Ibid., 4:9–10.

480. The hunter who returned was Shannon. Ibid., 4:17.

481. Lewis noted on the 27th that Goodrich had recovered from " the Louis Veneri," which he contracted from an amorous contact with a Chinook woman. "I cured him as I did Gibson last winter by uce of murcury." Ibid., 4:16.

482. These were Howard and Werner. Ibid., 4:18.

483. Joseph Field came to the fort asking for men to carry meat that Gibson and Willard were drying at the saltworks. Moulton, *Journals of the Lewis and Clark Expedition,* 6:253.

484. Lewis noted on January 31 that McNeal had the "pox," or venereal disease. Thwaites, *Original Journals,* 4:29.

485. Gass spoke of himself in the third person here. He and five men went up the Netul (now Lewis and Clark) River to get elk. Ibid., 4:30.

486. Lewis included in his entry on February 1 a wonderful description of the canoes of Northwest Indians. He said they were light, neat, and adapted for riding high waves, with fine ornamentation, and constructed in only a few weeks. Ibid., 4:30–33.

487. Clark wrote that R. Field whooped and fired across the marsh by the fort. Clark sent Gass to find out why. They found the lost Indian canoe on the way to Field, who reported his kill (See Table of Hunters, Appendix B) and said that Labiche and Shannon were still hunting. Ibid., 4:43.

488. Bratton and Gibson were sick. Ibid., 4:57.

489. Willard cut his knee with his tomahawk. Ibid.

490. Pryor and four men went to get the sick men, according to the captains. Ibid., 4:59.

491. Gass, R. Field, and Thompson went to hunt. Ibid., 4:60.

492. Gass well describes their leather clothing, its weight and vulnerability to the rainy climate. One can feel the disagreeable dampness on the wet buckskin clothes and the men's need to shelter beneath the elk hide.

On the 15th, Lewis wrote that Drouillard and Whitehouse went hunting, and Pryor returned with Gibson, who was very weak. Ibid., 4:72.

493. On the 17th, Clark wrote that Gass and his party arrived at 4:00 P.M. Ibid., 4:83.

494. Clark commented that he dispatched a party to the salt works with Ordway and another party with Gass to get the meat. Ibid., 4:84.

The entry here is a clue to campfire editing. On the 18th, Lewis reported that Ordway described the wave that prevented his party's progress, and Ordway said he had to return to the fort. Thwaites, *Original Journals,* 4:84 and Quaife, *Journals of*

Lewis and Ordway, 375. On the 18th, Gass was sent across the Netul to get meat, having perhaps a sizable backwater, not a bay, to cross. Lewis reported on the 19th that Ordway left again and Gass returned to camp with meat. Therefore, Gass's entry on the 18th reflected Ordway's writing, not his own experience.

495. Lewis wrote on the 19th that Gass returned in the evening with the flesh of eight elk and seven skins, having left one with Shannon and Labiche "who remained over the netul to continue the chase." Thwaites, *Original Journals,* 4:87.

496. According to Lewis, on the 20th they were visited by Tah-cum, a principal chief of the Chinooks and twenty-five men. He described the chief as good looking, about fifty, larger in stature than most Indians. The corps gave the Indians something to eat and smoked with them, presenting the chief with a small medal. Later, Lewis asked the Chinooks to leave at sunset; Lewis remarked that it was difficult to impress on the men to be on guard as they had become so accustomed to friendship with Indians. Ibid., 4:89–90.

497. On the 23rd, Ordway noted that six of the party were sick. He and three others had "the Enfluenzey." Quaife, *Journals of Lewis and Ordway,* 326.

498. Clark said these fish were superior to any fish he had eaten, delicate of taste. Thwaites, *Original Journals,* agrees with his judgment and identifies the fish as eulachon, a member of the smelt family. Thwaites, *Original Journals,* 4:108, 109 n. 1.

499. Shields, J. Field, and Shannon were sent to the Netul to hunt. Ibid., 4:109.

500. Drouillard and two others went to fish. Ibid.

501. Ordway wrote that Willard was very sick, but the rest of the sick men were better. Quaife, *Journals of Lewis and Ordway,* 326.

502. This was Gass himself, according to Lewis. Thwaites, *Original Journals,* 4:117.

503. Showing his preference for dog, even when they had elk and fish, Peter Cruzatte bought a dog on the 28th with his capote (a short blanket cloak with a hood), the customary garment of French engagés. Ibid., 4:119.

Chapter 18: March 1–April 8, 1806

504. Young's River Falls are 75 feet high. Clark estimated 100 feet, so Gass's guess of 60 feet was closer to reality. Moulton, *Journals of the Lewis and Clark Expedition,* 6:384 n. 15.

505. These fish were eulachon. See note 498.

506. This is the Klaskanine River. *National Geographic Atlas of the World* (Washington, D.C.: National Geographic Society, 1981), 74.

507. This is now the Lewis and Clark River in Oregon. Quaife, *Journals of Lewis and Ordway,* 327 n. 1.

508. Lewis noted on the 3rd that two pirogues were split by the tide from having been left partially on the shore. Thwaites, *Original Journals,* 4:127.

509. On March 5 Lewis surmised that if the elk had left the area, the corps might have to leave sooner than April 1 and proceed slowly up the Columbia. They had two days' provisions on hand, which were spoiled. Ibid., 4:135. The weather was so warm that game spoiled quickly.

510. Gass liked chewing tobacco, as did most of the corps. Trading and smoking with the Indians used up tobacco provisions, apparently presenting a significant hardship to all but seven of the men.

511. Lewis wrote on March 8 that McNeal and Goodrich had recovered from "Louis veneri," and he told them to quit using mercury. Ibid.

512. Ordway and ten men went to get meat. Quaife, *Journals of Lewis and Ordway,* 327.

513. Pryor had a small canoe loaded with fish that he got from the Cathlahmah Indians for a few articles. Dogs in the Indian camp chewed off the throng holding his canoe and it went adrift. He borrowed another from the Indians to retrieve his. Thwaites, *Original Journals,* 4:155.

514. Lewis wrote on March 11 that Gass and a party were sent to the Netul to search for a canoe, which was supposed to have been sunk in a small creek draining into the Netul when Shields, R. Field, and Frazer had been sent to hunt there. Gass and his party could not find the canoe; it had broken its cord and been carried off by the tide. Ibid.

515. This count of moccasins is the only one in the journals, a valuable contribution. The men wore moccasins when their shoes wore out or were traded, because they had

skins from which to make them and moccasins provided surefooted protection better than shoes for their travel. Patch leather were remnants used for mending or patching holes.

516. Pryor and two men went to look for the canoe. Quaife, *Journals of Lewis and Ordway,* 328.

517. Lewis sent Drouillard to buy two canoes from the Clatsop Indians. He and some Clatsops returned with an "indifferent canoe," but the corps could not afford to trade for it. The four hunters included Collins, J. Field, and Shannon. Thwaites, *Original Journals,* 4:167, 169.

518. Gass and six others went for the meat and soon returned with it. Quaife, *Journals of Lewis and Ordway,* 328.

519. Sheep sorrel is a small acid dock, or one of a coarse weedy member of the buckwheat genus. *Webster's Ninth Collegiate Dictionary* (1985), 371 and 1084.

On the 14th Clark said that the Clatsops informed the corps that they had lately seen an Indian from the Quinnachart nation, six days to the northwest, who had reported that four vessels, owned by Haley, Moore, Callamon, and Swipeton, had stopped to trade with his people. Thwaites, *Original Journals,* 4:169.

520. Lewis said they were visited "by Delashshelwilt a Chinook Chief his wife and six women of his nation which the old baud his wife had brought for market. This was the same party that had communicated the venerial to so many of our party in November last, and of which they have finally recovered. I therefore gave the men a particular charge with rispect to them which they promised me to observe." Ibid., 4:170.

521. On the 17th, Drouillard found Pryor's canoe and bought another from the Cathlahmahs in exchange for Lewis's uniform laced coat and a half carrot of tobacco. Ibid., 4:176.

522. Lewis, planning for the return, contemplated making contact with the trading ships. He said the party was too small to think of leaving anyone to return to the United States by sea. He thought they could return by land as quickly, because the ships might want to trade all summer with the Indians. He gave Delashshelwilt a certificate of good deportment and a list of all the names of the corps, which was also given to other natives and posted in the rooms at Fort Clatsop on their departure. Thus their presence would be documented. Ibid., 4:180–81.

523. For an excellent description of the Indians of the Columbia, see the March 19 entries by Lewis and Clark. Ibid., 4:183–92.

524. Gass's enumeration of the game killed at Fort Clatsop is the only one, and is quoted by scholars of the historiography of the voyage.

525. The other accounts that cover this issue and time period all agree there were six, not nine, girls accompanying the Chief Delashshelwit. See note 436. On the other hand, maybe Gass knew something they did not.

526. These were Nez Perce Indians; see notes 340 and 348.

527. The hunter who remained out the prior night was Colter. Thwaites, *Original Journals,* 4:197.

528. At this village, Clark saw two very elegant canoes inlaid with shells, but he described the village as the dirtiest and stinkingest place he had ever seen. Ibid., 4:199, 200.

529. These were Clatsops who had been trading with the Skilloots. Ibid., 4:200.

530. These were Skilloots, called "Chilutes" by Ordway. Quaife, *Journals of Lewis and Ordway,* 333.

531. Gass offers the best description of the garment of the Cathlapotles, called "quathalahpahtle" by Lewis. These people were an upper Chinookan language group who lived on the Washington shore of the Columbia in present-day Clark County. Moulton, *Journals of the Lewis and Clark Expedition,* 6:24 n. 6.

532. They bought twelve dogs, wapato, and two sea otter skins. Thwaites, *Original Journals,* 4:215.

533. Clark wrote, "Willard quit well & Bratten much Stronger." Moulton, *Journals of the Lewis and Clark Expedition,* 7:30. Perhaps Pryor's shoulder was the third ailment Gass mentioned.

534. This was Sauvie Island. Quaife, *Journals of Lewis and Ordway,* 334 n. 2.

535. Gass saw these boats with the eye of a craftsman.

536. Lewis called this the Shahhala nation. Thwaites, *Original Journals,* 4:223. Ronda, *Lewis and Clark among the Indians,* 215, calls it the Neerchekioo tribe of the Shahhala nation.

537. Pryor and two men explored six miles up this river, now called the Sandy River, and found it to fork. The Indians affirmed that it extended only to Mount Hood. Thwaites, *Original Journals*, 4:227.

538. The corps received word that Indians upriver were starving, so they decided to get more food before proceeding. Ibid., 4:231.

539. Clark had been assuming that there was a major river draining the country south, the range between the Cascades and the coast, as far south as California. He thought the Quicksand [Sandy River] was that river. When they discovered it went only to Mount Hood, Clark then assumed the Multnomah [Willamette] went to California. The Corps of Discovery missed the Willamette traveling both east and west because it enters the Columbia at Canoe Island and they had been on the wrong side of the island to see it enter the Columbia. They learned about it from a canoe-load of men from the Neerchekioo nation. Clark took Thompson, Potts, Cruzatte, Weiser, Howard, Whitehouse, and York to scout the river. He did not know his assumption that the river went south was erroneous. Ibid., 4:236, 243 (Clark's map). Also see Quaife, *Journals of Lewis and Ordway*, 336, 336 n. 1.

540. The Indians gave them wapato in exchange for the three bear cubs. Thwaites, *Original Journals*, 4:247.

541. They cut the elk into thin pieces and put it on the scaffold over a small fire to dry it for future use. Ibid.

542. This is Gass at his best, describing the beautiful trees.
     On the 6th, Lewis directed Drouillard and the two Fields to ascend the river to hunt. They set out the 7th. Ibid., 4:254.

543. This is another example of excellent reporting on Gass's part.

544. Clark noted on the 8th that John Shields repaired his gun and that the party owed much to Shields's ingenuity because he had repaired all the guns as a regular occurrence. Ibid., 4:257.

Chapter 19: April 9–May 4, 1806

545. This was the Wahclellah village, on the north side of the Columbia, where they ate breakfast. Colter found Clark's pipe tomahawk, which had been stolen the previous fall. Clark said the village was where two tribes of the Shah-ha-la nation wintered. Although these people were not hospitable, the party obtained from them five dogs and some wapato. Thwaites, *Original Journals*, 4:261–62.

546. While they were at the above village, a "Grand Chief" plus two other chiefs, eleven men, and seven women of the Chee-luck-kit-le-quaw nation came in canoes from downriver. They had been trading with other Indians in the "Columbia Valley" for wapato roots, beads, dried anchovies with berries, pounded fish, and bear grass. Members of this traveling group were friendly with the corps. Ibid., 4:262.

547. They camped at Brant Island, just below the lower Cascades. Quaife, *Journals of Lewis and Ordway*, 339 n. 1.

548. These were mountain goat skins.

549. They needed to get rosin or pitch from pine trees to seal the canoes. Collins, Gibson, and Gibson's crew were sent. Thwaites, *Original Journals*, 4:264.

550. The Clah-lah-lar Indians at the last village who caught the canoe and returned it were rewarded with two knives. Ibid., 4:264, 266.

551. Lewis described the portage of the Cascades on the 11th as being 2,800 yards along a narrow, rough, and slippery path. The river was high and rapid with the spring run-off. The portage was observed by many of the War-clel-lar Indians, who were "the greates[t] theives and scoundrels we have met with," according to the now testy Lewis. That evening Indians pushed J. Field off the portage path and took the dog he had just purchased. He drew his knife to protect himself and recover his goods. Then, three Indians stole Lewis's dog, Seaman. Lewis ordered three of the corps to pursue them, with orders to fire if they resisted returning his dog. The Indians fled and Lewis recovered Seaman. Another Indian stole an axe, an act that Thompson witnessed and he recovered the axe. Bratton was still too weak to work. Ibid., 4:266–68.
     Ronda, *Lewis and Clark among the Indians*, 216, calls these Indians "Watlalas." He sheds light on their culture and the captains' accusations of thievery.

552. Lewis wrote that it was the Y-eh-huh nation. Clark called it Y-ep-huh. Thwaites, *Original Journals*, 4:276, 278.

553. Clark noted thirteen large burial sepulchres, on which lay numerous bodies, on a small island in the river. Ibid., 4:285.

554. Lewis wrote on the 16th that he set "Gass and Pryor with some others at work to make a parsel of packsaddles." Ibid., 4:286. Pack saddles are made of wood to fit horses' backs. Covers of hides, wool, or other wrapping and articles themselves could have been roped onto the wooden frames with rawhide thongs. Horses and mules can carry packs that weigh up to several hundred pounds.

555. Clark sent Cruzatte, McNeal, Weiser, and Willard back to the Rock Camp to advise Lewis that he could not get horses, and he would now proceed to the Enesher nation above Celilo Falls to try to buy horses. Ibid., 4:293. Ronda, *Lewis and Clark among the Indians,* 218, spells this tribe "Eneeshur."

556. The great falls were Celilo Falls. Clark left the portage at the falls on the 19th to obtain horses from the Enesher nation, taking Pryor, Shannon, Cruzatte, and Labiche with him. The Indians wanted "emence prices" for "indifferent" horses. Thwaites, *Original Journals,* 4:301.

557. Lewis described these Eneshers as "poor, dirty, proud, haughty, inhospitable, parsimonious and faithless in every respect." Ibid., 4:304.

558. Ronda, *Lewis and Clark among the Indians,* 219, believes that the last two days at the Narrows (The Dalles), April 21 and 22, were the most unpleasant of any in the expedition. The corps burned their unneeded canoes to make sure the Indians got nothing from them.

559. Shapeleel, sap-o-lil (Chinook), or Cha-pel-el (Clark) are edible roots. See Moulton, *Journals of the Lewis and Clark Expedition,* 5:380 n. 7. They were also known as "coues." Cutright, *Lewis and Clark,* 283–84, 288–89, 370, 373.

560. The Shoshone, or Clark's, River is now called the Deschutes River. Quaife, *Journals of Lewis and Ordway,* 345 n. 1. Thwaites, *Original Journals,* 4:310.

561. Ordway wrote on the 22nd, "in the evening Serg[t.] Gass & R. Fields came across the river & joined us with one of the Small canoes." Quaife, *Journals of Lewis and Ordway,* 345. The other canoe with Colter and Potts was ahead, Clark noted. Thwaites, *Original Journals,* 4:316.

562. Lewis reported that a Choppunish family met them at the Wah how pum village, offering to hire out some of their horses to the party as far as their village, but, not wanting to feed the family, Lewis preferred to buy horses. Moulton, *Journals of the Lewis and Clark Expedition,* 7:160. Ordway noted on the 23rd that several of the "Flatheads" (Nez Perce) continued with the party and assisted them as much as possible. Quaife, *Journals of Lewis and Ordway,* 345.

The horse that got away belonged to Charbonneau. On the 23rd, Gass and Reuben Field left in the canoe at 8 A.M., according to Clark. Thwaites, *Original Journals,* 4:316.

563. This Indian was of the Wa-hapari tribe, from the river to the north, according to Ordway. Quaife, *Journals of Lewis and Ordway,* 346. Quaife, however, notes that Coues identified this as the Klikitat tribe. Ibid., 345 n. 1. The site is Rock Creek, Klickitat County, Washington.

564. Lewis said these were Pishquitpahs [Pisquow], a nation of about 700 souls. Thwaites, *Original Journals,* 4:321.

565. On the 24th, Clark wrote that most of the party complained of their feet and legs being sore from walking over rough rocks and deep sand after being used to soft soil. Ibid.

566. The corps was greeted by the Wallahwalla Indians. Their great chief, Yellepit, a man of influence among tribes other than his own, was glad to see the party. He entreated his people to furnish fuel and food. On the 28th he brought an elegant white horse to Captain Clark. Lewis said Clark gave him his sword, a hundred balls and powder, and other small articles in return. The chief convinced the corps to stay over and he invited the Yakimas for a feast and dance honoring the white men. A Shoshone slave among them made communication through Sacagawea possible. Ibid., 4:331–32. The village was near the confluence of the Snake and the Columbia in eastern Oregon.

567. Clark gave the Indians medical treatment on the 29th. The party received ten dogs as provisions for the trip. Yellepit loaned them two canoes to transport baggage and to lead horses across the river. Ibid., 4:333–35.

568. Lewis wrote on May 1, "I think we can justly affirm to the honor of these people that they are the most hospitable, honest, and sincere people we have met with in our voyage." Ibid., 4:345.

Lewis spelled the tribe's name "Wallahwollah." Ibid., 4:327. Clark spelled it "Wallahwallahs." Ibid., 4:329. Ronda, *Lewis and Clark among the Indians,* 280, calls them "Walulas."

569. This was Chief Wearkkoomt and ten Nez Perce men who had traveled a great distance to meet them. Thwaites, *Original Journals.,* 4:351.

570. The fork is the site of Lewiston, Idaho, and Clarkston, Washington. The party camped ten miles below. Quaife, *Journals of Lewis and Ordway,* 352.

571. This was their Nez Perce friend Tetoharsky, who informed them that Toby, the Shoshone guide, took two horses when he left. On May 4, Ordway was first to name "tobe" [*sic*]. Quaife, *Journals of Lewis and Ordway,* 352. The captains did not name Toby until May 12, 1806. Thwaites, *Original Journals,* 5:25.

Chapter 20: May 5–May 22, 1806

572. The Kooskooske was the Clearwater River, home of the Nez Perce.

573. Tetoharsky was the old chief Gass mentioned.

574. Toby's taking two horses when he left seems small compensation considering he and his son led the expedition over the Bitterroot Mountains on the Lolo Pass. They left after a canoe accident, apparently being afraid of the rapids on the Clearwater River. They departed without pay and, needing transportation to return home, took two horses.

575. Gass is the only journalist who gave this information about the Nez Perce lodge.
     Clark continued to give medical treatment. On the 5th, an Indian rewarded him with the gift of an elegant grey horse. Thwaites, *Original Journals,* 4:357. Clark was also given a young horse by a chief for treating an abcess on his wife's back. The horse was butchered for meat. Ibid., 4:363.

576. Gass expressed his appreciation here for the Walulas, the Nez Perce, and the Shoshone compared to more worldly Columbia River Indians used to trading with white men.
     Lewis projected concern on the 7th about the passage over the mountains. The Indians told them the snow was too high to pass until June, which he said was "unwelcom inteligence to men confined to a diet of horsebeef and roots, and who are as anxious as we are to return to the fat plains of the Missouri and thence to our native homes." Thwaites, *Original Journals,* 4:369.

577. The other old chief was Twisted Hair, who had kept the expedition's horses since the previous fall. Quaife, *Journals of Lewis and Ordway,* 354.

578. This is a rosy account that ignores a testy disagreement between Twisted Hair and The Cut Nose over the horses. After receiving the Corps of Discovery coolly, Twisted Hair argued with The Cut Nose, holding up the party for twenty minutes. The horses had been scattered and the saddles misplaced. The Cut Nose had been away at war with Shoshones when the party left the horses with Twisted Hair the preceding fall. When he returned, he had been displeased about Twisted Hair's authority over the expedition's horses. He quarreled with Twisted Hair who, being an old man, gave up his claim to the corps' horses. The Cut Nose had moved the saddles, some of which could have washed away at high water of the river. Drouillard was sent to make peace between the chiefs, and an effort was initiated to retrieve the horses and saddles. See Lewis's account. Thwaites, *Original Journals,* 5:5–8.

579. Gass's description of the Nez Perce horses shows their good condition and their importance both for transportation and as a sign of wealth in Nez Perce culture, even when the tribe did not have enough to eat. No mention is made of appaloosa coloring of horses, for which the Nez Perce are famous.

580. This was the village of Tunnachemootoolt, the chief whom they had presented a flag the preceding fall. They found it displayed on a staff near his lodge. Thwaites, *Original Journals,* 5:14.

581. One cannot help marveling at this act of generosity: to divide half of what they had when it was enough only for themselves. Apparently the Nez Perce desisted from eating the flesh of their valuable horses, but they gave "two fat young horses" to the corps to eat. The men ate one immediately. See Lewis's remarks, Thwaites, *Original Journals,* 5:15.

582. The evening of the 10th, the Nez Perce women pitched a leather lodge, brought wood, and made a fire in the lodge for the Lewis and Clark. The group played the fiddle and danced. Quaife, *Journals of Lewis and Ordway,* 355.

583. Lewis wrote on May 11, "The Choppunish [Nez Perce] notwithstanding they live in the crouded manner before mentioned are much more clenly in their persons and habitations than any nation. . . since we left the Ottoes on the river Platte." Thwaites, *Original Journals,* 5:20.

584. With the horses they brought and the horses retrieved at the Nez Perce village, Ordway counted sixty on the 13th, confirming Gass's count. Quaife, *Journals of Lewis and Ordway,* 356.

585. The corps would camp on the north side of the Clearwater until the snow melted. With the exception of Fort Mandan and Fort Clatsop, the explorers stayed here longer than at any other camp, from May 13 until June 10, 1806, about four weeks. Although the camp is called "Camp Choppunish," or "Long Camp," none of the journals used those names. It is located two miles downriver from Kamiah, Idaho, where a lumber mill now stands.

Ronda, *Lewis and Clark among the Indians,* 227, points out that the camp's location followed the suggestions of several chiefs to establish it along the north bank of the Clearwater River.

586. They castrated the stallions to ease the handling of their horses. One of the Indians helped them; his method of operation was different from Drouillard's. The Indian cut the testicles clean from the scrotum, scraping the connecting "string very clean and to seperate it from all the adhereing veigns before he cuts it." Thwaites, *Original Journals,* 5:35. Drouillard tied a string around the testicles to sever them, which was the conventional method for Euro-Americans. The Indian's method proved to promote faster healing.

587. In addition to the five grizzlies, the men also ate some troublesome stud horses. Quaife, *Journals of Lewis and Ordway,* 357.

588. Gass's description of the method Nez Perce used to cook bear meat is concise and complete.

On May 14, Lewis noted that the stallions castrated by Drouillard were more swollen. Those cut by the Indian bled more, but improved faster. Thwaites, *Original Journals,* 5:39.

Several men were sick, Lewis noted, including Frazer, J. Field, Weiser, Howard, and York. He attributed it to the diet of camas roots (which had also given them problems on the trip west). Ibid., 5:38.

589. This was Hohastillpilp, who wore a tippit of human scalps, ornamented with fingers and thumbs of men he had slain in battle. Ibid., 5:31.

590. Ordway noted on the 16th that they ate two more of their "unruly stud horses." Quaife, *Journals of Lewis and Ordway,* 357.

591. On the 16th, Lewis said that "Sahcargarweah" gathered roots of fennel which they enjoyed eating. (Note his spelling, the nearest phonetic rendition we have. She is usually referred to in the journals as "Charbonneau's squaw.") Thwaites, *Original Journals,* 5:41.

592. The Indians came for medical treatment. Ibid., 5:49.

593. Three more stallions were castrated by Drouillard. Ibid.

594. The captains became wet in the rain the night before, as the tent was not tight. Ibid., 5:51. This precipitated Gass's preparation of a shelter of willow poles and grass on the 21st. Ibid., 5:52.

595. Five men made a canoe for fishing. Ibid. Meanwhile, Gass was preparing the lodge for the captains.

596. Gass observed the outstanding horsemanship of the Nez Perce Indians, a culture thoroughly involved with horses.

597. On the 22nd it was noted by Clark that Charbonneau's [and Sacagawea's] child was ill. He was cutting teeth and had a swollen neck and jaw. Thwaites, *Original Journals,* 5:57–58. Clark was very fond of the child, offering to take him when his parents stayed at the Mandan village the fall of 1806. Later, Clark would be responsible for the boy's education in St. Louis.

Chapter 21: May 23–June 20, 1806

598. Bratton had been miserably ill and unable to work for over three months, so his apparent recovery due to treatment in an Indian sweathouse was a source of jubilation for everyone in the party. Lewis said that Bratton consented to the treatment,

was stripped, and put in a hole 3 feet across and four feet deep. He sprinkled water on rocks to make steam for about twenty minutes, and they carried him from the cold water to the sweat hole alternately. Thwaites, *Original Journals,* 5:60.

599. Gass is either uninformed or optimistic here. Clark, who was caring for the child, Jean Baptiste Charbonneau, said he was not as well as the previous day. Ibid., 5:64.

600. Lewis said the canoe would carry twelve people. Ibid., 5:67.

601. Referring to the sick Indian, a chief whose father was so caring that he went in the sweat house with his sick son, Captain Lewis observed also that the Nez Perce were attentive to elderly people and that women were treated with more respect that those of the Missouri tribes. Ibid., 5:68–69.

602. Ordway's journal indicates that he, Frazer, and Weiser went to "the ki-mooenim river" (Lewis's River or the Snake River). It was farther than Lewis thought. They went seventy miles west and did not return until June 2. Quaife, *Journals of Lewis and Ordway,* 360.

603. Charbonneau, York, and LePage got dried roots of "Cows" (cous; see Cutright, *Pioneering Naturalists,* 284) and bread from the village. Thwaites, *Original Journals,* 5:75.

604. Lewis noted on the 29th that Bratton, Charbonneau's child "Pomp," and the old Indian chief were recovering. Ibid., 5:80.

605. There were actually three men involved in this dramatic accident on the Clearwater River during spring runoff. Shannon, Collins, and Potts were aboard the canoe that struck some standing trees and sank. Potts could not swim well and made it to land with great difficulty. Captain Lewis sent Pryor in an Indian canoe to recover the canoe, but the spring run-off water was too swift and deep. Ibid., 5:86.

606. On May 30, Lewis noted that he sent Gass to get goat hair for saddle pads. Gass ascended the Clearwater but couldn't cross the river opposite the Indian village he wanted to visit (to trade for the goat hair). So Gass returned in the evening, unsuccessful in his mission. Ibid.

607. On June 1, Charbonneau's and LePage's horses fell in the river and lost the elk skins they were carrying. An Indian helped drive the horses back to the two hunters from the opposite shore. Ibid., 5:97.

608. These were Ordway, Frazer, and Weiser. See note 602.

609. This man was Frazer. Quaife, *Journals of Lewis and Ordway,* 362.

610. Gass, McNeal, Whitehouse, and Goodrich accompanied two young chiefs when they returned to their village to obtain pack ropes in exchange for old fishing nets, fish gigs, and pieces of old iron, files, and bullets. Thwaites, *Original Journals,* 5:114.

611. This man was Frazer, who had given Hohastillpilp a pair of shoes. Ibid.

612. Lewis wrote that several footraces were run between the Indians and the men of the corps the evening of the 8th. He said, "One of them proved as fleet as Drewyer [Drouillard] and R. Field, our swiftest runners." Lewis also wrote that the chief who was paralyzed and had received the sweat treatment could now bear his weight on his feet; Bratton was so well that he was no longer considered an invalid; and the child was nearly well. Ibid., 5:117.

613. Lewis recorded that they had extra horses for emergency food, and that they were "perfectly equiped for the mountains." Ibid., 5:120.

614. Gass's description of the beautiful "Com-mas flat" stands as unique in the journals. Lewis and Clark called the plant "quawmash," not as close to its present name of 'camas" as Gass's nomenclature.

615. Gass had his thirty-fifth birthday on June 12, 1806.

616. The man who returned with the horse was Whitehouse. Thwaites, *Original Journals,* 5:132.

617. On the 12th, Clark wrote that The Cutnose, who had come to their camp on the 10th before their departure, said that two young chiefs would accompany them to the Great Falls and perhaps to the "Seat of our Governm^t^." Ibid.

618. Ordway said that "the Snow must fall in these hollars in the winter 15 or 20 feet deep." Quaife, *Journals of Lewis and Ordway,* 367. Usually snow does not melt in deeper places until the end of June in the Bitterroots, and sometimes it stays in draws or arroyos on the north side all year.

619. Lewis wrote, "Under these circumstances we conceived it madnes[s]. . . to proceed without a guide who could certainly conduct us [over the snowy mountains] to the fish wears on the Kooskooske [the Lochsa at Colt Killed Creek, now Powell Ranger

Station]. . . this is the first time since we have been on this long tour that we have ever been compelled to retreat or make a retrograde march." Thwaites, *Original Journals,* 5:141–42.

620. Drouillard and Shannon went ahead to get an Indian guide. Ibid., 5:144.

621. Potts cut his leg with a big knife, Ordway said. Quaife, *Journals of Lewis and Ordway,* 367.

622. Colter was thrown from his horse. Ibid.

Chapter 22: June 21–July 2, 1806

623. Gass remained with Lewis and the Field brothers to hunt. Thwaites, *Original Journals,* 5:154.

624. This was Cruzatte's horse. Thompson's horse was choking and may have had distemper. Ibid., 5:153. At least four horses had fled to Camas Flat. Quaife, *Journals of Lewis and Ordway,* 368. The Indians brought back these three horses and a mule and told the captains that Drouillard and Shannon would not return for two days. The Indians promised to stay two days more. They dined with Gass and the Field brothers. Thwaites, *Original Journals,* 5:153.

625. There is a difference in reporting here because Gass had been separate from the main party. Ordway said they killed eight deer and two brown bear on the 22nd. Quaife, *Journals of Lewis and Ordway,* 369. Gass reported the kill the next day, when they returned, misquoting the number at ten deer.

626. Lewis wrote on the 23rd that Drouillard, Shannon, and Whitehouse returned at 3:00 P.M. They brought three Indians with them, who agreed to go to the Great Falls with the exploration party in exchange for two guns. Thwaites, *Original Journals,* 5:156–57.

627. Lewis had Gass, the Field brothers, and Weiser go ahead with the three Indians to clear the trail and blaze the trees (mark them so the party behind would not get lost) to Travellers Rest. Ibid., 5:157.

628. Lewis wrote on the 25th that an Indian had entertained the corps by setting fir trees on fire the evening of the 24th. Ibid., 5:159. The danger of fire spreading was minimal with snowclad ground and the moisture of spring runoff.

629. On the 25th, Clark noted, "One of our guides complained of being unwell, a Symptom which I did not much like as such complaints with an indian is generally the prelude to his abandoning any enterprize with which he is not well pleased. . . . The indians all continue with us and I beleive [sic] are disposed to be faithfull to their engagements. Capt. L. gave the sick indian a small buffalow robe which he brought from the Missouri, this indian having no other Covering except his mockersons and a dressed Elk skin without the hair." Ibid., 5:160–61.

630. Lolo Hot Springs, on U.S. Highway 12 in present-day Montana, near the Idaho border.

631. Lewis wrote on June 29 that they descended to the main branch of the Kooskooske (Lochsa) one and a half miles above Quawmash (Glade Creek), and "bid adieu" to the snow. They found the old road going east/west "more beaten" from the tribes that had used it on the way to hunt buffalo since the corps had used it. They made twelve miles that day and all bathed in the natural hot springs. Ibid., 5:169–70. The hot water is now called Boyle's Springs in Montana. Quaife, *Journals of Lewis and Ordway,* 370 n. 4.

632. Here, Shields repaired the guns again. Thwaites, *Original Journals,* 5:175.

633. After crossing with the explorers out of the snow into traversable country, the Indian guides wanted to go home. They agreed to show Lewis the right road to cross the mountains to Great Falls. Lewis gave one a medal and tied blue ribbon in the hair of all of them, which pleased them. They gave Lewis a horse in token of their wish to be at peace with the Gros Ventre (Big Bellies, or Minatarees). Ibid., 5:179–80.

634. The arrangements for the separation of the troops were based on a plan that split them into several groups with different missions:

Lewis and six men, Drouillard, R. and J. Field, Werner, Frazer, and Gass were to explore the Marias River to the north. McNeal, Goodrich, and Thompson, who also traveled with Lewis to the Great Falls were to prepare carriages for the portage around the falls. When horses were stolen, Gass Werner, and Frazer stayed at the falls while the Fields and Droulliard accompanied Lewis to the Marias.

Pryor, Hall, Windsor, and Shannon were to proceed by land with the horses to the Mandans with a letter to Hugh Haney, who Lewis wished would convince Sioux chiefs to accompany the corps to Washington, D.C. This part of the plan aborted when those horses were all stolen, so those four men had to kill buffalo and make two bull boats in which they descended the Yellowstone to meet Clark's party on the Missouri August 8.

The largest group would go with Captain Clark to explore the Yellowstone River. This party included Clark, York, Charbonneau, Sacagawea, the child Baptiste, Labiche, Shields, Gibson, and Bratton. At Three Forks, Clark separated from Ordway to ascend the Gallatin River and proceed to the Yellowstone overland. Ordway was in charge of nine men who were to descend the Jefferson, then the Missouri, to the Great Falls in the canoes recovered from the cache at Camp Fortunate. They included Colter, Collins, Cruzatte, Willard, Weiser, Whitehouse, Howard, LePage, and Potts. See Thwaites, *Original Journals*, 5:175–76 for the original plan, and 5:259 for Clark's party after Ordway left them and before Pryor separated from them.

635. Lewis wrote on July 2 that Shields continued to repair guns. In the evening some horse races and footraces were enjoyed with the Indian guides, who were about to leave the party. Goodrich and McNeal had a reoccurrence of the pox (which is why they were sent to the Falls, where they could work at their own pace , using mercury freely without the stress of rapid travel). Thwaites, *Original Journals*, 5:180.

Chapter 23: July 3–July 26, 1806

636. The stream called Clarke's River by Gass was called the Flathead River by Ordway; today it is known as the Bitterroot River. Ordway said that Clark's party went thirty-five miles down it on July 3. Quaife, *Journals of Lewis and Ordway*, 372. Meanwhile, Lewis's party with Patrick Gass proceeded up the river.

637. These were Nez Perce Indians, who had come to help the corps over the mountains. The sentiment was undoubtedly Gass's, as Lewis felt the same, but probably McKeehan turned the phrase. Thwaites, *Original Journals*, 5:188.

638. Isquet-co-qual-la is the same as Lewis's "Cokahlahishkit" but a reversal of the word "ishkit" or "Isquet." The Nez Perce words mean "road leading to buffalo." The "Cokahlahishkit River" is now the Blackfoot River.

639 Lewis called Werner's Creek and now is known as the Clearwater River. Thwaites, *Original Journals*, 5:190 n. 1.

640. Clark's party on the 6th stayed at the site where the Battle of the Big Hole later was fought between Chief Joseph and General Gibbon on August 9, 1877. Quaife, *Journals of Lewis and Ordway*, 373 n. 3. Sacagawea said she knew the country, identifying the creek as headwaters of the Jefferson River. Ibid., 373.

641. From the headwaters of the Big Blackfoot River, Lewis went to the headwaters of the Medicine River, by which he soon reached the Missouri. Thwaites, *Original Journals*, 5:194 n.1.

642. Reuben Field wounded a moose near camp the morning of the 7th, agitating Lewis's dog Seaman. Ibid., 5:194.

643. Meanwhile, on July 7, a hundred miles to the south, Clark sent Ordway to search for nine of their best horses, which were "scattered." Clark "thought it probably that they might be stolen by some skulking shoshones" or "they may have taken our back rout." Thwaites, *Original Journals*, 5:251–52. Ordway's party "got the track of the horses" and rejoined Clark's party on the 9th with the horses, having had nothing to eat the night of the 8th "but the head of a goat or antelope which the party had droped on the road." Quaife, *Journals of Lewis and Ordway*, 374.

644. On the 8th, Clark's party opened the cache on the Jefferson River and hauled out their canoes while it was raining on the Lewis and Gass party. On the 9th, the wind and sun were drying the canoes sufficiently for them to be ready for Clark's party to leave for the Three Forks area on the 10th. Thwaites, *Original Journals*, 5:255.

645. Surprisingly, Gass does not mention a significant experience: Lewis wrote on July 10 that he sent the pack horses on with Gass, directing him to encamp at the first timber in view, which was about seven miles ahead. Lewis recounted that a large bear had pursued Gass and Thompson, but their horses enabled them to keep out of its reach. Gass and Thompson were afraid to fire at the bear because their horses were not used to gunfire. Thwaites, *Original Journals*, 5:198.

646. On the 10th, Clark's group traveled a long ninety-seven miles downstream, passing six nights' camps of the outward bound journey. Ordway wrote that the party with

the horses "by land makes way with us," who are in the canoes. Quaife, *Journals of Lewis and Ordway,* 376.

647. Drouillard and J. Field went to track the horses but were not successful. Lewis credited Werner with finding the horses Gass claimed to have found. Thwaites, *Original Journals,* 5:200.

648. Lewis wrote of the contents of the cache at Great Falls Upper Portage Camp that his bear hides and plant specimens had been destroyed and much of his medicine was not recoverable because the river had risen so high that its water penetrated the cache; however, he was happy that the "Chart of the Missouri" escaped damage. Ibid., 5:201.

649. Lewis sent McNeal to the lower part of the portage to see if the large pirogue and cache were safe; Drouillard returned without the horses. Lewis, relieved to see him, constructed a new plan since they were short of horses: three of the party that had been slated to explore the Marias River would stay with Goodrich, Thompson, and McNeal, and four horses. These men were Gass, Frazer, and Werner. Lewis would take Drouillard and the two Fields with him. Ibid., 5:203.

650. This passage describes one of the most amazing episodes of the trip! After his horse shied and dumped him in fright of a grizzly bear, McNeal broke his rifle over the bear's head and climbed a tree, where he was forced to stay several hours. When the bear left, McNeal found his horse and returned to tell this story. Ibid., 5:203–4. Note the charming woodcut from the 1811 edition of Gass's journal, in which the grizzly appears more like an English sheepdog peering up at McNeal.

651. See note 649.

652. The remaining men with four horses were Gass, Werner, and Frazer. See note 649. McNeal, Thompson, and Goodrich were to have stayed at the portage according to the first plan.

Gass's journal is the only account of this portion of the voyage. Lewis was not writing; Clark and Ordway had separated from them. See note 634.

653. In Clark's party on the 18th, Charbonneau's horse tripped in a badger hole as they were charging a buffalo and threw him off. Charbonneau was bruised on his hip, shoulder, and face. The same day, after shooting a deer, Gibson fell on a snag while mounting his horse. The snag penetrated his thigh two inches, a very painful and bad wound, according to Captain Clark. Thwaites, *Original Journals,* 5:272–73.

654. The men in Clark's party searched for a tree large enough to make a canoe for Gibson to lie in, but Clark concluded that he would line a pack horse with soft skins and blankets for Gibson's comfort. Ibid., 5:275.

655. On the 19th, Ordway and nine men (see note 634) met Gass and his five companions. Quaife, *Journals of Lewis and Ordway,* 379.

656. Ordway wrote on the 20th that they stayed at this camp while Gass finished putting tongues on the wagons. Some of the men were dressing skins. All were tormented by mosquitoes. Quaife, *Journals of Lewis and Ordway,* 380.

657. On the 22nd, Lewis and his party proceeded up Cutbank Creek, the northern of the two forks of the Marias River. Thwaites, *Original Journals,* 5:213 n.1.

658. Weiser cut himself with a knife. Quaife, *Journals of Lewis and Ordway,* 380.

659. On the 24th, Pryor, Shannon, Hall, and Windsor separated from Clark on the Yellowstone with the horses to drive to the Mandans. Thwaites, *Original Journals,* 5:288–90.

660. On the 26th, an Indian dog entered the portage camp at morning and they fed it. The men opened the cache and got the white pirogue, which was in good shape. Ordway noted that they returned "with much hard fatigue" after portaging all the canoes and baggage to the cache. Quaife, *Journals of Lewis and Ordway,* 381.

661. On the 26th, Captain Lewis's party, a hundred miles north, began the only fatal Indian encounter of the journey: Lewis and the Field brothers ascended a hill and saw thirty horses, about half of them saddled. Using his spyglass, Lewis saw eight Blackfeet Indians looking at the river, probably at Drouillard. Lewis decided to approach them in a friendly manner, telling J. Field to show the flag. Lewis and the Field brothers advanced slowly. The Indians scattered. One, on horseback, ran up and then back. Lewis counted eight Indians as they approached each other. Within a hundred feet, all but one halted. He told J. Field to do the same. Lewis advanced, shook hands, and went to the men in the rear just as the Indian did. The Indian asked them to smoke and claimed three of them were chiefs. Lewis gave one a flag,

one a medal, and one a handkerchief. All of them mounted and rode to the river; Drouillard met them on the way. That night, Lewis and Drouillard slept with the Indians in a semicircular camp of dressed buffalo hides. J. Field was guard and R. Field slept by his brother, near the fire. These Indians were part of a large band camped near the foot of the Rocky Mountains a day and a half away. Apparently a French trader was with the main band. Thwaites, *Original Journals*, 5:219–22. The incident continues in note 664.

Chapter 24: July 27–August 21, 1806

662. The other man was Willard. Quaife, *Journals of Lewis and Ordway*, 381.

663. This was probably an antelope.

664. Early the morning of July 27, 1806, events with Captain Lewis and his party of three on the upper north fork of Marias River took a tragic turn. J. Field, on guard, had "carelessly" laid his gun by his sleeping brother. The Indian whom Lewis had given a medal snuck behind J. Field and took his and his brother's guns. When Joseph Field realized this, he called to his brother, Reuben, who leaped up, overtook the Indian in about fifty or sixty paces, seized his gun, and stabbed him in the heart. At the same time, two other Indians took the guns of Drouillard and Lewis. Drouillard swore and wrestled his gun and pouch back from the Indian. Lewis awakened when he heard Drouillard and ordered his men not to kill Indians unless they tried to run off the horses. This they promptly attempted. Lewis said he called the Indians as they drove the horses up a steep niche. One of the Indians jumped behind a rock. Another turned and found Lewis with a gun. Lewis shot him in the stomach. The Indian returned fire but missed. Lewis, being bareheaded, felt the wind of this bullet. Lewis returned to camp and got Drouillard to catch the Indians' horses. He put the Indians' shields, arrows, and baggage on the fire and took the gun they left and the flag, but left the medal on the dead man as a sign of who killed him. Lewis and his party left nine horses, took the best four and rode quickly away. Thwaites, *Original Journals*, 5:223–27.

665. Lewis and his three men met Gass and Ordway's party on the 28th after pushing their horses to their limits. They had ridden sixty-three miles on the 27th, resting only an hour and a half. Continuing seventeen more miles in the evening, then resting two hours, they feasted on a buffalo they killed. They did not stop riding until 2:00 A.M. on the 28th. They joined Ordway's party in the forenoon on the Missouri. At about 1:00 P.M. they met Gass and Willard. who brought the horses from the Great Falls portage. Thwaites, *Original Journals*, 5:226–28. Ordway said Lewis threw the saddles in the river, and let the horses go on the plains. Quaife, *Journals of Lewis and Ordway*, 383.

666. These were really Piegan Blackfeet Indians. Ronda, *Lewis and Clark among the Indians*, 242.

667. This Indian was Side Hill Calf, a Piegan Blackfoot warrior, identified by old Wolf Calf to George Bird Ginnell. Wheeler, *The Trail of Lewis and Clark*, 2:311–14.

668. Lewis wrote on the 28th that he heard rifles and felt the "unspeakable satisfaction to see our canoes coming down" after their long and rapid ride down the Marias River. He was so sore from the ride, he could hardly stand. Thwaites, *Original Journals*, 5:227–28.

   Ordway wrote that, after greeting Lewis's party, they arrived at the next cache on the 28th; by 1:00 P.M. Gass and Willard brought the horses to meet the men who had gone downriver by canoe. They left the horses there on the plains. When they opened the cache at the campsite, they found the red pirogue too rotten to use. Quaife, *Journals of Lewis and Ordway*, 383.

669. On the 29th, they passed the part of the Missouri where natural walls appear (the Missouri Breaks in Montana). Colter, Collins, and the Field brothers were sent ahead to hunt. They killed nine bighorn sheep, of which Lewis had two females and one male skeletonized, keeping the horns and skins. Thwaites, *Original Journals*, 5:229.

670. Ordway wrote, "We killed 15 of them mearly for the hides to cover our canoes." Quaife, *Journals of Lewis and Ordway*, 384.

671. On August 3, Clark made it to the Missouri with his party, some 100 miles ahead of Lewis's party. They had traveled 837 miles from the place where he struck the Yellowstone to the Missouri River, 636 miles of which they traveled in two small

canoes lashed together and holding Shields, Gibson, Bratton, Labiche, Toussaint Charbonneau, Sacagawea and young Baptiste ("Pomp"), York, and himself. Thwaites, *Original Journals,* 5:318–19.

672. Lewis set out at 4:00 A.M. He had Ordway and Willard exchanged with the Fields for the day. Ordway and Willard would use the small canoe and hunt. Collins and Colter had stayed out the night before. Ibid., 233.

673. Ordway wrote that the current of the river drew the small canoe into a jam of logs at 11 P.M.; the stern ran under a limb and caught Willard, who held onto it and was pulled from the canoe. In the bow, Ordway leaned one way and then another to get the canoe through the logs and then paddled to shore. Willard made a raft of two logs and held onto it, floating down clear of the many logs. Ordway paddled his canoe out to meet and retrieve Willard. Then they rejoined the party. Quaife, *Journals of Lewis and Ordway,* 385.

674. Meanwhile, Clark moved camp on August 4 because the mosquitoes were so bad and buffalo scarce, leaving a note for Lewis. Thwaites, *Original Journals,* 5:322–23.

675. On August 8, Pryor, Shannon, Hall, and Windsor came downriver in two buffalo skin canoes ("bull boats") and met Clark's party. Pryor said that on the second evening after he left Clark on the Yellowstone, the horses were grazing in a grassy area. The next morning all of the horses were gone. Indian tracks about a hundred paces away showed that all of the horses had been driven off. Pryor and his party followed the tracks, noting where they divided after five miles, then followed the larger party five more miles. There seemed no chance of finding them. Returning to camp, they retired. A wolf bit Pryor's hand that night. It prodeeded to attack Windsor when Shannon shot it. The next day, Pryor's men packed their articles on their backs and headed toward the Yellowstone River, which they found at Pompey's Tower (named by Clark for Sacagawea's baby). Shannon killed a buffalo, from whose hide the men made two bull boats (as a precaution; one normally held six to eight men) in the manner of the Mandans and Arikaras. In these they descended safely to meet Clark's party. Clark recounted this story in his diary, adding that now they would kill for skins to trade with the Mandans for corn and other foodstuffs, since all their horses were gone. Ibid., 5:325–26. It is ironic that Lewis's party and the Gass contingent had just turned eight horses loose on the plains.

676. On August 11, Lewis wrote that he went out alone with Cruzatte. They both fired at elk. Lewis killed one and Cruzatte wounded another. They reloaded their guns and took different routes through the thick willows in pursuit of the wounded elk. Lewis said he was in the act of firing the second time when a ball struck his left thigh, one inch below the hip joint, missing the bone. Lewis was dressed in brown leather, and Cruzatte could not see well. Lewis shouted and when Cruzatte did not answer, Lewis thought it might have been an Indian who shot him. So he proceeded to the pirogue. Cruzatte returned in about twenty minutes, much alarmed and apologetic in the event it had been his fault. Gass helped Lewis take off his clothes and dressed the ball holes with "tents of patent lint." The wound bled profusely. Miraculously, the ball had hit neither a bone nor an artery. Ibid., 5:240–42.

677. Gass referred to Pryor, with Shannon, Windsor, and Hall.

678. These men were Joseph Dickson and Forest Hancock, the first white men the party had seen since the Mandan village in the spring of 1805. They were from Illinois and had been out since the summer of 1804. Thwaites, *Original Journals,* 5:329; Quaife, *Journals of Lewis and Ordway,* 388 n. 1.

679. This is one of the rare references to God in the journals. It shows Gass's sincere expression of relief that all parts of the party had succeeded in rejoining each other after the harried episodes they had separately experienced. It is truly amazing that they all united within such a short time span after traveling such varied routes.

680. Clark had seven men including himself, and he had Sacagawea and Jean Baptiste with him.

681. These were Pryor, Shannon, Windsor, and Hall. See note 675 above.

682. Clark wrote on August 14 that they were opposite the principal village of the Mahhar-has, at which place he saw the principal chief of the Little Village of the Minetarrees, who was crying over the death of his son, recently killed by Blackfeet Indians. All of the Indians in the village seemed glad to see the Lewis and Clark party.

Later they went on to Black Cat's Village, where the Mandans were also pleased to see them. Drouillard went to ask Jessaume to interpret at the lower village. Clark sent Charbonneau to get the chief to talk to them. The captains explained where they had been, and invited the chiefs to return to the United States with them. The Indians responded that they were afraid of the Sioux. The chief of the Mah har has said he would give the party corn, so Clark sent Gass and two men to get it; they soon returned, loaded with corn. Thwaites, *Original Journals*, 5:338–39.

683. Colter wanted to be released to join Dickson and Hancock, the two trappers from Illinois whom they had met on the Missouri and had now come to the Mandans. The captains gave Colter permission to leave. He later returned to the Yellowstone River while employed with Manuel Lisa and became the first white man to describe the area south of Yellowstone Park. Ibid., 5:341 n. 2.

684. Big White, or Chief Sheheke of the Mandans, agreed to go if he could take his own wife and son, and Jessaume, his wife, and two children. Ibid., 5:343.

685. "The interpreter" refers to Toussaint Charbonneau. On the 17th, Clark wrote that they settled with him for his services, which amounted to the price of a horse and a lodge, or a total of $500.33 1/3¢. Before leaving at 2:00 P.M, Clark offered to take Pomp, "a butifull promising child" who was nineteen months old; both Charbonneau and Sacagawea were willing provided he were weaned. In a year he would be old enough, they observed. All agreed. Ibid., 5:344–45.

686. "A small piece of ordnance" consisted of a gun salute. Thwaites, *Original Journals*, 5:346.

687. They met three Frenchmen from the Arikara village, two of whom had wintered with Lewis and Clark at the Mandans, "Reeved [Francois Rivet] & Greinyea." Ibid., 5:350. The Frenchmen said that 700 Sioux whose camp was near the Big Bend had passed them on the way to war with the Mandans and Minetarees. Ibid.

688. The Arikara chief who went to the United States the spring of 1805 had died near the Sioux River on his return trip, according to the Frenchmen. Ibid.

689. On the 21st, Clark lectured an Arikara chief against banding with the Sioux to kill Mandans, who had heeded Clark's own advice and stayed home from war. Ibid., 5:354–55.

690. At the nation of Cheyennes, the party found a Frenchman named Rokey who was one of their engagés to the Mandans. He had spent all his money and requested passage down. The captains agreed. Ibid., 5:356.

Chapter 25: August 22–September 18, 1806

691. The chief who gave them corn was Arikara. Thwaites, *Original Journals*, 5:355. The party also visited with Cheyenne Indians on the 22nd, whom Clark aptly described. Ibid., 5:356–57.

692. On the 22nd, Lewis walked for the first time since his accident. Ibid., 5:358.

693. This fort was Regis Loisel's (not Landselle's) on Cedar Island, entirely empty when the party visited it. They had stayed here September 22, 1804. See note 94.

694. The party had named "Camp Pleasant" when they stayed at this agreeable site September 16 and 17, 1804, relishing the abundance of game and fruits nearby.

695. On the 29th, Clark noted that he must have seen 20,000 buffalo feeding on the plain, a greater number than he had ever seen at one time. Thwaites, *Original Journals*, 5:364.

696. Clark wrote on the 30th that with his spyglass he saw several Indians on horseback; there were about twenty above where they had seen the barking squirrels. One was probably a Frenchman in a capote, a loose cloak with a hood. Both parties fired salutes, and three Indians swam over to meet Clark. They were Teton Sioux, and their chief was Black Buffalo. Clark told them they were "bad" because they had been deaf to the councils that they had shared in 1804, and they had killed other Indians (the Mandans). With the use of their interpreter (Jessaume), Clark informed them that he had given the Mandans a cannon, and he warned them not to come near the party or they would be fired upon. Clark then noted that he was anxious for the return of the hunters, Shannon and the two Fields, who arrived about six. Ibid., 5:365–67.

Ordway wrote on the 30th that, when the Indians beckoned, the party replied that they were bad and there was nothing to say. The Indians signaled to come, and the party refused. Then the Indians threatened that if the party came to their side of the river, they would kill them. Quaife, *Journals of Lewis and Ordway,* 395.

697. One of the men knew that one of these Indians was the brother of Pierre Dorion's wife. These Indians saluted the Mandan chief, Big White, and they all smoked together. Thwaites, *Original Journals,* 5:371.

698. Here the group viewed a structure built by Robert McClellan, a scout in General Anthony Wayne's army from 1794 to 1795 when both Lewis and Clark knew him. It had been built for trade with the Yankton Sioux 1804–1805. In 1807, McClellan partnered with Ramsey Crooks in the St. Louis fur trade. Later he played a part in the Astorian enterprise. Ibid., 5:373 n. 1.

699. James Aird, a Scottish trader, was employed in 1806 with the House of Dickson and Company, which was trading with the Sioux. He had two bateaux loaded with merchandise for trading. Robert Dickson, a prominent Canadian trader, enjoyed great influence with the Indians of Wisconsin and the upper Mississippi country. Ibid., 5:374 n. 2.

700. On September 4, Clark wrote that they came to Floyd's grave and found it had been opened by the Indians and only partly covered. They refilled the grave and proceeded to camp near the Omaha Indian village. Ibid., 5:376.

701. This boat belonged to Auguste Chouteau, a prominent fur trader from St. Louis. Henry Delauney may have been the steersman who sold the party some whiskey. (They were to pay Chouteau later, but he would not accept money.) Clark noted also on this day that Big White and the Indian women and children were weary of traveling. Ibid., 5:378.

Ordway described Chouteau's boat as a keel boat with twelve Frenchmen aboard. Quaife, *Journals of Lewis and Ordway,* 397.

702. In this pirogue were Alexander Lafass and three Frenchmen from St. Louis, headed toward the Platte River to trade with the Wolf Indians. Clark learned from them that Zebulon Pike and General James D. Wilkinson had set out up the Arkansas River on an expedition to the West. Thwaites, *Original Journals,* 5:381, 381 n. 1.

703. In this large pirogue were seven men headed by Mr. LaCroix. They had come from St. Louis to trade with Omaha Indians. Ibid., 5:381, 5:381 n. 2., 381 n. 2.

704. Robert McClallan is described in note 698. His party included Joseph Gravelines, who was in charge of the bateaux sent back from the Mandans, and the elder Pierre Dorion, another man hired along the Missouri who had accompanied Gravelines on the return party from the Mandans the spring of 1805. They had taken with them an Arikara chief, who unfortunately had died in Washington, and were sending a speech from Jefferson back to the Arikara nation. President Jefferson asked McClallan to inquire about Lewis and Clark on his mission to the Arikaras. Ibid., 5:383. Quaife, *Journals of Lewis and Ordway,* 398.

Ordway noted that there were two Englishmen, besides McClallan, and the rest of the party were French. They had heard that members of the Lewis and Clark expedition had all been killed. People in the United States had been concerned about the party. Quaife, *Journals of Lewis and Ordway,* 399.

705. These boats were owned by LaCroix, Chouteau, and Aiten [sic] of St. Louis. Thwaites, *Original Journals,* 5:384.

706. This group of eight included Joseph Robidoux, a well-known French-Canadian fur trader. Their bateaux had six oars. Thwaites, *Original Journals,* 5:386. Quaife, *Journals of Lewis and Ordway,* 400 n. 1.

707. This was Captain John McClallan of New York, who was venturing forth on a speculative mission to New Spain by way of the River Platte, to see what the interest for trading might be there. He hoped that some of the Otoes and Pawnees would accompany him to Santa Fe. McClallan's group told the party that people in the United States had given up and forgotten them, but President Jefferson still had hopes of seeing them. Thwaites, *Original Journals,* 5:387 n.1.

708. The expedition passed the Two Charetons River on the 18th and found the current gentler than when they had ascended it in May of 1804. Ibid., 5:388.

709. On the 20th, they arrived at Charrette, a small French village. They fired guns. Two young Scotsmen furnished dinner and sold them whiskey. Astonished to see them return, the French and Americans said it had been surmised that they were lost. The party traveled sixty-eight miles the 20th. Ibid., 5:390–91.

At 7:00 A.M. the following day, on the 21st, the party passed twelve canoes of Kickapoos. Many people walked along the shore to see them. Towards evening they arrived at St. Charles. Ibid., 5:391.

On the 22nd they arrived in the evening at Fort Bellefontaine, the military headquarters of the department of Louisiana. Built in 1805, it was the starting place for many later explorations. Ibid., 5:392 n. 2. Quaife, *Journals of Lewis and Ordway,* 402.

710. Clark wrote that they arrived at St. Louis, where they received a "harty welcom," about 12 o'clock on September 23rd. An old acquaintance of Clark's, Major W. Christy, furnished them with storage for the baggage. Peter (Pierre) Chouteau offered them a room in his home. Captain Lewis wrote a letter to President Jefferson on the 24th. The next two days they bought clothes, dried baggage, and wrote letters. On September 26th, Clark ended the journal, noting, "commenced wrighting &c." Ibid., 5:393–95.

APPENDIX A

MEMBERS OF THE EXPEDITION

These people went from the Mandan Village to the Pacific Ocean and back:

Capt. Meriwether Lewis, U.S. Infantry
Capt. William Clark, U.S. Artillery
York, Clark's black servant
Sgt. Patrick Gass
Sgt. John Ordway
Sgt. Nathaniel Pryor
Pvt. William Bratton
Pvt. John Collins
Pvt. John Colter
Pvt. Peter Cruzatte
Pvt. Joseph Field
Pvt. Reuben Field
Pvt. Robert Frazer
Pvt. George Gibson
Pvt. Silas Goodrich
Pvt. Hugh Hall
Pvt. Thomas Proctor Howard
Pvt. Francois Labiche
Pvt. Jean Baptiste LePage
Pvt. Hugh McNeal
Pvt. John Potts
Pvt. George Shannon
Pvt. John Shields
Pvt. John B. Thompson
Pvt. Peter M. Weiser
Pvt. William Werner
Pvt. Joseph Whitehouse
Pvt. Alexander Hamilton Willard
Pvt. Richard Windsor
Interpreter George Drouillard
Interpreter Toussaint Charbonneau
Sacagawea
Jean Baptiste Charbonneau

The following joined on the Missouri:

Pierre Dorion Sr.
Joseph Gravelines
Phillipe Degie
Pvt. Jean Baptiste LePage (repaced Newman in permanent party
November 3, 1804)

The following joined at Fort Mandan:
Sacagawea
Toussaint Charbonneau
Jean Baptiste Charbonneau

Men who served only on the first leg of the trip to Mandan:
Sgt. Charles Floyd (cousin of Pryor) died August 20, 1804,
near Sioux City, Iowa, on Missouri River.
Cpl. John Boley
Cpl. John Dame
Cpl. Jean Baptiste DeChamps
Cpl. John Newman (court-martialed)
Cpl. John G. Robertson
Cpl. Ebenezer Tuttle
Cpl. Richard Warfington
Cpl. Isaac White
Pvt. Joseph Barter "La Liberte" (deserted)
Pvt. Moses B. Reed (expelled)
Engagé Alexander Carson
Engagé Pierre Roi
Engagé Charles Caugee
Engagé Roky
Engagé Paul Primeau
Engagé Francois Rivet
Engagé Joseph Collin
Engagé Jean Baptiste LaJeunnesse
Engagé Etienne Malboeuf
Engagé Peter Pinaut
Engagé Charles Hebert

APPENDIX B

Gass usually did not identify hunters. Often, they were not identified by anyone. This table names hunters identified in other journals. For full citations, see the bibliography.

Date		Hunter	Killed	Source
May 27, 1804		George Shannon	a deer	Quaife, 81.
May 28,	"	Reuben Field	a deer	Ibid.
May 31,	"	R. Field	a deer	Ibid., 82.
June 17,	"	George Drouillard	bear & 2 deer	Thwaites, 1:51.
June 18,	"	John Colter	1 bear	Ibid., 7:36.
June 22,	"	Drouillard	bear	Ibid., 1:37.
June 24,	"	Drouillard	2 deer	Quaife, 88.
		R. Field	a deer	Ibid.
		John Collins	3 deer	Ibid.
June 26,	"	Drouillard	8 deer	Thwaites, 7:38.
June 28,	"	R. & Joseph Field	young wolf	Quaife, 89.
July 7,	"	Colter	wolf	Thwaites, 7:40.
July 11,	"	Drouillard	6 deer	Ibid., 1:74.
July 12,	"	Drouillard	2 deer	Quaife, 95.
July 16,	"	R. Field	2 deer	Ibid., 96, 98.
July 17,	"	Drouillard	3 deer	Thwaites, 7:42.
July 18,	"	Drouillard	2 deer	Quaife, 99.
July 25,	"	Collins	2 deer	Ibid., 101.
July 27,	"	Shannon	1 deer	Thwaites, 7:45.
		William Clark	1 deer	Ibid., 1:91.
July 29,	"	Drouillard	a deer & elk	Quaife, 102.
July 30,	"	J. Field	badger	Ibid., 103.
July 31,	"	Drouillard	1 deer	Ibid., 104.
Aug. 1,	"	John Shields, J. Field & George Gibson	3 deer	Ibid.
Aug. 2,	"	Drouillard	an elk	
		Francois Labiche	a deer	
		Collins	a deer	
		R. Field	a fawn	
		Peter Cruzatte	a deer	Ibid.
Aug. 8,	"	Collins	an elk	
		John Dame	pelican	Ibid., 107.
Aug. 9,	"	Clark, Charles Floyd	a turkey	Ibid., 108.
Aug. 23,	"	R. Field	a deer & a buffalo	Ibid., 115.
		Clark	a deer	
		J. Field	a buffalo	
		Collins	a fawn	Ibid.
Aug. 25,	"	Shannon	an elk	Quaife, 117.
Aug. 29,	"	Drouillard	a deer	Ibid., 119.
Sept. 2,	"	John Newman & Thomas Howard	an elk	

Date		Hunter	Killed	Source
		Drouillard	2 elk	
		R. Field	1 bull elk	Ibid., 124.
Sept.5,	"	R. Field	1 deer	
	"	Drouillard, Newman	elk fawn deer & elk calf	Ibid., 126.
Sept. 6,	"	R. Field	1 deer, 1 fawn	Ibid., 126-27.
Sept. 7,	"	Shields	prairie dog	Ibid., 127.
Sept. 8,	"	Drouillard	1 elk, 1 fawn, 2 beaver, & 1 prairie dog	Ibid.
		Meriwether Lewis & party	2 buffalo	Ibid., 128.
Sept. 9,	"	Drouillard	deer & 2 fawns	Ibid.
		R. Field	buffalo	Thwaites, 7:57.
Sept. 10,	"	Newman	1 deer	Quaife, 128.
		Nathaniel Pryor	1 buffalo	Ibid.
		Richard Warfington	2 buffalo	Ibid., 128, 129.
Sept. 11,	"	John Ordway	porcupine	
		Clark	1 elk, 1 deer, 1 fawn	
		Gibson	1 elk, 1 deer, 1 fawn	Ibid., 129.
Sept. 13,	"	Drouillard	4 beaver	Ibid., 130.
Sept. 14,	"	Shannon	1 porcupine	Ibid., 132.
		Drouillard	3 beaver	
		Shields	a hare	
Sept. 16,	"	Collins	2 deer	
		Clark	1 deer	
		Lewis	1 deer,1 buffalo	
		Drouillard	1 deer	
		Bapt.DeChamps	1 buffalo	
		Peter Roi	1 fawn	Ibid.
Sept. 17,	"	Colter	antelope & mule deer	Thwaites, 1:152.
		Gibson	deer with 18"tail	Quaife, 132.
		Drouillard	a beaver, a coyote	Thwaites, 7:59
		Colter & others	coyote	Ibid., 1:152.
Sept. 18,	"	Clark	coyote	Ibid, 1:155.
		Clark, J. Field & Drouillard	11 deer	Ibid., 7:59
Sept. 19,	"	Clark	1 buffalo	Thwaites, 1:156
		boat crew including Ordway & Gass	2 buffalo	Ibid., 1:157, Quaife, 133.
		York	1 deer	Thwaites, 1:157.
Sept. 19,	"	Clark	1 buffalo	Quaife, 133.
		J. Field	1 deer	Ibid.
		Drouillard	2 deer	Ibid., 134.
Sept. 20,	"	R. Field	1 deer, 2 antelope	Thwaites, 1:158.
Sept. 22,	"	Drouillard & Shields	white wolf & 2 deer	Quaife, 135.
		Clark	1 deer	Thwaites, 1:161.
Sept. 23,	"	R. Field	antelope	Quaife, 136.
Sept. 24,	"	Colter	2 elk, 1 deer	Ibid.

Date		Hunter	Killed	Source
Oct. 17,	"	Clark, an Arikara Chief & another hunter	6 deer	Thwaites, 1:194, 197.
Oct. 20,	"	Clark	3 deer	Ibid., 1:201.
Oct. 21,	"	Clark	1 buffalo	Ibid., 1:202.
Dec. 13,	"	J. Field	2 buffalo	Ibid., 7:237.
Jan. 14,	1805	Shannon & Collins	buffalo, wolf, 2 porcupine & hare	Quaife, 177.
Feb. 16,	"	Lewis, Ordway, Gass & others	36 deer & 14 elk	Moulton 3:296, 297 n.1
Apr. 17,	"	Lewis	1 buffalo	Quaife, 197.
Apr. 20,	"	Lewis	2 deer	Ibid., 198, 199.
		Drouillard	a beaver	Ibid., 199.
Apr. 22,	"	Drouillard	a beaver	Ibid., 200.
May 22,	"	Lewis	a deer	Ibid., 216.
May 25,	"	Drouillard	mountain sheep	Thwaites, 2:72.
		Clark	mountain sheep	Quaife, 218.
June 2,	"	Drouillard	grizzly bear	Thwaites, 2:109.
June 12,	"	Clark	1 elk, 1 deer	Ibid., 2:146.
June 21,	"	Alexander Willard	1 elk	Thwaites, 2:179.
June 24 [23],"		Drouillard & R. Field	16 buffalo, 5 deer	Ibid., 2:184, Quaife, 235.
June 25,	"	Gass & Shields	2 elk	Thwaites, 2:186.
June 26,	"	Gass & Shields	7 buffalo	Ibid., 2:189.
June 27,	"	Drouillard & J. Field	9 elk & 3 bears	Ibid, 336.
July 3,	"	Drouillard	grizzly bear	Thwaites, 2:205.
July 21,	"	Clark	buck deer	Ibid., 2:256.
		J. Field	buck & doe deer	Ibid., 2:259.
Aug. 1,	"	Drouillard & Lewis	2 elk	Ibid., 2:293.
Aug. 8,	"	R. Fields	1 deer, 1 antelope	Quaife, 261.
Aug. 10,	"	Drouillard	3 deer	Thwaites, 2:235.
Aug. 14,	"	R. & J. Field	4 deer, 1 antelope	Quaife, 261.
		Clark	1 deer	Thwaites, 2:349.
Aug. 16,	"	Drouillard	3 deer	Ibid, 2:355.
Aug. 25,	"	Shannon	1 beaver	Ibid, 2:336-37.
Sept. 8,	"	Drouillard	1 deer	Ibid, 3:57.
Sept. 9,	"	Drouillard	2 deer	Ibid.
Sept. 10,	"	Colter & others	4 deer, a beaver, 3 grouse	Thwaites, 3:61.
Sept. 21,	"	Lewis	1 wolf	Quaife, 289.
Sept. 27,	"	Colter	a deer	Thwaites, 3:89.
Sept. 29,	"	Drouillard	2 deer	
		Collins	1 deer	Ibid., 3:90.
Nov. 2,	"	Labiche	14 brants	
		Collins	1 brant	
		J. Field	3 brants	Ibid., 3:190.
Nov. 3,	"	Collins	1 deer	Ibid., 3:192.
		Labiche	3 geese	Ibid.
		Lewis	swan & several ducks	Ibid., 3:193,194.

Date		Hunter	Killed	Source
Nov. 16,	"	York	2 geese, 8 speckled brants	Ibid, 3:227.
Nov. 18,	"	Labiche	48 plover	Ibid., 3:230.
		R. Field,	California Condor	Ibid., 3:231.
Nov. 20,	"	J. Field,		
		Colter & Labiche	3 deer, some brants	Ibid., 3:237.
		R. Field	8 ducks	Ibid., 3:238.
Dec. 2,	"	Joseph Field	1 elk	Ibid., 3:264.
Dec. 3,	"	Gibson & Pryor	6 elk	Ibid., 3:265.
Dec. 10,	"	Drouillard & Shannon	1 elk	Ibid., 3:273.
Dec. 13,	"	Drouillard & Shannon	18 elk	Ibid., 3:279.
Dec. 28,	"	R. Field & Collins	1 deer	Ibid., 3: 291, 293.
Dec. 30,	"	Drouillard, R. Field, Shannon, Labiche, & Collins	4 elk	Ibid., 3:291, 297.
Jan. 4,	1806	Shannon	1 elk	Ibid., 3:309.
Jan. 10,	"	Gibson & Shannon	7 elk	Ibid., 3:335.
Jan. 17,	"	Colter	1 deer	Ibid., 3:354.
Jan. 21,	"	Labiche & Shannon	3 elk	Ibid., 4:4.
Jan. 24,	"	Drouillard & LePage	2 deer, 3 elk	Ibid., 4:11.
Jan. 27,	"	Shannon, Labiche, & R. Field	10 elk	Ibid., 4:17.
Jan. 31,	"	J. Field	2 elk	Ibid., 4:26.
Feb. 3,	"	Drouillard	7 elk, 1 beaver	Quaife, 232.
	"	Gass, R. Field, Shannon & Labiche	4 elk	Thwaites, 4:39.
Feb. 4,	"	R. Field	6 elk & 1 pheasant	Ibid., 4:43.
Feb. 8,	"	Shannon & Labiche	4 elk	Ibid., 4:52.
Feb. 9,	"	Drouillard	1 beaver	Ibid., 4:54.
Feb. 11-17,	"	Gass, John Thompson & R. Field	8 elk	Ibid., 4:60, 83.
Feb. 26,	"	Collins	1 elk	Ibid., 4:114.
Feb. 28,	"	Shields, J. Field, & Shannon	5 elk	Ibid., 4:117.
Mar. 7,	"	Labiche & Drouillard	1 elk	Ibid., 4:140.
Mar. 8,	"	Collins	3 elk	
		Drouillard & Labiche	1 elk	Thwaites, 4:133.
Mar. 13,	"	Drouillard, J. Field, & Robert Frazer	2 deer & 2 elk	Ibid., 4:162.
	"	Collins	2 elk	Quaife, 328.
Mar. 14,	"	R. Field & Thompson	1 brant	Thwaites, 4:168.
Mar. 18,	"	J. Field	1 elk	Ibid., 4:181.
Mar. 23,	"	Colter	1 elk	Ibid., 4:196.
	"	Drouillard & R. & J. Fields	2 elk	Ibid., 4:198.
Mar. 28,	"	Gibson, Drouillard & party	7 deer	Ibid., 4:207, 209.
Apr. 1,	"	Pryor	1 deer	Quaife, 335.
Apr. 2,	"	Gass & party	1 elk, 6 deer	
		Collins	1 bear	Thwaites, 4:244.
Apr. 4,	"	Gass & party	4 elk	

Date		Hunter	Killed	Source
Apr. 6,	"	Shannon	5 elk	Ibid., 4:250, 251.
Apr. 7,	"	R. Field	1 partridge	Ibid., 4:252.
Apr. 8,	"	Drouillard	1 duck	Ibid., 4:258.
Apr. 10,	"	Collins	3 deer	Ibid., 4:263.
Apr. 13,	"	Shields	2 deer	Ibid., 4:277.
Apr. 14,	"	Drouillard &		
		J. & R. Field	4 deer	Quaife, 341.
Apr. 15,	"	Drouillard	1 deer	Ibid., 342.
Apr. 16,	"	J. Field	pheasant	
		R. Field	3 squirrels	Thwaites, 4:286
	"	Labiche	2 deer	Ibid., 4:287.
Apr. 17,	"	Sheilds	1 deer	Ibid., 4:291.
May 1,	"	Labiche	1 deer	Ibid., 4: 346.
May 8,	"	Drouillard	1 deer	
		Shields	1 deer	
		Collins	1 deer	
		Cruzatte	1 deer	
		Sheilds	1 deer	Ibid., 5:3.
May 11,	"	Drouillard	2 deer	Quaife, 356.
May 14,	"	Collins	2 grizzlies	Ibid., 357.
		Labiche	3 grizzlies	Ibid.
May 16,	"	Drouillard & Cruzatte	1 deer	
		Shannon	1 deer	Thwaites, 5:43.
May 17,	"	Pryor & Collins	1 large bear	Ibid., 5:44.
May 18,	"	Drouillard, R. Field, &		
		Baptiste LePage	1 large hawk	Ibid., 5:48.
May 20,	"	Labiche	1 deer	Ibid., 5:51.
May 22,	"	Drouillard, R. & J. Field,		
		Gibson, & Shields	5 deer	Thwaites, 5:55.
		Lewis, Clark, & 3 men	1 deer	Ibid.
May 23,	"	Pryor	1 deer	Quaife, 359.
May 27,	"	Drouillard, Labiche,		
		& Cruzatte	5 deer	Thwaites, 5:72.
May 28,	"	Collins, Shannon,		
		& Colter	8 deer	Ibid., 5:75.
May 30,	"	J. & R. Field	3 deer	Ibid., 5:89.
May 31,	"	J. & R. Field	2 deer	Ibid., 5:91.
June 3,	"	Colter, J.Field,		
		& Willard	5 deer, 1 bear	Ibid., 5:103.
June 4,	"	Shields	2 deer	Ibid., 5:106.
June 5,	"	R. Field, Shannon,		
		Labiche & Collins	5 deer, l bear	Ibid.,5:107.
June 10,	"	Collins	1 deer	Quaife, 365.
June 11,	"	Labiche	1 bear & large buck	
		Gibson	1 fat buck	Thwaites, 5:123.
June 12,	"	Shields	2 deer	Quaife, 365.
June 13,	"	Collins, J. Field, Gibson,		
		Shields, Shannon, Labiche,		
		& Drouillard	8 deer	Ibid., 365-66.
June 14,	"	Colter	1 deer	Ibid., 366.

Date		Hunter	Killed	Source
June 15,	"	R. Field & Willard	3 deer	Ibid.
June 19,	"	Labiche	1 deer	
		R. Field	2 deer	Ibid., 368.
June 20,	"	R. Field	bear	Ibid.
		Labiche & Cruzatte	1 deer	Ibid.
June 21,	"	Shields	1 deer	Ibid, 369.
June 29,	"	Colter & J. Field	1 deer	Thwaites, 5:170.
June 30,	"	R. Field	a deer	
		Shields	2 deer	
		Drouillard	3 deer	Quaife, 371.
July 2,	"	Collins	2 deer	Ibid.
July 5,	"	Shannon	1 deer	Ibid., 373.
July 8,	"	R. Field	1 deer, 1 antelope	Thwaites, 5:196.
July 9,	"	J. Field	1 buffalo	Ibid., 5:197.
July 10,	"	Lewis, R. Field,		
		& Drouillard	3 elk, 1 bear	Ibid., 5:198.
		Collins	a goose	Quaife, 376.
July 27,	"	Frazer	1 buffalo	Ibid., 382.
July 28,	"	Gass & Willard	6 antelope	Quaife, 383.
July 29,	"	Collins, Colter,		
		& R. & J. Field	9 bighorn sheep	Thwaites 5:229.
July 30,	"	Willard	7 buffalo, grizzly bear	Quaife, 383.
July 31,	"	J. Field	1 bighorn sheep	Ibid., 384.
Aug. 1,	"	Drouillard & Lewis	1 bear	Ibid.
Aug. 3,	"	R. & J. Field	24 deer	Ibid, 385.
Aug. 4,	"	Ordway & Willard	2 deer, l bear	Thwaites, 5:234.
Aug. 5,	"	R. & J. Field	2 bear	Ibid., 5:235.
		Ordway & Willard	a bear, 2 deer	Ibid.
Aug. 8,	"	Drouillard	2 deer	Quaife, 387.
Aug. 9,	"	R. & J. Field	1 elk, 1 deer	Ibid.
Aug. 23,	"	Shields, R. & J. Field	3 elk & 3 deer	Thwaites 5:358.
Aug. 25,	"	Drouillard	1 deer	Ibid., 5:360.
		Shields & Collins	2 deer	Ibid., 5:359-360.
		Shannon & J.& R. Field	2 deer	Ibid., 5:360.
Aug. 28,	"	Drouillard, Labiche,	1 deer	Ibid., 5:363.
		Pryor, Shields, Gibson,		
		Willard & Collins	4 deer, 2 buffalo &	
		Wm Bratton & Frazer	2 barking squirrels	Ibid.
Sept. 2,	"	Clark & party	2 buffalo	Ibid., 5:373.
Sept. 11,	"	Drouillard	1 deer	Quaife, 398.
Sept. 15,	"	R. & J. Field,		
		Shannon	1 elk	Thwaites, 5:385.

APPENDIX C

LEWIS LETTER, MCKEEHAN REPLY, AND GASS PROSPECTUS

Lewis to the Public[*]

City of Washington
March 14th, 1807.

Having been informed that there were several unauthorised and probably some spurious publications now preparing for the press, on the subject of my late tour to the Pacific Ocean by individuals entirely unknown to me, I have considered it a duty which I owe the public, as well as myself to put them on their guard with respect to such publications, lest from the practice of such impositions they may be taught to depreciate the worth of the work which I am myself preparing for publication before it can possibly appear, as much time, labor, and expense are absolutely necessary in order to do justice to the several subjects which it will embrace: With a view therefore to prevent the practice of those deceptions the public are informed that the lists for subscriptions which have been promulgated by myself are headed with the subjoined Prospectus, and that those who wish to possess the genuine work, may obtain it by entering their names on those lists. The Prospectus will serve to shew the distribution and contents of the work.

The map will most probably be published by the latter end of October next, and the first volume of the work about the 1st of January 1808; the two remaining volumes will follow in succession as early as they can possibly be prepared for publication.

As early as a just estimate of the price of the several parts of this work can be formed, public notice will be given of the same through the medium of the Press.

To Robert Frazier only has permission been given either by Gen. William Clark or myself, to publish any thing in relation to our late voyage. When the proposals were first drawn in October last for the publication of the journal of that man, they were submitted to me for correction; I then expunged the promise which had been made, that the work should contain certain information in relation to the natural history of the country through which we had passed and cautioned the persons concerned in the publication not to promise the world any thing with which they had not the means of complying; but as the hope of gain seems to have outstripped their good faith to the public in this respect; I think it my duty to declare that Robert Frazier, who was only a private on this expedition, is entirely unacquainted with celestial observations, mineralogy, botany, or zoology, and therefore cannot possibly give any accurate information on those subjects, nor on that of geography, and that the whole which can be expected from his Journal is merely a limited detail of our daily transactions. With respect to all unauthorised publications relative to this voyage, I presume that they cannot have stronger pretensions to accuracy of information than that of Robert Frazier.

MERIWETHER LEWIS.

National Intelligencer, 18 March 1807. A propectus similar to No. 262a follows the letter, concluding with the note: "Editors of Public Prints in the United States, disposed to aid the publication of this work, are requested to give the foregoing a few insertions." The *National Intelligencer* ran the prospectus without the letter in its 23 March issue, then used both together in the issues of 25, 27, and 30 March, and 1 April. The *Aurora* ran both the letter and prospectus 23 March. This letter provoked a stinging reply from David McKeehan (No. 264).

Excerpts of David McKeehan's reply to Meriwether Lewis,**
printed in the *Pittsburgh Gazette,* 14 April 1807, p. 2.

To his Excellency Meriwether Lewis, Esquire, Governor of Upper Louisiana.

Sir,
  Your publication in the National Intelligencer, dated the 14th of last month, has forced into notice an obscure individual, who, of course, has had the misfortune of being "entirely unknown to you," to defend his character and his rights. . . . Your rapid advancement to power and wealth seems to have changed the polite, humble and respectful language of a *Sir Clement* into that of him who commands and dispenses favours; even your subscription lists, when you offer your learned works for publication must be *"promulgated."* . . .
  The public are then referred to the lists for subscriptions which have been *promulgated* by yourself, and the prospectus with which they are headed; and obligingly informed, "that those who wish to possess the genuine work, may obtain it by entering their names on those lists." But . . . we are told that the price of this "genuine work" is to be fixed at a future day; that the map *will most probably* be published the latter end of October next; the first volume of the work *about* the first of January, 1808; and that the two remaining volumes will follow in succession as early *as they possibly can be prepared for publication;* or . . . at *as early periods as the avocations of the author will permit.* Next you tell the public that to Robert Frazer only permission has been given to publish any thing relative to your late voyage. But even the *proposals* of Frazer must feel the effect of your expunging fingers. . . . Do you yet stop here? No, but in order to defeat the ostensible object of your own permission, and to deprive poor Frazer, or those who may have purchased from him, of all benefit arising from his publication, you attack his capacity, and "declare that Robert Frazer, *who was only a private on this expedition,* is entirely unacquainted with *celestial observations, mineralogy,*

botany, or *zoology,* and therefore cannot possibly give any accurate information on *those subjects,* nor that of geography, and that the whole which can be expected from his journal is merely a *limited detail* of our daily transactions." Limited perhaps in proportion to your expunging operations! Having thus attempted to expose Frazer and his work, you conclude your notice with the following sweeping clause intended to affect all other persons interested in any of the journals; "With respect to all unauthorised publications relative to this voyage, I presume that they cannot have stronger pretensions to accuracy or information than that of Robert Frazer." . . .

Without soliciting either your permission or authority, I have purchased the journal of one of the persons engaged in the late expedition from the mouth of the Missouri to the Pacific ocean, "performed by order of the government;" that I have arranged and transcribed it for the press, supplying such geographical notes and other observations, as I supposed would render it more useful and satisfactory to the reader; that a large edition of it is now printing in this place, and will be published and ready for delivery . . . the latter end of next month. . . .

With respect to the hazardous nature of the enterprize and the courage necessary for undertaking it, candour compels me to say, that public opinion has placed them on too high ground. Mr. M'Kenzie with a party consisting of about one fourth part of the number under your command, with means which will not bear a comparison with those furnished you, and without the *authority,* the *flags,* or *medals* of his government, crossed the Rocky mountains several degrees north of your rout, and for the *first time* penetrated to the Pacific Ocean. You had the advantage of the information contained in his journal, and could in some degree estimate and guard against the dangers and difficulties you were to meet. . . .

What compensations did your Excellency receive? By an act of congress passed the 3d of last month, double pay was allowed you as captain of infantry, during the expedition, and also a grant of 1600 acres of land; to these may be added the value of your rations and your pay as private secretary or master of ceremonies to the president, the latter of which it is alledged and believed you pocketed though you could perform no part of the duties or ceremonies attached to the office. Have we got through the items of the account? No. To these perquisites the executive adds the honorable and lucrative office of Governor of Upper Louisiana! Why, sir, these grants and rewards savour more of the splendid munificence of a Prince than the economy of a republican government. . . . There is besides a good deal of tinsel thrown into the scale with these solid considerations; such as the praises of the president . . . the honor of leading such an expedition; of knighting or making chiefs (an act perhaps not strictly constitutional) of the poor savages of the west; of immortalizing your name and those of your friends by giving them to the mighty streams which flow from the Rocky mountains; and what I had almost forgot, the warblings of the Muses, who have been celebrating the *"Young Hero's name."* Who could have thought that after so much liberality shewn by the country, your Excellency would have been found contending with the poor fellows, who for their small pittance were equally exposed with yourself to the toils and dangers attending the expedition, about the publication of their journals, which cost them so much trouble and anxiety to keep and preserve! I am afraid Captain Clarke, who appears to have acted during the whole of the tour with the greatest prudence, firmness and courage, will be forced to blush for the man he has called his friend. . . .

Where was your journal during the session of Congress? Snug, eh! No notice is given in the government paper of an intention to publish it. . . . Some of the members begin to wince, complain that they are called upon to legislate in the dark, that no journal of the expedition was laid before them; others boldly assert that the grants they are asked for are extravagant— that double pay is a sufficient compensation. . . . This was the time to keep the journal out of view; and to be silent about the fortune to be made out of the *three* volumes and a map. "I'll squeeze, (says his Excellency in embrio) the nation first, and then raise a heavy contribution on the citizens individually: I'll cry down these *one*-volume journals, and frighten the publishers; and no man, woman, or child shall read a word about *my* tour, unless they enter their names on *my* lists, and pay what price I shall afterwards fix on my *three* volumes and map." . . . Every man of sense must agree that these journals are either *private* property of the individuals who took them, or *public* property; for none but an ideot could for a moment suppose, that any officer upon the expedition could have a property in any but his own. . . . There may be cases where the journals, maps, surveys, and all other documents taken during a military expedition, especially where policy and the interest of the country requires secrecy, ought to be considered the property of the public and delivered up to the government; but where no such policy, interest or secrecy exist; and where it is for the public advantage that the information collected shall be diffused as widely as possible . . . where other persons belonging to the expedition, who had taken journals or other documents, were discharged from public service with these journals and documents in their hands, and no claim made of them as public property when other public property in their possession was delivered up; where the commanding officers have been allowed by the government to publish their journals, maps and other documents for their private emolument; will it be said that in a country governed by equal laws, and where equal rights and privileges are secured to all the citizens, these persons who have been so discharged from public service and become private citizens, have not also a right to publish the documents they have taken and preserved? . . . The object of multiplying journals of the tour was that, in case of defeat or other misfortune affecting the safety of those taken by the commanding officers, the chances of preserving information with respect to the country through which the expedition was to pass might also be multiplied. . . . Was it not a part of your duty to see that these journals were regularly kept, and, if necessary, to supply from your journal, any defects or omissions? Were not all the journals belonging to the corps brought together at certain resting places, examined, compared and corrected? If Mr. Gass (from whom I purchased) "is unacquainted with celestial observations" (which I will grant) was it not your duty, and did you not supply him with the result of those made by yourself? How else did Mr. Gass find out the latitude of certain places where your observations were taken to the exactness of minutes, seconds and tenths of seconds? Without information from Captain Clarke or yourself, how did he ascertain the distances of places, the breadth of rivers and bays, height of falls and length of portages? But it is unnecessary to multiply questions: you know that these journals will furnish the necessary information relative to the tour; and that the publication of them will *"depreciate the worth of the work you are preparing for publication."* This is what alarms your insatiable avarice. . . . Why purchase them at high prices in order to have them supressed? Did you not lately purchase the journal of sergeant Prior or Sergeant Ordway, for that purpose?. . . [Gass] may in some respects be considered as having the advantage; for while your Excellency was star-gazing, and taking celestial observations, he was taking observations in the world below. If Mr. Gass and the publisher of his journal can lead their readers along the rout of the expedition and make them acquainted with those things which were the objects of the external senses, and as they appeared to those senses, the greater number will willingly dispense with "scientific research.". . .

The publication of the journal of Mr. Gass I expect will have the following good effects: first, It may save many the trouble of purchasing your *three volumes* and map, by affording them at a cheap rate, a plain and satisfactory account of the tour; in the second place, it will so *depreciate the worth of your work* that there may be a chance of getting it at a reasonable price; and in the third place, as it will contain plain matter of fact, it may deter you from swelling your work with such *tales of wonder* as have sometimes issued from the *Ten-mile-square.* . . .

I, however, assure you that I shall wait with some impatience for your voluminous work; and shall willingly subscribe for it, when a reasonable price is fixed; but hope you will be cautious in magnifying trifles. . . .

Pittsburgh, 7th April, 1807   The Editor of Gass's Journal

The Patrick Gass Prospectus[***]
[23 March 1807]

PROPOSALS for publishing by subscription, By David M'Keehan,[1] Bookseller, a Journal of the Voyages & Travels of a Corps of Discovery, under the command of Captain Lewis and Captain Clarke of the Army of the United States, from the mouth of the river Missouri through the interior parts of North America to the Pacific Ocean, during the years 1804, 1805 & 1806. Containing An authentic relation of the most interesting transactions during the expedition;—A description of the country, and an account of its inhabitants, soil, climate, curiosities, & vegetable and animal productions. By Patrick Gass, one of the persons employed in the expedition; with geographical & explanatory notes, by the Publisher.

To recommend the correctness of this work, the publisher begs leave to state, that at the different resting places during the expedition, the several journals were brought together, compared, corrected, and the blanks, which had been unavoidably left, filled up; and that, since he became the proprietor, in order to render it more useful and acceptable, he has undertaken and completed the labourious task of arranging and transcribing the whole of it. To this he will add, the following extract from a certificate delivered by Captain Lewis to Mr. Gass, dated St. Louis, 10th Oct. 1806.

"As a tribute justly due to the merits of the said *Patrick Gass,* I with chearfulness declare, that the ample support, which he gave me, under every difficulty; the manly firmness, which he evinced on every occasion; and the fortitude with which he bore the fatigues and painful sufferings incident to that long voyage, intitles him to my highest confidence and sincere thanks, while it eminently recommends him to the consideration and respect of his fellow citizens."[2]

CONDITIONS.

I. This work will be published in one volume duodecimo; and is expected to contain near 300 pages.

II. The price to subscribers will be one dollar, handsomely bound in boards. As the expence, however, of publishing an edition sufficiently large to meet the demands for this work, including the original purchase money, will be very considerable; those who pay in advance, will be intitled to a discount of 12 1/2 per cent.

III. Those who obtain ten subscribers and become responsible for the payment of the subscription money shall receive one copy gratis.

The work will be ready for delivery in two months from this date.

Subscriptions will be received at the Store of the publisher, and at of Office of the Pittsburgh Gazette.

Pittsburgh, March 23d, 1807.

---

[*]Donald Jackson, *Letters of the Lewis and Clark Expedition with Related Documents 1783-1854,* vol. 2, Document #253 (Urbana: University of Illinois Press, 1978), 385-86.

[**]For a complete transcript of this letter, please see Donald Jackson, *Letters of the Lewis and Clark Expedition,* Vol. II., (Urbana: University of Illinois Press, 1978), Item 264, pp. 399-408.

[***]Jackson, Document #259, 390-91.

1. *Pittsburgh Gazette,* 24 March 1807 and later issues. McKeehan was a bookseller who ran a "Book and Stationary Store, in front of the court House," in Pittsburgh. His name appears as signer of advertisements from the Pittsburgh land office, appearing in the *Gazette* in 1807; he may have been the register of that office. He may also be the David McKeehan who was graduated from Dickinson College in 1787 and was admitted to the Pennsylvania bar in 1792. Perhaps he had lived at one time in Wellsburg, (West) Virginia; Gass's biographer, John G. Jacob, associates him with that place.

2. Lewis wrote similar testimonials for all his men. Bratton's has survived as No. 215 in Donald Jackson, *Letters of the Lewis and Clark Expedition with Related Documents 1783-1854* (Urbana: University of Illinois Press, 1978).

BIBLIOGRAPHY

Adams, Mary P. "Jefferson's Reaction to the Treaty of San Ildefonso." *Journal of Southern History* 21, 2 (1955): 173–88.

Allen, John Logan. *Passage Through the Garden, Lewis and Clark and the Image of the American Northwest*. Urbana: University of Illinois Press, 1975.

Appleman, Roy E. *Lewis and Clark*. Washington, D.C.: United States Department of the Interior, National Park Service, 1975.

Bakeless, John. *The Journals of Lewis and Clark*. New York: New American Library, 1964.

Bergon, Frank, ed. *The Journals of Lewis and Clark*. New York: Viking Penguin, 1989.

Biddle, Nicholas, ed. *The Journals of the Expedition under the Command of Capts. Lewis and Clark to the Sources of the Missouri, thence across the Rocky Mountains and down the River Columbia to the Pacific Ocean Performed during the Years 1804–5–6 by Order of the Government of the United States*. 2 vols. New York: Heritage Press, 1962.

Bishop, Beverly D. "The Writingest Explorers: Manuscripts of the Lewis and Clark Expedition." *Gateway Heritage* 2, 2 (1981): 22–29.

Bolas, Deborah. "Books From An Expedition: A Publications History of the Lewis and Clark Journals." *Gateway Heritage* 2, 2 (1981): 31–35.

Chuinard, Eldon G., M.D. *Only One Man Died: The Medical Aspects of the Lewis and Clark Expedition*. Glendale, Calif.: Arthur H. Clark, 1979.

———. "The Western End of the Lewis and Clark Trail,"*We Proceeded On* 12, 3 (August 1986): 7–13.

Clark, Ella E., and Margot Edmonds. *Sacagawea of the Lewis and Clark Expedition*. Berkeley: University of California Press, 1983.

Clarke, Charles G. *The Men of the Lewis and Clark Expedition, a Biographical Roster of the Fifty-one Members and a Composite Diary of Their Activities from All Known Sources*. Glendale, Calif.: Arthur H. Clark, 1970.

Coues, Elliott, ed. *History of the Expedition of Lewis and Clark*. 4 vols. New York: Frances P. Harper, 1893.

Crawford, Anthony R. "Exploring the Wilderness: The Lewis and Clark Expedition." *Gateway Heritage* 2, 2 (1981): 8–21.

Cutright, Paul Russell. *A History of the Lewis and Clark Journals*. Norman: University of Oklahoma Press, 1976.

———. *Lewis and Clark: Pioneering Naturalists*. Urbana: University of Illinois Press, 1969; Lincoln: Bison Books, 1989.

———. "Meriwether Lewis on the Marias." *Montana The Magazine of Western History* 18, 3 (Summer 1968): 30–43.

DeVoto, Bernard, ed. *The Journals of Lewis and Clark*. Boston: Houghton Mifflin, 1953.

Dillon, Richard. *Meriwether Lewis, A Biography*. New York: Coward-McCann, 1965.

Ellis, Edward S. *Ellis's History of the United States*, Vol. 2. Philadelphia: Syndicate Publishing, 1899.

Ewers, John C. "Plains Indian Reactions to Lewis and Clark." *Montana The Magazine of Western History* 16, 1 (Winter 1966): 2–12.

Fields, Wayne D. "Meaning of Lewis and Clark." *Gateway Heritage* 2, 2 (1981): 3–7.

Forrest, Earle E., ed. *Journal of Patrick Gass*. Minneapolis: Ross & Haines, 1958.

———. "Patrick Gass, Carpenter of the Lewis and Clark Expedition." *Bulletin of the Missouri Historical Society* 4 (July 1948): 217–22.

———. "Patrick Gass, Lewis and Clark's Last Man." Independence, Pa.: Mrs. A. M. Painter, 1950.

Gass, Patrick. *A Journal of the Voyages and Travels of a Corps of Discovery, under the Command of Capt. Lewis and Capt. Clarke of the Army of the United States from the Mouth of the River Missouri through the Interior Parts of North America to the Pacific Ocean, during the Years 1804, 1805, & 1806*. Pittsburgh: David M'Keehan, 1807.

———. *A Journal of the Voyages* . . . London: J. Budd, 1808.

———. *A Journal of the Voyages* . . . Philadelphia: Mathew Carey, 1811.

———. *Lewis and Clarke's Journal to the Rocky Mountains in the Years 1804-5-6*. Dayton, Ohio: Ells, Claflin & Company, 1847.

Gill, Larry. "The Great Portage—Lewis and Clark's Overland Journey Around the Great Falls of the Missouri River." *We Proceeded On* 1, 4 (Fall 1975): 6–9.

Goetzmann, William H. *Exploration and Empire: The Explorer and the Scientist in the Winning of the American West*. New York: W. W. Norton & Company, 1978.

Graveline, Paul. "Joseph Gravelines and the Lewis and Clark Expedition." *We Proceeded On* 3, 4 (October 1977): 5–6.

Hermann, Binger. *The Louisiana Purchase and Our Title West of the Rocky Mountains, with a Review of Annexation by the United States.* Washington, D.C.: Government Printing Office, 1898.

Hosmer, James K., ed. *Gass's Journal of the Lewis and Clark Expedition.* Chicago: A. C. McClurg & Company, 1904.

Howard, Harold P. *Sacajawea.* Norman: University of Oklahoma Press, 1989.

Hunt, Robert R. "The Espontoon: Captain Lewis's Magic Stick." *We Proceeded On* 16, 1 (February 1990): 12–18.

Jacob, John G. *The Life and Times of Patrick Gass, Now Sole Survivor of the Overland Expedition to the Pacific, under Lewis and Clark, in 1804–5–6.* Wellsburg, Va.: Jacob & Smith, 1859.

Jackson, Donald, ed. *Letters of the Lewis and Clark Expedition with related Documents, 1783–1854.* Urbana: University of Illinois Press, 1962.

———. "Thomas Jefferson and the Pacific Northwest." *We Proceeded On* 1, 1 (Winter 1974–75): 5–8.

Kubik, Barbara. "John Colter—One of Lewis and Clark's Men." *We Proceeded On* 9, 2 (May–June 1983): 10–14.

Lange, Robert. "$2,500.00 Vs. $38,722.25—The Financial Outlay for the Historic Enterprise." *We Proceeded On* 1, 2 (February 1975): 17–18.

———. "The Brig *Lydia* Misses a Rendezvous with History." *We Proceeded On* 3, 4 (October 1977): 10–12.

———. "The Expedition's Brothers—Joseph and Reuben Field." *We Proceeded On* 4, 3 (July 1978): 15–16.

———. "George Drouillard (Drewyer)—One of the Two or Three Most Valuable Men on the Expedition." *We Proceeded On* 5, 2 (May 1979): 14–16.

———. "John Shields: Lewis and Clark's Handyman: Gunsmith-Blacksmith-General Mechanic for the Expedition." *We Proceeded On* 5, 3 (July 1979): 14–16.

———. "Private George Shannon: The Expedition's Youngest Member—1785 or 1787–1836." *We Proceeded On* 8, 3 (July 1982): 10–15.

———. "William Bratton—One of Lewis and Clark's Men." *We Proceeded On* 7, 1 (February 1981): 8–11.

Large, Arlen J. "Additions to the Party." *We Proceeded On* 16, 1 (February 1990): 4–11.

Lavender, David. *Land of Giants: The Drive to the Pacific Northwest, 1750–1950.* Lincoln: University of Nebraska Press, 1979.

———. *The Way to the Western Sea.* New York: Doubleday, Anchor Book, 1988.

Loos, John L. "They Opened the Door to the West." *The Humble Way* (Fall 1964): 10–15.

Lottinville, Savoie. *The Rhetoric of History*. Norman: University of Oklahoma Press, 1976.

Macapia, Mary E. *Lewis and Clark's America: A Contemporary Photo Essay*. Seattle: Seattle Art Museum, 1976.

MacGregor, Carol Lynn. "The Role of the Gass Journal." *We Proceeded On* 16, 4 (November 1990): 13–17.

Mackenzie, Alexander. *Voyages From Montreal . . . with a Preliminary Account of the Rise, Progress and Present State of the Fur Trade of that Country*. London, 1801.

Moulton, Gary E. "A Note on the White Pirogue." *We Proceeded On* 12, 2 (May 1986): 22.

———. *The Journals of the Lewis and Clark Expedition*. Vols. 1–10. Lincoln: University of Nebraska Press, 1986–1995.

Munford, James Kenneth, ed. *John Ledyard's Journal of Captain Cook's Last Voyage*. Corvallis: Oregon State University Press, 1963.

M'Vickar, Archibald, ed. *History of the Expedition under the Command of Captains Lewis and Clark to the Sources of the Missouri thence across the Rocky Mountains, and down the River Columbia to the Pacific Ocean: Performed during the Years 1804–1805–1806, by the Order of the Government of the United States*. New York: A. L. Fowle, 1900.

Nasitir, A. P. *Before Lewis and Clark*. 2 vols. Lincoln: University of Nebraska Press, 1990.

Osborne, Kelsie Ramey. *Peaceful Conquest: Story of the Lewis and Clark Expedition*. Portland: Beattie & Company, 1955.

Osgood, Ernest S., ed. *The Field Notes of Captain William Clark, 1803–1805*. New Haven: Yale University Press, 1964.

Peebles, John J. "On the Lolo Trail: Route and Campsites of Lewis and Clark." *Idaho Yesterdays* 9, 4 (Winter 1965–66): 2–15.

———. "Rugged Waters: Trails and Campsites of Lewis and Clark in the Salmon River Country." *Idaho Yesterdays* 8, 2 (Summer 1964): 2–17.

———. "Trails and Campsites in Idaho." *Lewis and Clark in Idaho*. Boise: Idaho Historical Series No. 16, December 1966.

Quaife, Milo M., ed. *The Journals of Captain Meriwether Lewis and Sergeant John Ordway*. Madison: The State Historical Society of Wisconsin, 1916.

Peterson, Merril D., ed. *The Portable Thomas Jefferson*. New York: Penguin Books, 1987.

Preston, Ralph N. *Early Idaho Atlas*. Portland, Oreg.: Binford & Mort, 1978.

Rees, John E. "The Shoshoni Contribution to Lewis and Clark." *Idaho Yesterdays* 2, 2 (Summer 1958): 2–13.

Rickman, John. *Journal of Captain Cook's Last Voyage to the Pacific Ocean*. London: E. Newbery, 1781; Ann Arbor: University Microfilms, 1966.

Ronda, James P. *Lewis and Clark among the Indians*. Lincoln: University of Nebraska Press, 1984.

——. "The Names of the Nations." *We Proceeded On* 7, 4 (November 1981): 12–17.

Saindon, Bob. "The Abduction of Sacagawea." *We Proceeded On* 2, 2 (Spring 1976): 6–8.

——. "The Flags of the Lewis and Clark Expedition." *We Proceeded On* 7, 4 (November 1981): 22–26.

Salisbury, Albert, and Jane Salisbury. *Two Captains West*. Seattle: Superior Publishing, 1950.

Schwantes, Carlos A. *The Pacific Northwest*. Lincoln: University of Nebraska Press, 1989.

Skarsten, M. O. *George Drouillard: Hunter and Interpreter for Lewis and Clark and Fur Trader, 1807–1810*. Glendale, Calif.: Arthur H. Clark, 1964.

Smith, James S., and Kathryn Smith. "Sedulous Sergeant, Patrick Gass: An Original Biography by Direct Descendants." *Montana The Magazine of Western History* 5, 3 (Summer 1955): 20–27.

Snyder, Gerald S. *In the Footsteps of Lewis and Clark*. Washington, D.C.: National Geographic Society, 1970.

Space, Ralph. *The Lolo Trail: A History of Events Connected with the Lolo Trail Since Lewis and Clark*. Lewiston, Idaho: Printcraft Printing, 1984.

——. *The Clearwater Story*. Northern Region [Missoula, Mont.]: U.S. Forest Service, Department of Agriculture, 1964.

Steffen, Jerome O. *William Clark: Jeffersonian Man on the Frontier*. Norman: University of Oklahoma Press, 1977.

Tomkins, Calvin. *The Lewis and Clark Trail*. New York: Harper & Row, 1965.

Thwaites, Reuben Gold, ed. *Original Journals of the Lewis and Clark Expedition 1804–1806*. New York: Arno Press, 1969.

Werner, Wilbur P. "Disaster at Montana's Two Medicine River Fight Site." *We Proceeded On* 6, 3 (August 1980): 12–13.

Willingham, William F., and Leonor Swets Ingraham. *Enlightenment Science in the Pacific Northwest: The Lewis and Clark Expedition*. Portland, Oreg.: Dynagraphics Incorporated for the Lewis and Clark College, 1984.

Wheeler, Olin D. *The Trail of Lewis and Clark*. Vol. 2. New York: G. P. Putnam's Sons, 1904.

INDEX TO BOOK I

Book II

The Account Book of Patrick Gass 1826-1837 and 1847-1848

INTRODUCTION

The recent discovery of Patrick Gass's account book yields exciting new information about the literacy, numeracy, record-keeping abilities, and community and family life of its author.[1] The legible, handwritten account book unfolds in reasonable spelling and remarkably accurate math over an extended period of time, 1826–1837 and 1847–1848. It offers convincing evidence that Patrick Gass was not just a "tough, untutored, tobacco-chewing sergeant" whose journal became a "bowdlerization" by David McKeehan from sketchy, ill-written notes.[2]

Twentieth-century scholars of the Lewis and Clark expedition summarily pushed Gass into the background as a series of stimulating manuscript discoveries came to light, including the original journals of Ordway, Whitehouse, and Floyd, Lewis's journal of his trip down the Ohio River, Clark's field notes, and numerous letters (see the Introduction to Book I). Gass's journal, the first and only record of the expedition to enjoy publication during the seven years following its return—from 1807 to 1814—unfortunately still lacks the original manuscript to back it.[3] Therefore, an assumption gained credence that Gass's hand was somehow less influential in the manuscript as it went to press than that of his editor, David McKeehan. Returning to the original publication of the Gass journal in 1807, McKeehan's preface stated that "in determining the form in which the work should appear, the publisher had some difficulty. Two plans presented themselves. The one was to preserve the form of a daily journal (in which the original had been kept) and give a plain description of the country and a simple relation of occurrences equally intelligible to all readers. . . . The other plan was to more fully digest the subject, make the narrative more general, and assuming less of the journal form and style, describe and clothe the principal parts of it as his fancy might suggest." McKeehan chose the first alternative and kept the book close to the original manuscript.[4] Yet scholars persist in believing that McKeehan did far more than he stated he had done to Gass's manuscript.

John Bakeless dispensed with Gass swiftly in his introduction to the 1962 update of Biddle's edition of the Lewis and Clark journals. He implied that Biddle might have had access to Gass's manuscript but "used only the printed version, which a local parson had zealously expurgated and rewritten, in rolling literary periods, very nearly ruining what had originally been one of the liveliest and saltiest narratives ever written. ('Paddy' was, for instance, very explicit about the amours of the expedition with the Indian girls—not even the parson could quite disguise everything.)"[5] Bakeless undoubtedly referred here to a rare instance of McKeehan's flowery and intellectual language that appeared in the text at the end of the section describing the group's departure from the Mandan villages.[6] But Bakeless expected his readers to accept this supposition in general and without references. Undaunted, and apparently unchallenged, he proceeded in 1964 to assume in the introduction to his own book, *The Journals of Lewis and Clark,* "the complete bowdlerizing of Patrick Gass's [journal] through the revision of a well-meaning clergyman who had no appreciation of its frankness and earthy vigor."[7] No citation pointed to Bakeless's source ascribing the bookseller McKeehan an ecclesiastical role. And his presumption about the tone and style of text lost for more than a century and a half astonishes careful readers.

In 1976 Paul Russell Cutright presented a thoughtful chapter on Patrick Gass and his expedition journal in *A History of the Lewis and Clark Journals.* Cutright's display of the caustic volley of letters between Meriwether Lewis in the *National Intelligencer* and David McKeehan in the *Pittsburgh Gazette* demonstrated to the reader Lewis's proprietary feeling about written accounts of the expedition he led. In addition to Cutright's opinion that McKeehan played the part of a "jackass" in this exchange,[8] one wonders why Cutright blasphemed McKeehan and held Biddle and Coues, editors who clearly took license with original manuscripts, in such high esteem.

Were legal or personal understandings about the rights of expedition personnel to publish their own accounts of the voyage clearly or universally communicated? Apparently not. Patrick Gass believed that he had the option to turn over his manuscript to David McKeehan, a bookseller and teacher he considered capable of publishing the travel diary. Beyond the dialogue of 1807 and closer to our current concern about the place of the Gass journal in the historiography of the expedition stand Cutright's charges about Gass's authorship. In support of his claim that McKeehan changed Gass's text, Cutright selected the same passage Bakeless identified, one of very few obvious examples of a change in tone and language that appear in the journal at points of summary.[9] He assumed that McKeehan corrected "spelling, punctuation, capitalization, and the like," besides changing the "language of the tough, untutored, to-bacco-chewing army sergeant into the resolutely correct precepto-rial prose of the early-nineteenth-century schoolmaster."[10] This state-ment must be broken apart: Yes, Gass liked tobacco, and yes, he told his biographer, J. G. Jacob, that he had not benefited from more than nineteen days of formal education.[11] Before discovery of Gass's account book, many might conclude that he was less literate, less numerate, and generally less savvy than his account book proves him to have been. In the few months that he possessed the manu-script, McKeehan probably corrected grammar, occasionally embel-lishing its prose, but he did not intervene to the extent he has been accused. Overall, his interference in the text apart from footnotes was slight.

Gass's personal interviewer, J. G. Jacob, was quick to point out in 1859 that Gass "took lessons from men and things . . . [he] closely observed and shrewdly reasoned."[12] The body of the journal reads in Gass's style, matter-of-fact and terse, accounting for daily events that only he, not McKeehan, could have known. Cutright threw his considerable weight as a scholar too far toward twentieth-century presumptions about Gass. His conclusions are now overwhelmed by new evidence, obvious in studying the account book, of Patrick Gass's abilities to record, spell, account, and interrelate with myriad friends and neighbors in congenial business and personal exchanges over an extended period of time. Gass was not just a tough, unlettered army sergeant, nor was he incapable of having written, organized, maintained, and arranged to publish his almost daily account of the expedition.

Unfortunately, McKeehan did very sparsely interject comments in Gass's text in addition to his thirty separate footnotes. Jacob af-firmed that Gass's original manuscript "was but very slightly al-tered, either in verbiage or arrangement from the original" by David McKeehan, whose editorial commentary is general in nature, posed at specific demarcations in the journal. McKeehan's style, with its erudite and flowery prose, jumps out. The journal overall reflects the style of Patrick Gass, which Jacob calls "the very plainest and most unadorned style possible."[13] Jacob continued to remark on the conscientious accuracy of Gass's observations and on his personal style:

> for contrary to the received aphorism in regard to travellers tales, we have never perused a work so devoid of the imaginative or where

was manifested so little desire to garnish plain prose with poetic tinsel. All is plain unpretending matter of fact, just such notings as a
mathematician might make in a scientific traverse of the land.[14]

Nevertheless, doubters and critics have abounded. William F.
Willingham and Leonoor Swets Ingraham echoed Bakeless two de-
cades later at a one-day symposium given on February 18, 1984, at
Lewis and Clark College in Portland, Oregon, called "Enlightenment
Science in the Pacific Northwest: The Lewis and Clark Expedition."
In their introductory program, the authors proceeded farther than
Bakeless down the briar path of supposition, stating that Patrick
Gass's 1807 journal "lacked accuracy due to a heavy handed editor."
Twentieth-century students have been taught wrongly that Patrick
Gass's journal of the Lewis and Clark expedition was really David
McKeehan's journal and that it was not a true account of the voy-
age. In fact, Gass included unique experiences and comments in his
journal, thus adding to the large body of literature composed by several members of the expedition. As the captains instructed, journal
keepers copied and coordinated their logs along the trail as time
allowed, adding personal observations.

Patrick Gass's specific contributions to the historiography of the
expedition underscore his authorship of the journal. He wrote about
things that interested him, such as the number of moccasins made
and elk shot, details of construction of Fort Clatsop and the Mandan
fortress, and descriptions of many types of trees along the way. Simi-
larities in entries among accounts show campfire editing and on-
the-trail collaboration among journalists, practices that McKeehan
noted in the first edition of the published journal. Had McKeehan
changed Gass's original notes, they would not parallel those of his
companion writers. These multiple writings become clearly evident
when one compares a day-to-day account in the different journals.
Endnotes to Book I point to examples of campfire editing in chap-
ters 3, 4, 5, 8, 12, 17, 20, and 24.

Gass's journal should enjoy the same presumption of authentic-
ity that subsequently discovered journals command. Patrick Gass's
account book shows that he was quite literate despite any seem-
ingly modest statements that he made about the limits of his formal
education. The speculation by Gass's own descendants that his manuscript "must have exceeded that of Captain Clark for uniqueness of
spelling and punctuation" no longer seems credible.[15] Indeed, the
spelling in his account book, while somewhat irregular and inconsistent, supersedes Clark's creative orthography in correctness.
Gass's account book shows that he bought nine magazine almanacks,
one for every year in the period of accounting except 1830 and 1833.

Gass kept books in his home, including his own journal, a Bible, a spelling book, and David Coyner's *The Lost Trappers*. Jacob described Gass to Eva Emery Dye, an early-twentieth-century Oregon author and suffragette, as a man of "more than ordinary natural ability and of good address and of very considerable acquired information from reading &c &c."[16] At eighty years of age, Patrick Gass continued to subscribe to and read the local newspaper, the *Wellsburg Weekly Herald*. Its publisher, J. G. Jacob, wrote in that paper on May 14, 1852, "[Gass] is a subscriber to *The Herald,* walks to town, three miles regularly, rain or shine, and gets it, pays always in advance and prides himself on being a democrat of the old school, true blue Jeffersonian stamp."

The evidence that Patrick Gass could organize his thoughts and records well lies in his account book and in his attention to organizing support and execution of his pension appeals. Gass's pension of $96 per year stands as the only means of support noted in this record. The pension provided for full disability on account of losing his left eye in September of 1813 at Fort Independence on the Mississippi, Territory of Missouri.[17] At intervals, when problems arose in receiving his pension or when the need to increase it pressed on him, Gass rallied professional help to write letters to advocate increased and regular payments or land grants.[18] When the federal agent at Richmond challenged him and required him to have biannual check-ups, Gass complied in a timely fashion, arranging doctor's examinations and sending an affidavit signed by Doctors Cook and Allison on March 25, 1829. He made subsequent payments to Cook. Gass appealed directly to Secretary of War John Eaton, arguing that the law of March 3, 1819, should have exempted him from such examination.[19] He was, therefore, aware of the requirements of the law of 1819 even ten years later, at age fifty-seven.

In the endeavor to increase his bounty land and pension, Gass garnered support from an array of substantial Wellsburg citizens. For instance, in 1851, the cover letter for his "Samuel Marks Petition" lists signatures of ten local luminaries: Campbell Tarr, a leading citizen and later a partner in Tarr and Crothers and Company, a dry goods establishment;[20] Hugh W. Crothers, Tarr's partner, who constructed a home costing $8,000 in 1858;[21] John C. Perry, member of the Board of Health in the 1850s;[22] Peter Curran, president of the Wellsburg and Bethany Turnpike board of directors in 1851;[23] William Marks, leading merchant;[24] James Agnew, chairman of the 1852 Democratic Party meeting in Bethany;[25] O. W. Langfitt, an attorney and leading Democrat;[26] Wilson Beall, proprietor of Wilson Beall and Company;[27] Dr. N. W. White, a doctor and attorney;[28] and C. H. Gist of Baltimore. The accompanying petition erroneously listed the number of Gass's children as eight. According to the family Bible, the Jacob biography, and family tradition, Gass had seven children, the first of whom died in infancy in 1832.[29] On January 1, 1852, Eli Boring's affidavit attested erroneously again that Gass had eight children, one having "recently" died. [30] These errors complicated Gass's extensive effort to enhance his petition and secure more bounty land. Gass employed the services of Samuel Marks in his 1851 petition, of William McCluney[31] and Joseph Applegate [32] in his 1854 petition, and of Joseph Applegate and Dr. N. W. White in his 1855 petition.

Gass's 1854 petition to the government stressed his concern that his meager pension and his inability to work, at eighty-three and with complete disability, would rob his children of the chance for a proper education. Such a preoccupation would not emanate from a man illiterate and heedless of the value of education. Likewise, the reader soon realizes Gass's excellent ability with numbers. Over a period of ten years of regular record-keeping, the margin of mathematical error is slight, with only six discernible arithmetic errors. Thus, "The Account Book of Patrick Gass" establishes his literacy and numeracy, grounding his authorship of the expedition journal on a firm foundation.

Even though Gass proved to be a man who could organize people, events, and data important to him, he unfortunately did not extend his organizational skills to the maintenance of land granted him by the U.S. government. For his role in the Lewis and Clark expedition, he received 320 acres in 1807 (Warrant number 6), which appears to have been cashed and not collected.[33] In 1816, the government awarded him 160 acres of bounty land for his service in the War of 1812 (Warrant number 7460). Jacob indicated that Gass did not cash his second warrant, but, "The land he suffered to lie, until eaten up and forfeited from non-payment of taxes."[34] In August of 1854, he received a special double bounty, Warrant number 24,894 1/2 in the amount of 320 acres, which he assigned to John Tweed of Wellsburg.[35] None of these grants comprised Grog Run or Pierce's Run, land to which Gass held title and where his family lived. Proceeds from these sales, in addition to the 1827 sale of his father's land, occasionally provided Gass with a great deal of money apart from his pension.[36] The accounting for these transactions does not show in this account book.

Although the income accounted for in this book came solely from his government pension and not from carpentry work, Patrick Gass's trade as a carpenter began while he was a young man and followed him through life.[37] Periodically in the era of this account book, he bought carpentry tools including a morticing chisel, a pegging awl, an auger, an axe helve, a cross-cut file, and steel. Although it appears that he continued to practice his lifelong trade, there is no income attributed from its practice. A trading arrangement must have taken place for his carpentry services, or such payments were accounted for outside of this record.

Gass no doubt performed all the construction and repair necessary at his own homes. Earle Forrest claimed that Gass built a small house shown in two pictures in his publications.[38] First, after their wedding, Patrick and Maria lived at the small house they rented from "Cricket on the Crawford farm."[39] On March 24, 1837, Gass, age sixty-six, with a wife and three young children, bought six acres on Grog Run for $180.93, which he held until selling it on April 17, 1845, for $120.[40] On March 22, 1848, after Maria's death, Gass paid Frances Wells $500 for a parcel of land on Pierce's Run. He resold this land only nine months later, on December 30, 1848, to George Oram for $547.94, keeping a five-acre pie-shaped piece of land with the house.[41] Money paid to Jonathan Brady in fairly regular biannual sums of $28 between December 12, 1833, and April 6, 1837, poses a big question. The size of payment and the activities reflected indicate it could have been land rental or purchase, but no documents exist to support any such purchase. The business Gass transacted with Jonathan Brady—renting land, buying stock or machinery—remains unknown, but the family's sparse buying pattern at this time suggests they were probably living on land away from town.

Gathering facts about Patrick Gass's life and fitting them with new information from his account book presents a more composite picture of his life than has been known so far. Now, as Coues mused a century ago, it is finally possible to "float Gass with an air of novelty."[42] All of Gass's own and his family's purchases from 1826 through 1836, and some in 1847, give a wonderful portrait of his life. Gass now comes alive as a vital man with many community ties, a man who formed a marriage and a family in the 1830s, and lost his wife in 1847. Numerous names in the account book link Gass to a wide and rich variety of acquaintances in Wellsburg.

Patrick Gass's purchases provide portraits of the man before and after his marriage in 1831 to Maria Hamilton. One can envision the stocky Celt, five foot seven inches tall, with "keen grey eyes, red cheeks fairly good teeth,"[43] and "tawny" or "white" hair (formerly black[44]), walking to Wellsburg at a good clip to shop,[45] wearing home-made pants and shirts, a fashionable hat, and Jefferson shoes, and chewing tobacco. There he would have visited with numerous friends about his adventures on the Lewis and Clark expedition, his encounters with Indians and knowledge of other myths about them,[46] and his acquaintance with famous people. He had met Jimmy Buchanan, who later became president, when the boy's father was constructing a house. At Carlisle, Pennsylvania, Gass saw George Washington in 1794.[47] And he made the acquaintance of the infamous Indian killer Lewis Wetzel and Captain Samuel Brady.[48] He could call on these connections and the many adventures of his very long life to entertain friends and neighbors while going about his daily business of getting the newspaper, buying merchandise, or drinking a couple of beers in Wellsburg.[49]

In town, Gass bought goods for friends who must have lived near him and borrowed money that he later repaid. Frequently he bought goods labeled for other people, and he paid back debts, but there are few clues about when or why he incurred them. The text shows that Gass was comfortable with borrowing and lending. He seemed to have a warm, ongoing exchange with women for whom he bought merchandise and with men for whom he bought merchandise or performed services and from whom he borrowed money, paying them in return. People knew Gass for the stories that accompanied whatever business they had with him. His garrulous nature colored the memories of neighbors, family, and his biographer. It is easy for the reader to imagine, for instance, Patrick Gass entertaining John Hamilton and his young daughter Maria over more than a few drinks in an evening at Hamilton's boarding house, where Gass resided and courted Maria.

The Gass family's diet can be surmised by seeing what they bought and what they did not buy. Like most of rural America at that time, the Gasses probably raised a good deal of food. Thus, meat, poultry, eggs, milk, cheese, vegetables, and fruit do not appear, for the most part, as purchases. Purchased staples included flour, sugar, salt, and bacon (cured pork was easier to buy than to prepare). They likely obtained homemade yeast from potato juice, eggs from hens, and milk and cream (for making butter) from cows. They purchased cheese occasionally. Regular purchases of fish—mackerel, shad, and bass—show that they amplified their diet of bacon and, possibly, of locally killed meat, with lean, vitamin-packed fruits of the sea not obtained right at Wellsburg.

Frequent and ample purchases of shirting, muslin, flannel, lincey, dowlass, jean, linen, and other fabrics indicate that Maria made the family clothing. Just before his wedding day, Gass purchased fabric for his own nuptial suit of clothes. Expenditures for appropriate fabric for baby clothes and bedding appear when their baby, Elizabeth, was born. Sewing expenses still appeared in 1847, after Maria's death. Perhaps Mrs. Kinder was making the children's clothes.

After Maria's death came an interim period during which Gass was trying to provide the best future for his young family. According to Rachel's letter to Eva Emery Dye, all of the six surviving children (Elizabeth died in infancy) were eventually placed with others. The two oldest boys, Benjamin and William, were placed out to work, and the youngest children were put with good families.[50] An agreement of record in 1849 shows that Gass bound Rachel at three and a half years of age to Samuel Morrow of Wellsburg until she was eighteen. Gass provided $60 in trust for her medical or possible funeral expenses, which his daughter received with interest on April 1, 1864, the day after her eighteenth birthday. In exchange, Morrow "covenants that he will give to the said Rachel at proper periods within her time of service aforesaid six months schooling, and will during the entire period of her service provide good & sufficient board lodging washing & clothing for the said Rachel, suitable to her condition."[51] The census of 1850 shows Gass living with seven-year-old son James. The next census, ten years later, states that James resided, probably as a bound worker, in the Isaac McIntyre (age sixty-nine) household, wherein John (age forty-six) and Eliza (age thirty-five) had several children and a female domestic.[52] James later became a teacher at Walker, Vernon County, Missouri, and most of his five daughters became teachers.[53] In 1850, ten-year-old Annie Gass was living with George and Ruth Nunamaker (both age thirty-two) and George Brown (age twenty-nine); both men were listed as carpenters.[54] By 1860 eighteen-year-old Annie Gass lived with her eighty-seven-year-old father, Patrick, and her one-year-old son, James W. Gass. Another James Gass, age nineteen, "farm hand," lived with them.[55] Rachel later wrote that Annie kept house for her father, as "he was too old to stay alone as small sums of money had been taken and other valuables such as Books relics & clothing."[56]

The largest part of the purchases noted in the Gasses' account book do not comprise items necessary for survival. Yet these clearly describe the individual characteristics of their purchasers. Before his marriage, Gass bought silk scarves, probably as gifts, labeled only in the instances of "Miss Bowls," and then "Miss Hambleton," who later became his wife. Combs, jews' harps, scarves, hats, handkerchiefs constitute relatively large purchases, considering his disposable income. Candy appears sporadically after Gass's marriage to Maria, who appeared to like chocolate and other sweets. But none loom like the composite body of Gass's purchases to support his own habits.

Throughout the journal, Gass bought whiskey, tobacco, coffee, and patent medicines. Gass tended his health with regular purchases of gum guaicum, camphor, castor oil, magnesia, salt peter, calomel, "Sparrow" pills, pink root, and other remedies. Gass loved coffee and tobacco, but his particular fondness for spirituous drink can now be grounded. Rumors of it arose from literature, a notation on his service record for drunkenness in December 1813,[57] and traditional stories among his descendants. Now it appears on the hard pages of his purchase records. J. G. Jacob explained Gass's position after returning to Wellsburg after the War of 1812:

> His subsequent career has been that of an old soldier, subsided into the realities of every-day life, and struggling against poverty for an honest subsistence . . . A life of settled industry was irksome to his temperament, and altogether contrary to his habits. Like too many others in his position, he gave way to intemperance, and during the succeeding forty years of his life, occur many chapters, over which we gladly draw the veil of charity . . . Let us not judge too harshly . . . Still . . . the fact cannot be denied, that, like too many others, he acquired, during his campaigns, a taste for intoxicating liquors, and was, for many years, a slave to the debasing habit that degrades and demoralizes so many of the best, most brilliant and most generous of our race. Intemperance was his besetting sin, but drunk or sober, he was ever honest, sincere and truthful, and a patriot to the very core of his heart.[58]

Patrick Gass purchased a goodly quantity of liquor in gallons, quarts, and pints throughout the decade of the account book. Although it appears he bought a steady supply, his use waned and waxed according to events in his life. This correlation is made clear in Appendix Z, which shows that his purchases of whiskey accelerated during the period preceding his marriage to the sixteen-year-old Maria Hamilton on March 31, 1831, during the illness of their first child, Elizabeth, who died November 7, 1832, and following the birth of their first son, Benjamin, on September 10, 1833. Gass celebrated or grieved these important events with a liquid aide. Following the last binge, after Benjamin's birth, an interesting comment in his own hand, "Take care patric" (November 9, 1833), with no financial extension, piques the reader's imagination. The coincidence of purchases of liquor, his previous fine "for taking too much grog on Sunday" (May 22, 1833), and the new responsibility of a son after having lost a daughter the previous year seem to have combined to produce this warning to himself. Whatever its motivation, the line sits there, out of context in an account book, in his own hand.

Every year of the account book, Patrick Gass spent his pension. The social garrulity accompanied generosity, according to both J. G. Jacob and W. M. Horner, a contemporary of Gass who lived in Wellsburg. After his marriage to Maria, they both bought various fabrics frequently. When his first child was born, Gass celebrated with the unusual purchases of rum, cinnamon, allspice, cloves, muslin, and "callico." And when she died, he immediately bought black crepe, two black silk handkerchiefs and a new pair of worsted hose. During a ten-year period, Gass bought many combs, three jews' harps, numerous handkerchiefs, several hats, and several flasks. These may have been gifts; perhaps some of these durable goods were lost. This was not a man who budgeted, nor one who held back when his own spirit was moved.

In family relations and patriotic feelings, Gass's emotions shone. Upon the birth of his first son on September 10, 1833, Patrick Gass penned a personal note in his account book with no extension: "Son born." Rachel described Gass as a loving father, saying, "He was very fond of little ones his songs were mostly nursery rhymes to them he loved flowers often carr[y]ing the first violets of spring in his hand for several miles to me."[59] Jacob wrote of Patrick Gass, "In his married life he was kind and affectionate—a good husband and father." He described Gass's life as "pleasant, albeit impoverished."[60]

> With the pittance of $96 a year, which he has been for many years in the habit of drawing in half yearly instalments [sic] from the agent of the government at Wheeling, and the small amount he has been enabled to eke from his spot of stony land, he has lived in patriarchal simplicity, scrupulously honest, owing no man anything, and apparently contented and happy as a millionaire.[61]

Patrick Gass's allegiance to his family, to the Democratic Party, and to his country continued until the end. In December of 1854, he was chosen to attend a convention of old soldiers in Washington, D.C., in January of 1855 with John Miller, William Tarr, and Ellis C. Jones. After their meeting on the 8th, the delegation "formed in procession and preceded by all the military of the city, and various bands of music, marched to the President's [Pierce] house, which they reached at about 2 o'clock, and found the President and most of the Cabinet in waiting to receive them."[62] Jacob added that though the soldiers did not succeed in the aims of their meeting to better veteran pensions, they did attract citizens' attention to the issue. On the front of his hat, Gass continued to wear the spread eagle of brass, which had been presented to him as he was lionized in Washington.[63]

The publication of *The Life and Times of Patrick Gass* in 1859 brought the elder Gass much attention. Again, his adventures with Lewis and Clark, his exploits in the War of 1812, and his wanderings as a youth came to the fore. At the Fourth of July celebration in 1861 W. M. Horner said:

> [Gass] appeard to be the most sot after as the other soldiers had a grand carriage sent for Patrick and had a big Platform made with kind of legs to it which they histed Patrick up on and carried him a round and then set it on the table or near it and gatherd round to lisson while he made a Patriotic speech and told the new soldiers that they must not go out with the intention of expecting they was going to had [*sic*] a Picnic but O far from it and they would not see so much spread before them of a table to eat as they could look now and see no no for if you go through and see what I have seen of war and starveation [*sic*] . . . for three days without one Bite to eat of any thing at all . . . and while he was talking and telling of hardships he Brought many tears to eyes of mothers of sons and husbands who was standing ner by in there uniforms and guns he made a long speech had many apploses and much cheering done and fireing of the cannon and guns and they wanted him to set upon the table while they would eat around him with the big flag floating over his head that kind of ruffled the old fellow he down out off [*sic*]that in a hurry and says far enough is far enough and be the dievel will yes try to make sport of meself.[64]

Patrick Gass's patriotism became legendary. At ninety-one, on March 1, 1862, during the Civil War, citizens toasted various people at a supper given for Lieutenant Hall. A. P. Kirker saluted Patrick Gass, "All honor to the noble veteran who has lived to see that country, for whose liberties he so nobly contended, advance to the highest position of national renown. May he yet live to see our country united, prosperous and free." And Gass responded, "May the American Eagle never lose a feather." Then John Blankensop offered a more humorous toast to Patrick Gass, "Eat horse, eat dog, killed Indian and played the devil generally."[65]

Three years before his death, Gass was baptized. On April 28, 1867, he was immersed in the Ohio River at Wellsburg and became a member of the Disciples Church.[66] Jacob wrote in 1901, "I witnessed the Ceremony of putting the old man under, one beautiful Summer Sunday afternoon, the Congregation at the water side— singing the then new hymn of the "Beautiful river."[67]

A Note on the Text

Patrick Gass's account book at Fort Canby, Washington, is a leather-covered notebook with forty leaves, or eighty pages, bound with heavy thread. The book will lie flat when opened to any page. The front cover design includes an expandable pouch to allow storage of receipts, bills, and other paper documents. The lower half of the front cover is torn and missing. The covers consist of a heavy-weight card stock covered with leather. The leather on both front and back covers is old, dry, and crumbly. The original pages measure four and one-half inches wide by seven and five-eighths inches tall.

Each page of the account book reproduced here represents a page of the original book, excepting the blank pages at the front and back of the original. The account book is printed with each of the sixty-one pages on the recto with notes for that page on the facing verso as their length allows. The page number in the original account book is provided by the editor at the bottom of the page. Certain editorial conventions have been employed:

—Three different type styles indicate the three different writing styles that appear in the journal: regular type identifies the hand of Patrick Gass; italic shows what Maria entered; and the larger type, Avant Guard, represents the script of Connell Wells & Co.

—Meaningless horizontal lines and place-holding ditto marks were omitted for readability.

—When the editor could not decipher meaning: [?]

—When the book was illegible: [illegible]

—When the editor wished to confirm spelling in the original text: [*sic*]

—No clarification of spelling was attempted when phonetic spelling seemed obvious.

—In the mathematical column, if there was no small wavy line to indicate a fractional cent, none was applied; but if a mark existed, it became necessary to interpret the meaning. This was done by the conventions of pricing of the day as seen previously in the account book, and by the pricing of the time. For example, whiskey was usually 6 1/4 cents a pint, and, for years, it was 37 1/2 cents a gallon. A magazine almanac was 12 1/2 cents. Tea sold for $1.25 a pound, so a quarter pound would have sold for 31 1/4 cents. Unfortunately, the accounting for such fractional cents was handled in unpredictable ways, sometimes being rounded up or down. The editor has pages of detailed spreadsheets prepared by Ludd A. Trozpek, who checked each and every calculation. Trozpek states, "There are two examples of failure to extend a credit or expenditure. But over the course of more than ten years of account keeping, the noticeable arithmetic errors amount to only a half-dozen and a few dollars. Patrick and Maria Gass were comfortable—perhaps even facile—with numbers."

Hazel Buxton (widow of Owen Buxton, Rachel Brierley's grandson and Patrick Gass's great-grandson) and her only child, Jane Bridge, offered to all of us the opportunity for a new appreciation of Patrick Gass by allowing me access to his fascinating account book. From them I obtained permission and copyright for this work.

Throughout the course of my work on Gass's account book, Ludd A. Trozpek has researched, calculated, collected, and discussed this fascinating account book with me. Without him, this could not have been possible, and heartiest thanks are not enough to give him.

End Notes to the Introduction

1. The account book, owned by descendants of Patrick Gass, is safely housed at the Lewis and Clark Interpretive Center at Fort Canby, Washington. The family graciously permitted this editor publication rights to share their forebear's records with the public.

   Authorship of the account book can be ascertained not only through handwriting analysis, but also through significant internal references. An analysis of the handwriting studied all signatures of Patrick Gass, including his petitions for pension, the Jacob biography, an inscription at the front of a book he owned and inscribed (David H. Coyner, *The Lost Trappers*, 1847, now owned by a member of the Lewis and Clark Trail Heritage Foundation), and a promissory note at the end of the account book *that bears his signature in the same writing as the note and the account book*. Careful comparison of the handwriting of each line of the account book made possible recognition of three hands, which are represented by different type styles (see "A Note on the Text" at the end of this introduction).

   A Questioned Documents Examiner from the Bureau of Investigative Services of Boise, Idaho, Richard L. Miller studied the editor's conclusion, verifying that, aside from numerous internal clues of authorship, the primary handwriting was that of Patrick Gass, signer of the note, the letters of petition to the government, the frontispiece to the Jacob biography, and the autograph in *The Lost Trappers*.
2. These quotations come from Cutright and Bakeless, to be expanded and cited completely in the following text.
3. Nicholas Biddle wrote to William Clark from Philadelphia on July 7, 1810, regarding his preparation of the captains' journals for their first publication. He understood that "Gass's journal in the original manuscript is also deposited in our library, & at my service." Donald Jackson takes "our library" to mean either the American Philosophical Library or the Library Company of Philadelphia. Regardless of Biddle's supposition, the manuscript has eluded two centuries of scholars eager to find it. Biddle referred to his desire to circumvent the 1810 Philadelphia edition of Gass with publication of his own prospectus for the captains' journals, feeling at the same time that the successful reception of Gass's journal in England boded well for his own (Donald Jackson, The Letters of Lewis and Clark (Urbana: University of Illinois Press, 1978), 550–55.
4. See Book I preface, section 3, historiography.
5. John Bakeless, introduction to *Journals of the Expedition under the Command of Capts. Lewis and Clark,* ed. Nicholas Biddle (New York: Heritage Press, 1962), xv.
6. See the second paragraph of the journal entry for Friday, March 5, 1805, in Book I.
7. John Bakeless, ed., *The Journals of Lewis and Clark* (New York: Mentor Books, 1964), x.
8. Paul Russell Cutright, *A History of the Lewis and Clark Journals* (Norman: University of Oklahoma Press, 1976), 27.
9. Ibid., 28–29.
10. Ibid.
11. J. G. Jacob, *The Life and Times of Patrick Gass* (Wellsburg, Va.: Jacob and Smith, 1859), 12.
12. Ibid.
13. J. G. Jacob to Mrs. Eva Emery Dye, November 25, 1901, Oregon Historical Society, Portland.
14. Jacob, *Life and Times,* 106–7.
15. James S. Smith and Kathryn Smith, "Sedulous Sergeant, Patrick Gass," *Montana The Magazine of Western History* (Summer 1955), 22.
16. Jacob to Dye.

17. Patrick Gass's military discharge papers dated June 10, 1815, affirm that Gass lost his left eye at Fort Independence on the Mississippi River. He was granted a full disability pension for life because the loss occurred while in the service of his country. In 1851, Gass erroneously swore in the "Samuel Marks Petition" that he lost the eye at the Battle of Lundy's Lane. Earle Forrest's reference must have stemmed from that petition. Paul Cutright, *History of the Journals,* 25, perpetuates this error. But J. G. Jacob, Gass's 1859 biographer, states that Gass lost an eye constructing a fort at Bellfontaine,"by being struck with a splinter from a falling tree." (*Life and Times,* 148). Donald Jackson (*Letters,* 650–51 n. 2) correctly points out the error of the Marks petition.

18. There are five outstanding examples of this: the 1829 letter to John Eaton, Secretary of War (Jackson #408); the Samuel Marks Petition of December 23, 1851 (Jackson #410); the Joseph Applegate Petition of February 17, 1854 (Jackson #411); the McCluney Petition of February 22, 1854 (National Archives, Record Group 15A, file 24097); and the Joseph Applegate Petition of March 9, 1855, Claim #527 (National Archives, Record Group 15A, file 24097).

19. Chapter 81, 15th Congress, 2nd session, of laws passed, p. 514, confirms that no affidavit was necessary in cases of total disability.

20. *Wellsburg Weekly Herald,* February 22, 1850. Campbell Tarr (1819–1879) was treasurer of the new state of West Virginia by early 1863. Later, he was instrumental in the establishment of Sabetha, Kansas. George W. Atkinson and Alvaro F. Gibbons, *Prominent Men in West Virginia: Biographical Sketches of Representative Men* (Wheeling, W.V.: W. L. Callin, 1890), 585–91.

21. *Wellsburg Weekly Herald,* July 23, 1858.

22. Ibid., May 17, 1850.

23. Ibid., August 8, 1851.

24. William Marks could have been the son of Samuel Marks, creator of Gass's 1851 petition. William Marks's store sold leather goods, saddles, trunks, fire hose, and other like products, advertising continuously during the first half of the 1850s in the *Wellsburg Weekly Herald.*

25. *Wellsburg Weekly Herald,* May 21, 1852.

26. O. W. Langfitt's name frequently appears for two decades in the *Wellsburg Weekly Herald* as a leading attorney in the area.

27. Wilson Beall & Co. sold dry goods and hardware, frequently advertising in the *Wellsburg Weekly Herald* of the 1850s.

28. One of the most colorful characters of early Wellsburg, Dr. N. W. White, embraced several professions, including physician, surgeon, and dentist (*Wellsburg Weekly Herald,* February 22, 1850). Later he became an attorney while still maintaining his medical practice (*Wellsburg Weekly Herald,* December 19, 1851). He was a member of the Board of Health (*Wellsburg Weekly Herald,* May 17, 1850). Gass employed him in 1854 as the agent for his pension collection, and in that capacity he filed the petition of 1855 in Gass's behalf. In 1856 and 1857, White served as Gass's agent to pursue the land patent Gass received and assigned to John Tweed, which became misplaced at the Fort Des Moines Register's office. (Record Group 49, Bureau of Land Management, National Archives)

    In June of 1861 White had taken an oath to support the Constitution of the United States as Prosecuting Attorney of Brooke County, but by 1862 the doctor was seen about Richmond supporting the cause of Dixie. The editor of the *Wellsburg Herald* (shortening its name by 1855) wrote this epitaph on March 7, 1862, "Poor Doc. We shall probably see his rubicund visage no more forever. His effects are in the hands of the constable, his body and soul in the hands of the devil." Dr. White was indicted for treason at Wheeling five weeks later (April 18, 1862) and later still was known to continue his practice as a surgeon for the Confederacy.

29. Earle Forrest extensively interviewed members of the Gass family during the 1920s and concurred that the Gasses had seven children: Elizabeth, Benjamin, William, Sara (Sallie), Annie, James, and Rachel. *Patrick Gass, Lewis and Clark's Last Man* (Independence, Pa.: Mrs. A. M. Painter, 1950.) Rachel in the 1902 letter confirmed seven children and gave their names. Rachel Gass Brierley to Eva Emery Dye, January 6, 1902, Oregon Historical Society, Portland.

30. N. W. White's letter to the Virginia Congressman George W. Thompson on January 1, 1852, referred to several outstanding Wellsburg citizens who affirmed Eli Boring's

statement as Gass's "nighest neighbor," further confusing the issue of the number of Gass's children, but unquestionably showing the strong support his petition for more money or land enjoyed in the community. (Gass's Pension File at National Archives, Record Group 15A, file 24097; this copy obtained at Brooke County Library.)

31. Captain William McCluney handled the receipt of Gass's pension for at least the eleven years of the account book. A resident of Brooke County in Virginia (later West Virginia) since 1795, McCluney was a native of Antrim County, Ireland. The 1854 petition states that McCluney had known Gass personally since 1794, before Gass left Brooke County to join Captains Lewis and Clark.

   By 1814, McCluney was conducting a manufactory of delft ware at Charlestown, the earlier name for Wellsburg, Virginia. Zadoc Cramer, *The Navigator,* 8th ed. (Pittsburgh: Cramer, Spear, and Eichbaum, 1814), 84. He served in numerous capacities in Brooke County, including clerk of the Turnpike Commission and clerk of the Board of Overseers of the Poor. See *Wellsburg Weekly Herald,* June 7, 1850; January 24, 1851; and April 25, 1851. At the Fourth of July celebration of 1851, F. M. Reynolds toasted William McCluney, eulogizing him: "Although the frost of ninety winters crowns his venerable brow; may his patriotism, prove as vigorous, until he becomes a Centenarian." *Wellsburg Weekly Herald,* July 4, 1851. Gass's petition of 1854 shows McCluney, at age 83, living south of Wellsburg in Ohio County, Virginia, "a man of undoubted veracity, of respectability." National Archives, Record Group 15A, file 24097.

32. In 1854, Joseph Applegate was President Judge of the Brooke County Court. He was a prominent Democrat until becoming an elector for Abraham Lincoln and Hannibal Hamlin for the new Republican Party (*Wellsburg Herald,* November 2, 1860).

33. According to a "Statement of the Number of Warrants granted to the Companions of Messrs. Lewis and Clark, received by T. A. Smith Receiver of Public Monies at Franklin from 2 November 1818 up to 30 May 1822," Gass had cashed his warrant for bounty land described in five parcels as follows: on September 17, 1819, to Edward Finch in the amount of $160.00 and to George Tenniels in the amount of $160.00; on February 7, 1821, $97.69 from John Brunt, $81.11 from Price Arnold, and $141.20 from John Johnson. The total of these five transfers (all 320 acres of Gass's bounty land) amounted to $640.00. National Archives, Record Group 15A, file 24097; and McGirr, Newman F., "Patrick Gass and His Journal of the Lewis and Clark Expedition," *West Virginia History,* vol. 3 (April 1942), 205–212.

34. Jacob, *Life and Times,* 179. This land was located in Illinois Territory and the patent sent to the post office at Wellsburg on November 24, 1817. National Archives, Military Bounty Land Warrant, Record Group 49 of the Bureau of Land Management, Washington, D.C.

35. National Archives, Record Group 15A, file 24097.

36. On September 12, 1827, Patrick Gass and his mother, Mary, widow of Benjamin Gass, sold forty-eight acres and thirty-three poles on Buffalo Creek at Pierce's Run to Eli Boring for $450.00. Deed Book 8, p. 217, Brooke County Courthouse, Wellsburg.

37. J. G. Jacob tells the story of Gass building a house in 1794 for James Buchanan's father (*Life and Times,* 29). Gass's military discharge papers list his trade as "carpenter." Lewis wanted Gass for his expedition because of Gass's skills, used in building the forts at Camp Dubois, the Mandan village, and Fort Clatsop, constructing Lewis's abortive "Experiment" boat of hides, and creating pack saddles and canoes on the expedition.

38. Forrest, *Patrick Gass, Lewis and Clark's Last Man,* 9; and *Patrick Gass, A Journal of the Voyages and Travels of a Corps of Discovery,* ed. Earle Forrest (Minneapolis: Ross & Haines, 1958), n.p., different view of same house.

39. Jacob, *Life and Times,* 178.

40. Gass as grantee: Deed Book 11, p. 506; Gass as grantor: Deed Book 15, p. 206.

41. Brooke County Deed Book 16, pp. 188 and 292.

42. Elliot Coues to Francis Perego Harper, February 17, 1894, marked "Confidential," indicates that Coues would have liked to have reprinted Gass's journal if he could have found Ordway's or Floyd's journal or any other unpublished papers to print with it. Elliot Coues papers, Beinecke Rare Book and Manuscript Library, Yale University.

43. Rachel Gass Brierley to Eva Emery Dye, January 6, 1902, affirmed her father's mother, a McLane, was Scottish. She described Patrick Gass's "keen grey eyes" along with her opinion that he was "Aristocratic by nature," then stating that "his likes and dislikes were both strong. He did not like colored people. He was riding along with a man once

during the Civil War & they were discussing that matter. The driver said he thought the negro as good as any white man. Father said he prefered to walk rather than ride with a man that expressed himself that way." In spite of Gass's prejudiced viewpoint, J. G. Jacob in December 1901 said Gass's good eye was "bright and sharp with a very distinct twinkle of humor, for his age. He was then in the neighborhood of 80." Jacob to Dye.

44. Gass's discharge papers of June 10, 1815, stated his height, hair color, complexion, and eye color. Jacob to Dye on December 9, 1901, said Gass's hair in his elder years was "yellowish or tawny." However, his youngest child, Rachel, stated that her father's hair was always white in her memory. Brierley to Dye, January 6, 1902.

45. Gass, in his eighties, walked the four miles to Wellsburg with a cane "without complaint of fatigue," Jacob said, adding, "I don't believe he would have complained though, even had he been tired." Jacob to Dye, December 9, 1901, Oregon Historical Society, Portland.

46. W. M. Horner (to Eva Emery Dye, February 7, 1902, Oregon Historical Society, Portland) described how Gass bent his ear for a long dissertation on Indians carrying off a Mrs. Morgan in a gulch up Buffalo Creek to be rescued later by her husband and his friend. Horner and Gass were walking between Pierce's Run and Wellsburg when Gass, with a cane in one hand and a hat in the other, "yelled out at me hay he says the divil to you are you going to run off and leave me all to me self come now and be going along with me and I will show you and tell you more than you no a bout here."

47. Jacob, *Life and Times,* 29.

48. Ibid., 41. Wetzel and Brady were famous scouts in the upper Ohio frontier at the end of the eighteenth century.

49. A letter from Hammond Tarr (February 27, 1902) to Eva Emery Dye stated, "I remember the old man with his staff would come to the Brewery (I lived next to it) and was at home there) [*sic*] & drink 2 glasses of beer and then take up his staff & go back home." Hammond Tarr was the son of Campbell Tarr and his second wife Nancy, sister of his first wife, Mary. Atkinson and Gibbons, *Prominent Men in West Virginia,* 590. See note 20 above.

50. Brierley to Dye.

51. Deed Book 16, p. 457, Brooke County Courthouse. This trust deed was released May 2, 1864. Deed Book 20, p. 190.

52. Brooke County Census, 1860, p. 12; dwelling house, p. 86; family, p. 175.

53. Brierley to Dye.

54. Eileen Avery, Brooke County Historical Society, to Ludd A. Trozpek, May 8, 1995.

55. This James Gass could possibly have been Patrick's nephew. His son James was seventeen and residing in the McIntyre household. Wellsburg 1860 Census, p. 106; dwelling house, p. 722; family, p. 689. See also note 52.

56. Brierley to Dye.

57. The notation states that Gass was court-martialed ("C.M") on December 16, 1813, for being drunk; his whiskey was removed for fourteen days. Again on December 27, 1813, Gass was tried for the same offense. He was confined a week and released January 1, 1814. National Archives, M233, roll 5, *Register of Enlistments in the U.S. Army 1798–1914,* 200.

58. Jacob, *Life and Times,* 176–77.

59. Brierley to Dye. Rachel's memories of her father could have been of him visiting her at the Morrow household in Wellsburg where she was bound. See note 51.

60. Jacob, *Life and Times,* 179.

61. Ibid, 182.

62. Ibid, 187.

63. Ibid, 192–93.

64. Horner to Dye, February 19, 1902.

65. *Wellsburg Herald,* March 7, 1862.

66. J. H. Newton, G. G. Nichols, and A. G. Sprankle, *History of the Panhandle* (Wheeling, W. Va.: J. A. Caldwell, 1879), 349.

67. Jacob to Dye, November 25, 1901. Elder Alexander E. Anderson was the minister for the Disciples Church in Wellsburg. Renee Britt Sherman, *Brooke County Virginia / West Virginia Licenses and Marriages,* 1797–1874 (Bowie, Md.: Heritage Books, 1991), 309.

Wellsburg March 4th 1826

To	Balance Brot forward	4.19
"	Medsn for M Cluny	1.00
"	¼ ℔ Tea @ 1.25	31¼
"	Bag	06½
"	1 Comb	33
"	Cash	50
"	Cash	50
7	2 ℔ Coffee	50
	1 Doz Nedles	06
	1 ℔ Nails	12¼
12	1 Hat of P. Plattenburg	6.00
"	Cash	1.50
25	" Cash Do	.50
April	" 2 ℔ Coffee	.50
"	1 Oz Camphor	" 18
"	¼ ℔ Ring	" 31¼
"	½ ℔ Tea	" 31¼
"	amt Settled with	4 " 00
"	Hans Elson	
"	1 Montecurie Pipe	" 50
"	6 Rolls Tobacco	" 12
"	Cash	" 50
"	1 pr Spectacles	" 75
18	" 1 white Robe	1 " 75
	1 ℔ whiskey	" 12
"	...	2 . 0
		26 "

Page 1 of Gass's account book.

1. "To Balance Brot forward" shows that this account book continues from a previous account book, indicating at least one other full account book existed, the whereabouts of which is unknown.

2. Captain William McCluney handled the receipt of Gass's pension for at least the eleven years of the account book. McCluney held Gass's power of attorney, charging for his services as noted in this account book. (For more on McCluney, see note 31 in the introduction to Book II.)

3. Gass bought this expensive hat from P[erry] Plattenburg. On October 26, 1835, he bought another hat from Plattenburg for $1. Palm hats usually cost only 25 cents; therefore, this $6 Plattenburg purchase—constituting a large percentage of Gass's disposable income—must have been an elegant felt hat. During the decade, Gass bought a total of ten hats. J. G. Jacob, in *The Life and Times of Patrick Gass* (Wellsburg, Va.: Jacob & Smith, 1859), wrote that during Gass's trip to Washington, D.C., in 1855 to the soldiers' convention, the "old hero" wore a "spread eagle of brass which was attached to the front of his hat." (p. 192).

According to the *Wellsburg Herald,* Perry Plattenburg was serving as a commissioner (with Peter Curran, D. Brown Jr., James McCluney, and Adam Kuhn) on February 28, 1851. On January 21, 1853, he was paid $10 as state commissioner for 1852. In April of 1852, he was advertising his daguerrean gallery. On July 14, 1854, P. D. Plattenburg appeared on the delinquent list for the year 1853 for nonpayment of county taxes. Yet by March 17, 1857, he was "formerly of Wellsburg," having left for Illinois with a group of Brooke County emigrants. When they suffered in an Illinois flood, he "had a large amount of lumber in the river at the time of the breakup, but did not lose any." William D. Plattenburg, perhaps a brother to Perry, advertised a tailor shop at the M'Keevers Hotel in Wellsburg on December 17, 1852, but there is no indication that he sold hats.

The Plattenburg family seems to have been extensive in Wellsburg. It appears that Jacob (seventy years old on September 27, 1861, when he broke his leg while still working at his occupation of shoveling out cellars) and John, who died in 1845, were brothers in the older generation. Jacob filed suit against John's widow and six children regarding a contract between George and John, both deceased, and another contract between John and Jacob. Jacob hoped to recover title to the south half of lot Number 60 in Wellsburg and money and interest of the other half of the same lot from John's estate (*Wellsburg Herald,* February 8, 1856). The senior Perry would probably have been a brother of George, John, and Jacob.

4. Camphor was a drug or remedy used to avoid disease or to assuage aches. *Dictionary of American English.*

5. Hans Elson appeared to have had relatives and progeny in Wellsburg in the 1850s, but he is not mentioned in the newspaper at that time. Captain John H. [Hans?] Elson served in the War of 1812 as captain of the First Virginia Regiment, mustered from Brooke County. Virgil A. Lewis, *The Soldiery of West Virginia* (Baltimore: Genealogical Publishing Company, 1978),

Wellsburg March 4$\underline{th}$, 1826

	To Balance Brot forward[1]	4.19
[March 4]	" Mcdse for McCluney[2]	1.00
	1/4 lb tea @ 1.25	.31 1/4
	" Bass	.06 1/4
	" 1 Comb	.33
	" Cash	.50
7	2 lb Coffee	.50
	1 Doz Nedles [needles]	.06
	1 lb Nails	.12 1/2
12	1 Hat of P. Plattenburg[3]	6.00
"	[To] Cash	1.50
25	" Cash Do [ditto]	.50
Apr 1	" 2# Coffee	.50
	" 1 oz Camphor[4]	.18 3/4
	" 1/4# Pinz [pins]	.31 1/4
	" 1/4# Tea	.31 1/4
	" amt Settled with Hans Elson[5]	4.00
	" Morticeing Chissell[6]	.50
	" 6 Rollz Tobacco	.12 1/2
	" Cash	.50
	" 1 pr Spectacles	.75
18	" 1 white Robe	.75
	" 1 Qt whiskey	.12
	" cash	2.00
	[missing due to wear of book]	26.15

[1]

181. John Elson had an unclaimed letter in the post office (*Wellsburg Herald,* October 3, 1851) and was assessed $29.79 for income tax. (*Wellsburg Weekly Herald,* September 1, 1865). Other family members were mentioned in the local paper: A. M. Elson and Mrs. Charlotte Elson had unclaimed letters in June of 1855 (*Wellsburg Weekly Herald,* July 7, 1855). In 1859, A. M. Elson's name appeared in an advertisement as purchaser of a combined reaper and mower. (*Wellsburg Herald,* April 1, 1859). Elson's Run appears on the 1852 map of Brooke County.

6. A morticing chisel is used to fashion a hole or slot for a tenon to fit into. Gass's carpentry skills, which he used from time to time throughout his life, proved very useful during the Lewis and Clark expedition. His purchases of tools herein reflect his ongoing practice of carpentry, although no receipts in this account book are shown to have originated from such work. Gass's pension was based on his complete disability; however, oral tradition in Wellsburg credits Gass with construction of numerous local buildings, including the Yellow Hammer's Nest and various public and private houses.

7. Mackerel (spelled various ways in Gass's account book) is a highly edible ocean fish that grows up to eighteen inches long. Constituting an important element of Gass's diet, mackerel accounted for thirty purchases of eighty-one fish during the period covered herein. A couple of times Gass noted purchases of mackerel for friends. He also bought herring, bass, and shad to balance his diet of fat, carbohydrates, and probably seasonal fruits and vegetables.

8. John Berry printed and published the *Wellsburgh* [*sic*] *Gazette* in 1821. He had an unclaimed letter January 4, 1834 (*Brooke Republican*), and again on October 11, 1850 (*Wellsburg Herald*).

9. Boot webbing refers to the webbing or material to recover the "boot" of a buggy, the cover for the seat that protected passengers from water and mud that might splash up from the road. *Dictionary of American English.*

10. The "15 may" notation in the original account book appears above the word "yarn" with a caret pointing to it, showing that Gass forgot the entry in May and interlined it in June. A storekeeper would not have kept books this way; Gass did until Connell Wells & Co. took over the bookkeeping.

11. Patrick Gass purchased twenty handkerchiefs during the course of the account book, including two of black silk, one of silk, one of Madras, one headwrap handkerchief, a flag handkerchief, and one specified to have been cotton.

1826		Amt Brought over		$26.15
Apr	24	To 2# Coffee .25		.50
	"	To Cash		2.00
May	15	To 2# coffee	.50	
		" 1/2" tea	.62 1/2	
		" 1# Tobacco	.12 1/2	
		" 4 Mackeral[7]	.25	
		" 1 ps [piece] tape	.12 1/2	
		" bass	.06 1/4	
		" Cash	<u>1.00</u>	2.68 3/4
		a/ct [account] for Jno [Jonathan] Berry[8]		1.87 1/2
June	1	To Cash		3.00
	"	" Bottle whisky		.12 1/2
	"	" 15# Bacon 5 1/2		.82 1/2
	"	" 1 Cross Cut file		.18 1/3
	"	" 1 1/2 yd Boot webing[9]	8	.12
	24	" 1 Qt why. [whiskey]		.12 1/2
	"	" 2# Coffee 25		.50
	"	" 1# Tobbacco		.12 1/2
	"	" Cash		1.00
	"	" 1# cotton yarn 15 may[10]		.37 1/2
	"	" 1 Pocket Handf[11]		.20
July	9	1 Parrissall		1.8?
	"	1 Qt why		[.12 1/2]
	"	" 4 1/2 # Coffee for [missing]		[1.12 1/2]
	"	" Cash	[missing 1.50]	

[2]

12. "Do" is an abbreviation for "ditto," used throughout the account book.

13. Throughout his journal, Gass attributed cash and sometimes goods for himself to "Self," a clear internal indication of his authorship.

14. Castor oil, a purgative or lubricant, was a popular remedy of the time.

15. During this record-keeping, Gass bought seven "combs," four "side combs," six "fine combs," two "pairs of combs," and "dressing combs," as well as a gift specified as a "hair comb for Miss Hambleton," before he married Maria Hamilton.

16. "By pension due last March" refers to Gass's semiannual government pension for complete disability, granted because of his losing an eye during his military service in the War of 1812. For more information on this pension, and errors surrounding it, see note 17 in the introduction to Book II. Full disability was granted Patrick Gass on June 10, 1815, in the amount of $48 semiannually ($96 per year), payable in March and September. In this September 1826 entry, Gass received his pension nearly six months late.

17. Before his marriage in March of 1831, Gass bought a total of four silk scarves (perhaps for Miss Bowls or others in addition to Maria Hamilton). After that date, he bought none.

1826		To amt brot up		43.73
July	8	To 1/4# pepper		.12
"	29	To 1 1/2 # Tobacco	.25	
		" 1 pt wine	.37 1/2	
		" 1 Qt whiskey	.12 1/2	
		" Cash	<u>1.00</u>	1.75
Augt	4th	do for Cheese[12]		1.00
"	20	do for Self[13]		.25
"	"	Castor Oil[14]		.25
"	25	4 macrell		.25
"	"	To Cash		.50
Sept	2	" do		.25
		" 1/4# tea 31 1/2		.31 1/2
		" 1 Comb[15]		<u>.12 1/2</u>
				48.56
		postage of Pension last March		<u>.50</u>
				49.05
		pension due last March[16]		<u>48.00</u>
			Balance	$1.05
Sept	4	To 1/2# Salts [sic]	.18 3/4	
		" Cash	<u>2.00</u>	2.18 3/4
"	"	" A/ct to McGluney [McCluney]		1.00
"	"	" 1 Handf		.18 3/4
"	"	" 4# Coffee		1.00
"	12	" 1" Tobacco	.12 1/2	
		" 1 Bottle whisky	.12 1/2	
		" 1 Scarv [scarf] Silk[17]	<u>.06 1/4</u>	
				<u>.31 1/4</u>
				$5.73

[3]

18. Gum guaiacum is a sticky substance yielded from the inner bark of American trees of the genus *Gauzuma,* used in medicine as a remedy for gout or rheumatism. *Webster's Third New International Dictionary.*

19. Dr. William J. Cook and James Allison signed Gass's petition of March 25, 1829, validating his total disability. Nevertheless, Gass's letter to Secretary of War John Eaton on March 12, 1829, stated that the federal agent at Richmond wanted biannual medical certifications of his disability, for which Gass claimed exemption under the law of March 3, 1819. National Archives, Record Group 15A, file 2409, reprinted in Donald Jackson, ed., *Letters of the Lewis and Clark Expedition* (Urbana: University of Illinois Press, 1978) 2:646–48. Chapter 81, 15th Congress, sess. 2, p. 514 confirms that no affadavit was necessary in cases of total disability. Entry of payment for medical services in the amount of $13 proved crucial to receipt of Gass's pension. Gass referred to Dr. Cook again on page 12, paying him $9 on March 21, 1829, and the pension continued.

News of Dr. Cook continued in Wellsburg where he married Drusilla, age twenty, on February 2, 1830. In 1832 the couple joined the Methodist Episcopal Church. She died December 7, 1854, in Springfield, Jefferson County, Ohio. (*Wellsburg Herald,* February 2, 1855).

20. A magazine almanack forecasted weather and reported news. He bought nine almanacks between 1827 and 1837, missing only 1830 and 1833. This one could have been *Cramer's Pittsburg Magazine Almanack,* published from 1806 at Pittsburgh. Gass's regular purchases of almanacks and the daily paper in Wellsburg testify to his literacy and interest in public affairs.

21. Cassinette (or casinet) was a lightweight twilled fabric, usually with cotton warp and wool filling used to make men's trousers. *Webster's Third New International Dictionary.*

22. Comments such as "to castor oil last summer" are evidence that Gass wrote entries. Notations of this kind would not be the work of an account manager or storekeeper.

1826		Amt Brought over		5.73
Sept	18	1/4# allspice		.12
"	"	Cash		1.00
"	"	Do for Miller		1.50
"	24	To 1 oz Gum Guacum[18]		.12 1/2
"	"	" 1/2 oz Camphor	18 1/2	.09 1/4
Oct	7	To Cash for Cook[19]		13.00
"	"	To 1# Tobacco		.12 1/2
"	"	" 2 pt. Bowls		.18 3/4
Nov	2	" 4 pt Bowls	9	.36
	"	Cash		1.00
	"	1 mag^z allmanac[20]		.12 1/2
	8	4# Coffee		1.00
	"	1/4# Pepper		.12 1/2
	"	1 Qt Why		.12 1/2
"	9	3 1/2 yd Cassinett[21]	100	3.50
	"	1 " flannell		.44
	"	2 scarv Silk	12 1/2}	
		Why	6 1/2}	.18 1/2
	11	Cash 50 Tea 31 1/4 Tobacco 12 1/2		.94
	25	Cash		3.00
	"	whiskey		.12 1/2
Dec^r		To Castor oil last summer[22]		.31
	18	To 4 1/4# Coffee 25		1.06 1/4
	"	To 1# Tobacco		[missing .12 1/2]
	23	" Cash		[missing 3.00]

[4]

23. Jonathan Gass could have been Patrick Gass's brother, who in this case would probably have come to Wellsburg sometime in 1827 when their father Benjamin died there (Jacob, *Life and Times,* 177; Deed Book B, 217, Brooke County Courthouse, records the sale of Benjamin's property by Patrick, the estate administrator, and his mother, Mary, to Eli Boring on September 12, 1827, after having been appraised in May). It could have been Patrick Gass's nephew, John, who was born in 1798.

24. Saltpeter, potassium nitrate, was used to make gun powder or as a medicine to relieve asthma. *Dictionary of American English.*

25. Probably the son of Captain William McCluney, James McCluney served as a Brooke County Commissioner in 1851 (*Wellsburg Weekly Herald,* February 28, 1851), an assistant marshall to the Fourth of July celebration of 1851 (*Wellsburg Weekly Herald,* July 4, 1851), an agent for bounty land (*Wellsburg Weekly Herald,* December 6, 1850, and March 21, 1851), an agent for the Knox Insurance Company (*Wellsburg Weekly Herald,* May 17, 1850), and as a seller of "Cheap Novels, Magazines," etc. (*Wellsburg Weekly Herald,* May 24, 1850), as well as a book dealer of cultural offerings like "Goldsmiths's Works, Cromwells [*sic*] Letters and Speeches . . . Rollins Ancient History," and a seller of paper, ink, and stationery.

26. "Tea in two papers" was a term used to describe the envelope in which tea was wrapped for sale.

27. Shirting was a fabric suitable to make men's shirts. *Webster's Ninth New Collegiate Dictionary.*

28. Jonathan Murray could have been the principal of Murray and Barnes Cigar Manufactory. (*Brooke Republican,* August 4, 1836).

		Amt Brought over	37.31
1827			
Jany	24	4 1/4# Coffee	$1.00
"		1# Tobacco	.12 1/2
"		Cash this day	1.00
"		Leather for Jn° Gass[23]	1.50
Feby	14	To 1/2# Salts	.18 3/4
"		" 1 Qt why	.12 1/2
"		" Cash	1.00
"		" 1 Box wafers	.10
			$42.34
"	24	To Cash	4.00
"		To Goods for Jn° Gass	4.00
"	"	To 1 Sett Tea Spoonz	.25
		" error	.38
			50.97
		By his pension due last Sept. 48	

March 5, 1827	To balance	2.97
	To 2 1/2# Coffee	.50
	To 1 oz Gum Guacum	.12 1/2
	" Salt Peter[24]	.06 1/4
	" 1# Tobacco	.12 1/2
	" Cash	1.00
	" Ditto for Jas McCluny[25]	1.00
	" 1# Coffee	.20
	" 1/2# tea in 2 papers[26]	.62
	" Cash	1.00
	" 29 1/2 yds shirting[27].12 1/2	3.68
	To [illegible] Jno Murray[28] 15th Inst	.9 ?

29. Solomon Connell was probably a principal of the store Connell Wells & Co., in Wellsburg, which would in 1847–48 keep Gass's account in this book. This particular entry indicates that Gass had an account at the store that he paid with a cash disbursal. Unfortunately, Gass seldom noted the reason for cash expenditures.

30. A John Groves, at about age ninety-five, died in Brooke County on August 27, 1864. At that time, he was supposed to be the oldest inhabitant of the area (*Wellsburg Herald,* September 2, 1864). Patrick Gass would have been 93 at this time.

31. Muslin is a plain woven, coarse to sheer, cotton fabric. *Webster's Ninth New Collegiate Dictionary.*

32. Green coffee indicates that the beans were not roasted. *Webster's Ninth New Collegiate Dictionary.*

33. A quire of paper comprised twenty-four to twenty-five sheets the same size and quality, or one-twentieth of a ream. *Webster's Ninth New Collegiate Dictionary.*

34. Cotton hose refers to men's socks.

1827		To amt Brought over		12.17
March 26		To Cash		$1.00
"	"	To amt. P[d] S. Connell[29]		2.00
"	27	To Cash		1.00
April	2	To Goods for Jacob Groves[30]		3.03 1/2
"	2	To 2 1/2# Coffee 20		.50
	"	" 1 1/2 yd Muslin[31]		.31 1/4
	"	" 3 mackerell		.25
	"	" 1 Qt whisky		.12 1/2
	"	" Cash		3.00
	21	" Cash		1.00
	"	" 1 Qt Port wine		.75
	"	" 2# Green Coffee[32]		.50
	25	" 1 Silk handf.		.62
	28	" 2# coffee @	50	
	"	" 2 yd crape [crepe]	50	
	"	" 1 Qt whiskey	12 1/2	
	"	" 1 oz Gum guacum	12 1/2	1.25
	"	" a/ct for Sol. Connell		1.37 1/2
	"	To 1/2 Quire paper[33]		.12
	30	" 1 Qt why		.12
		" 2# Tobacco		.25
	"	" Cash		1.00
May	12	" do		1.00
"	"	To 2 pr Cotton hose[34]		1.25
				32.64

[6]

35. Powder is an explosive used with shot to charge a muzzle-loading gun for firing. *Webster's Ninth New Collegiate Dictionary.*

36. Shot, small lead or steel pellets, was used as the projectile to be pro-pelled by gun powder from the barrel of a muzzle-loading gun. *Webster's Third New International Dictionary.*

37. In the 1860 census, Elizabeth Patterson, age sixty-four, was married to James, age sixty-two, which would make her thirty-one at the time of this entry.

38. Probably this refers to William Burt, the late husband of Martha Burt, noted in her obituary *(Wellsburg Weekly Herald,* October 17, 1857). It could have been William E. Burt, probably the son of the above couple. See note 98 below.

39. Indigo, obtained from plants of the genus *indigofera,* in a powder form produced a popular and lovely blue dye. *Dictionary of American English.*

40. "Error" acknowledges a discrepancy, but, overall, Patrick Gass's numeracy is excellent: the account book from March 1826 through April 1835, the decade of his family's personal record-keeping, is quite accurate. He made only six identifiable arithmetic errors of any substance. Editorial conventions regarding numbers and arithmetic errors in the account book are explained in the Introduction to Book II.

1827		To amt brot up			32.00
May	17	To 4 Mackeral @ 8 1/3			.33 1/2
"	18	" 1/4# powder[35]	.12 1/2		
		" 1# Shott[36]	.12 1/2		.25
"	25	To goods for Betsy Patterson[37]			3.00
	"	" 3 mackerel 8			.24
"	28	" Cash	1.00		
		" 2# Coffee	.50		
					1.50
	30	" order as per Burt[38]			3.00
1 June		" Cash			1.00
	"	" Lary McDowl			3.00
"	12	" Cash			2.00
					46.32
		To postage on Pension			.50
					46.82
July 3^d		To 2 1/2# Coffee 20	50		
	"	" 1/4# pepper	12 1/2		
	"	" Cash	1.00		1.62 1/2
"	"	" 1 pr Sizsors [scissors]			.25
"	17	" 1 Cheese			.37 1/2
	"	" 1# Tobacco 12 1/2 fish .25			.37 1/2
		" 1 oz Indigo[39]			.25
		" 1 1/2# tea 31 1/4 June 15)			
		" 1 pr Suspenders 18 3/4 " ")			.50
		error[40]			.62 1/2
					50.82
		By his pension to the 4 ^th}			
		of March 1827 }		48.00	
		" balance		2.82	
				50.82	$50.82

[7]

41. "Jefferson shoes" describe a calfskin shoe that laced up the front to or above one's ankle. Thomas Jefferson was fond of wearing them and they became popular about the time of his presidency. *Dictionary of American English.*

42. Gingham is a fabric of yarn-dyed cotton in plain weave and often in checkered pattern. *Webster's Ninth New Collegiate Dictionary.*

43. Bunting was a lightweight woolen fabric. Flags were often made from bunting. *Dictionary of American English.*

44. Brown holland was a plain linen fabric with little or no bleaching, retaining the natural color of the flax fiber. *Dictionary of American English.*

45. A penknife was used for making and mending quill pens. *Webster's Third New International Dictionary.*

46. Three Jeffers appear in the *Wellsburg Herald* during this time: John, Henry, and William. In January 1852, J. H. Pendleton foreclosed on property owned by John Jeffers and other property owned by Henry Jeffers. (*Wellsburg Weekly Herald,* January 23, 1852) Henry Jeffers advertised "Money Wanted" on July 27, 1855, to advise those who owed him money to pay him and avoid further "dunning" as "he needs money to pay hands and buy stock and must have it." (*Wellsburg Weekly Herald*) John Jeffers lost his son Andrew to typhoid in Placerville, California, December 31, 1852, making him of an age consistent with Patrick Gass's 1827 entry. He lost another son, John, to a disease of the heart at the Eastern Virginia Lunatic Asylum, Williamsburg, Virginia, on May 31, 1859, aged thirty (*Wellsburg Herald,* June 24, 1859). The Jeffers to whom Gass referred may have been the John Jeffers reported in the *Wheeling Gazette* of May 14, 1825, as having run away from an apprenticeship in the baking business at age nineteen. That young man was probably the same John Jeffers above. Another kinsman, H. Jeffers, operated the Jeffers Boot and Shoe Establishment. *Wellsburg Weekly Herald,* July 22, 1853.

47. A pocketbook is a small notebook suitable for carrying in the pocket; a pocket case of leather or other material for holding paper money or papers. *Dictionary of American English; Wellsburg Herald,* May 31, 1850. Patrick Gass's account book was in fact a pocket book.

1827

July	17	To balance from other page		2.82
"	24	" 1 pr Jefferson Shoes[41]		1.75
		" 1 Dble Bladed knife		.37 1/2
Augt	13	" 5# Coffee	1.00	
		" 3 Mackeral	25	
		" Needle & Camphor	<u>12 1/2</u>	1.37 1/2
"	18	" 2 doz Buttons	25	
		" tobacco	6 1/4	.31 1/4
Sept	4	" Cash		.50
	5	" do p^d McCluney		1.00
	8	" 4 yds Gingham[42]		1.60
	10	" 7 " Blk [black] Bunting[43]		3.15
	"	" Cash		.50
	"	" 1/2 yd Gingham		.20
	"	" 1 1/2 " Shirting .17		.26
	13	" 1 3/4 " Brown Holland[44]		.44
	"	" 5 Skane [skein] Silk 3		.15
	"	" Cash for Jno Carter		6.00
	18	" Pocket Handf		.25
	"	" 1# Tobacco		.25
	22	" Cash		1.00
Oct	6	" 1 Razor		.31 1/4
	"	" 2 1/2# Coffee		.50
	"	" 1 Penknife[45]		.25
	"	" Cash for Jeffers[46]		3.00
	"	" 1 Pocket Book[47]		<u>.25</u>
				26.28

[8]

48. The only outside reference to elucidate Larry McDowl's identity or that of "Miss McDowl," probably his daughter, are notices for two unclaimed letters for Elizabeth McDowel in 1834 (*Brooke Republican,* January 4, 1834) and another to her, addressed "Miss Eliza McDowel," in 1835. (*Brooke Republican,* April 9, 1835). See Gass's entries of June 1, 1827, and February 12, 1828. In this second reference to "McDowl," however, we do have the item purchased for him, showing that Gass bought building materials as well as food staples for others. How he was repaid, or if this favor was repayment of debt, is unclear.

1827		To amt brot up			26.26[*sic*]
Oct	15	To 2 1/4 yd Blue cloth @ 3[.00] =		6.75	
		" 2 " holland		50	
		" 1 1/3 doz buttons @ 62 1/2 =		83	8.08
"	"	" Iron for McDowl[48]			4.00
Nov	1	" thread		12 1/2	
		" 1 pr Spectacles		62 1/2	
		" 1 comb		12 1/2	.87 1/2
	3	Cash			.50
	8	1 Flag Handf			.87 1/2
Dec^r	5	" 3/4 yd Cassinett @ 96^c			.72
		" 3/4 " flannell 37 1/2			.28
		" silk & thread			.12 1/2
		" Cash			1.00
					42.73
"	14	" do			.50
		" Postage			.37
					43.60
"	25	" 2 1/2# Coffee 20			.50
	"	" Cash			1.00
1827 [*sic*] }					
Jany1 }		To 1# Tobacco			.12 1/2
"	"	To 1 Almanac			.12 1/2
"	"	To Cash			1.00
"	7	" Cash			.50
"	15	" Cash			1.00
Feby	9	" Do			.50
"	12	" Mds for Miss McDowl			1.00
		" 1/2# Tobacco			.06 1/4
					49.41
		By pension to the 4th Sept last}	48.00		
		" balance carried over	1.41		
			49.41		

[9]

49. The name of Mrs. Sarah Wingate appears on the list of unclaimed letters in the spring of 1835. *Brooke Republican,* April 9, 1835.

50. Sparrow pills comprise one of the many patent medicines of the time, which Gass bought several times. Contemporary references researched yield no references to them.

1828		To Balance brot over	1.41
March	7	To Cash	1.00
"	24	" 1# Tobacco	.12 1/2
Apr	1	" Cash on a/c	.50
"	28	" Do	1.00
	"	" a/ct for Captn McCluney	1.00
		" Cash Self	1.00
May	8	" 10 yd Muslin @ 16^c	1.60
		" 1# Tobacco	.12 1/2
March	24	" amt paid Captn McCluney	.75
		" 5# Coffee @ 20^c	1.00
		" 2# sugar @ 12 1/2^c	.25
June	3	" Dinner plate 9^c	.09
		" Cash 6 1/4 1 hdkf 25	.31 1/4
		" 1 Pt. whiskey	.06 1/4
		" 1 Silk hdkf (if not charged or paid for)	.87 1/2
		" 2 1/4# Coffee 50 4# Sugar 50	1.00
July	9	" Cash	2.00
"	29	" Goods for Mrs Wingate[49]	1.00
Aug^t	16	" Sugar 25 Rice 6 1/4^c Salt 12 1/2	.44
			15.55
Sept	5	" Cash	.25
"	22	" 2# Coffee a 20	.40
	"	" 2# Sugar 12	.25
	"	" 1 Paper Sparrow Pills[50]	.12 1/2
	24	" 2 Side Combs	.06 1/4
	"	" Cash	.50
Oct	20	" 2 1/2# Coffee	.50
	"	" 3 1/2# Sugar @ 12 1/2	.44
	"	" 1/2# Candles	.06
	"	" Cash	1.00

[10]

51. This entry begins a series of twenty-three in less than two years labeled for the Boles family. Most of the purchases made on their behalf are large quantities of food supplies specified for "Mrs. Bowls." Gass's purchases for "Miss Bowls" are for a gymp bonnet, calico, bobbinett, and "goods."

In the 1830 census, James Boles is listed as the head of a household that included a male and female between ages forty and fifty (probably him and his wife), a male between twenty and thirty, a male and a female between fifteen and twenty, a female between ten and fifteen, and two females between five and ten years old. In addition, there is a male listed between ages fifty and sixty. At this time, Patrick Gass was fifty-nine. It seems probable that Gass stayed in the Boles home at this time when he was making a large number of purchases in their name. 1830 Virginia Census, Brooke County. National Archives, series M19, reel 189:134.

52. The roots of madder, a European climbing plant, produces a red dye frequently used in Gass's times to dye cloth. *Dictionary of American English*.

53. Alum is a mineral salt. *Dictionary of American English*.

54. "Hambleton" or "Judge" John Hamilton entered Gass's diary here as the recipient of a gallon of whiskey. It is not clear if this was a gift or a favor for which Gass would be reimbursed. Hamilton was his future landlord and father-in-law; Gass moved to the Hamilton boarding house the fall of 1829. Jacob, *Life and Times,* 178.

When Patrick Gass and Maria moved to Grog Run, Hambelton (age 60-70) and his wife (age 50-60) lived on adjacent property in 1840. (1840 Virginia Census, Brooke County National Archives, series M704, reel 552:22A)

On April 25, 1856, S. L. Marks received $100 for the yearly keep of J. Hamilton (*Wellsburg Weekly Herald,* April 24, 1856). He was not on the poor list in 1859. The Board of the Overseers of the Poor noted in 1855 the higher prices and greater unemployment, causing expansion of those receiving aid. (*Wellsburg Weekly Herald,* May 4, 1855) Gass's biographer, J. G. Jacob referred to Hamilton in 1858 as "a wreck of a powerful and once influential man."

Another man, Judge S. C. A. Hamilton, with John Wier, built a building for a Steam Planing Mill near the Foundry at Wellsburg in 1853. Noted as "very ingenious," this man could have been related to John and Maria Hamilton. Later this Judge Sam Hamilton, formerly of Wellsburg, managed the steam press at the *Intelligencer* office at Wheeling by 1858. Known as a "true-blue 'unwashed' Democrat," this Judge Hamilton had a "portly" figure. *Wellsburg Weekly Herald,* April 29, 1853, and January 29, 1858.

55. Blacking paste was a paste applied to objects, usually shoes, to make them black. *Webster's Third New International Dictionary*.

1828	To am^t brot up	19.14
Oct^o 25	To Cash 100 tobacco 6 1/4^c	1.06 1/4
	" Postage on obtaining Pension to the }	
	4th March 28 process having been returned }	
	& several letters per mail on the subject }	2.00
Oct 4	To Cash	13.00
" 25	" Sundries for Wingate	6.37 1/2
" 29	" Cash Self	1.00
Novr 5	" do do	1.00
		$43.58
Sept 22	By his pension to the }	
	4th March last }	48.00
Novr 5	To balance to new a/ct	4.42
Novr 5	By balance	4.42
Sept 12	To postage 50 a/ct to McCluny 1.00	1.50
" 12	To Cash	3.00
" 7	" 3# Sugar 37 1/2 }	
	" 3" Coffee @ 20^c } Bowles[51]	.97
" 12	" 1# Nails for Bowles	.10
" 15	" 5" madder[52] for Mrs Bowles	1.00
	" 2 1/2 yd Muslin Do	.37 1/2
" "	" 1# allum[53] @ 12 Do	.12
	" 2" Sugar Do	.25
	" 7 yd Plaid trimings Do	4.93
Decr 3	" 1 pr Socks self	.25
1829		
Jay 8	" Cash	1.00
	" 1 Gal whiskey for Hambleton[54]	.37 1/2
12	" 3# Coffee @ 22 for Mrs Bowles	.66
	" 2" Sugar @ 12 1/2^c Do	.25
	" 29# flour @ 3^c Do	.87
19	" Cash	1.00
24	" 1 Box Blacking past[e][55]	.12 1/2
	" 1 Comb	.12 1/2
		16.81

[11]

56. This refers to a special sugar from New Orleans. For instance, an ad in the *Wellsburg Weekly Herald,* November 28, 1851, noted that a "Flat Boat Fairy" had just brought "New Orleans, Crushed and Loaf Sugar . . . Superior Coffee" and other items.

1829		Amt. Brought over	16.84 1/2
Jan^y	27	To 1 Pt why	.06 1/4
"		" 1 Mag^z. Almanac	.12 1/2
"	28	" 50# flour for Mrs Bowles	1.50
	30	" Cash	2.00
Feby	4	" Do	1.00
		$21.53	22.53 1/2
"	12	" Cash	1.00
"	18	" Do	1.00
"	23	" Do	1.00
"	"	" 2/3# Tobacco 12 1/2	.08 1/3
March	2	" 3# Coffee per Mrs Bowls	.60
"	"	" Cash for Self	3.00
"	"	" do	1.00
"	10	" do	1.00
"	15	" do	1.00
"	21	" do for Dr. Cook	9.00
"	"	" do for Self	1.00
"	25	" do "	.50
"	30	" Do "	2.00
April	2	" Do "	2.00
"	7	" 2# Coffee Mrs Bowls	.40
"	"	" 2# Orlean Sugar⁵⁶ do	.25
"	11	To 47 1/2# flour @ 3^c do	1.42 1/2
	14	" 1 Dble B^d [bladed] Penknife	.12 1/2
	17	" 3 Mackeral for Mrs Bowles	.25
	19	" Cash	1.00
	24	" Do	1.00
			~~49.27~~
			50.17

[12]

57. Elizabeth Maxwell died in 1835 at age sixty-six after an illness of several months. (*Brooke Republican,* July 9, 1835) James Maxwell had an unclaimed letter in 1821 (*Wellsburgh Gazette,* October 20, 1821) and received $5 for burying a deceased person in 1851. *Wellsburg Weekly Herald,* July 11, 1851.

58. Gymp, an ornamental braid or binding, was used to trim clothes or furniture, so this bonnet or girl's hat would have featured such trim. *Dictionary of American English.*

59. Sarcenet refers to a soft, thin silk in plain or twill weave used for dresses, veils, or trimmings. *Webster's Ninth New Collegiate Dictionary.*

60. A jean vest would be made of strong cotton.

61. Gass bought his future wife a hair comb, calling her "Miss Hambelton" in this first reference to the woman more than forty years his junior, the daughter of "Judge" Hamilton.

62. Calomel, mercurous chloride, was used as a purgative or as a specific cure for ague. During the Lewis and Clark expedition, on Thursday, October 10, 1805, Gass thought he had ague. He probably had fever from a canoe accident two days earlier. Dr. Eldon G. Chuinard, *Only One Man Died: The Medical Aspects of the Lewis and Clark Expedition* (Glendale, Calif.: Arthur H. Clark , 1979), 175 n. 19, missed Gass's reference to ague.

		To amt brot	50.17
1829			
May	2	To Cassinett & trimings coat for Bowles	6.00
		" 2# Coffee .40 }	
		" 2" Sugar .25 }	
		" 4" Bacon .28 }for Do	
		" 72" flour 2.16 }	3.09
May	1	" 1/2 Gal whiskey for Do	.18
"	4	" 1 Cotton hdkf	.25
		" Cash	1.00
		" Goods for Mrs Maxwell[57]	3.50
"	5	" 1 Gymp[58] Bonnett for Miss Bowls	1.75
		" 1/2 yd Sarcenett[59] for Do	.28
		" 2 " Ribbon @ 25^c Do	.50
		" 1 " do – 12 1/2^c Do	.12
		" 1 Scarv Silk 6 1/4^c wire 3^c Do	.09
May	9	" Cash	.50
"	18	" 2 1/2 yd [vest?] Jane [jean][60] @ 22^c	.55
		" Cash	1.00
"	23	" 1 Hair comb for Miss Hambleton[61]	.12 1/2
		" 2 1/2 # Coffee 50^c 4# Sugar 50^c	1.00
"	27	" Cash	1.00
June	2	" 5 yd Blue callico @ 20^c for Miss Bowls	1.00
		" 1/2# tobacco 6 1/4 Cash 50^c	.56 1/4
"	10	" 1 Gal whiskey 37 1/2 1 pt Flask 12 1/2	.50
"	12	" 1 Cake Shaving Soap	.06 1/4
		" 1 " do do	.12 1/2
"	20	" 1/2 Gal whiskey	.18 1/2
		" a/ct for Captn McCluny [sic]	5.00
		" 1 oz Calomel[62] Feby 2 6 1/4	.25
			78.81

[13]

63. The calfskin could have been used as a rug or table throw or to make leather objects.

64. Since this entry constitutes a cash disbursement, "Rice" probably refers to a person by that name, perhaps Edward Rice, who had an unclaimed letter. *Wellsburg Herald,* February 26, 1858.

1829	To amt brot over		78.81
1828	By bal of acct brot forward	4.42	
Sept 4	" his pension	48.00	
1829			
May 22	" do 48.00		
	" ded^t for expences 1.00	47.00	
Jun 20	To balance to new a/ct		20.61
		99.42	$99.42
June 20	By balance	20.61	
24	To 1 Pt why		.06 1/4
"	To Cash		1.00
25	" 1 Pt whiskey		.06 1/4
29	" 1 " do 6 1/4 Cash 1.00		1.06 1/4
July 4	" Cash		1.00
13	" Do 50^c		.50
21	" Do		2.00
27	" Do 50^c		.50
"	" 1 pt whiskey & flask 15^c		.15
Augt 3	" Cash		1.00
" 6	" 1 Shaving Glass		.25
	" 1/8# pepper		.06 1/4
9	" 16 1/2# Bacon @ 7^c		1.15 1/2
	" 1 Calf Skin[63]		2.00
	" Cash		.50
	" Do		1.00
			12.32
17	" Do for Rice[64]		7.00
24	" Gal whiskey for Hambelton		.37 1/2
	" 1/4 Bag Salt do		.23
	" 1 Gal whiskey do		.37 1/2
29	" 7# Cheese @ 8^c		.56
	" 1 hdkf		.25
		.52	21.13
		21.13	21.13

[14]

65. A Jew's harp is a small metal lyre-shaped instrument played with the mouth and a finger. It was named by the French after Jewish peddlers who frequently made music with them.

66. John C. Perry and nine others would later sign a letter on December 24, 1851, to the Honorable George W. Thompson accompanying a petition to benefit Patrick Gass to assist him in caring for his large and young family. (*Wellsburg Weekly Herald,* May 17, 1850) Although the writing looks like "Pinsy," there are no references to such a name, and Perry did play an important role in the community as well as in Gass's behalf regarding his pension appeal.

Here Gass informs us about a cash expenditure with "do," indicating the cash reimbursed Perry is for whiskey, the expense directly above. Unfortunately, Gass did not usually note the purpose of cash dispensed to "Self" or other people.

67. Purchase of this barrel of whiskey completes the drinking binge Gass and "the Judge" had enjoyed since August 24, involving about seven gallons of whiskey specified in the account book. In addition to this, Gass apparently borrowed $5 from Perry for liquor. Please refer to Appendix Z, Liquor Purchases, which notes only entries specifically for whiskey, not cash expenditures or loans possibly made to obtain liquor.

68. This reference is probably to Samuel Herdman, deputy sheriff of old Brooke. He was probably a carpenter, since his name appears in the list of many estate sales in the early 1800s for buying large amounts of tools. In August 1852, Samuel Herdman was involved in a lawsuit that forced him to call in all of the debts owed to him. (*Wellsburg Weekly Herald,* August 6, 1852). His wife was probably Ellenor (sometimes called Ellen) Herdman. (*Wellsburg Weekly Herald,* January 30, 1852). By January 1851, the Herdmans were $71.40 delinquent in taxes on their land for the years 1842 through 1849. (*Wellsburg Weekly Herald,* January 17, 1851). Samuel Herdman died in Wellsburg on November 29, 1855, aged eighty-nine years, nine months, and a few days. He "left only his fair name, and unspotted integrity, as a memorial to his friends." *Wellsburg Herald,* December 5, 1856.

69. Here Gass refers to "Maria," not "Miss Hambleton," showing a changing relationship and clearly indicating hereby his own authorship of this account book. Furthermore, this notation comprises a credit to his account, so she repaid him for the goods purchased on September 19, 1829, amounting to $1.75.

1829		To balance from old acct	.52
Sept	4	" 1 pt whiskey	.06 1/4
		" 1 Gal do for Hambleton	.37 1/2
"	8	" Cash	1.00
"	12	" 1 Gal whiskey Self 37 1/2 Jewharp[65] 3c	.40 1/2
"	15	" 1 do per Hambleton	.37 1/2
		" 2 Mackeral	.12
	16	" 1 pt whiskey 6 1/4 1/2# candles 6 1/4^c	.12 1/2
"	19	" 1 " do	.06 1/4
		" 1 pr Socks 31 1/4^c 1/4 yd flannell 12^c	.44
		" Cash 100 4 Buttons 4^c	1.04
		" 1 Bandanna	1.12 1/2
"	19	" Goods for Miss Hambleton	1.75
"	21	" 12# Bacon 96^c 1 pt whiskey 6	<u>1.02</u>
			8.43
	22	" 1 box blacking	.12 1/2
		" 1/2# tobacco	.06 1/4
	24	" 1 Gal whiskey	.37 1/2
"	30	" Cash for Pinsy [probably Perry][66] do	5.00
Oct	5	" 1 whiskey bbl[67] 37 1/2 2 Mackeral 12 1/2	.50
"	26	" a/ct for Jno Hambleton	3.47 1/2
"	29	" Cash p^d Herdman[68]	10.56
	"	" do	1.00
Nov	4	" order to Service	4.00
"	18	" Cash 100^c 1 pr Socks 25	1.25
		" 1/2# tobacco	.06 1/4
"	28	" Cash	2.00
Dec	4	" do	.50
"	10	" do	1.00
"	13	" do	<u>2.00</u>
			40.35 1/2

Sept 18	By pension 48. ded^t postage 50^c	47.50
Nov 12	" Cash of Maria[69]	<u>1.75</u>
		<u>49.25</u>
		8.89 1/2

[15]

70. Eli Boring (born September 6, 1794; died May 1, 1852) served as affiant to an affidavit of January 1, 1852, swearing that Patrick Gass had eight children, one having died recently. (Gass actually had seven children, the first of whom died the same year she was born in 1832, according to the family Bible, descendants' records, and Jacob's contemporary biography.) See note 29, Introduction to Book II.

Boring hung himself at age fifty-eight, ending an outstanding life as a "sterling citizen." Yet his tribulations had been manifold: of his thirteen children, nine were "idiotic and blind." A son of "exemplary character" had his arms and hands "so mangled in a threshing machine that both arms had to be amputated above the elbows." Boring was remembered as a man "not blessed with a liberal education . . . [but] a man of close thought and much practical sense . . . proverbially industrious." (*Wellsburg Weekly Herald,* May 14, 1852). Hanson Boring, Eli's son, served as administrator of his father's estate and lived at Pierce's Run (Ibid., August 6, 1852), where, as N. W. White put it (to Honorable George W. Thompson, January 1, 1857, National Archives, Record Group 15A, file 24097, copy obtained at the Brooke County Library), Eli Boring was "Gass's nighest neighbor."

71. Bobbinette or bobbinet is a machine-made net usually of hexagonal shape made of cotton or silk and used to trim curtains or dresses. *Webster's Third New International Dictionary.*

1829		By bal brot over	8.89 1/2	
Decr	22	To Cash		1.00
		" 1/2# tobacco		.06 1/4
	24	To 2# Coffee 40 2# Sugar 25 Mrs Bowls		.65
		" Cash		.50
	26	" 1 pr Ladies gloves		.25
	29	" Cash		.50
1830		" 1 fine comb		.12 1/2
Jany	1	" Cash		.50
	6	" Tobacco		.06 1/4
	"	" 2# Coffee		.40
	8	" Cash		2.00
	"	" 6 1/2# Cheese Mrs Bowls		.52
	16	" Cash		.50
	25	" Do 50 Tobacco 6		.56
	27	" Goods for Eli Boring[70]		1.55
	28	" 4# tea 31 1/4 1# Coffee for Bowls		.51 1/4
	"	" Cash		.25
Feby	5	" Good for Bowls per Order		3.00
	13	" Tobacco		.05
	22	" 1 yd Bobbinett[71] for Miss Bowls		1.50
March	1	" 5# Cotton yarn for do		1.62 1/2
	"	" 1# Coffee do		.20
	"	" 1/2 Gall. Molasses do		.31 1/4
	4	" Cash		5.00
	"	" do McClunys a/c		1.00
	17	" Cash		.50
	19	" Goods Miss Bowls		1.00
	22	" Cash per Self		.25
				$24.39

72. Meslin or maslin is a mixture of rye and other grains.

73. Here begins another's handwriting, feminine and interspersed throughout the text from this notation through 1837, when Gass abandoned keeping the record. All evidence points to it being the handwriting of Maria Hamilton, in whose father's boarding house Gass was living by the time of this notation and whom he married on March 31, 1831. After the marriage, their handwritings interspersed regularly, sometimes on the same day, such as May 7, 1831; June 25, 1831; January 7, 1832; March 5, 1832; March 10, 1832; November 10, 1832; May 4, 1833; June 15, 1833; January 24, 1834; and November 13, 1834.

74. J. H. stands for John Hamilton. See note 54 above.

75. Linen is a fabric made of woven flax.

76. An assumpset or assumpsit is a promise taken on oneself to pay another.

1830	To amt Brought up	24.39
March 22	" Coffee 20 Sugar 25 for Bowls	.45
24	" Cash	.50
29	" do	1.00
	" do	.25

April

7	" Coffee 20 Sugar for Bowls	.44
"	" 1/4 Tea for do	.31 1/4
"	" Cash for Self	.25
9	" Cash	1.00
13	" 17 3/4# Mestling[72] @ 7 Bowls	1.25
"	" 1# Sugar do	.12 1/2
"	" 1# Coffee do	.12 1/2
"	" 7 yds Muslin @ 12 1/2	.94 [sic]
"	" Cash	1.00
20	" 1# Tobacco	.12 1/2
"	" Cash	1.00
27	" 15 2/4# Bacon for Hamilton[73]	1.16
"	" 1 Qt molasses for Bowls	.12 1/2
"	" Cash 3.00 why 12 1/2	3.12 1/2
March 7	" 1/2 gallon Molasses per order	.31 1/4
13	" 26# Bacon @ 6 1/4 1 pt why for J H[74] 6 1/4	1.68 3/4
May 18	" 4 yd Linnen[75] @ 25	1.00
"	" Camphor & Thread	.12 1/2
"	" Cashe	.50
24	" order p^d Bearer March	.75
June 1	" 2 Mackerall @ 6 1/4	.12 1/2
"	Cashe	1.00
3	"assumiset [assumpsit][76] of Mrs Bowls @	1.06 1/4
		$44.13

[17]

77. This constitutes the last of twenty-three purchases Gass made for "Bowles," "Mrs. Bowles" and "Miss Bowles." See note 51 above. Maria Hamilton had been writing in Gass's journal for about six weeks.

78. Sweet oil could refer to any mild, edible oil.

79. This entry looks like "Gassage," but there are no references to such a name, whereas Gossage appears as a local name. Perhaps this referred to either William or Samuel Gossage. In 1833, William Gossage was paid $1.50 as a bounty for a fox scalp. (*Brooke Republican,* June 5, 1833) In 1851, Samuel Gossage received $4.30 and $2 as part of the list of approved expenditures by the trustees of the town of Wellsburg. (*Wellsburg Weekly Herald,* January 24, 1851) S. Gossage was delinquent in his taxes in 1851. *Wellsburg Weekly Herald,* January 21, 1853.

80. Bounce was a cordial, usually flavored with fruit juices, or it also could be a mixture of two parts beer and one part wine. *Dictionary of American English.*

81. A flask on display at Fort Canby, Washington, is reputed to be the one Patrick Gass had on the Lewis and Clark expedition. It seems unlikely that army personnel would have been allowed to carry individual flasks for liquor on the voyage. The decrease of the community liquor supply is noted in the journals, as are specific times that the captains rewarded the men with a dram or a gill of liquor. Patrick Gass's account book reflects the purchase of four flasks, including this one; he also bought flasks on June 10, 1829, July 29, 1829, and September 17, 1832. In any case, we can guess that Gass lost or gave away flasks, combs, jew's-harps, and handkerchiefs.

1830		To Amt Brot over	44.13
June	3	" 1# Tobacco	.12 1/2
	"	" 1/2# Raisins @ 25	.12 1/2
	4	" goods p^d Mrs Bowls[77]	2.00
	5	" 22 3/4# Bacon @ 6 1/4	1.42 1/2
	"	" 26# flour @ 1 3/4^c	.45 1/2
			48.26
	14	" Cash	.50
	19	" Tea	.12 1/2
	"	" 1# Sugar	.12 1/2
	"	" 2 Mackrell	.12 1/2
	"	" W D Wilson	3.25
	"	" Cash	.50
	24	" do	.50
July	5	" do 50^c Bacon 63	1.13
"	20	" do 25^c Sweet oil[78]12 1/2	.37 1/2
"	25	" 15 3/4# Bacon @ 7^c	1.10 1/4
	"	" 1 Qt Whiskey	.12 1/2
	31	" 1 pt do 6 1/4 1/2 dz herron [sic] 12 1/2	.18 3/4
		" Cash 50^c tobacco 9	.59
Augt	5	" 1 Gal whiskey for Hambleton	.31 1/4
"	9	" Mdse for G[o]ssage[79]	1.00
	13	" Cash	.50
	16	" 10 1/2 Bacon 73 1/2^c Bounce[80] 6 1/4^c	.80
	21	" Cash for self	.50
		" Flask[81] & whiskey	.18 1/2
	25	" Cash	.25
		" Postage on pension	.50
			$60.95

[18]

82. J & D Brown advertised in the *Brooke Republican* of January 4, 1834, as a retailer of scores of items in the categories of dry goods, hardware and cutlery, groceries, queensware, and drugs and dyestuffs. (Other advertisement entries appear in the *Brooke Republican,* July 9, 1835; *Western Transcript,* September 17 and December 17, 1835, August 25, 1836; *Wellsburg Weekly Herald,* August 26, 1847.) J. D. Brown Jr. (James D. Brown, proprietor) and J. & D. Brown Jrs. each placed ads on October 7, 1848 in the *Wellsburg Herald,* the first for flour and the second for "cloths" (fabric). Gass here paid off the balance on his charge account.

83. The sheriff served as tax collector in the early and middle nineteenth century in this area. Gass's payment could well have been for taxes.

84. Valentine Mendel was a soldier in the First Virginia Regiment, mustered from Brooke County and commanded by John H. Elson in the War of 1812. Thus he would have been Gass's contemporary. (Lewis, *Soldiery,* 181). In 1835, a 100-acre parcel of land owned by Valentine and George Mendel was sold in satisfaction of a trust deed. They had inherited this land, possibly prior to 1831, from Valentine Mendel Sr. (*Brooke Republican,* June 4, 1835).

The same day, an ad for wool was placed in the newspaper by Mendel and Gist, "The highest price in cash will be given for clean wool, washed on the sheep's back." Eliza Mendel owned a millinery shop in Wellsburg in 1851, offering all kinds of bonnets and repairing old ones "done in the best and most fashionable style" (*Wellsburg Weekly Herald,* October 17, 1851). H. J. Mendel was assessed for $8.26 in 1845 (*Wellsburg Herald,* September 1, 1865).

85. "Y. H." tea refers to young hyson tea, listed among produce available in Wellsburg at the time (*Brooke Republican,* September 17, 1835). It sold at $1.26 per pound, making it more expensive than Imperial tea (*Wellsburg Herald,* May 18, 1847). Lewis and Company, in *Tea and Tea Blending* (London, 1887) described young hyson as a green tea with "young to medium leaf made in Congou fashion; the finest and closest make is known as 'Gomee.'"

1830	To amt brot up			60.95
Augt	By Bal bro^t forward	}		
	the bal for acc^t 22 Dec	}	8.89 1/2	
	" his pension to the 4	}		
	March last	}	48.00	
			$56.89 1/2	
	To bal due for J & D Brown[82]			4.05 1/2
Sept 6	" Cash for Sheriff[83]			10.50
" 9	" order on V. Mendal[84]			9.00
Augt 31	" *13# Bacon per Self 7^c*			*.91*
" "	" *Cash*			*.25*
Sept 4	" *Ditto*			*.50*
6	" *Headrap Hdkf*			*.25*
" 11	" *Tobacco*			*.25*
22	" *Cash*			*1.00*
25	" *1/4# Y. H. Tea*[85]			*.31 2/4*
	" *13 3/4# Bacon @ 7*			*1.01*
[Oct] 2	" *Cash*			*.50*
4	" *7 yds Muslin 12 1/2 Buttons 3*			*.90*
7	" *1 gal Salt p. Hambleton*			*.12 2/4*
	" *Cash*			*1.50*
16	" *order p^d Hambleton*			*1.25*
22	" *1 pr Socks 25 Coffee 12 1/2*			*.37 1/2*
	" *why 6 1/4 Tobacco 6 1/4*			*.12 1/2*
	" *1 Almanack*			*.12 1/2*
30	" *Cash*			*.50*
	Amt C^d over			*$33.44*

[19]

86. This ended the spate of drinking preceding Gass's wedding. For the next two months, immediately leading up to the event, he bought no liquor. The day after the wedding, on April 1, he bought three pints, perhaps to celebrate with friends.

Acct C^d Over			*$33.44*
Nov	*2*	*3 Mackerall*	*.12 1/2*
	"	*assumst [sic] of Mariah*	*.75*
	12	*p^d Capt McCluny*	*1.00*
	20	*Cash 150 Tobacco 12 1/2*	*1.62 1/2*
Decr	*12*	*1/4# Pepper*	*.06 1/4*
	17	*Cash*	*2.00*
	22	*1 Qt Why*	*.12 1/2*
	24	*Cash*	*.75*
1831			
Jany	*1*	*1 Qt Why*	*.12 1/2*
	5	*1 " Do Tobacco 6 1/4*	*.18 3/4*
	8	*2 Balls blue Bass*	*.06 1/4*
	13	*1 Qt Why*	*.12 1/2*
		Cash to buy Thread	*.06 1/4*
	19	*1 Qt Why 12 1/2 Coffee 6 1/4.*	*.18 3/4*
	26	*1 Qt Why 12 1/2 Tobacco 12 1/2*	*.25*
Feby	*1*	*1 " Whiskey*[86]	*.12 1/2*
	8	*1 " Do 12 1/2 1 gal Salt 12 1/2*	*.25*
	15	*1 " Do 12 1/2 Coffee 12 1/2*	*.25*
	21	*1 " Do 12 1/2 Cash 12 1/2*	*.25*
	26	*1 " Do 12 1/2 Needles 03*	*.15 1/2*
March	*1*	*Cash*	*.25*
	3	*Ditto*	*.50*
	4	*p^d ~~Capt McCluney~~*	*~~1.00~~*
		Amt C^d up	*$42.66*

87. An ax helve is its handle. When a handle breaks, a new one can be fitted upon the ax head.

88. From the November 16 entry through the December entry on his pension, Maria inserted purchases made during the end of 1830 after she had already begun recording 1831.

89. On March 31, 1831, Maria Hamilton and Patrick Gass married (Gass family Bible). The purchases of a fur hat, new suspenders, casinett for new trousers, and a skein of silk, and the receipt of $5 cash prepared Patrick Gass, age fifty-nine, for his nuptials with the sixteen-year-old Maria Hamilton (see note 24 in Book I of this volume for more on Maria's age). J. G. Jacob wrote that the couple moved to a house Gass rented "from a certain Crickett, who resided on the Crawford farm, in the vicinity of Wellsburg." *Life and Times of Patrick Gass,* 178.

90. Pasteboard refers to a stiff, firm material made by compressing and rolling sheets of paper or pulp. *Dictionary of American English.* Maria might have used this to fashion a bonnet or small home decoration to be covered by fabric.

Amt Brot up			*$42.66*
[1830]			
Nov	16	*To Cash 25 cheese 25 omitted*	*.50*
	25	*" 5 3/4# Bacon @ 7 Do*	*.41*
		" Cash 50 1 pt why 6 1/4	*.56 1/4*
Decr	3	*" Cash*	*.12 1/2*
	11	*" Cash 50 Axe Helve* 87 *12 1/2*	*.62 1/2*
			$44.88 1/2
		" Postage	*.50*
			$45.38 1/2
		By his pension to 4th March 1831	*48.00*
		$48.00	
		*To Cash in full*88	*2.61 1/2*
			$48.00
1831			
March	11	To 1 Fur Hat	2.50
		" 2 1/2 yds Casinett	2.50
		" 1 pr Suspenders	.25
		" 1 Skein Silk	.06 1/4
		" Cash89	5.00
April	1	" 3 pts whiskey	.18 3/4
		" 7# flour @ 2c	.14
"	7	" 1 Sett knifes & forks	1.00
		" 1 " teaspoons 25c 3 spoons 18 3/4 c	.44
		" 2 " plates 40c 1 oven 1.10	1.50
		" 1 yd callico	.20
		" 1 wire & past[e] board90	.06 1/4
		" 1 Gal Salt 12 1/2c tobacco 6 1/2	.18 3/4
		" 1# Sugar 12 1/2c 1# Coffee 16	.28 1/2
		" Cash 100c	1.00
"	9	" 1 Spade 87 1/2 1 Qt whiskey 12 1/2	1.00
		" 1 hand saw file	.12 1/2
			16.44

[21]

91. Dowlass was a kind of coarse linen cloth. *Dictionary of American English*.

92. Here "Miss Hambleton," who became "Maria" in the account book, now became "wife." This evolution clearly reflects the changing relationship to the book's author, providing firm internal ground for the conclusion that the book's author is Patrick Gass.

93. This chocolate is the first of several subsequent purchases of candy, so one could easily conjecture that Maria had a sweet tooth, since Gass in several years had not bought candy. (See also account book pages 25, 29, 36, and 49 for candy purchases.)

1831		To amt brot over		16.44
Apl	14	" 1 Pitcher		.31 1/4
	19	" Cash		2.00
	"	" 1 Pt why		.06 1/4
	23	" 1 " do		.06 1/4
	"	" 1 Bag [salt?] 56 1/2^c		.56
	"	" 1 1/4 yd Muslin 12		.16
	"	" 1# Coffee		.16 1/2
	25	" 2 1/2 yds Dowlass[91] 22		.55
	"	" 1 Pt why		.06 1/4
	"	" 1 Dressing combs		.12 1/2
	27	" 1# Sugar		.12 1/2
		" 1/4 yd Muslin per Wife[92]		.03
	30	" 1 Pt why		.06 1/4
	"	" Cash		.12
	"	" 1/2# Tobacco 12 1/2		.06
May	1	" 19 3/4# Bacon @ 7^c 1 pt whiskey 6 1/4^c		1.45
	4	" *1 yd Flannell Ch^d to Hambleton*		*.33*
	7	" *Dry apples 12 1/2 Why 6 1/4*		*.18 1/2*
		" 1/4# pepper		.06 1/4
"	14	" 1 Inkstand 6 1/4 whiskey 6 "	12 1/2	
		" 1/2# Chocolate[93]	12 1/2	.25
"	16	" Cash for himSelf		.50
	19	" 1 pt why		.06
	"	" order p^d Jas Bell		<u>2.43</u>
		Carried forward		26.16

[22]

94. Samuel L. Marks, a prominent citizen of Wellsburg, appears three times in Gass's account book. President of the Board of Overseers of the Poor in 1850, Marks kept John Hamilton in 1855 (*Wellsburg Weekly Herald,* June 7, 1850, April 27, 1855) Marks was justice of the peace in Brooke County by 1851 (*Wellsburg Weekly Herald,* May 28, 1852), and in that capacity he composed and signed Gass's impressive petition to the government for enhanced support the same year, swearing to a falsehood about Gass's loss of an eye at Lundy's Lane (see note 16 above). Marks became sheriff in February 1852. (*Wellsburg Weekly Herald,* March 12, 1852) Samuel Marks maintained a cabinet shop in Wellsburg. (*Wellsburg Herald,* August 9, 1850) He was elected mayor in 1856 as a member of the American Party, following adoption of a new town charter. (*Wellsburg Weekly Herald,* April 11, 1856) Marks had been married to Caroline T. Marks, who died in 1857. (*Wellsburg Herald,* January 30, 1857). Their son Theodore F. died September 19, 1851, age seven (*Wellsburg Weekly Herald,* September 26, 1851) Their daughter Mary Louisa died of consumption at age thirty on January 23, 1857. (*Wellsburg Herald,* January 30, 1857) In May of that year, their eight-year-old son broke his thigh and dislocated his hip while playing on the courthouse steps. (*Wellsburg Herald,* May 3, 1857) In February of 1860, S. Marks was chastised for selling a slave as "a vicious member of the community." (*Wellsburg Herald,* February 17, 1860) Marks died of consumption in 1865 and was buried with Masonic honors. A prominent newspaper editorial described him then as "widely known and highly respected." *Wellsburg Herald,* December 8, 1865.

95. Madras refers to goods imported from Madras, India, usually made of a cotton and silk blend, and checkered or plaid in design. Florence M. Montgomery, *Textiles in America 1650–1870* (New York: W. W. Norton & Company, 1984), 287.

1831		Amt Brought forward	26.16
May 23		To 1 1/2# Coffee	.25
"	"	" 1 Qt Molasses	.12 1/2
"	"	" 1 Pt why	.06
"	"	" Cash	.50
"	26	" 1/2# Salts 12 1/2 1/2# Candles /12 [1/2]	.18 3/4
	31	" *1 pr Shoes*	*1.81 1/4*
		" *6 yd Stress^d Cotton 18 1/4*	*1.12 1/2*
		" *1/2 " Muslin*	*.06 1/4*
		" *Bass 03 Camphor 6 1/4*	*.09*
		" *1 Straw Hat*	*.25*
	"	To 1/2# Tobacco	.06 1/4
June 4		"1 pt whiskey 6 1/4 }	
		" 1 ax halve [sic] 12 1/2 }	.18 3/4
		" Cash	.50
	11	" *Do*	*1.00*
		" *1 Qt Whisky*	*.12 1/2*
	14	" *1# Sugar*	*.10*
	"	" *a/ct of S L Marks*[94]	*2.50*
	25	" 1 1/2# Coffee	.25
	"	" 1/4# Raizins 25	.06
	"	" Cash in Change	1.00
	"	" 1/2# Tobac[c]o	.06 1/4
	"	" *1 Madrass Hdkf*[95]	*.25*
	30	" *Bal on goods p[er] Wife*	*.27 1/2*
	"	" *Sallad [sic] Dish*	*.22 1/2*
"	9	" *Order p^d Hambleton*	*.50*
"	30	" Cash for <u>Rice</u>	2.00
July 1		" 1/2 [doz] Herrings	.12 1/2
	"	" Cash	<u>.50</u>
		add for error 9[c]	40.35[sic]

[23]

		Amt Bot over		*40.44*
1831				
July	16	*To 1 1/4# Sugar*		*.12 1/2*
"	23	" 1/4 Tea 6 1/4 why @ 6 1/4		.12 1/2
April	28	a/ct for Capt. McCluney		1.00
"	"	" postage of pension		.50
				42.19
July	23	" Cash		1.00
				43.19
		By pension to the}		
		4th March last }	48.00	
July	26	To 2 Measurs Salt		.12 1/2
Augt	1	" *Order p^d Hambleton*		.37 1/2
	18	" *Cash*		.50
	"	" *1 Coffee Bag*		.18 3/4
	"	" *3# Choccolate*		.12 1/2
	"	" *1 1/4# Sugar*		.12 1/2
	20	" Cash		1.00
	"	" 2# Shad 18th @ 10		.20
				45.82 1/2
Sept	5	" Cash		2.17 1/2
	"	[A?] By Pention [pension]		48.00
		due the 4th March	$48.00	" "
"	15	To 7 yd Muslin @ 12 1/2^c		.87 1/2
		" 6 Shirt Buttons		.06 1/4
		" 4 Mackerel		.25
		" 1 pr Shears		.25
		" 1/2# tobacco		.06 1/4
Sep^t	17	" 1 Basket 25^c Cash 50^c		.75
		" 1# Candles		.12 1/2c
	24	" 1 1/2 yd linnen		.33
				2.71

[24]

96. Ticking describes a strong, firm fabric made of cotton or linen, usually striped and used for upholstery or covering pillows or mattresses *Webster's Third New International Dictionary*.

97. A "cut of thread" is a unit indicating yarn size based on the number of fixed length hands per pound. A cut, hank, or spool depends on the thread's diameter or thickness. Therefore, thread could be 12-, 16-, 20-, or 24-cuts (hanks, or spools) to the pound.

1831	To amt brot up	2.71
Sept 29	" 1 Gal Salt 12 1/2 1 Seive 56 1/2	.69
Oct 5	" 5# Bacon 7	.35
	" Cash	1.00
	" Liquorice Ball	.06 1/4
	" 1/2 oz Camphor	.06 1/4
7	" Cash	1.50
15	" 1/2# Tobacco	.06 1/4
24	" 9 yds Ticking⁹⁶ 33 1/3	3.00
	1 Cut Thread⁹⁷	.06 1/4
"	Cash	2.00
	1 Almanack	.12 1/2
Novʳ 5	To 2 Macrell	.18 1/2
"	" 1# Sugar	.10
"	" 1/8# Tea 1.25	.15
"	" 1/2# Tobacco 12 1/2	.06 1/4
12	" 1 Candle Stick	.15 1/4
21	" Cash	1.25
"	" Coffee 25 Candles 12 1/2	.37 1/2
"	" 2 1/2 yds Flannell 50	1.25
	" 1 pr Socks	.37 1/2
25	" 4 1/4 yds Flannell 62 1/2	2.65
	" Thread	.06 1/4
	" 1 Butcher Knife	.18 1/2
	Amt over	$18.39

[25]

98. Martha Burt was born November 24, 1788, in Brooke County. She married William Burt of December 4, 1806, and moved to Wellsburg in 1817. She died October 2, 1851 (*Wellsburg Weekly Herald,* October 17, 1851). Her age makes it likely she is the one here mentioned. Martha and William's son, William E., married Laura A. and had a daughter named for his wife. The infant died at a year and nine days of "hooping cough." (*Wellsburg Weekly Herald,* December 20, 1850) After his wife also died, William E. married Anna E. Howe of St. Louis, Missouri. *Wellsburg Weekly Herald,* January 24, 1856.

1831		Amt Brot over	18.39
Dec	2	To Cash 25 1 1/4 Sugar 12 1/2	.37 1/2
		" 1 peck Salt	.22 1/2
		" 1/2# Tabacco	.06 1/4
"	5	" Cash 100^c 1/4# pepper 6 1/4^c	1.06 1/4
"	24	" Cash	1.00
	"	" 1 pr Spectacles	.68
	"	" 1 Coffee Mill	.62 1/2
	"	" 1 Cotton Shawl	1.06 1/4
		" 1 " Hkf	.18 3/4
	30	" 1 Jug & why	.37 1/2
	"	" Cash	1.00
1832			
Jany	7	" 2 1/2# Sugar 10	.25
	"	" 1 1/2# Coffee	.25
	"	" 2/3# Tobacco 18 3/4	.12 1/2
		" order p^d Mrs Burt[98]	3.50
			29.19
		" order p^d Whittake omitted	1.15
		" postage & Clerk's fees p^d W^m McCluney	2.31
		1 Molasses Bbl omitted	.25
		Cash	1.00
			$33.90

[26]

99. "Sackinet" probably is Maria's spelling for sarcenet.

100. Bed cord is a stout cord passing from side to side of a bed frame to support the mattress. *Dictionary of American English.*

1832	*Amt Brot over*			*$33.90*
Jany 14	*To 1 1/2 Calico 30*	*45*		
	" 1 1/2 Do 18 1/2	*28*		
	" 1/8 Sackinet[99] *@ 62*	*7 1/2*		
	" 2 Caps 16 12 1/2	*28 1/2*		
	" 1 Bass	*06 1/4*		
	" 1 yd Muslin	*20*		
	" 1 " Lace	*18 1/2*		
	" 1 bolt Tape	*06 1/4*		
		1.61		
	" 1 1/3 flannell .56	*.75*		
		2.36		
	By Butter	*.25*	*bal*	*2.11*
	To 1 1/4 flannel	*50*		*.62 1/2*
	" Bass			*.03*
	" 1# Sugar			*.10*
	" 1 Cake Soap			*.12 1/2*
	" Cash			*1.00*
21	*" 1* ℔ [measure] Sparrow Pills			*.12 1/2*
"	*" Cash*			1.00
28	*" 1/2 Gall Molasses*			.25
"	*" 1 1/4# Tobacco*			.15 1/2
Feby 6	*" 2# Coffee*			.33 1/2
	" 2 " Sugar			.20
	" 1 Bed cord[100]			.25
	" Nutmeg			.06
	Continued			*$40.27*

[27]

101. The series of purchases for rum, cinnamon, allspice, and cloves prepared for a celebration of the birth of the Gasses' first child, Elizabeth, on February 24, 1832.

102. Two days after Elizabeth's birth, the Gasses bought a chamber pot, probably so Maria would not have to walk to an outhouse after childbirth.

1831		Amt Brot over	18.39
Dec	2	To Cash 25 1 1/4 Sugar 12 1/2	.37 1/2
		" 1 peck Salt	.22 1/2
		" 1/2# Tabacco	.06 1/4 1832

Amt Continued			40.27
Feby	6	To Cash	1.00
"	17	" 1# Candles 12 1/2 Salt 6 1/4	.18 3/4
		" tobacco	.06 1/4
		" 2 1/2 yd Muslin 14^c	.35
		" 3 1/2 " Callico 14^c	.49
	21	" 1 Bottle rum	.46 1/2
	"	" 1 oz cinnamon	.06 1/4
	"	" Allspice	.06 1/4
	"	" Cloves	.03
	"	" Cash[101]	.25
Feby	26	" 1 Tea Kettle	.87 1/2
		" 1/2 gal whiskey	.18 3/4
		" 1 Chamber[102]	.25
March 5		" Cash	.50
	"	" 1 1/4# Sugar	.12 1/2
			$45.15
	"	" Cash in full	2.85
			$48.00
		By Pension due 4th Sept Last	$48—

103. Perhaps Gass's $6 payment was for tailoring clothes. In 1822, Nathan Reeves took out the following advertisement: "N. L. Reeves, Tailor, Late From Philadelphia, Tenders his services to the inhabitants of Wellsburgh [*sic*], & its vicinity.— From his long experience in the above business, he hopes to be able to render general satisfaction to all who may please to favor him with their custom; on reasonable terms." In the same newspaper, Nathan Reeves was bonded for $31.56 by the collector of the revenue. (*Wellsburgh Gazette,* July 20, 1822). Nathan Reeves's name appeared often during the 1850s in public matters. In the town hall on February 22, 1851, he chaired a meeting of the Democratic Party. (*Wellsburg Weekly Herald,* February 28, 1851) His son Samuel died at age eighteen on August 4, 1861 (*Wellsburg Herald,* August 23, 1861) Reeves himself died on January 13, 1862, at age sixty-six, after a lingering illness. *Wellsburg Herald,* January 17, 1862.

1832	Continued from last page	
March 10	To 1 1/3# Coffee 18 3/4	.25
"	" 1 1/4 do 10	.12 1/2
"	" 1/2# Tobacco 12	.06
"	" *1 Vest Pattern*	*.62 1/2*
13	" *1/8 YH Tea 16 1 Tea Pot 31 1/4*	*.47 1/4*
17	" *1# Candles*	*.12 1/2*
	" *Cash*	*.25*
30	" order on Nathan Reeves[103]	6.00
"	" Cash	3.00
"	" 2 1/2# Sugar	.25
Apl 7	To 1# Chocalate	.20
	" 1# Tobacco	.12
	" Castor Oil	.06
9	" 1/8# Tea 100	.12 1/2
13	" *6 yd Muslin 12 1/2*	*.75*
	" *4 " Calico @ 18*	*.75*
	" *1# Candles*	*.12 1/2*
	" *1 pr Socks*	*.12 1/2*
21	" *1 Qt Molasses*	*.12 1/2*
28	" *3 Cord*	*.62 1/2*
	" *3/4 Muslin*	*.09*
	" *1 pr Shoes*	*1.62 1/2*
	" *1/8# Tea*	*.12 1/2*
	" *1/2# Tobacco*	*.06*
	Carried over	16.17

[29]

104. Pink root, used as a vermifuge to eradicate worms, came from the root of an herb of the genus *Spigelia. Dictionary of American English.* During this period, pink root appeared among advertisements for "drugs, medicines, paints & stuffs." *Wheeling Gazette,* May 14, 1825.

105. Buckram was a fabric of fine linen or cotton used in millinery and bookbinding. (*Webster's Ninth New Collegiate Dictionary.* Used with padding, muslin, and buttons, next on the account list, Maria could have ingeniously fashioned a mattress and bed for their baby.

106. Rosin or rozin is the resin or solid substance remaining when crude turpentine is distilled. An export of North Carolina, rosin could be used as a sealer. *Dictionary of American English.* In 1847, rosin sold in Wellsburg for $3.50/bbl. Used in a bar for soap, rosin sold six for 8¢. *Wellsburg Weekly Herald,* May 18, 1847.

107. "Batts" probably batting, describes layers of raw cotton or wool, used for lining quilts. *Webster's Third New International Dictionary.*

108. Jackson whiskey traces its name to the era of President Andrew Jackson's popular military leadership. Jackson was president from 1829 to 1837. *Dictionary of American English.* Gass bought this quart on his sixty-first birthday.

1832		Brot over		$16.17
May	1	To Pink root[104]		.12 1/2
	"	" Calomel		.06 1/4
	4	" *2 yds Cloth 375*	*7.50*	
		" *3/4 " Buckram*[105]	*.18 3/4*	
		" *1/2 " Padding*	*.25*	
		" *1 1/4 " Muslin*	*.18 3/4*	
		" *16 Buttons*	*.50*	
		Silk	*.258*	*.87 1/2*
		" *1 gal Salt*		*.12 1/2*
		" *1/2# Tobacco*		*.06 1/4*
		" *1 1/4 Sugar*		*.12 1/2*
	22	" *2# Havana Sugar*		*.30*
		" *1" best Coffee*		*.18 3/4*
		" *1" Rozin*[106]		*.06 1/4*
		" *Cash*		*1.00*
June	5	" *2# Batts* [107] *37 1/2 Thread 12 1/2*		*.50*
		" *1 Mug 8 Ribbon 3*		*·.11*
		" *1# Tobacco 12 1/2 Tea 12 1/2*		*.25*
		" *Cash*		*1.00*
	12	" *ps Tape*		*.06 1/4*
		" *1# H. Sugar*		*.15*
		" *1 Qt Jackson whiskey*[108]		*.12 1/2*
				29.30

[30]

109. Maria referred to herself as "wife," whereas Gass usually referred to himself as "Self" or "himSelf."

110. "Cash paid your brother" is in Gass's handwriting; the personal reference points to his authorship as well. In 1830, the Brooke County census listed three Hamilton brothers. This one remains unidentified.

111. Check linen is linen fabric of a checkered design.

112. Perhaps Mrs. Smith is the wife of Dr. Edward Smith. See note 143 below.

		Brot ove——	*29.30*
June 12		*To pr Combs p/ Wife*[109]	*.06 1/4*
		" *1/4# Raisens*	*.06 1/4*
"	16	" Cash p^d your brother[110]	3.00
"	23	" 1 1/2# Coffee	.25
		" Penknife	.12 1/2
		" 1 whet Stone	.12 1/2
	26	" *1/8# Tea*	*.12 1/2*
		" *1# Sugar*	*.15*
		" *1 yd Check Linen*[111]	*.28*
		1/2 " Calico 23	*.11 1/2*
			33.60
		" *Cash*	*4.00*
	30	" Salt 12 1/2 Cheese 15	.27 1/2
July 10		" *a/ct. of Timons*	*5.06*
		" *order p^d Mrs Smith*[112]	*.50*
		" *2 # Sugar 15*	*.30*
		" *1 " Tobacco*	*.12 1/2*
		" *1/8" Ginger*	*.03*
		" *1/2 Dz Herring 25*	*.12 1/2*
	18	" *1# Rice p/wife*	*.06 1/4*
		" *1 Qt Molasses*	*.12 1/2*
		" *Pins*	*.03*
	23	" *order p^d Hambleton*	*.75*
		" *1/2 gal Why*	*.18 3/4*
		Over	*$45.17*

[31]

113. Adam Kuhn appears to be the primary legal advisor of Brooke County, his name appearing as "clerk: in civil actions from the 1830s through the 1850s. He served as commissioner to the Wellsburg Female Seminary in 1851, along with Joseph Applegate, Perry Plattenburg, A. P. Wheeler, and others. (*Wellsburg Weekly Herald,* May 9, 1851) His views on congressional reform while a candidate for a seat in the convention to reform the constitution of Virginia are stated at length in the newspaper. (*Wellsburg Weekly Herald,* June 16 and 21, 1850) In 1851, Kuhn was elected president of the board of trustees of the "N.W. Bank of Virginia." (*Wellsburg Weekly Herald,* January 24, 1851) After the death of his first wife, Priscilla, of consumption on May 27, 1850 (*Wellsburg Weekly Herald,* January 24, 1851), Adam Kuhn married Miss Julia Gant of Wellsburg on February 2, 1854 (*Wellsburg Weekly Herald,* February 3, 1854). His twenty-two-year-old daughter died in April of the same year. (*Wellsburg Weekly Herald,* April 7, 1854) Mrs. Kuhn headed the list of ladies thanked for generous donations of blankets for Union soldiers in 1861. *Wellsburg Herald,* June 21, 1861.

1832	Amt brougt over		$45.17
July 24	*To Mackeral*		*.12 1/2*
31	" 1 1/2# Coffee		.25
Augt 7	*" 3/4 yd Blk [black] Muslin 20*		*.15*
	" 1 Skein Silk		*.06 1/4*
	" 1# Sugar		*.10*
" 10	" 1 1/2# Coffee 25 Tea 15ᶜ		.40
	" 1# tobacco		.12 1/2
	" Cash		.25
			46.64
	To postage on pension }		
	it being returned }		2.25
	To Wm MᶜCluney		1.00
			49.89
	By his pension to		
	the 4ᵗʰ March last	48.00	
		Balance	$1.89
	To Cash for Mr Kuhn omitted[113]		.25
			$2.14
17	Cash		.25
27	*Salt*		*.06 1/4*
	1# Sugar		*.10*
	Cash		*.12 1/2*
Sepᵗ 4	Do for Kuhn		.25
11	1 Measure Salt		.06
	1# Best Sugar		.10
"	Cash for Letter	JnH[John Hamilton]	.25
			3.34

[32]

114. Lensa or linsey is a fabric of wool or linen and cotton. Linseys "striped and plain" were advertised for sale by J. & D. Brown in 1835. *Brooke Republican,* September 17, 1835.

115. Spider and lid refers to an iron frying pan or skillet, sometimes with long legs on which it stands. *Dictionary of American English.*

Sept		Amt Brought up	3.34
	11	[entries crossed out and illegible]	
	17	[To] Flask 10 Why 6 1/4	.16 1/4
	22	" *3 1/2 yd Flannell 62 1/2*	*2.18 3/4*
		" *1 1/2# Coffee*	*.25*
		" *1/8" Tea*	*.15 1/2*
		" *1 pt Why*	*.06 1/4*
		" *Cash*	*.50*
	25	" Pt Gin	.06 1/4
	"	" 1# Candles	.12 1/2
	"	" 1/2 yd flannel	.31 1/2
	29	" *15# Bacon @ 7ᶜ*	*1.05*
		" *1" Tobacco*	*.12 1/2*
		" *1 pt Whiskey*	*.06 1/4*
		" *Cash*	*.50*
Oct	1	" 1 Pt why	.06 1/4
	"	" 1 1/4# Sugar 10	.12 1/2
	6	" 1 M[easure] Salt 6 1/4 1 pt why 6 1/4	.12 1/2
	8	" 1 pt why	.06 1/4
	"	" 2 1/2 yd. Brown Lincy [linsey][114]	.94
	13	" 1 Pt why	.06 1/4
	"	" Cash	.50
	20	" 1 Pt why	.06 1/4
	25	" Sugar & Coffee	.37 1/2
	"	" Gin 6 1/4 Tea 18 1/2	.25
	"	" 6 yds Muslin	.75
	"	" 1 Spider & Lid[115]	.62 1/2
	31	" 1 1/4# Sugar @ 10	.12 1/2
		" 1# tobacco 12 1/2ᶜ Gin 6 1/4ᶜ	<u>.18 3/4</u>
			13.15 1/2

[33]

116. Cambric is a thin, closely woven plain white linen fabric. *Webster's Third New International Dictionary.*

117. Book was a fine kind of muslin so called because of the book-like manner in which it was folded. *Dictionary of American English.*

118. The last three expenditures were probably made in preparation to bury their baby, Elizabeth, who died November 7, 1832, age eight months and eleven days. Patrick Gass's heavier drinking pattern in October must relate to the baby's illness.

119. Matthias Ebberts joined Patrick Gass as one of the old soldiers of the war of 1812 who gathered on Christmas Day of 1854 to elect delegates to attend the national convention of soldiers to be held at Washington, D.C., on January 8, 1855. Patrick Gass, Major John Miller, Ellis C. Jones, and William Tarr were elected. President Pierce met these delegates at the White House. Jacob, *Life and Times,* 185–87.

In March 1851, Ebberts received $2 for services from the Overseers of the Poor of Brooke County. (*Wellsburg Weekly Herald,* April 25, 1851) An old and respected citizen of Wellsburg, he died on January 9, 1856. (*Wellsburg Weekly Herald,* January 18, 1856) A year later, his heirs were selling his lot and house in Wellsburg: "a good, substantial and comfortable Frame Dwelling, 1 1/2 stories high, smoke house, stable, and a number of choice bearing fruit trees. *Wellsburg Herald,* January 9, 1857.

120. An auger is a tool for boring holes in wood. It has a handle for turning and a spiral channel; at its end is a tapered screw with cutting lips. *Webster's Third New International Dictionary.*

121. Although no mention of L. Timmons appears in contemporary newspapers, a large family of this name headed by Ephram Timmons, age thirty-three (possibly the son of L. Timmons), was listed in the 1860 census.

1832		To amt brot over		13.15 1/2
Nov	3	To Cash		1.00
"	10	" 1 1/2# Coffee		.25
		" *1* " *Candles*		.12 1/2
"	8	" 1 1/2 yd Cambrick[116]	.66	
		" 1/4 " Book[117]	.12 1/2	
		" 1 " Blk crape	.50	
		" 1 pr worsted hose	.50	
		" 2 Blk silk hdkf[118]	1.62 1/2	
		" 1 ps tape	<u>.03</u>	3.44
"	20	" a/ct for M Eberts[119]		1.50
		" do for S L Marks		1.25
		" 1 measure Salt	6 1/4	
		" 1/4# Sugar	12 1/2	
		" 1 " Candles	<u>12 1/2</u>	.31 1/4
"	27	" 1 peck Salt 18 3/4^c pepper 6 1/4^c		.25
		" 1# tobacco		.12 1/2
		" Cash		8.00
	28	" *p^d Marks*		.50
	29	" order p^d Hambleton		.56
Dec^r	22	" 1 1/4 Brn Sugar @ 10^c		.12 1/2
		" 1 1/2# Candles		.18 3/4
		" 1/2# tobacco 6 1/4^c		.06 1/4
		" 1 pr Shoes		1.31 1/4
		" 2 1/2 yd Muslin @ 12 1/2		.31 1/4
		" 1 pr side combs		.06 1/4
	29	" 9 ft Chain 15		1.35
		" 1 3/4 In. augur[120]		.37 1/2
		" 1 1/4# Sugar		.12 1/2
		" Good for L. Timmons[121]		<u>.41</u>
				34.80

[34]

122. A plowline or ploughline are the reins to guide a plow horse. *Webster's Third New International Dictionary.*

123. A U.S. Spelling Book provided standardized English spelling after 1750 for students and users of the language. Numerous spelling books existed during this era, such as *Cramer's United States Spelling Book,* published at Pittsburgh, and *The United States Spelling Book,* published in Noyes, Pennsylvania.

124. "Bible" probably refers to the Gass family Bible on display at Fort Canby, Washington, published at Philadelphia by McCarty & David, 171 F Street, in 1832. This purchase at the beginning of 1833 accompanied others aimed at self-improvement and industry, perhaps revealing resolutions for the new year.

125. A pegging awl is a pointed tool for making holes into which pegs fit.

126. A shingling hatchet is a small hatchet used for cutting shingles for roofs. *Dictionary of American English.*

127. Imperial tea featured older leaves, made in Gunpowder style or rolled in balls ranging from "Pinhead" to "Pea Leaf" (Lewis and Company, *Tea and Tea Blending,* 79). In 1847 it sold in Wellsburg at 87 1/2¢ per pound.

1833	Amt Continued		34.81
Jany 1	To Bal on Scissors		.12 1/2
"	1 Plow Line[122]		.06
	1 U S Spelling Book[123]		.12 1/2
5	1/2# Tobacco		.06
"	1# Coffee		.18 3/4
11	*3 / 4 Yd Flannell 31 1 / 2*		*.24*
	Scotch Thread		*.06 1 / 4*
	order p^d Mrs Smith		*1.00*
	1 Bible[124]		*.12 1/2*
" 26	1# Sugar 10 1# Coffee 18 3/4		.28 3/4
"	1 pegging all [awl][125]		.03
"	1 Shingling Hatchet[126]		.50
Feby 2	Tobacco 6 1/4^c paper 6 1/4^c		.12 1/2
9	*5 Yds Linen & Cotton Th[read]*		*1.56 1/4*
"	*1# Coffee*		*.18 3/4*
16	*1# Candles*		*.12 1/2*
"	*1 / 2# Tobacco*		*.06*
23	1/8# Imperiall Tea[127]		.18 3/4
"	Cash		1.00
March 4	To 1# Coffee		.18 3/4
	" p^d Postage		*.87 1/2*
			$41.91
	" p^d McCluney	*1.00*	
	" Bal to new a / ct	*5.09*	*6.09*
	By pension up to 4th}		*48.00*
	Sept 1832 }	*48.00*	

[35]

1833

March	*4*	*By Bal due*	*5.09*	
	"	To Cash on a/c		2.00
	"	" 1 p̸ſ [measure] Sparrow Pills		.06 1/4
	18	*" Tobacco*		*.06 1/4*
		" Mackerel		*.10*
	25	" 1 measure [*sic*]		.06 1/4
	31	" 1# Coffee		.18 3/4
		" 3 Mackeril		.15
		" 1 keg		.12 1/2
April	1	*" 2 yd Calico*	*.28*	
		" 1/2# Tobacco	*.06 1/4*	
		" Mint Stick	*.06 1/4*	
		" Pot	*.62 1/2*	*1.03*
		" 1 HKf		.25
	15	" Cash		2.00
	"	" 1# Coffee	18 3/4	
	"	" 1/2# Tobacco	6 1/4	
	"	" Camphor	6 1/4	
	"	" Why 6 1/4 Bot 6 1/4	12 1/2	.44
	"	" 17# Bacon 5		.85
	22	" Cash		1.00
	23	*" 2 Calico 28 1/4 Ribins 6 1/4*		*.34 1/2*
	29	" 5 yd Muslin @ 10		.50
		" 1 measure Salt		.06 1/4
		" Candles		.06 1/4
		" Bass		.06 1/4
		" 1/4# tea		.25
		" 1" Cotton bats		.18 3/4
May	1	" 50# flour @ 1 3/4[c]		.87 1/2

128. A John Lyons was on the *Wellsburg Weekly Herald* list of delinquent titheables dated July 11, 1851.

129. This fascinating entry noted a fine imposed on Patrick Gass for drinking "too much" on Sunday, probably May 26, 1833. Noting the purchase and consumption of spirits throughout this book, one can see he might have been out of practice in 1833 because he had purchased only one pint of whiskey since the end of October. However, he had a few large cash withdrawals in March, April, and May. The fact that he wrote the cause of the expenditure denotes candor and authorship, revealing an upright character in spite of his drinking habit. The 83¢ fine was not subtracted from the running total. The curious amount of this fine for social transgressions seems typical of the era and place. Newton, Nichols, and Sprangle, *History of the Panhandle* (Wheeling, West Virginia: J. A. Caldwell, 1879) 311.

1833		To amt brot up		10.65
May	4	" 2 Mackerel		.10
		" 1/2# tobacco		.06 1/4
		" Cash		1.00
		" *1 3/4 yd Silk*	*1.10*	
		" *3/4 " Sarcinett*	*.28*	
		" *paste Board*	*.06 1/4*	
		" *3 wire*	*.06 1/4*	
		" *3/4 Yd Muslin*	*.09*	
		" *cord 3 Silk 6*	*.09*	
		" *3 Ribbons 12 1/2*	*.37 1/2*	2.06
	12	" 1 1/3# Coffee		.25
	"	" 1/2# Tobacco		.06
	22	" Cash for Lyons[128]		9.00
	"	" *3 Yd Bard [sic] Cotton .25*		.75
		" *1/2 Dz Buttons*		.02
		" *1 Hkf*		.12 1/2
		for Taking too much }		
		grog on Sunday 83 }[129]		" "
	27	To 1# Tobacco		.12 1/2
	"	" 1 Pt why		.06 1/4
	"	" 1/2 yd callico		.06 1/4
	"	" Salt		.06 1/4
June	*3*	" *1 3/4 Yds Calico 12 1/2*		*.21 1/2*
		" *3 mackerel*		*.15*
		" *1 Stran Beads*		*.03*
"	8	" 50 # flour @ 2		1.00
		" 1/4" tea		.25
		" 1 pt Pecons [pecans] May 4		.06 1/4
		" order to Hambleton May 24		1.00
				27.10

[37]

130. Three references to Freemans include Mr. Freeman, Mrs. Freeman (October 1, 1833), and Miss Freeman (November 4, 1835). John Freeman was a soldier in the First Virginia Regiment, mustered from Brooke County, commanded by John H. Elson in the War of 1812. Thus he would have been more or less a contemporary of Gass's. Lewis, *Soldiery,* 181. In the 1820s, Freeman purchased a large number of tools at estate auctions in Wellsburg, so he, like Gass, apparently was a carpenter. Brooke County Courthouse Inventory Book.

131. Magnesia, a white highly infusible oxide of magnesium, used in antacids and as a mild laxative. *Webster's Ninth New Collegiate Dictionary.*

1833			
June 15	To amt brot up		27.10
	" 22# Bacon @ 5		1.10
	" Error in extending entry 15 April		.06 1/4
	" do in addition		<u>.06</u>
			28.32
	" *5 yd Muslin*	*12*	*.60*
	" *3 Mackerel 5^c*		*.15*
	" *3/4# Coffee*		*.12 1/2*
	" Cash for Timmons }		
	March 16th }		11.00
	" Postage & Clerks certificate on Pension		.87 1/2
	" Capt McCluney		<u>1.00</u>
			42.07
	By a/c bal brot forward	$5.09	
	" Pension to 4th March last	<u>48.00</u>	
		<u>53.09</u>	
	Bal	11.02	
"	To 1 1/2# Coffee		.25
	" Cash		1.00
	" Ditto for Stevenson		<u>9.77</u>
		11.02	$ 11.02
" 17	To Bacon for Mr Freeman[130]		.80
	" 1/2 oz magnesia[131]		.06 1/4
" 25	" *1# Tobacco*		*.12 1/2*
	" *1 gal Salt*		*.12 1/2*
July 4	" *5 Calico @ 10*		*.50*
	" *5 Muslin 10*		*.50*
	" *1 1/2 Paper 5*		*.07*
	" *1 1/2 Do*		*.09*
	" *Magnesia*		*.06 1/4*
	" *1 Dish 12 1/2 6 1/4 Crocks*		*<u>.22</u>*
			2.56

[38]

132. "By Butter" appears as the second credit for produce. January 14, 1832, (account book page 27) showed the first. By this time, Patrick and Maria Gass must have owned a milk cow from whose cream Maria made butter to sell.

133. "By cucumbers," another credit for produce sold, shows that the Gasses had a garden ample enough to sell vegetables and exhibited enough enterprise to do so. However, the credit is not extended by subtraction.

134. Sugar was sold in loaves as well as by the pound.

1833		Brought up		2.56
July	4	Allspice & Cinnamon		.06 1/4
"		goods p^d Stephens in	}	
		full of Note	}	2.23
	8	1/2 gal Why		.19
	12	1 pt Do		.06 1/4
		75# Flour @ 2		1.50
	19	Coffee 1 1/2#		.25
	"	1/2# Tobacco		.06 1/4
	"	Why		.06 1/4
	"	1 1/2# Tobacco		.18 3/4
	"	3# Macrell		<u>.15</u>
Augt	7	To Why 6 & Tobacco	12 1/2	
	"	" 1/4# Tea	25	
	"	" Salt	<u>12 1/2</u>	
			50	
	"	By Butter[132]	<u>22 1/2</u>	.27 1/2
	"	To 50# flour		1.00
	"	By cucumbers[133]	<u>6 1/4</u>	" "
July	22	To Why omited	6	
		" 2 oz magnesia	<u>16</u>	.22
"	26	" 1 Qt Bowl	9	
	"	" 1 Comb	<u>19</u>	.28
Augt	*8*	*6 Calico 18 3/4*	*1.12*	
		" 2 1/4 Muslin	*<u>.28</u>*	*1.40*
	13	*" 6 "[1/4] Ditto 12*	*.75*	
		" Cut Thread	*.06 1/4*	
		" 1 Bot Rum	*.25*	
		" Pins	*<u>.03</u>*	*1.09 1/4*
	"	*" 1# Loaf Sugar[134]*		*.18 3/4*
	17	*" 1# Coffee*		*<u>.18 3/4</u>*
				11.96

[39]

135. This is one of several entries in the account book with no monetary significance. "Son born" underscores Gass's authorship.

Original of opposite page: shows nonaccounting entry "Son born" as well as the handwriting of both Patrick and Maria Gass.

Amt Continued				*11.96*
Augt 20	*3 mackerel 5*		*.15*	
	1/2# Tobacco		*.06 1/4*	
	1 pt Brandy		*.12 1/2*	*.34*
" *31*	1 1/3# Coffee			.25
27	Buttons 2^c Cash 25^c			.27
Sept 4	1/2# Tobacco		.06 1/4	
	1/4# Tea		.25	
	Flour for Hambleton		.50	.81 1/4
7	" 1 pt why			.06 1/4
10	Son born[135]			"
11	[To] 3 Macrell			.15
"	" Why 6 1/4 Ginger 6 1/4			.12 1/2
"	" 1 Handf			.12 1/2
17	*" 1/4# Tea*	*25*		
	" Nutmeg	*.03*		
	" Cash	*1.00*		*1.28*
24	*" Flour*	*50*		
	" Tobacco	*06 1/4*		
	" 1/2# nails0	*4 1/2*		*.61*
Oct 1	" 2 measurs Salt			.12 1/2
"	" 1/2# Candles			.06 1/4
"	" 1 qt why			.06 1/4
"	" order for Hambleton			.87 1/2
"	" order for Mrs Freeman			2.81 1/4
3	" Cash			.50
8	" 1 3/4 yds flannel @ 43			.75
"	" 1 1/2# Coffee			.25
"	" Candles			.06 1/4
"	" 1 Pt why			.06 1/4
"	" Cash			.50
10	" 1 Oz Indigo			.12 1/2
	" 1 pt why			.06 1/4
				22.23 1/4

[40]

136. "P nails" means penny nails.

137. Joshua Mendel was probably a son of Valentine Mendel. See note 84 above.

138. Again, we see an entry not related to accounting, "Take care Patric—." One could guess that the frequent purchases of whiskey (see Appendix Z) between his son's birth and this notation has to do with the comment.

1833		Amt Brot up			22.23 1/4
Oct	15	To 5 3/4# Bacon	36		
		" Candles	6 1/4		
		" Tobacco	6 1/4		
		" Why	6 1/4		.55
Oct	*16*	*" 4 3/4 yds Calico*	*@ 12 1/2*		*.59 1/4*
	"	*" 1/2 yd Do @ 25*			*.12 1/2*
	"	*" 2 1/2 yds Casinett*	*@ 87 1/2*		*2.18 3/4*
		" 1 yd Calico			*.18 3/4*
		" 1 Comb			*.12 1/2*
		" 1 Past[e] Board			*.06 1/4*
		" Cash			.06 1/4
	21	" 1 Why 6 1/4 Tea 25			.31 1/4
	26	*" 1 lb candils*			*.12 1/2*
		" 1/2 lb Tobacco			*.06 1/4*
		" 1 pt Whisky			.06 1/4
Nov	1	" 1# P nails[136]			.08
	"	" 1 Qt why			.12 1/2
	"	" 2 1/2 yds Lensa [linsey] 40			1.00
	9	" 1 Pt why			.06 1/4
	"	" Joshua Mendel[137]			.92
	"	" 1 umbrell [*sic*]			1.25
	"	" 2 measurs Salt			.12 1/2
		" Take care Patric —[138]			
	26	" 1 allmanac 12 1/2 whiskey 6 1/4			.18 3/4
		" 1# Candles			.12 1/2
	20	" Coffee 25 tea 25 tobacco 6 1/4			.56 1/4
					31.12 1/2
		" error			.14
Oct	19	" postage 37 1/2 Certificate 37 1/2			.75
	"	" Capt McCluney			1.00
					33.01 1/2

[41]

139. This December 12 entry, the first mention of Jonathan Brady, is followed by a series of payments of larger sums, $28 paid in installments from April 1834 through 1837, when Gass's record-keeping ceased. (See entries on April 24 and September 20, 1834, September 4, 1835, May 6, 1836, and March 6 and April 6, 1837.) It is not clear what these payments bought. Records show that Gass bought a parcel of land in 1837 on Grog Run from Samuel Moore. But leases were not recorded. The Gasses, at the time of this entry, were living out on a farm; their specific purchases and sparse buying pattern at this time indicate both that Gass was farming and not spending much time in town.

Jonathan P. Brady was a substantial livestock man in the area. In 1833 Brooke County paid him $1.50 for fox scalps (*Wellsburg Weekly Herald,* July 5, 1833). In 1850 Brady served as secretary to a public meeting held to discuss the Virginia constitutional convention held in West Liberty (*Wellsburg Weekly Herald,* July 5, 1850). Brady lived in Ohio County, just south of Brooke County, and had a daughter, Drusilla (*Wellsburg Weekly Herald,* July 12, 1850). At the Autumnal Exhibition of the Ohio and Brooke Agricultural Society, Jonathan Brady won a prize for having the three best Spanish merino ewes (*Wellsburg Weekly Herald,* October 17, 1850). In 1859 Brady purchased a combined reaper and mower (*Wellsburg Herald,* April 1, 1859). His family had its own burial grounds at his home site overlooking Buffalo Creek, where Brady's grandson, Joseph Ray, was laid to rest in 1859 after dying from a head injury due to a horse kicking him. The boy, son of Brady's widowed daughter Pamela, was only thirteen years old (*Wellsburg Herald,* April 1 and 8, 1859). John Brady and his son William were both guilty of insufficient returns of income for taxation in 1864 (*Wellsburg Herald,* November 24, 1865).

140. Thomas Kirk was paid $10 by Brooke County out of the county levy for 1833 (*Brooke Republican,* June 5, 1833). A Democratic Party stalwart like Gass, Kirk was representing Pierce's Run in 1850 (*Wellsburg Weekly Herald,* March 15, 1850). He had been appointed to take the 1850 census in Wellsburg (*Wellsburg Weekly Herald,* June 28, 1850). In October 1850, T. Kirk advertised his services as agent to collect bounty land under the act of Congress of September 28, 1850 (*Wellsburg Weekly Herald,* October 25, 1850). He married Abigail Caldwell on June 5, 1851 (*Wellsburg Weekly Herald,* June 13, 1851).

1833	To amt brot over			33.01 1/2
Nov 26	By his pension		48.00	
		Bal	14.98 1/2	
" "	To Cash			.50
Decr 12	To Cash Pd Jno Brady	}139		
	for sider [*sic*]	}		2.75
"	To Cash for Kirk140			4.50
"	" 1 Pt why			.06 1/4
"	" 1/2# Tobacco			.06 1/4
"	" Cash for Self			.50
18	To 1/2 Bus [bushel] Salt			.31 1/4
	" 1# Candles			.12 1/2
23	" 1 Yd Flannel			.50
"	" 2 1/2 " Muslin 12 1/2			.31 1/4
"	" Bass			.04
"	" 1 Pt why			.06
"	" 1/2# Tobacco			.06 1/4
30	" 1 Qt Molasses 14			.14
"	" 1 Pt why			.06 1/4
1834				
Jany 8	" 1 " why			.06 1/4
16	" 1/2# Candles			.06
"	" 1/2# Tobacco			.06 1/4
21	" *2 1/2 Yds Lincy*	*@ 37 1/2*		*.93 3/4*
	" *1 doz Buttons*			*.06 1/4*
24	" *1/4# Tea*			*.25*
"	" *1 1/2# Coffee*			*.25*
"	" *1 pt whiskey*			*.06 1/4*
"	" Cash			.12 1/2
Feby 1	" 1/2# tobacco 6 1/4^c pipes 2^c			.08 1/4
8	" Magnesia 6 1/4 Candles 6 1/4			.12 1/2
16	" forward			12.09

[42]

141. A curry comb is used to brush a horse. Gass rode horses all his life. One assumes he kept a horse also to pull a buggy, which was indicated by his purchase of "boot webbing" on June 1, 1826.

142. Rhubarb, the medicinal cure, comes from dried rhizome and roots of herbs of the genus *Rheum* grown widely and used as a purgative. *Webster's Third New International Dictionary.*

143. In 1853, Dr. Edward Smith ran for the office of Delegate to the General Assembly of Virginia (*Wellsburg Weekly Herald,* May 6, 1853). Dr. Smith continued his medical practice in July 1853 (*Wellsburg Weekly Herald,* July 8, 1853). Three years later, he was confined to his room for twelve weeks with rheumatism but could "receive friends for a good humored chat" (*Wellsburg Herald,* December 16, 1856).

144. Power of attorney, apparently given to Captain William McCluney for representing Gass at the time of this payment to Jonathan Brady, cost $1. Postage and certificate for pension cost 75¢ while processing cost 50¢. Using 1860 as 100, the consumer price index would put 1834 dollars at 103, and 1991 dollars at 1629, so the total of $2.25 would have equaled approximately $40 in 1991. "How Much is That in Real Money?" *Proceedings of the American Antiquarian Society* 101 (October 1991).

1834	Brot forward			12.09
			14.98 1/2	
Feby 15	To 1 curry comb[141]			.12 1/2
	" 1 pt whiskey 6 1/4	} Dec[r] 23		
	" Tobacco 6 1/4	} omited		.12 1/2
				12.34
21	" 1 Pt why			.06
"	" 1/2 Oz Rhubarb[142]			.06 1/4
"	" Cash			.25
				12.70
	" error in calculation			.37 1/2
March 4	" 1/2# Candles			.06 1/4
				13.14
	" Cash			1.84
			$14.98	$14.98
" 20	To Coffee 25 Tea 25			.50
"	" 1 Handf			.12 1/2
"	" 1 Pt why			.06 1/4
25	" Edward Smith[143]			3.00
"	" Cash 100 why 6 1/4			1.06 1/4
Apl 5	To 6# Bacon 6 1/4			.37 1/2
"	" why 6 1/4 Tobacco 6 1/4			.12 1/2
18	" 13 3/4 Bacon @ 6 1/4			.86
"	" Tobacco 6 1/4 why 6 1/4			.12 1/2
"	" 1 Palm hat			.25
25	" 1/4# tea 25[c] whiskey 6 1/4			.31 1/4
	" Cash			.50
	" order in f[avor] Jno Brady			28.00
	" Cap[t] M[c]Cluney charges			
	Power of atty[144]	1.00		
	Postage & certificate	.75		
	processing	.50		2.25
				37.54 1/2

[43]

145. "Best" could have referred to sugar (see account book page 32) or coffee (see account book page 30).

146. "Cash for wheat" indicates that in May of 1834 the Gasses farmed the land where they had moved.

1834		To am^t bro^t over		37.54 1/2
		By his pension to the }		
		4th March }	48.00	
			$10.45 1/2	
May	*3*	*To 4 1/2 Yds Calico @ 12 1/2^c*		*.56 1/4*
	"	*" 1 Handkerchief*		*.12 1/2*
		" 1/2 Yd Muslin @ 12 1/2		*.06 1/4*
		" 1 " Do		*.16 1/2*
		" 2 Mackeral		*.12 1/2*
	6	" Cash		1.00
	7	" 1 Pt why		.06 1/4
	"	" Cash		.25
"	*17*	*" 7 3/4# Bacon*	*.46*	
"	"	*" 1/2# Tobacco*	*.06*	
"	"	*" 1/4# Pepper*	*.06*	
	"	*" 1 pt whisky*	*.06*	
	"	*" Cash*	*.12 1/2*	*.76 1/2*
		" order p^d J Hamilton		*1.00*
	24	" 1 1/2# Coffee 25 Molasses 12 1/2		.37 1/2
		" Raisins		.06 1/4
	30	" 16 3/4# Bacon 6 1/4		1.04
	"	" 1/4# Best[145]		.25
	"	" Camphor 6 1/4 Tobacco 6 1/4		.12 1/2
	"	" Cash for wheat[146]		1.00
	"	" Cash		1.00
	31	" 1 pt why		.06
June	3	" Cash to Spend		.25
	14	" why 6 1/4 Salt 6 1/4		.12 1/2
				8.41

[44]

147. Probably the Gass milk cow could be turned out to pasture farther away from the house and a cowbell would be needed to help locate her.

148. The first entry of meat besides bacon brings to mind that all the Gasses bought was not all that they ate, and it poses questions. Did Gasses slaughter chickens before this? Did Gass hunt and provide wild meat and or fowl for the family? Why are they buying pork now that they have a farm on which to raise it? Was it just too hot the end of August to slaughter and eat it before it rotted? Heretofore, they had purchased only fish and bacon.

1834	Amt Brought forward		8.41
June 17	To 1/2# Tobacco		.06
24	" 3 Macrell		.24
"	" 1 Cow Bell[147]		.56
26	" 5 Yds Calico @ 12 1/2		.62 1/2
"	3/4 " Check @ 16^c		.12 1/2
"	" 1 3/4 " Calico @ 18 3/4		.32 1/2
"	" 1 " Cotton for	[sic]	.12 1/2
"	" 1 pr Blk Cotton Hose		.37 1/2
"	" 1 pt Whiskey		.06
July 3	" 2 1/4 Yds Calico @ 12 1/2 .28		
"	" 4 3/4 Yds Muslin @ 10	.47	
	" 1 Thimble	.03	.78
July 22	1/2 Gal whiskey		.18 3/4
" 24	1 " do per order		.37 1/2
30	1/2 do		.18 3/4
"	7 3/4# Bacon @ 7^c		.55 1/4
"	1 Pt why		.06
May 10	" 1 3/4# Steel @ 25^c		.44
			$13.50
Augt 5	To 1 Hdkf	25	
	" Bass	3	.28
	" 1 Crock for	[sic]	.12 1/4
" 29	" 10 3/4# pork @ 7^c[148]		.75 1/4
"	" 1 Yd Calico		.12 1/2
Sep^t 1	" 12 1/2 cts worth of Salt		.12 1/2
4	" 1# Candles 12 1/2 why 6 1/4		.19
"	" 1 1/8# Sugar		.12
	Carried over		15.22

[45]

149. A pair of small shoes would be in order for young Benjamin, who would have been a year old on September 10 and was probably beginning to walk.

1834		Brought forward		15.22
Sept	4	To 2# Cheese @ 6 1/4		.12 1/2
	20	To 1 Pt Why		.06 1/4
	"	" Cash		1.00
	25	*" 7 1/2 Yds Ticking @ 25*		*1.87 1/2*
	"	*" 1 Comb 6^c Thread 4^c*		*.10*
	"	*" 2 # Cheese 07^c*		*.14*
	"	*" 8 " Pork @ 6 1/4*		*.50*
Oct	*2*	*" 1 p[air] Small Shoes for*[149] *[sic]*		*.31 1/4*
	"	*" 1 Measure Salt*		*.06*
	"	*" 1 pt whiskey*		*.06*
	"	*2 1/2 Yds Muslin @ 11^c*		*.27 1/2*
	9	" 1 pr men Shoes		1.25
"	14	" 1 Bed cord		.25
Sept	10	" 2 1/4 Yd linnen @ 28		.56 1/2
Oct	6	" order p^d Mrs Freeman		.50
		" 1 auger		.30
	30	" Cash		<u>1.00</u>
				23.60
		" error		.13
Sept	20	To order in f[avor] J Brady		28.
		" McCluney's charges o	}	
		Pension	}	<u>1.87 1/2</u>
				53.60 1/2
		By ba^l bro^t forw^d	10.45 1/2	
		" his pension to the		
		4th Sept last	<u>48.00</u>	
			58.45 1/2	
Nov	6	To bal to new a/ct		<u>4.85</u>
			58.45	58.45

[46]

150. Here appears another charge account that Gass was paying with cash. In this case, he was refunded an overcharge. F. Priest does not appear in contemporary newspapers of Wellsburg; but Susannah Priest had two unclaimed letters at the post office on October 20, 1821 (*Wellsburgh Gazette*). Stephen Priest had an unclaimed letter in 1835. *Brooke Republican,* January 22, 1835.

151. Comic almanacs became increasingly popular during this period of history in England and America. Most likely this one would have been *The American Comic Almanac,* published at Boston by Charles Ellms and sold by all the principal booksellers and traders throughout New England.

1834

Nov	6	By bal		$4.85	
"	"	By wrong charge for	}		
"	"	Steel See F. Priest a/c	}150		
"	"	10th May last	}	.44	
"	13	To 1 Yd Lincy			.56 1/4
	"	" 3/4 " Casinett @ 100			.75
	"	" 1 " flannell			.25
		" 1 Skind [skein] Silk			.04
	"	" 1# Candles			.12 1/2
	"	" 1/2# Tobacco			.06
	"	" 1/4 Tea			.12 1/2
	20	" 1 1/2# Coffee			.25
	27	" 1/4 yd Red Flannell			.11
	29	" Cash per Self			.12 1/2
		" Comic almanac151			.10
Dec	6	To 1/2# Tobacco 12 1/2			.06 1/4
	"	" Cash			1.00
"	10	" 1/2 Bush[el] Salt			.37 1/2
	"	" 1 Jews Harp			.03
	"	" 1# Candles			.12 1/2
	"	" 1/4# Pepper			.06 1/4
	20	" 1/2# Tobacco			.06 1/4
1835					
Jany	1	" 1 1/2# Coffee			.25
	15	" 1# Candles			.12 1/2
Feby	6	" 1 1/2# Coffee			.25
		" 2 Measures Salt			.12 1/2
					4.97
	21	" vial British oil			.12 1/2
				5.29 [sic]	5.09 1/2
Mar	4	To Cash in full			.20
		Continued next page			

[47]

152. Probably this was Mrs. E. F. Moore, whose husband owned a fine daguerreotyping business in Wellsburg and took the ambrotype from which the frontispiece of *The Life and Times of Patrick Gass* was engraved. E. F. Moore's name was listed for an unclaimed letter in 1850 (*Wellsburg Weekly Herald,* July 19) and for being delinquent $1.25 in taxes (*Wellsburg Weekly Herald,* January 17, 1851). "Captain" Moore's office adjoined that of the *Wellsburg Weekly Herald.* As his business burgeoned, Moore added new equipment the first year of operation (*Wellsburg Weekly Herald,* July 28, 1854). Meanwhile, Mrs. E. F. Moore had been selected by the ladies executive committee of the Farmers and Mechanics Industrial Society to judge quilts at the upcoming exhibition and competition at the fair (*Wellsburg Weekly Herald,* September 29, 1854). She won a first prize for spiced quinces and he won the miscellaneous category with beautiful specimen daguerreotypes (*Wellsburg Weekly Herald,* October 20, 1854). In the Civil War, E. F. Moore was commissioned a lieutenant, receiving a testimonial letter from Lieutenant Colonel Joseph Darr for his duties at the Atheneum Prison as a "faithful and reliable officer." (*Wellsburg Herald,* July 29, 1864).

153. E. Barnes was partner in a cigar manufactory that also sold hats in the mid-1830s (*Brooke Republican,* January 22, 1835). On April 16, 1835, Barnes took out an advertisement proclaiming "HATS of every description, cheap for cash or country produce" (reprinted in *Brooke Republican,* August 20, 1835). Gass apparently bought a hat on April 30 as a result of the ad.

154. Gass has bought, at this point, three hats in six weeks. This purchase on his sixty-fourth birthday, June 12, duplicates a palm hat purchased on April 18, 1834, and probably the one bought on May 4, 1835.

1835	Continued from last paid [*sic*]	
March26	" 1 Handkerchief	.12 1/2
"	" 1 1/2# Coffee	.25
Apl 16	" Cash	.50
"	" 2 Measurs Salt	.12 1/2
"	" 3 Mackrell 6 1/4	.18 3/4
"	" Cash	2.00
27	" do	1.00
30	" order Mrs Moore[152]	1.00
"	" 2 Mackrel	.12 1/2
"	" M^r. Barns for hat[153]	<u>3.50</u>
		8.81
May 4	" *3 Mackrel @ 5*	*.15*
	" *1 Hat*	*.25*
	" *Cash to buy Flour*	*2.00*
	"*1 1/2# Coffee*	*.25*
June 9	" Sal^t 6 1/4^c tobacco 9 1/2	.15 3/4
12	" 1 Palm Hat[154]	.20
16	" *1/2 Doz Herrings*	*.15 1/2*
23	" Tobacco 9 Camphor 6	.15
	Cash	.25
July 3	" Cash	.50
" *14*	" *1 1/2# Coffee*	*.25*
	" *1/2# Tobacco*	*.09 1/2*
"	" *1 Phial [vial] Terpentine*	*.06*
" *15*	" *1 oz Indigo*	*.12 1/2*
20	" Cash	.50
28	" Cash 1.00 & Goods 25	1.25
"	" do .50	.50
	forward	

1835		Amt Brought forward			15.75 1/2
Aug^t	1	Cash 50 chocalate 10			.60
	3	28# C [*sic*] flour 2			.56
	5	2 1/4# Cheese 8	.18		
	13	1 Qt Mollasses	18 3/4		
	14	1/2 Oz Camphor	.06		.44
	31	To 1 Measur Salt			.06 1/4
					17.40

To Cap^{tn} McCluney charge for
   collecting pension   1.87 1/2
By amt of pension from   }   19.27 1/2
Captn McCluney to 4th March }
                                    48.00
By Bal $28.72 1/2

Sept	4	To 1 1/2# Coffee 25 tobacco 9 1/2			.34 1/2
		" Cinnamon & nutmegs			.12 1/2
		" Sundries of John			.12 1/2
					.59
		" 1# Candles			.12 1/2
		" Cash in full			28.00
				28.74	$28.71 1/2

Sept	*15*	*To 1 1/2 Yd Bro[wn] Holland 31 1/2*	*47*	
		" 3 Skeins Silk @ 4	*12 1/2*	
		" Threadz Irish _	*12 1/2*	*.72*
"	*16*	*" 1/2 Sett Teas*	*.12 1/2*	
		" 1 1/2 Yds Muslin	*.26*	
		" 1 Fine Comb	*12 1/2*	
		" 1/2 paper pins	*06 1/4*	*.57 1/4*
	24	" 1 Bed cord		.25
	29	" 1# tobacco		.18 1/2
Oct	3	" 4# Cheese @ 8	.32	
		" 1 Pt Brandy	.25	.57
				2.30

[49]

155. William L. Gass was born on October 24, 1835, to Patrick and Maria Gass. On December 1863, at age twenty-eight, his name appeared on a list of enrollees for the Board of Enrollment of the First District, Provost, liable for the draft (*Wellsburg Herald,* December 4, 1863). William Gass was a cooper by trade, "worked industriously, saved his money and mostly carried all he had about him" (*Wellsburg Herald,* October 27, 1865). His early death and its subsequent investigation was well covered by the *Wellsburg Herald.* On October 7, 1865, he had been to Burgettstown with a friend, Edward Nicholls. Being too late for the train to Wellsburg, they began to walk from Steubenville. An acquaintance loaned them a "dug out" to cross the river, but it filled with water and partly overturned. Gass began to swim while Nicholls held fast to the craft. Gass was unable to reach shore. His body was recovered four days later. A small sum of money, a flask partly full of whiskey, and a knife were found on it, but there were no signs of violence (*Wellsburg Herald,* October 13, 1865). Yet two weeks later the paper announced "Foul play suspected," as the corpse of young Gass was exhumed for further examination. This spawned from the allegation that he had considerable money on him, while only a small sum was recovered from his body. The inquest jury, however, did not find cause other than accidental drowning. William's younger brother, James Waugh Gass, wrote a poem of five stanzas in memory of his departed brother, showing a high degree of both literacy and sentiment (*Wellsburg Herald,* October 27, 1865).

1835		Brought over		2.30
Oct 5th		To 1# Candles	J [sic]	.12 1/2
"	"	" 1 Jews Harp		.03
	6	" 1 Measur Salt		.06
	12	" 1 pt best Brandy		.25
		" 1 1/2# Coffee 25c tobacco 9c		.34
	14	" 6 1/4# Bacon		.50
	20	" Cash for Candles 12 1/2		.12 1/2
	"	" 1/2 oz Camphor		.06 1/4
	"	" 1 yd Muslin		.12 1/2
	24155	" 1 Pt why		.06 1/4
	26	" 1 " do		.06 1/4
	"	" Cash		2.00
		" Do		2.00
		" 1 hat of Platenberg		1.00
	31	" 1 Bus Salt	75	
	"	" 1/2 Gall why	25	1.00
Nov	3	" why	6 1/4	
"	"	" 1# Candles	12 1/2c	
	"	" 1 1/2# coffee	25	
	"	" Cash	2.25	2.68
"	7	" 1 1/4 Yds Flannell		.62
		" magazine almanac		.12 1/2
	9	" 2 plates 12 1/2c knitting pins 5		.17 1/2
		" tea		.12 1/2
	14	" Cash Self		.50
	24	" Candles 12 1/2 tea 12 1/2		.25
		" order pd. Miss Freeman		1.37 1/2
	"	" Candles 12 1/2 Tea 12 1/2		.25
				16.15

[50]

156. This could have been the James Lawhead listed with unclaimed letters in 1834 and 1835 (*Brooke Republican,* January 4, 1834, January 7, 1836), or it could have been James Loughhead, Sr., whose name appeared on a list of delinquent titheables (*Wellsburg Weekly Herald,* July 11, 1851) and who was assessed $41.10 in income tax in 1864 (*Wellsburg Herald,* September 1, 1864).

		Amt Brought up		*16.15*
Dec	5	*Cash*		*.50*
"	"	*To 1 Pair Blankets*		*3.00*
"	8	*" 1 1/2# Coffee*		*.25*
"	"	*" 1/4# pepper*		*.06 1/4*
"	"	*" 1# Candles*		*.12 1/2*
"	"	*" 1 Mackerel*		*.08*
"	19	*" Tobacco*		*.09*
"	"	*" Cash*	*self*	*1.00*
	23	*" do*		*2.00*
	26	*" do*		*1.00*
	"	*" 1# Candles*		*.12 1/2*

1836

Jany	11	To 1/8# tea 12 1/2^c 2 yds Muslin 12 1/2^c		.37 1/2
		To Cash		1.00
	14	" Cash 100 Linsa [linsey]	200	3.00
	"	" Jas Lawhead order[156]		3.00
	30	" 1# Candles	12 1/2	
		" 1 1/2# Coffee	25	.37 1/2
Feby	11	*" 1/2 Qt Tea*		*.09 1/2*
				$35.23
		McCluneys Charge on pension		.87 1/2
				37.10 1/2
By his pension to [illegible] Oct 6			48.00	
				$10.89 1/2
March 11		*To Cash*		10.00
		" 1 1/2# Coffee		.25
	19	To 2 1/2 yds Muslin 12 1/2		.31
	"	*" 1# Candles*		.12 1/2

[51]

157. "Twilled jeans" denotes a fabric of durable twilled cotton. *Webster's Ninth New Collegiate Dictionary.*

158. James Marshall and Brothers were defendants in an action filed by Adam Kuhn on February 7, 1851. *Wellsburg Weekly Herald,* February 28, 1851.

159. A wheat riddle is a coarse sieve used to separate the grain from the chaff. *Webster's Ninth New Collegiate Dictionary.*

1836	By & To amt Brot over	10.89	10.69
May 6	To 1 1/2# Coffee 25 1/2 tobacco		.33
		10.89	11.02
	Balances		.13
	To Capt McCluneys charge		2.00
May 6	" Cash for Jno. Brady		28.00
"	" 2 mackerel @ 6^c		.12
" 21	" 6 yd twild [sic] Jeans[157] @ 25		1.50
"	" Cash some days ago		1.00
24	" Cash for Jas. Marshal[158]		1.50
June 23	" 1 1/2# Coffee	25	
	" 1/8# ginger	3	
			.28
July 4	" Cash		1.50
18	" do		.50
18	" 1/8# Im[perial] Tea		.12 1/2
"	" 1# Rice		.07
"	" 1/2 Doz Herring		.12 1/2
Augt 5	" order in f[avor] of Hambleton		3.00
	" 1/2# Tobacco 8^c 1 1/2# Coffee 25		.33
	" amt p^d Jno Hambleton		5.75
			$45.94
Sept 10	" 1/2 Oz Indigo		.06 1/4
"	" Cash		1.00
14	" 11# Bacon @ 10		1.10
"	" 1 1/2# Coffee		.25
Oct 8	*" 1 Wheat Riddle*[159]		*1.12 1/2*
	" Cash		*1.00*
" "	*" 1 Measure Salt*		*.06*
			50.53

[52]

160. "Head and ribs" is boiling meat to make broth for stew, noodles, soup, etc. The bones themselves could have been broken to expose the marrow.

1836		*To & By Amt Brot up*		*50.53*
Oct	12	~~To 1 pr Small Shoes~~		~~.50~~
"	31	To 1 vest & trimings		1.26
		" 2 1/2 yd Red flannell @ 62 1/2		1.56 1/2
Nov	7	" 2# Coffee		.25
"	14	" 2 3/4 yd fulled linsey @ 68 1/2		1.88 1/2
		" 4 2/4 " linsey @ 55^c		2.47 1/2
		" 1 measure Salt		.06 1/4
	17	" 1/2 Bus[hel] Salt		.50
Dec^r	10	" 43# head & ribs[160] @ 3^c		1.29
		" 9# Pork @ 6 1/4^c		.56 1/4
	17	" 12" Ribs 36^c 1 allmanac 10^c		.46
	19	" 1 1/2# Coffee	25	
	"	" 1 1/2# Tobacco	8	.33
1837				
Jany	20	" 1 Bottle British oil		.12 1/2
Feby	4	" tea 12 1/2^c Candles 6 1/4^c		.18 3/4
	18	" 1 1/2# Coffee		.25
	"	Cash		.25
	22	One Coffee Bag		.12 1/2
		Cash to get		.25
		To Captn McCluneys charge }		
		for Pension last }		2.00
				64.36 1/2
		By his pension to the }		
		4th March last }	48.00	
		" his pension to the		
		4th Sep^t last	48.00	
			96.00	
		By bal due P Gass	31.63 1/2	
March	4	To Cash		2.00
	"	" 18 hog jowls @ 4 2/4^c		.81
	"	" do for Hambleton		.50

[53]

161. The cash Maria noted is "lent," a different notation from her husband's "cash for himSelf."

162. Pearlash, potassium carbonate, was advertised to take out grease spots from a carpet or any woolen cloth. A piece the size of a pea was dissolved in a half teacup of water to make a solution to rub into the soiled area (*Brooke Republican,* March 29, 1834). A warning against putting pearlash in bread advised cooks that eating too much pearlash would cause skin to turn yellow. *Wellsburg Herald,* March 23, 1860.

		Amount brought Over		
		To amt brot over	*31.63 1/2*	*3.31 1/2*
Ma[sic]	*6*	*Cash Order p^d Brady*		*10.00*
	22	*To 1/8# peper 3 1/8# alspice 3*		*.06 1/4*
	"	*" 2# Coffee @ 16 2/3^c*		*.33 1/3*
	"	*" Cash lent pr. Self*[161]		*5.00*
	"	*" tea*		*.12 1/2*
	29	*" 1/2# Candles*		*.08*
	"	*" Pearlash*[162]		*.03*
				18.95
		" 10 1/4# hog Joles @ 5^c		.51
				19.46
April	6	" Cash		12.
		" Goods		.17 1/2
			31.63	$31.63 1/2

[54]

163. A ten-year gap in record-keeping in this account book occurred between April 1837 and January 1847 marked by one blank page in the account book. During that time, according to the Gass family Bible, four more
Gass children were born. On March 24, 1837, Patrick Gass bought six acres
at Grog Run, near Wellsburg, for $180.93 (Deed Book 11, p. 506, Brooke
County Courthouse). He then sold it on April 17, 1845 (Deed Book 15, p.
216).

[The Gasses stopped keeping these records in 1837. A ten-year gap follows.][163]

164. The reopening of the account book featured a different format, a different handwriting, a balancing accounting for each page, the heading "Patrick Gass in a/c with Connell Wells & Co.," and the notation "settled" when each page closed. Clearly, it was the work of a storekeeper.

165. Methuen drilling is a coarse linen or cotton fabric. *Dictionary of American English*.

166. "Sermon for Wife's Funeral" marks a retrogressive entry of cash spent February 16, 1847, added after the July 31 entry. Maria died on February 16, so probably Gass remembered this day, not the day of the funeral, to have this entered and perhaps paid. Measles had appeared in the Gass family in the fall of 1846, prostrating all of the children before it took their mother early the next year. Jacob, *Life and Times*, 179; Gass family Bible. Confusion over Maria's death comes from Earle Forrest's work, the gravestone, the Bible, and some genealogical reports.

   Close examination with a magnifying glass of the date in the Gass family Bible shows that the original and correct date of 1847 has been written over with heavier ink to loop the top of the seven into a big nine. Rachel stated that she was eleven months old at the time of her mother's death. Therefore the Bible entry of her birth that caused the change in Maria's death date is erroneous (Rachel Brierley's letter to Eva Emery Dye, Oregon Historical Society, Portland). Undeniable proof lies in the deed of trust between Patrick Gass, Eli Boring, and Samuel Morrow, stating Rachel's birthday to be March 31, 1846 (Deed Book 16, p. 457, Brooke County Courthouse). Jacob's interview with Patrick Gass placed Maria's death exactly when the account book listed it, in February 1847. Earle Forrest had the date correct in his article, "Patrick Gass, Carpenter of the Lewis and Clark Expedition," *Bulletin of the Missouri Historical Society*, 4 (July 1948), 217–22. However, his later perusal of the family Bible convinced him to alter the date in his subsequent work, *Patrick Gass, Lewis and Clark's Last Man* (Independence, Pa., 1950).

Patrick Gass   Db

in a/c with Connell Wells & Co[164]

Jany 8			
1847	Coffee Sugar & Tobacco		.50
24	Tea 12 paper 12 1/2		.25
Feb 1	Coffee	.25	
	Candles	5	.30
16	2 1/2# Coffee	.25	
	1 " Sugar	.10	
	1 " Candles	.10	.45
18	Tobacco		.13
Mar 4	To 2 1/2# Coffee		.25
	" 1/8# Tea		.12 1/2
16	" Jeans & Trim(min)gs		2.42
	" 1 Hdkf		.13
	" Tobacco		.12
	" 1# Candles		.13
27	" 2 1/2 Coffee		.25
	Tobacco		.13
Apr 7	" 15 Yds Methuen (*sic*) Drillg (drilling)[165] 18 3/4		2.81
May 1	" 1 pr suspenders		.25
12	" Hat 25 coffee 25		.50
July 31	" 10 yds Muslin		1.00
Febr 16	" Sermon for Wife's Funeral[166]		3.19
		$12.93	$12.93

[56]

167. This interlined entry "By butter" shows that Maria sold butter she made at the end of January, shortly before her death.

Cr

1847

Jany 20	By 8 1/4 Butter[167] 10		.82
May 8	" Cash		3.25
			$4.08
Sept 30	Cash in full		8.85
			$12.93

Settled

Sept

30
/
47

168. Mrs. Kinder's identity is unknown. Perhaps she helped take care of the children until Gass placed them with others. (Brierley to Dye) For more details on their placing, see the Introduction to Book II.

Db   Patrick Gass   In a/c

Sept	30	To 9 Yds Jeans	$2.25		
		" 3 " Drilling	37 1/2		2.62 1/2
Nov	30	" 3 " Flannel	84		
		" 1 Knife	31		1.15
		" 1 pr Socks			.25
1848					
Jany	10	3 yds Jeans 25	75		
		Hd^c (Handkerchief)	06		
		2 fine Combs	13		.94
Apl	3	" 13 yds Blue Drillg	12 1/2		1.63
May	8	" 4 " Ditto	50		
		" 2 1/2 # Coffee	25		.75
	13	" 2 1/2 # Ditto			.25
	23	" 2 1/2 # Ditto			.25
June	22	" Amt p^d Mrs Kinder[168]			1.50
		" 2 yds Gingham			.25
July	19	" 7 " Muslin	.56		
		" 1 doz Buttons	.03		
		" 2 1/2 # Coffee	.25		.84
Aug	8	" 2 1/2 # Ditto	.25		
		" 5 yds Muslin	.45		
		" Buttons	.03		.73
		" 1 P L Hat [palm leaf]			.26
	16	" 2 1/2 yds Jeans			.63
		" Tobacco			.06

[58]

With Connell Wells & Co   Cr

1847			
Sept	30	By Cash	$1.15
Apr	2	Ditto	1.00
Sept	24	ditto	11.10

Db   Patrick Gass   In

1848

Oct 26   To 2 1/2 yds Jeans   .62 (1/2)
           " 2 1/2 # Coffee   .25
           " Tobacco   .06 (1/4)
           " Candles   .06 (1/4)
                                     1.00

a/c With Connell Wells & Co

W^m   S   M $275.40

169. This upside-down notation on the account book's final page is not a formal accounting but a promissory note. It provides a valuable link in handwriting analysis, because it combines Gass's signature (recognizable from other sources) and his writing of other text.

[UPSIDE DOWN ON LAST PAGE]

P

A

I

D

Patrick Gass[169]

in acct with Evers [?] & Co

1 3/4 # Nail Rod [illegible]

P

A

I   .14

D

May 13

1848   43 "[lb] Bacon slab   4 1/2

Appendix X

Number of Purchases

	January	February	March	April	May	June	July	August	September	October	November	December	Total # of Purchases
1826		1 1	3	2	1	1	1+1B	2 2 4	3	1	4 1	2	29
1827	1	1 1	3	4	3 4	1	1 1	2	7	1 1	3	1 1	39
1828	2 1	2	1B 1	1 1	1 1	1	1	1	1+2B P 2+1B	4	4+1B 1	1	32
1829	2 6+1B	2	1 12	3 1	4+P+1B 4+1B	2 5	1 5	1	14+P+1B	3	1+1B 4	4	77
1830	3 1 3	1 1 1 1	6 6	3 1 1	6	3	3	12+3B	2	2 3	2+2B	4+P+2B	68
1831	3 5 2	1 5 1	1	11+1B	9+1B	3	1 3+P	2	2 4	1 1 1	4	2	63
1832	1 1 1 1	3	1 4	3 1	1	1 2 3	3	3 1 2 1	11	5+1B	4	2	58
1833	3 1	2 1 1 1	1+1P 4	1	4	3+P	1+2B 3	5	6+1B	10+1B	1+P+1B 1	3 1	62
1834	1 3	1 1 1 2+1B	1	4+P+1B 1	4	2 2	3	1	2+P+1B 3+1B	3+1B 1	1 1 1 2	2 1	52
1835	1	1 1	1	3	1	3 1	3 1	2 4	2+P 2	15	1	2 3	49
1836	2	1 1+P	1 1	1	1 2	1	1	1	2	2	2 1	1 2	23
1837	1	1 2+2P	1 1 1	1									9

KEY: 2 = 2 Transactions   2B = 2 Back Dated Transactions   P = Pension Entries

Appendix Y

Unspecified Cash Expenditures

	January	February	March	April	May	June	July	August	September	October	November	December	Total Cash Entries
1826			¢ $ ¢	¢	$	$	$	$	$ $	$	$ ¢ $	$	$26.25
1827	$	$ $	$	$	$	$ $	$	$	¢ $	$	¢	¢	$41.50
1828	¢ $ ¢ $	¢	$	¢	$ $	¢	$		¢ $	$ $	$		$19.05
1829	$	$ $ $ $	$	$	$	$	$ $ $	$	$		$ ¢ $	$ ¢	$64–74.50
1830	¢ $ $ ¢	¢ ¢	$ $	¢ $ ¢	$	¢ ¢	$	$	¢ ¢ $ $	¢	$ ¢ $	$ ¢	$49–59.00
1831	¢		¢	$ ¢	$	$	$ ¢	$	$		$	$	$30.50
1832	$ $	$	$		$	$	$	¢ ¢ ¢	¢ ¢ ¢	¢	$ $ ¢		$31.00
1833		$	$		$ $	$ $			$ $	$ ¢	¢	$ ¢	$44.00
1834	¢	¢	$	¢ $ ¢	¢ $	¢ $			¢ $ ¢	$	$ ¢ $		$11.00
1835			¢	$	$	$	¢ $	$ ¢	$	$	¢	¢	$17.00
1836	$		$		$ $ $		$ $ ¢						$8.50
1837		¢	$ $	$									$8.00

Cash Entries for Gass
¢ = less than $1.00
$ = $1.00 - $8.00
$ = $8.01 and over

Cash Entries for Others
¢ = less than $1.00
$ = $1.00 - $8.00
$ = $8.01 and over

440

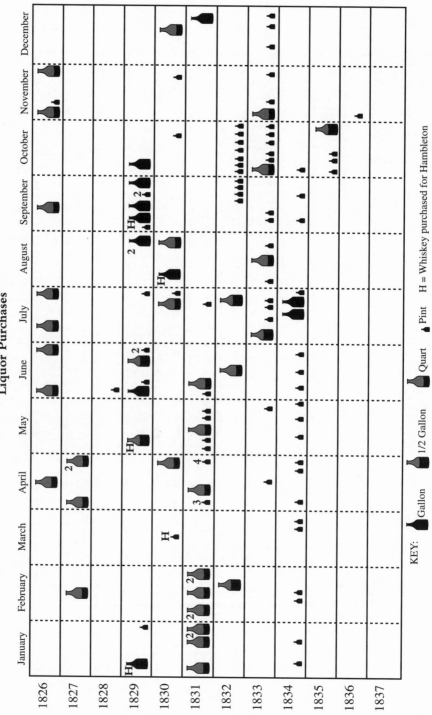

Appendix Z

Liquor Purchases

KEY: Gallon   1/2 Gallon   Quart   Pint   H = Whiskey purchased for Hambleton

INTERPRETATION OF
APPENDICES X, Y, Z

Comparing the figures showing the number of purchases Gass made (Appendix X), the amount of cash he took (Appendix Y), and his purchases of liquor (Appendix Z) during the ten-year period of the journal, several important patterns yield clues to changes in his lifestyle and habits. In 1827, the first year of this accounting, Gass, at age fifty-six, spent about one-fourth of his pension in cash and noted sporadic, moderate purchases of liquor. The following year his total purchases (39) seemed moderate and his drinking notations sparse, but over half of his pension was spent on cash dispersals, and we do not know their nature. The next year, 1828, Gass appeared to be working. His purchases of bottled liquor were very sparse, with only one pint noted. He had few purchases overall (32), and only one-fifth of his pension disappeared in "cash." The year 1829 witnessed sporadic purchases of gallons of liquor, with a heavy binge featuring John Hamilton, his future father-in-law, and Gass in September and October. Purchasing was very high (77 purchases), and cash expenditures equaled two-thirds of his pension. He was buying goods for the Bowles, courting Maria, drinking with John Hamilton (into whose boarding house he moved that fall), and apparently living in town. The following year, 1830, Gass's cash expenditures equaled more than one-half of his pension, with the heaviest months being March and September. His purchases totaled 68. The crescendo of his drinking as reflected in liquor purchases continued through May of 1831, except for a twenty-day hiatus preceding his marriage to Maria Hamilton on March 31. He slowed his cash expenditures to 30 percent of his pension, making 63 purchases overall, many directly after his marriage, apparently to set up a new household. Into Maria's pregnancy with their first child by summer, Gass's expenditures waned. In 1832 Gass purchased only a half gallon when Elizabeth was born, February 24, until June; but when the baby became ill in the fall, Gass bought about two pints a week during September and October. The baby died November 7, 1832. That year Gass spent about one-third of his pension in cash and made only 58 total purchases.

The beginning of 1833 appears to be a time of new resolve. The Gasses bought the family Bible (now kept at Fort Canby, Washington), a spelling book, a plow line, and no liquor for months. But by May 26, Patrick Gass was fined for "drinking too much grog on Sunday." Maria was pregnant with Benjamin, who was born September 10. Most of their cash during 1833 was spent during April and May; over 40 percent of the pension was spent in cash. They made 62 purchases. In mid-1834, Gass seems to have made another resolution. Regular liquor purchases, about a pint every ten days, continue until June, with a binge in July, but there are no liquor purchases from September until the end of the year. Very little cash was spent, hardly any of which was specified "for himSelf." Only about 10 percent of the pension was noted as undesignated cash, and total purchases went down to 52.

The Gasses must have moved farther out of town to farm during 1834, when the cash payments of $28 biannually to John Brady started. There are no deeds filed for the Gasses in 1834, but their purchases and cash expenditures show a marked change at that time. This trend continued through 1835, when no spiritous beverage appeared except at harvest time in October. No cash was spent until planting time in April and May. Fewer purchases (only 49) were recorded, with about one-sixth of Gass's pension being spent in cash. The end of October, when William was born, there seems to have been a period of jubilation and expense. But 1836 had no liquor purchases noted, only $8.50 in cash spent all year, with only one-fifteenth of his pension being designated "for himSelf" and a mere 23 purchases overall. Gass, age sixty-five and father of three youngsters, had certainly found an occupation away from town, probably farming outside Wellsburg. This pattern continued into 1837, when no liquor purchases appeared until the end of the accounting period in April. Nine purchases were made in three months; Brady got $22.00 while $7.25 went for cash. In March 1837, the Gasses moved to Grog Run and discontinued the account book. By the next period, 1847, the accounting system had changed completely. Connell, Wells & Company kept the books, and there was no deposit of pension or purchase of liquor noted, although disbursements for cash, coffee, and tobacco continued as usual. Maria's industry shone until the end. Right before her death from measles in February 1847, there was a notation on January 20 "By butter," showing a credit for her butter.

INDEX TO BOOK II

Photograph by Ural Latham

ABOUT THE EDITOR

Carol Lynn MacGregor became interested in Partick Gass while working on her master's degree in history at Boise State University. In 1991 her work on Gass won an award from the Eastern Washington State Historical Society for the best manuscript on Inland Empire history. She continued her studies in American history at the University of New Mexico at Albuquerque, where she's now completing her Ph.D.

A member of the Western History Association and the Lewis and Clark Heritage Trail Foundation, she has recently been appointed cochairman for Idaho on the Governor's Committee on Lewis and Clark. She continues her study of the West from her home in Boise, teaching at Boise State University and managing her ranches near Emmett and Cascade, Idaho.